HANG ON SLOOPY

THE HISTORY OF ROCK & ROLL IN OHIO

NICK TALEVSKI

GUARDIAN EXPRESS
Green, Ohio U.S.A.

Copyright © 2008, 2010 by Nick Talevski

All rights reserved. No portion of this book may be reproduced, copied or electronically stored, by any means or technique, without the express written consent of the publisher.

Library of Congress Control Number: 2007908069
ISBN: 978-0980056105

Library of Congress Cataloging-in-Publication Data

Talevski, Nick
    Hang on Sloopy: The history of rock & roll in Ohio / Nick Talevski
    Includes bibliographical references
    ISBN 978-0980056105

    1. Rock music – Ohio. 2. Rock music – History and criticism. 3. Rock music – Bio-bibliography. 4. Ohio State University – Football – History.
    I. Title

Chapter 2 "Alan Freed & The Rise Of Rock And Roll In Cleveland" and Chapter 13 "The Rock And Roll Hall Of Fame" were originally published in *The Encyclopedia of the Rock and Roll Hall of Fame*, and have been revised and updated. The chapters appear with the permission of Greenwood Publishing Group. The Ohio State University and the Rock and Roll Hall of Fame did not participate in the writing, editing, or publishing of this book.

Organizations and other groups interested in purchasing quantities of this book should contact the publisher.

Please contact the publisher to report any errors or omissions.

Guardian Express
P.O. Box 205
Green, Ohio 44232

Printed in the U.S.A.

CONTENTS

PREFACE	v
ACKNOWLEDGMENTS	vii
INTRODUCTION	1
CHAPTER 1. Hang On Sloopy: The Ohio State University Tradition	11
CHAPTER 2. Alan Freed and the Rise of Rock and Roll in Cleveland	27
CHAPTER 3. Cincinnati: WLW and King-Federal Records	53
CHAPTER 4. Pop-Rock in the 1960s & 1970s	67
CHAPTER 5. The Rise of Album Rock	79
CHAPTER 6. The Arrival of Punk Rock in Cleveland	97
CHAPTER 7. New Wave and the Akron Sound	105
CHAPTER 8. Hard Rock and Heavy Metal	117
CHAPTER 9. Alternative Rock: 1980s and Beyond	125
CHAPTER 10. Soul and R&B	141
CHAPTER 11. Singer-songwriters, etc.	171
CHAPTER 12. Rock on TV: WKRP in Cincinnati, Drew Carey & Upbeat!	187
CHAPTER 13. The Rock and Roll Hall of Fame	195
CHAPTER 14. Conclusion	213
BIBLIOGRAPHY	217
INDEX	229

PREFACE

During the 1950s, Ohio was at the forefront in the rise of rock and roll. While Cleveland deejay Alan Freed gave the new musical form its name and played records by pioneering Ohio rockers such as Bull Moose Jackson and The Moonglows, Cincinnati entrepreneur Sydney Nathan singlehandedly built King-Federal Records into one of the most-successful independent labels in the nation.

A wide variety of musical styles have thrived in the Buckeye State. Beginning in the 1960s, Cincinnati and Dayton played a central role in the development of soul and funk. By the 1970s, punk rock was emerging in the urban enclave of Cleveland, while new wave was simmering in nearby Akron. An industrial state with traditional sensibilities, Ohio has also nurtured heartland rock and heavy metal.

In the 1980s, Cleveland was rewarded for its contributions to rock and roll with a prestigious museum. Housed in a massive pyramid-shaped, metal and glass structure, the Rock and Roll Hall of Fame became the focal point of a city in need of a jewel. Since the Hall of Fame's opening in 1995, millions of rock and roll pilgrims from around the globe have trekked to the House that Rock Built.

This book does not attempt to chronicle every musician, singer, producer or deejay that graced the Buckeye State. Instead, the objective is to honor the musical pioneers, the hit makers and those who defined the stylistic trends that made Ohio both a birthplace and proving ground of rock and roll.

ACKNOWLEDGMENTS

The idea for this book was conceived in the late-1980s. After amassing several boxes of magazine articles, newspaper clippings and various other source materials, I began writing some of the chapters in 1995. In addition to my own personal research, a debt of gratitude must be paid to the following institutions and individuals: William L. Schurk of the Music Library and Sound Recordings Archives at Bowling Green State University; the interlibrary loan office at Kent State University; the always helpful librarians in the Popular Culture division at the Akron Public Library; John M. Riley; Robert West; James A. Reed; Dan Kane; Rod Lockwood; Lisa Wise; and Gary Felsinger. Lastly, I'd like to acknowledge the late Alan Freed, whose contribution to the birth of rock and roll was the inspiration for this book.

INTRODUCTION

Beautiful Ohio. The rolling hills that dominate the eastern half of the state contrast with the flat terrain of the western portion. The state's northern boundary reaches the shores of Lake Erie – a region that was dubbed the North Coast by Cleveland rocker Michael Stanley. The southern boundary, the Ohio River, has served as a busy trading route for much of the state's existence. With the construction of the Erie and Miami Canals, Lake Erie was linked with the Ohio River. Suddenly, inland towns such as Akron and Massillon blossomed into centers of commerce.

Ohio was the first of five states carved from the Northwest Territory, a region ceded to the United States by Great Britain in the Treaty of Paris of 1783. At the time, Ohio was situated in the western-most part of the young, pioneer nation. But as the country's borders expanded westward, the region was later known as "the Middle West," and eventually, the Midwest.

The northeastern corner of Ohio – which would include the cities of Cleveland, Youngstown, Akron and Kent – was previously claimed by another state. Known as the Western Reserve of Connecticut, the region was intended for veterans of the Revolutionary War and civilian victims of British attacks. As a result, many of the area's older structures are indicative of New England architecture. On the opposite side of the state in Southern Ohio, a small region just east of Cincinnati was declared the Virginia Military District.

Once sparsely populated by Indian tribes such as the Ottawa, Delaware, Wyandot and Chippewa, Ohio retained many of these Indian references in the naming of counties, cities and rivers. Emptying into Lake Erie near downtown Cleveland, the Cuyahoga River took its name from the Mohawk word for crooked river, "cahagaga."

Beginning with William Harrison, Ohio has produced several presidents. As a result, the state is dotted by presidential monuments. A pro-abolitionist state, Ohio served as a gateway on the Underground Railroad. A museum in Cincinnati celebrates the state's role in the transportation of Southern slaves to Northern states and Canada.

The home of tycoon John D. Rockefeller, Cleveland prospered in the late-19th century. Rockefeller's ever-expanding conglomerate, Standard Oil, was chartered by the state in 1870. By the turn of the century, Rockefeller commanded one of the most formidable business empires in the Western Hemisphere.

During the automobile age, Ohio was second in the production of cars, right behind Michigan. And in Akron, rubber factories churned out tires by the millions. The rampaging industrialization in the northern Ohio cities of

Toledo, Cleveland, Akron, Canton and Youngstown, drew immigrants from Southeastern Europe as well as from neighboring states, with a disproportionate number of workers journeying north from West Virginia. Additionally, all around Ohio – particularly in Columbus and Cincinnati – large pockets of German immigrants established communities.

The growth of mass media at the start of the industrial age had its roots in Ohio. The most widely-used textbook of the 19th century, *McGuffey's Reader*, was compiled by Cincinnati educator William Holmes McGuffey. And while songwriter Stephen Foster wrote his first hit, "Oh! Susanna," during his stint as an employee at his brother's company in Cincinnati, banjo player Dan Emmett of Mount Vernon composed minstrel-era standards such as "I Wish I Was In Dixie" and "Turkey In The Straw."

At the dawn of the recording industry, Akron-raised tenor H. Evan Williams was the top-selling American opera singer of the era. Meanwhile, Cleveland-born composer and balladeer Ernest R. Ball scored a perennial hit with a song he co-wrote, "When Irish Eyes Are Smiling." And America's rodeo sweetheart, Annie Oakley of Darke County in Western Ohio, charmed the nation with her sharpshooting skills as a member of Buffalo Bill's Famous Wild West Show.

Ohio's contribution to the science of recording was provided by one of the greatest inventors in history, Thomas Alva Edison, who was born in Milan, a quiet town midway between Toledo and Cleveland. Though severely deaf as the result of a childhood incident, Edison refused to use the disability as a crutch. Later saving a 3-year-old from being crushed by a tumbling train boxcar, Edison was rewarded by the child's father with training as a telegraph operator.

While working as a telegraph operator in the lakefront town of Port Clinton, Edison built a homemade laboratory. In 1868 at the age of 21, Edison patented his first device, the Electrical Vote Recorder. After relocating several times, Edison abandoned his telegraph position to work as an inventor on a full-time basis.

Settling in Menlo Park, New Jersey, and opening a laboratory – which he later nicknamed "an invention factory" – Edison continued to create new devices. After constructing a telephone transmitter which improved upon Alexander Graham Bell's invention, Edison applied the technology to sound recording. Achieving only rudimentary playback, Edison had recorded himself, reciting "Mary Had A Little Lamb." Edison did not foresee the music-related potential of his revolutionary device, which he designed as an office dictation machine. Setting aside his work on sound recording for a time, Edison later sold the rights to entrepreneur Jesse H. Lippincott. But when Lippincott fell ill and his company went bankrupt in 1894, Edison acquired complete control of The North American Phonograph Company. Though improving upon the quality of both phonographs and records, Edison was slow to abandon cylinder-shaped records for the far more popular flat-disc format. While Edison eventually manufactured flat-disc records, they were playable only on Edison phonographs. Though fairly successful, Edison ended the production of records in 1929.

In addition to the phonograph, Thomas Edison also invented the modern incandescent light bulb, the alkaline storage battery, and another revolutionary mode of entertainment, the motion picture camera and projector.

One Ohio family made great use of Edison's movie projector. Several young brothers – the Warners of Youngstown – were the offspring of Polish immigrants. The only thing of any true monetary value their father brought with him from the old country was a prized, gold pocket-watch, which he kept in a hidden pocket inside his woolen pants. But with the Warners working hard to eke out a living, the family patriarch was willing to take a financial gamble. Pawning the watch as well as the family's horse, the Warners spent $1,000 to purchase a movie projector and a 24-minute silent film, *The Great Train Robbery*. Renting out a storefront in nearby Niles, the brothers screened their sole film for mesmerized audiences, earning $300 in a week for their efforts. Taking their projector and solitary film to other nearby towns, the brothers persevered until the brittle film wore out and could no longer be repaired. After a while, the Warners opened their first theater, the Cascade, in nearby New Castle, Pennsylvania. At the small storefront operation, the brothers screened rented films.

Eventually realizing that the film rental business was a far more lucrative venture, the Warner family sold its theater. Moving their operations to Pittsburgh, the brothers rented movies to regional theaters. Taking the next step, the Warners launched a movie production firm. Under the Warner Brothers banner, the company grew exponentially over the next two-decades by buying out a number of competing movie-production companies and theater chains.

Then in 1930, Warner Brothers expanded into the music business with the purchase of Brunswick Records, then the nation's third-largest label. But with the worsening Depression, the label was sold at a bargain-basement price at the end of 1931, a move which cost Warner Brothers $8 million in losses. At Jack Warner's insistence, Warner Brothers re-entered the music business in 1958, with Jim Conkling heading the new division. Although financially unsteady at first, the record company soon had successes with The Everly Brothers, Peter, Paul & Mary, Cleveland-born composer Henry Mancini and comedian Bob Newhart. Over the next five decades, the label swallowed up many of its competitors and would emerge as a conglomerate, the Warner Music Group.

POP SINGERS IN THE PRE-ROCK ERA

In the world of popular music before rock and roll, the Buckeye State spawned a series of leading vocalists and bandleaders. Many of these talented Ohioans dominated both the silver screen and Hit Parade, including Bob Hope, Dean Martin and Doris Day.

One of the era's top vocalists, Doris Day was also the nation's highest-grossing actress for nearly a decade. Projecting a wholesome persona, the Cincinnati native starred in a number of hit films including *The Pajama Game* and *April In Paris*. Also pursuing a musical career, Day was the featured singer for several bandleaders, most notably Les Brown, and provided the vocals on the 1945 smash, "Sentimental Journey." Pursuing a solo career in 1947, she scored dozens of hits including "Secret Love" and "Whatever Will Be, Will Be (Que Sera, Sera)." Day later hosted a popular, daily television program from 1968 to 1973.

Another female Buckeye vocalist, Rosemary Clooney emerged from a showbiz family. Born just across the Ohio River in Kentucky but raised in Cincinnati, she joined her sister Betty on a popular radio show at WLW in 1945. The following year, Rosemary Clooney headed for New York City and began a three-year recording stint as the featured vocalist in Tony Pastor's orchestra, reaching the pop charts with hits such as "You Started Something" and "Grieving For You." (Meanwhile, Betty would soon date Frank Sinatra.) Launching a solo recording career, Rosemary Clooney enjoyed a strong hit run from 1951 to 1957 with "Come On-a My House," "Mambo Italiano," and the double-sided entry, "Hey There" / "This Ole House." Also an actress, she appeared in a string of films including the 1954 holiday classic with Bing Crosby and Danny Kaye, *White Christmas*.

One of the leading bandleaders of the era, Lakewood-born Sammy Kaye was noted for his "sweet" sound. After building a fanbase while enrolled at Ohio University, he was hired by a Cincinnati radio station. Settling in Pittsburgh, Kaye became a national sensation with his popular radio program, *Sunday Serenade*. Meanwhile, Canton-born bandleader Enoch Light was trained as a classical violinist in Vienna. Scoring his first hit in the 1930s with "Summer Night," Light enjoyed a resurgence in the 1960s after launching a pair of record labels.

Nicknamed "the King of Swing," jazz giant Artie Shaw began his professional career in Cleveland. Dropping the saxophone for his soon-to-be trademark clarinet in 1927, Shaw joined a Cleveland-based jazz combo, The Joe Cantor Band. Excelling as an arranger, Shaw was offered a position with the city's top act, The Austin Wylie Orchestra. Forming his own orchestra in 1936, Shaw became a major star with his rendition of Cole Porter's "Begin The Beguine." In 1938, Shaw became the first bandleader to break the color barrier in jazz, when he hired singer Billie Holiday.

Meanwhile, Akron native Vaughn Monroe was a baritone vocalist and trumpet player who successfully crossed-over to network radio, movies and television. Also a popular bandleader, he signed with RCA-Victor and scored a hit in 1941 with what would become his theme song, "Racing With The Moon." Placing more than fifty hits on the pop charts, Monroe is best remembered for his 1949 classic, the haunting "(Ghost) Riders In The Sky." In the early-1950s, Monroe was briefly a singing cowboy.

Bob Hope

An actor and comedian, Bob Hope played the comic joker alongside the poised and polished Bing Crosby. Born in England but raised in Cleveland, Hope emerged from the vaudeville tradition. Trying his luck at boxing, shining shoes and other trades, Hope turned to dancing and, later, acting. After spending several years on the Broadway stage, Hope appeared in his first major feature film, *The Big Broadcast Of 1938*.

Hope first met screen partner Bing Crosby on the popular radio program, *Capitol Family Hour*. By 1938, Hope was hosting his own radio show, which quickly became the highest-rated program in the nation. Simultaneously working in movies, Hope signed a longterm contract with Paramount, and often co-starred with Crosby and Dorothy Lamour in a series of "road" picture comedies, which were filmed in exotic locales.

Although Crosby would become one of the most prolific singers of the 20th century, Hope would manage just a smattering of hits, including his signature piece, "Thanks For The Memories." A lifelong patriot, Hope flew around the globe to entertain U.S. troops in periods of both war and peace.

Much like Bob Hope, Danny Thomas was primarily known as an actor. Though born near Detroit, he was raised in Toledo, which he considered his hometown. Thomas is best remembered for his long-running television series, *Make Room For Daddy*. He also starred in several music-related films, including the 1952 remake of *The Jazz Singer* and opposite Doris Day in the biography of songwriter Gus Kahn, *I'll See You In My Dreams*. Surprisingly, Thomas' only chart hit came in 1967 with the holiday song, "The First Christmas."

Dean Martin

The king of cool and straight man to Jerry Lewis' slapstick humor, Dean Martin was a popular actor, singer and star of his own television program. Suave, tanned and good looking, Martin enjoyed a six-decade-long career.

The son of Italian immigrants, Martin was reared in the Appalachian steel town of Steubenville. Dropping out of high school and ignoring his father's advice to become a barber, the former Dino Crocetti toyed with a variety of vocations in his youth. While still a teenager, he boxed in the welterweight division, ran bootleg whiskey across the Ohio River and dealt blackjack in the hidden backroom of a cigar store. Exposed to the entertainment industry during a brief visit to Hollywood, Martin made the decision not to spend his life toiling in the sweltering steel mills of Ohio.

Possessing the ability to mimic crooner Bing Crosby, Martin went from singing for friends to appearing on local stages. In 1939, Martin was given a new stage name, Dino Martini, by Columbus-based bandleader Ernie Kay, who employed the 22-year-old singer on a full-time basis. Subsequently hired as the featured vocalist for The Sammy Watkins Orchestra, the renamed Dean Martin sang mostly romantic ballads. In Cleveland, Martin's performances drew large crowds to a downtown nightspot, the Vogue Room at the

Hollenden Hotel. Here, Martin would meet his first wife.

Leaving for New York City to pursue a career as a solo act, Martin struggled over the next few years. But at a performance in 1945, he became friends with one of the opening acts, a lanky vaudeville-style comedian named Jerry Lewis. The following year when Martin was hired as a last-minute replacement at Atlantic City's 500 Club, he created a stir with a series of ad-libbed performances with another act on the bill – his friend from New York, Jerry Lewis. Within weeks, the pair cultivated a popular stage show which drew lines out the door. Soon, Martin and Lewis were filling the biggest clubs in the nation with their music and comedy routines. Lured to Hollywood, they made their film debut in the comedy, *My Friend Irma*. A major box-office draw, the duo appeared in a series of lighthearted comedies including *The Caddy* and *Living It Up*.

Also pursuing a singing career, Martin managed only occasional chart success until finally breaking through in 1953 with the smash hit, "That's Amore." Lewis had secretly paid a pair of leading songwriters $30,000 to compose the Italian-flavored piece for Martin. (A perennial favorite, the song enjoyed newfound popularity after its inclusion in the 1987 film, *Moonstruck*.) Although Jerry Lewis would have a limited career as a singer, his son would form the pop-rock group Gary Lewis & The Playboys, and score several hits in the 1960s.

But after a simmering feud, Martin and Lewis dissolved their partnership in 1956, exactly ten-years to the date after their first nightclub performance. Although Martin was slow to cultivate his solo film career, he soon thrived as a member of the boozy and boisterous Rat Pack, alongside Frank Sinatra, Sammy Davis Jr., Joey Bishop and Peter Lawford.

Martin's daughter Deana later recalled, "He could hardly believe how much his fortunes had changed. 'Who'd have thunk it' he would say. 'For a boy from Steubenville, Ohio?' He was always proud of where he came from, and mentioned it whenever he could." Martin would later slip in the name of his hometown into the lyrics of the song, "Mr. Wonderful."

PRE-ROCK VOCAL QUARTETS
Two of the most important cogs in the evolution of big band-era, vocal music into rock and roll were a pair of all-male singing acts with Ohio credentials. The Ink Spots and The Mills Brothers were the most popular vocal groups – black or white – of the 1940s. Breaking down racial barriers in the process, these two groups dominated the pop charts.

The Mills Brothers were assembled in the Northwestern Ohio town of Pique in the mid-1920s by John Mills Sr. Formerly a member of a popular, barbershop quartet called The Four Kings, he supervised his four sons, all of whom received their musical training in local church choirs.

Initially using a primitive kazoo as their only musical accompaniment, the quartet later stumbled upon a successful gimmick. When Harry Mills forgot his kazoo, he improvised by blowing into his clasped hands and mimicking a trumpet. A sensation around the Midwest, the group landed its own program on WLW in Cincinnati.

Befriended by Duke Ellington, The Mills Brothers relocated to New York City in 1930. Nicknamed "the Four Boys and a Guitar," The Mills Brothers played to packed houses, appeared in several feature films and were signed to their own CBS network radio show. As a matter of pride, the following was printed on the labels of the group's early record releases: "No musical instruments or mechanical devices used on this recording other than one guitar." In 1936, John Mills Sr. joined the group upon the death of his son, John Jr.

Embraced by pop radio, The Mills Brothers scored a long string of hits beginning with "Tiger Rag" and continuing with "Paper Doll" and "You Always Hurt The One You Love." Enjoying success into the rock era, the group topped the charts in 1952 with "The Glow-Worm" and charted in 1958 with a cover version of the doo-wop song, "Get A Job."

A similar vocal group, The Ink Spots also have Buckeye roots. In the late-1920s, singer "Ivory" Deek Watson was a member of the Indianapolis-based Percolating Puppies. Arrested for disturbing the peace after a sidewalk show, the group escaped punishment after impressing the judge with an in-court performance. With the trial garnering press coverage, the group was offered a nightly radio show.

Watson subsequently formed The Four Riff Brothers. The group was hired by WLW in Cincinnati, replacing jazz pianist Fats Waller. Later relocating to Cleveland, Watson teamed with Indianapolis-natives Jerry Daniels and Charlie Fuqua. Initially billed as The King, Jack And The Jester, the vocal group later added cello-player/bass-vocalist Orville "Hoppy" Jones. After performing around the Cleveland area, the group headed south to Cincinnati and enjoyed a two-year residency at WLW.

Renamed The Ink Spots, the quartet was hired by the flagship station of the NBC-Red radio network, WJZ in Newark. With the replacement of Daniels with lead tenor Bill Kenny in 1936, the group gelled into its classic lineup. Beginning with their debut 1939 hit "If I Didn't Care," The Ink Spots enjoyed a long hit run which included "My Prayer," "Java Jive" and "The Gypsy."

Though frequently in competition with The Mills Brothers, The Ink Spots had a more distinct sound, with most of their songs featuring a spoken verse by Hoppy Jones.

Often ignored by music historians, The Charioteers were another popular African-American musical group of the 1940s. Formed in 1930 as The Harmony Four at Wilberforce University (a historically black institution in Ohio), the group was assembled and mentored by professor Howard Daniel. Featuring the radiant voice of lead tenor Billy Williams, the group was renamed The Charioteers, after the old spiritual, "Swing Low, Sweet Chariot."

Veering away from religious material and embracing the pop hits of the day, The Charioteers won a statewide, vocal quartet contest in 1931. After landing a radio show on WLW, the group was later hired by a New York City radio station. Despite recording for a series of record labels, the group had limited success on the charts. Instead, The Charioteers had far greater fortune as the backing vocalists for the leading stars of the day: Pearl Bailey, Frank Sinatra and Bing Crosby. As frequent guests on Crosby's network radio show, the group garnered further exposure. But due to changing musical tastes, The Charioteers did not survive into the rock era.

THE ARRIVAL OF ROCK AND ROLL
A crucial, but often-overlooked artist who aided in the transition of jazz and blues into R&B and rock and roll was Dayton-born vocalist Mildred Cummings, better known as Little Miss Cornshucks. Atlantic Records founder Ahmet Ertegun recalled in his autobiography: "In 1943, when I was 19 or so years old, I went to a nightclub in the northeast black ghetto section of Washington [D.C.] and heard a singer whose name was Little Miss Cornshucks and I thought, 'My God!!!' She was better than anything I'd ever heard. She would come out like a country girl with a bandana around her head, a basket in her hand, and so forth, which she'd set aside fairly early on into the show. She could sing the blues better than anybody I've ever heard to this day. I asked her that night if she would mind if I made a record of her for myself. We cut 'Kansas City' along with some other blues and she also sang a song called 'So Long.' She had such a wonderful sound and I remember just thinking, 'My God! My God!' And I didn't have a record company, I just made those records for myself."

After wowing audiences at talent shows in Dayton, the musically-unschooled 17-year-old singer was taken to Chicago in 1940 by a gospel-music promoter. An overnight sensation, Little Miss Cornshucks captivated audiences in Windy City nightclubs such as Club De Lisa and the Rhumboogie Club. Though poised to become a star, she instead turned to liquor to numb the pain of her tumultuous marriage to a musician.

When Ahmet Ertegun launched Atlantic Records several years later, he wanted to record Little Miss Cornshucks, but could not locate her. Instead, Ruth Brown scored a breakthrough hit with a note-for-note rendition of Little Miss Cornshucks' signature song, a bluesy re-working of Russ Morgan's 1940 pop hit 'So Long' (which had also been a hit for The Charioteers). Brown later admitted in *No Depression* magazine, "I *stole* that from her! It was a big hit for me – and it should have been hers." Atlantic Records struck again when it signed another female vocalist, LaVern Baker, and initially billed her as Little Miss Share Cropper.

Meanwhile just as rock and roll was taking hold, an Ohio-based, pop-vocal trio took America by storm. Hailing from Middletown, The McGuire Singers – Christine, Dorothy and Phyllis – were hired in 1953 by television and radio host Arthur Godfrey as the replacements for The Chordettes. As was commonplace during the early years of rock, The McGuire Sisters recorded a series of middle-of-the-road cover versions of rock and R&B hits, including the syrupy "Goodnight, Sweetheart, Goodnight" and "Sincerely."

But a growing number of deejays such as Alan Freed realized that the "cover record" practice was hurting both rock artists and independent labels, and as a rule, would play only the original versions. With the public clamoring to hear the original, unsanitized renditions of hit songs, most radio stations stopped playing cover records by the end of the 1950s.

CHAPTER 1
HANG ON SLOOPY:
THE OHIO STATE UNIVERSITY TRADITION

Middle-America, the heartland and the nation's pulse have all been used to describe the mid-Ohio city of Columbus. Locals have given the city another nickname – cow town. Also considered a college town, Columbus became synonymous with the Ohio State Buckeyes.

The Ohio legislature selected Columbus as the state capital in 1816, not because the town was along a water or train route, but because of its central location. Unlike the state's other large cities – Cleveland, Toledo, Akron and Cincinnati – which owe their growth to waterways such as wide rivers, lakes and man-made canals, Columbus was merely a village when it was designated the state capital. As such, Columbus owes its progress to a prime industry – government – as well as to a celebrated university with a strong sports program.

Isolated from the population centers of Northeast and Southwest Ohio, Columbus expanded its borders into the suburbs and significantly increased its population during the last half of the 20th century. By the 1990s, Columbus emerged as the state's most populous city, surpassing Cleveland. But unlike shrinking Cleveland or Cincinnati, Columbus was shut out of professional basketball, baseball and football (although the city did eventually snag a professional hockey team). Consequently, sports fans focused on Columbus' most successful and dynamic franchise – the Ohio State Buckeyes football team. A sensation not only in Columbus, the team came to represent the entire state of Ohio.

An eclectic assortment of musical acts sprang from Columbus: jazz diva Nancy Wilson, jazz multi-instrumentalist Rahsaan Roland Kirk, rock-funksters Royal Crescent Mob, rapper Bow Wow, bebop saxophonist Rusty Bryant, country-rockers The Pure Prairie League, jam band O.A.R., crooner Michael Feinstein, and folk troubadour Phil Ochs.

But the song that defined the city was a rock classic from 1965 called "Hang On Sloopy." And no, it's not Snoopy, Charlie Brown's smart-alec beagle.

OHIO STATE UNIVERSITY
Ohio State University was founded in 1873 as the Ohio Agricultural and Mechanical College. Despite receiving state funding, the institution struggled financially over the next two decades. Meanwhile in 1890, 182 of the school's 493 students signed a petition requesting $200 in annual funding for athletics, including the construction of football and baseball fields, a quarter-mile running track and tennis courts. A trio of students selected scarlet and gray as the school's colors, after administrators rejected their first choice,

orange and brown, a combination already claimed by Princeton.

As interest in football grew, a statewide, collegiate league was established in 1890. With only four scheduled games in their first season, the Buckeyes opened with a 14-to-10 win over Ohio Wesleyan. A rowdy encounter, the game was played in the town of Delaware, just north of Columbus.

By 1912, Ohio State joined a Midwestern athletic conference which would later evolve into the Big-10. Initially formed in 1896, the configuration was known by various names including the Western Conference. When a co-founding member, Michigan, rejoined in 1917 following a nine-year absence, the conference was informally dubbed the Big-10. (The Big-10 designation was officially adopted in 1987.)

After winning three conference championships between 1916 and 1920, Ohio State's football program had outgrown its playing field. The final game played at Ohio Field was a post-season charity event which pitted a group of college all-stars from around the nation against a team of former Ohio State players. One of the athletes playing that day was the great Jim Thorpe.

By 1918, the University approved the construction of a large, modern, football stadium. The planned structure would be an open-ended, horse-shoe-shaped edifice, situated along the banks of the Olentangy River. With one-million dollars raised in donations – about half of which came from Columbus residents – construction proceeded in 1920. That same year, the American Professional Football Association was founded in Canton. With Jim Thorpe as its first president, the consortium featured teams from Ohio and nearby Midwestern states. Two years later, the organization was renamed the National Football League. (Canton's historic role in the creation of the league was later acknowledged with the establishment of the Pro Football Hall of Fame.)

Initially budgeted at $930,000, the Ohio Stadium would eventually cost $1.7 million to build. A massive undertaking, the project required 6,000 steel beams and 70,000 tons of concrete. Though the structure boasted a seating capacity of 62,110, the project's architectural draftsman M.A. Carter considered the number inadequate. The first game played at the stadium was against Ohio Wesleyan on October 7, 1922. The stadium was officially dedicated two weeks later when the Michigan Wolverines came to town.

With college football growing in popularity, the Heisman Trophy was awarded to the best collegiate player in the nation. Named after Cleveland-born coach John W. Heisman who had introduced many innovations to the sport, the award was inaugurated in 1935. Beginning his career at Oberlin College as both a player and coach in 1892, he twice shut out Ohio State University that season. The following year, he was hired by Buchtel College (later renamed the University of Akron), where the faculty resisted his brand of competitive football. He subsequently returned to Oberlin for a season before coaching at a series of schools over the next four-decades, including Clemson and Rice Institute. In all, Ohio State University players would earn seven Heismans, with quarterback Archie Griffin winning twice. Meanwhile, in 1936, OSU athlete Jesse Owens emerged as the big winner at the summer Olympics held in Berlin.

An Ohio State alumnus and former high school coach, Paul E. Brown took over lead coaching duties at Ohio State in 1941. While heading the football program at Massillon's Washington High School, the 32-year-old Brown had amassed an impressive record of 81 wins, eight losses and one tie. During his first three seasons at OSU, he lost just one game. Brown later coached both the Cincinnati Bengals and the Cleveland Browns, and was the namesake of the Cleveland franchise. (Meanwhile, shortly after going on the air in 1949, Columbus television station WLWC began broadcasting OSU football games.)

Then in 1951, OSU officials considered rehiring Brown but instead selected former Denison and Miami (of Ohio) University coach Wayne Woodrow Hayes, better known as Woody Hayes. During his 28-year reign as head coach, Hayes took the Buckeyes to numerous Big-10 championships and bowl games. And in the process, "Woody" became an institution for his passionate and colorful outbursts. According to a history of Buckeyes football, "Hayes' many antics made the headlines. Unfortunately his humanitarian deeds did not receive as much exposure. He, in order, loaned money to players, which cost Ohio State a year of probation; evicted Big Ten writers and officials from pre-season practice; had locker room battles with California sportswriters; ripped down sideline markers; and had an altercation with a Los Angeles photographer. Woody worked seven days a week, 12 to 14 hours, and he could not understand why everyone else could not do the same." In 1967, Hayes introduced the practice of placing small, buckeye leaf stickers on the helmets of his players to mark the execution of a good play.

But it was the impulsive punching of Clemson linebacker Charlie Bauman following an interception run at the 1978 Gator Bowl that would stain Hayes' proud coaching career, and lead to his sudden resignation. A full 25-years after the career-ending incident, a *Los Angeles Times* sportswriter noted that Hayes' "legend in Columbus has only grown; you'd be surprised how many of the middle-aged men attending Ohio State games look like Hayes."

Every year since 1935, the Buckeyes have closed out their regular season by playing the University of Michigan Wolverines. While Ohio State dominated the series throughout most of the 1960s, Michigan managed an upset victory in 1969, giving then-rookie coach Bo Schembechler bragging rights. An Ohio native, Schembechler was born in Barberton. While earning a graduate degree at Ohio State University, Schembechler was an assistant coach under Woody Hayes.

By the 1970s, the Buckeyes and Wolverines had cultivated the greatest college rivalry of any sport. Since 1934, every Buckeyes player and coach that beat Michigan was awarded with a small "gold pants" charm. The tradition began when embattled OSU head coach Francis Schmidt told an interviewer that Michigan players "put their pants on one leg at a time just like we do."

THE BEST DAMN BAND IN THE LAND

As an essential facet of college football, the marching band performs throughout the game and during halftime festivities. Ohio State University debuted its first band at the start of the 1878 football season. Evolving from the drum corps and military band tradition, the inaugural OSU band was an informal, student-managed ensemble which consisted of just three fifes, eight snare drums and a single bass drum. Then in 1896, the university assembled an "official" marching band, with Gustav Bruder installed as director. A multi-instrumentalist who had gained experience as a member of a Marine band under the leadership of the legendary conductor John Philip Sousa, Bruder had also led a circus band. Transforming a small, undisciplined group of student musicians into a world-class university marching band was no easy task. Although membership in the marching band remained sparse over the next two decades, the number of participants ballooned to 100 by the time of Ohio State's third Big-10 champion win in 1920.

The Ohio State marching band began employing formations during the 1921 season, and would soon launch the "O-H-I-O" configuration. By 1924, floating formations were introduced. During this same time, C. Edwin "Tubby" Essington revolutionized the role of the frontman in the OSU marching band. With his showmanship, attitude and exuberant high-stepping, Essington became an Ohio State legend.

In 1929, Ohio State alumnus Eugene J. Weigel left his supervisory post in the Cleveland Public Schools to accept a position as director of the OSU marching band. After expanding the unit to 120 musicians, Weigel revolutionized the marching band in 1934 by eliminating all instruments outside of brass and percussion, due to their inability to be heard in large stadiums. He also required the musicians to memorize their parts instead of using sheet music.

More changes were to come. Members of the marching band would no longer just walk onto the field to spell "O-H-I-O." With a high-kicking drum major leading in front, the Best Damn Band In The Land paraded down a ramp into the perpetually packed, horse-shoe-shaped stadium. Twirling an elongated, single-ended baton, the drum major would drop into an acrobatic, gravity-defying, back bending march, touching the ground with just the tip of his hat's red plume. Then throwing his baton 100 feet into the air, a clean catch is considered good luck. According to OSU historians Wilbur Snypp and Bob Hunter, "The Marching Band has pioneered many techniques that have been copied by other bands. Such innovations as floating formations, animated movement of formations, scriptwriting, measured step marching, and the fast cadence and the high step were first tried and proven at Ohio State." Weigel patterned the revolving "O" in the "O-H-I-O" formation after airplane skywriters at the Ohio State Fair as well as the revolving lights of the landmark sign at New York City's Time Square.

The ceremonial dotting of the "I" in "O-H-I-O" was introduced in 1936, when a trumpet player, John Brungart, performed the task. The following year, the honor was bestowed to a senior sousaphone player. At exactly 16 measures from the end of the song "Le Regiment," a drum major struts toward the top of the "I," with the sousaphone player high-stepping at two paces behind. As the drum major comes to a halt and points to the location, the sousaphone player leaps to the spot, removes his black hat and dramatically bows to both sides of the stadium. (Guests who have dotted the "I" include Woody Hayes, Bob Hope, John Glenn and Ohio State alum Jack Nicklaus.) With the halftime festivities practically as important as the game itself, Buckeye fans still show up by the thousands for the marching band's Saturday-morning practice sessions at St. John Arena.

Yet for all of the OSU band's innovations, a controversy still rages concerning the origin of the celebrated "script Ohio" formation. According to a 1932 article in the University of Michigan student newspaper, the Michigan marching band had spelled out a number of phrases in script-writing – including "M-I-C-H" and "O-H-I-O" – during that year's Ohio State-Michigan match-up.

THE REAL SLOOPY

A jazz-styled cabaret singer, Dorothy Heflick was the inspiration for the song, "Hang On Sloopy." Her father, Fred Jr., ran a music store in Findlay, Ohio, before moving across the state to Steubenville. There he led a jazz combo, which on occasion, featured a budding local vocalist named Dino Crocetti, who would later emerge as Dean Martin.

Born in Steubenville on September 26, 1913, Dorothy Heflick learned to play the piano at a young age. Nicknamed "Dottie," she left Ohio in the early-1930s to join a New York City, jazz-flavored musical troupe, The Southland Rhythm Girls. The all-female act appeared in a 1935 film short, *Speedy Justice*.

When one of the troupe's members, Yvonne "Dixie" Fasnacht, quit in 1939 to open a nightclub with her sister in their hometown of New Orleans, Dottie Heflick soon followed. It was Fasnacht who gave Heflick her nickname, "Sloopy." At Dixie's Bar of Music, the pair soon began performing as "Dixie and Sloopy." By 1949, the bar relocated from its St. Charles Avenue location to Bourbon Street, and was promoted as "New Orleans' Biggest Little Club." In 1957, Dixie and Sloopy released their only album, a jazz-inflected project called *Sloopy Time*.

In the early-1960s, songwriters/musicians Bert Berns and Wes Farrell stumbled upon a performance by Dixie and Sloopy during a visit to New Orleans, and were smitten by the act. In between sets, Berns and Farrell chatted with Sloopy. Although Dorothy Heflick would rarely talk about the incident, her daughter Jane Heflick recalled in *Columbus Monthly*: "The club was a little rambunctious that night... Patrons were heckling a bit, and giving Sloopy a rough way to go. The musicians Sloopy had spoken to came to her defense... shouting out their encouragement: 'Hang in there, Sloopy,' they'd yell. 'Hang on, Sloopy.' They thought her nickname was just so cute." It was this fateful encounter which was the inspiration for what would become a rock and roll standard.

Born in Florida, Wes Farrell began his career in music at age 19. As a Brill Building songwriter in New York City, he penned hits for Freddy Cannon, Chubby Checker, Dion and Timi Yuro.

A Bronx-native, Bert Berns was born to Russian-Jewish immigrants. Studying classical piano during his childhood, he spent the rest of his life nurturing his love of music. His heart damaged by a teenage bout with rheumatic fever, Berns knew that his days were numbered.

After passing through a series of entry-level jobs in the music industry – including as a session pianist and music copyist – Berns spent some time in Cuba. Returning to New York City, he found work as a songwriter for music publisher Bobby Mellin in the Brill Building district. Often assuming the pen-name of Bert Russell, Berns wrote numerous hits, including "A Little Bit Of Soap" by The Jarmels and "Tell Him" by The Exciters. During this period, Berns also attempted a solo career. Releasing a handful of singles on the Laurie and Wand labels, he also appeared on *American Bandstand*.

Meanwhile, in the wake of Atlantic Records' fortunes with independent songwriters-producers Leiber & Stoller – who had great successes with both The Coasters and The Drifters – the label hired Bert Berns in 1963 to work in a similar capacity. At Atlantic, Berns collaborated with Solomon Burke, The Drifters, Barbara Lewis, Esther Phillips and others. One of Berns' compositions, "Twist And Shout," had been recorded at Atlantic by The Top Notes, but failed to reach the charts. Convinced the song could be a hit, Berns produced a new version by The Isley Brothers, which would reach the top-20 and later spawn a hit remake by The Beatles.

Atlantic Records co-owner Jerry Wexler recalled in his autobiography that Berns "was intrigued by the wiseguys, loved hanging out with hoodlums and trading gangster stories. Bert was also an adventurer who had haunted pre-Castro Cuba, where, he claimed, he'd run guns and dope; he boasted about owning a nightclub in Havana. All this may have been a romantic exaggeration; but his feelings for Latin rhythms was right as rain. His affinity for the Cuban [music] was deep, and he practically made a cottage industry on the chord changes of 'Guantanamera'.... He used those identical [chord] changes in 'Twist And Shout,' 'A Little Bit Of Soap,' and 'My Girl Sloopy.'"

Originally recorded by an R&B act called The Vibrations, "My Girl Sloopy" would later evolve into the rock standard, "Hang On Sloopy." The Vibrations were a group of veteran singers whose sound was rooted in the doo-wop tradition. Formed in 1955 as The Jayhawks by students at a Los Angeles high school, the group enjoyed a lengthy and varied career.

Featuring tenor Jimmy Johnson on lead vocals, The Jayhawks scored a crossover, novelty-styled hit in 1956 with their second single, "Stranded In The Jungle." But the group soon found itself competing on the charts with a quickly-recorded cover-version of the song by The Cadets. While both records reached the pop top-20, The Cadets' remake eclipsed the original by two notches, peaking at #16.

After experiencing some personnel changes and wanting to escape their image as a novelty act, The Jayhawks changed their name in 1959, first to The Vibes and then The Vibrations. Returning to the pop charts in 1961, The Vibrations had success with a dance record, "The Watusi."

Though under contract with Chicago-based Chess/Checker Records, the group members moonlighted at Arvee Records as demo singers. One of their demos, "Peanut Butter," was intended for an Arvee act, The Olympics. But with The Olympics touring on the East Coast, Arvee impatiently decided to release the demo as a single without notifying The Vibrations. A surprise hit, "Peanut Butter" was issued as by The Marathons. But after a lawsuit, The Vibrations remained with Checker and issued a new version of the song. Meanwhile, Arvee would assemble a group to record an album's worth of material as The Marathons.

Following their stint at Checker, The Vibrations teamed with the songwriting/production team of Bert Berns and Wes Farrell. Though the group had never signed with Atlantic, their single – a Berns/Farrell composition called "My Girl Sloopy" – was a hit on the label. A raucous and spirited track, the song had a slight Latin feel and borrowed elements from another Bert Berns composition, "Twist And Shout."

Believing that "Sloopy" had not achieved its full potential, Berns planned to pitch the composition to Van Morrison. But instead, fate intervened and the song returned to the charts after a series of unlikely events involving a trio of New York songwriters who posed as Australians and an obscure, teenage garage-band from the Dayton area.

THE STRANGELOVES & THE MCCOYS

In 1965, Bert Berns formed Bang Records, a label which was distributed by Atlantic. Bang took its name from the first initials of Berns and a trio of Atlantic Records owners, brothers Ahmet and Nesuhi Ertegun and Gerald (Jerry) Wexler.

One of the first artists signed by Bang was The Strangeloves. The group was formed by a trio of professional songwriters/producers – Bob Feldman, Jerry Goldstein and Richard Gottehrer. Feldman and Goldstein had been writing music together since their early-teen years, and enjoyed their first success when deejay Alan Freed used their song, "Big Beat," as the theme for his television program. The duo subsequently recorded some singles in 1960 as Jerry and Bob. Feldman and Goldstein were soon joined by Richard Gottehrer – a Bronx-born, classically-trained pianist who was drawn to rock music after hearing Alan Freed's radio show. Hired by April-Blackwood Music, the trio wrote songs for a number of acts including Pat Boone, Dion, The Jive Five, Freddy Cannon and Bobby Vee.

With Goldstein dating a member of the girl-group The Angels, he wanted them to record a composition called "My Boyfriend's Back." Written by Goldstein and his two partners, the song was inspired by an argument

Feldman had witnessed between two teenagers in front of a high school. But with April-Blackwood Music insisting that the song go to The Shirelles, Goldstein and his two songwriting partners held firm. Locked out of their office and fired from the publishing company, Goldstein and his associates produced the song themselves. A prudent move, their production of The Angels' rendition of the song topped the charts in 1963.

But when The Angels refused to record an exotic song called "Love, Love" (an updated version of the pop standard "A Little Love"), Feldman, Goldstein and Gottehrer decided to tackle the track themselves. Motivated by the popularity of the British Invasion, the budding rockers created false identities. Pretending to be Australian, the trio emerged as The Strangeloves.

Released by Swan Records, The Strangeloves' debut track received only spotty airplay. But when a Virginia Beach deejay invited The Strangeloves to perform the song at a radio station event, they accepted the offer. After performing the song for a screaming mob of young fans, The Strangeloves followed up with the only other song they knew – the R&B standard "Bo Diddley." With the audience reaction equally strong for the second song, The Strangeloves decided to record the track as their next single.

But during the sessions for "Bo Diddley" at the Atlantic Records studios in New York City, Atlantic chief Ahmet Ertegun advised the group to record an original composition. Merging the signature beat of "Bo Diddley" with a portion of the melody from Silverno Merano's "Anna," The Strangeloves masterminded an upbeat rocker called "I Want Candy."

Expanding on their phony pedigrees, The Strangeloves pretended to be a set of Australian brothers named Giles, Miles and Niles, who had amassed a fortune as sheep farmers. The trio dressed in bizarre, jungle-inspired outfits and spoke with phony accents, which they patterned after a British colleague. Bob Feldman told *Goldmine*, "I did a lot of talking in our interviews until Jerry and Richie developed their own accents. It was amazing – our stories never matched. We'd give separate interviews with answers that didn't match anything, and nobody picked up on it. They'd ask who was the oldest, and I'd make up something, and Jerry and Richard's order would be totally different. So finally we got together and got some basics down, like the reason we didn't look alike was we had different fathers."

But with one of the members professing to be the boomerang champion of Australia, the group was nearly outed. When a Pittsburgh deejay demanded to see a demonstration, a poorly-thrown boomerang struck a cameraman.

With "I Want Candy" becoming a sizable hit, The Strangeloves toured across the country. Further complications arose when the group's opening act, The Dave Clark Five, became enamored with a catchy song The Strangeloves were performing every night – an updated, rock-styled version of the recent Vibrations' hit, "My Girl Sloopy." Then when The Dave Clark Five informed The Strangeloves of their intention to record the song as their next single, the pseudo-Australians panicked. After the completion of the tour, The Dave Clark Five flew back to England with a tape of The Strangeloves' performance of the song from a show in Tulsa, Oklahoma.

Meanwhile, with one of the members of The Strangeloves afraid to fly, the group decided to drive back to New York City. Taking advantage of the situation, the group's agent scheduled a last-minute gig at Forest Park Arena in Dayton. At the concert, The Strangeloves were amazed by their young backing band, a group of teens with Beatles-inspired clothing and haircuts calling themselves Rick And The Raiders. Rick, of course, was Rick Zehringer (or as he was later known, Rick Derringer).

Rick Zehringer was raised near Dayton in the small town of Fort Recovery, Ohio. After showing an interest in his uncle's guitar, Rick received an electric guitar and amplifier for his ninth birthday. Quickly mastering the instrument, young Rick also began experimenting with home recording. Meanwhile, Rick's younger brother, Randy, soon abandoned the accordion for the drums. Schooled in harmony and music theory by their mother, the young brothers advanced quickly, with Rick especially proficient. Almost immediately, the duo began performing at functions around town.

In 1961, the Zehringers relocated just across the Ohio border to Union City, Indiana, when their railroad worker father was transferred. The brothers were soon joined in their garage sessions by a neighbor named Dennis Kelly, who asked his parents to buy him an electric bass. After several weeks, Kelly became proficient on the instrument by playing along to a 45-rpm record of "The McCoy" by the surf-rock band The Ventures. Kelly told interviewer Dan Muise, "In a very short period of time, we became the top band in the area. When I say 'the area,' I mean Dayton, Ohio. And I think the entire phenomenon was due to Rick's talent on the guitar. Randy was an OK drummer. I was an OK bass player. But Rick was phenomenal then as he is now. If you can imagine a kid of fourteen or fifteen at the time, that good at the guitar, it was incredible."

But just as the group began booking bigger gigs, Dennis Kelly had started college and could perform only on weekends. Hiring a weekday bassist named Randy Joe Hobbs – who originally used an old, rhythm guitar that was tuned low – the group eventually fired Kelly. Performing under various names including The Rick Z Combo, the group then hired keyboardist Ronnie Brandon. As Rick And The Raiders, the group recorded the single, "I Know That I Love You," for a tiny label, Sonic Records.

But just as Rick And The Raiders were about to break out of Dayton, the group was presented with an offer by The Strangeloves. Impressed by the young musicians, the anxious members of The Strangeloves hatched an idea to hire Rick's band to provide the vocals for "My Girl Sloopy." The recording sessions were arranged after obtaining permission from the Zehringer brothers' parents, who accompanied the band to New York City to act as chaperones.

Rick Derringer later told author Bob Shannon that after arriving in New York, The Strangeloves "gave us a small record player and a copy of the musical track and told us exactly what they wanted us to sing. We went out into the park for a few days, practiced singing it, and put the vocal on it. They jumped up and down in the control room and yelled, 'Number One!' and a few weeks later, it was. That's how easy it was for us."

On the recording, Rick Zehringer provided the pleading lead vocal while the rest of the band contributed harmonies and backing vocals. Additionally, he unleashed a blistering guitar solo after the first verse. And since the lyrics never actually say "My Girl Sloopy," he convinced the label to issue the single as "Hang On Sloopy."And although the completed track included an extra verse, it was edited down – not because of any foul language – but because it had to be shortened for airplay on top-40 radio stations.

Wanting to avoid any confusion with the similarly-named Paul Revere & The Raiders, Zehringer and his group reverted to one of their earlier monikers, The McCoys. And inspired by the pistol logo on the Bang label, Rick Zehringer changed his last name to Derringer. With The McCoys' single racing up the pop charts, The Dave Clark Five wisely chose not to issue their version of the song. But the news had not reached Canada where Little Caesar & The Consuls (a group which included Robbie Robertson and Gene McLennan) released "My Girl Sloopy" as a single.

Debuting on August 14, 1965, The McCoys' "Hang On Sloopy" topped the pop charts seven-weeks later on October 2, 1965. Spending only one-week at that position, the song was bumped by The Beatles' "Yesterday." While Caesar & The Consuls managed to reach the U.S. charts, their version of the song just missed hitting the top-40. And with many listeners continuing to confuse "Sloopy" with "Snoopy," The Royal Guardsmen took advantage of the situation by inserting a brief chorus of "Hang On Sloopy" into their top-10 novelty hit, "Snoopy vs. The Red Baron."

Touring across the country in late-1965 as the opening act for The Strangeloves, The McCoys were well received. But on the strength of "Sloopy," the billing was reversed midway through the tour, with The McCoys suddenly promoted to headlining status. Though receiving top billing, the young group did not see an increase in its wages.

Bob Feldman of The Strangeloves later recalled in *Goldmine* magazine: "If we had gotten back to New York without discovering The McCoys, we probably would have released the song ourselves under some other name. You must understand, we believed we had a number one record."

OSU BAND DIRECTOR CHARLES SPOHN

Meanwhile in 1964, Charles Spohn had been appointed the new director of the Ohio State University marching band, after more than a decade as an assistant under Jack Evans. Unlike his predecessor, Spohn wanted to infuse elements of rock and roll music into the marching band's repertoire. No longer considered a shortlived fad, rock music had permeated American culture and Spohn recognized that fact.

Spohn hired a former member of the marching band, John Tatgenhorst, to write arrangements of pop and rock songs for the OSU band to perform alongside traditional favorites such as "Buckeye Battle Cry" and "Across The Field." Paid a sum of $200, Tatgenhorst provided arrangements for nine songs, including Stan Getz's "Girl From Ipanema" and The Serendipity Singers' "Crooked Little Man." The new songs were popular with both the marching band and the audience, and as a result, Spohn ordered more arrangements from Tatgenhorst.

Then while visiting the Ohio State Fair in Columbus during the summer of 1965, Tatgenhorst was mesmerized by a song that blared from the speakers, "Hang On Sloopy" by The McCoys. Tatgenhorst told *Columbus Monthly*, "Just immediately, I heard an arrangement for the band. I liked its rhythmic quality. It rocked." Wanting to arrange "Sloopy" for the OSU band, Tatgenhorst played the 45-rpm single for Spohn. But when Spohn "heard the recorded version, he said, and I quote, 'The Ohio State Marching Band will never play that kind of music.' And 'music' wasn't the word he used."

But with Spohn eventually relenting, Tatgenhorst spent nearly five-hours arranging a marching band version of the song. Teaching the song to the OSU band, Spohn introduced what would soon be known as "The Sloopy Step." But initially, the band members were unhappy performing the new dance step.

"Hang On Sloopy" was introduced during the halftime of the Buckeyes' second game of the 1965 season, on October 9, versus the University of Illinois. Performed during a heavy rainstorm, the song apparently went unnoticed as drenched fans expressed little reaction. But the following week when fans in the stands kept yelling "Sloopy," the band reluctantly complied. Tatgenhorst told *The Akron Beacon Journal*, "The next week we played it in the C-Row, way up at the top, and the people behind the band started swaying back and forth, and before long the whole section was swaying to 'Sloopy,' and then four sections, and week after week they just kept yelling it and it just caught on to the whole stadium. And finally the PA announcer had to start asking students to not stand on top of each other (to sing)."

In his examination of the song, *Columbus Monthly* writer Eric Lyttle declared that "'Sloopy' stands out as an anomaly. The Best Damn Band In The Land is one of the nation's most traditional – steeped in a crisp, military marching style. Yet here's 'Sloopy,' one of the TBDBITL's most popular numbers, flying directly in the face of everything the OSU band stands for: a rock and roll tune from the 1960s, performed with a swinging-and-swaying dance step more resembling a show-style band." With the song's popularity broadening on a weekly basis, it quickly emerged as an Ohio State tradition.

Also in 1965, another OSU tradition made its debut when the school's costumed mascot Brutus Buckeye first hit the field. The mascot was the brainchild of students, Ray Bourhis and Sally Huber. After a campus-wide contest to name the mascot, student Kerry Reed provided the winning selection.

THE OFFICIAL STATE OF OHIO ROCK SONG

When *Columbus Citizen-Journal* columnist Joe Dirck read a wire story in April 1985 about how residents of Washington State wanted to proclaim The Kingsmen's "Louie Louie" as that state's official rock song, he experienced a moment of inspiration. Penning a column to promote "Hang On Sloopy" as the official Ohio rock song, Dirck would start the ball rolling. As a musician in his youth, Dirck had opened up for Rick Derringer's band on several occasions. Contacting politicians on both sides of the political aisle, Dirck enlisted the aid of Democratic state representative Mike Stinziano and Republican state senator Gene Watts.

Then on November 20, 1985, the measure to make "Hang On Sloopy" the official state rock song was approved. The legislature declared: "The members of the 116th General Assembly of Ohio wish to recognize the rock song 'Hang On Sloopy' as the official rock song of the great state of Ohio." But since the state already had an official song, the state declared that the "adoption of 'Hang On Sloopy' as the official rock song of Ohio is in no way intended to supplant 'Beautiful Ohio' as the official state song, but would serve as a companion piece to that old chestnut."

With the recognition of "Sloopy" by the state legislature, it joined other formal designations such as the state bird (cardinal), animal (white tail deer), beverage (tomato juice), insect (ladybug), wildflower (white trillium) and motto (With God, all things are possible).

AFTER SLOOPY

Despite the fact that "Hang On Sloopy" had sold six-million copies, The McCoys would earn very little for their effort. In the wake of "Sloopy," The McCoys returned to the top-10 with a cover of Little Willie John's R&B chestnut "Fever," which heavily borrowed the guitarwork and tempo of "Hang On Sloopy." During this period, The McCoys recorded mostly remakes and material composed by Feldman-Goldstein-Gottehrer. Although The McCoys would place seven more singles on the pop charts, their cover version of Ritchie Valens' "Come On Let's Go" would be their last top-40 entry. Another McCoys track, "Sorrow," became a top-10 cover hit in the U.K. for The Merseys. Meanwhile, in 1966, The McCoys were opening up for The Rolling Stones.

Leaving Bang Records in 1968, The McCoys took a stylistic turn toward psychedelia and hard rock. Wanting more artistic control, the group signed with Mercury Records. Produced by Rick Derringer and featuring the musical backing of the brass section from Blood, Sweat And Tears, the album *Infinite McCoys* was a major departure from their previous pop-oriented efforts. Though their followup album, *Human Ball*, was equally creative, The McCoys had fallen out of favor in pop music. At the time, The McCoys had settled into a long residency as the house band at Steve Paul's Scene nightclub in New York City. Eventually, the club's owner teamed The McCoys with another act he was managing – a blues-rock virtuoso named Johnny Winter. Beginning with the 1970 album *Johnny Winter And*, various members of The McCoys recorded and toured with Winter.

Rick Derringer would also collaborate with Johnny Winter's brother in the group, Edgar Winter's White Trash, and produce Winter's chart-topping, hard-rock smash, "Frankenstein." Then in 1974, Derringer scored a solo hit with the timeless rock anthem, "Rock And Roll, Hoochie Koo." Subsequently launching The Derringer Band in 1976, he released four albums. Then in 1983, he went solo with the album, *Good Dirty Fun*. A respected guitarist, Derringer would also work with Steely Dan, Alice Cooper and Kiss. As both a guitarist and producer, Derringer later teamed with Weird Al Yankovic on many of his hit parodies. A reunion with Edgar Winter would result in the 1990 album, *Edgar Winter And Rick Derringer Live In Japan*.

Meanwhile, "Sloopy" would occasionally return on the charts. Just months after The McCoys took the single to number-one, The Ramsey Lewis Trio nearly reached the top-10 with a Grammy-winning, instrumental rendition of the song. "Sloopy" would return to the U.S. pop chart on two more occasions: a pop-styled rendition in 1970 by The Lettermen and a rock/reggae version in 1975 by Rick Derringer. In the U.K., "Hang On Sloopy" reached the charts in 1976 with a disco-styled version by an American group, The Sandpipers. (Ironically, The Sandpipers' biggest U.S. hit was "Guantanamera," a song which inspired Bert Berns to write "Sloopy.")

Because The Vibrations had never signed a recording contract with Atlantic Records – despite the fact their hit "My Girl Sloopy" had been released on the label – the group was picked up by Columbia/Okeh Records in 1964. Hoping to capitalize on the "Sloopy" craze, the group issued a sequel called "Sloop Dance." The song was less catchy than the original and merely bubbled under *Billboard's* Hot 100 in late-1964, reaching just #109. The group would return to the charts with a cover of Erroll Garner's "Misty," a soulful rendition of The Beatles "And I Love Her," and two minor hits, "Pick Me" and "Love In Them There Hills." The Vibrations disbanded in 1971, at which time, member Rick Owens joined The Temptations for a very short stint. After briefly reuniting, The Vibrations split for good in 1976.

After "I Want Candy," The Strangeloves would score two more hits, "Cara-Lin" and the often recorded garage-rock anthem "Night Time," which was later used in a Miller Beer commercial. Becoming a rock standard, "I Want Candy" was a hit in 1983 for British new wave act, Bow Wow Wow. The song was reprised in 2000 by pop singer Aaron Carter.

Eventually, The Strangeloves would release their own version of "Hang

On Sloopy" as an album cut. Though employing the same musical backing as The McCoys' version, the song sounded strained. During this period, Feldman and Goldstein launched a side project called Rome And Paris, and scored a regional, doo-wop styled hit with "Because Of You."

After The Strangeloves disbanded in 1966, the individual members would achieve various levels of success. Strangeloves member Richard Gotterher teamed with Seymour Stein to launch Sire Records, and worked with rock acts such as Renaissance, Climax Blue Band and Focus. Leaving Sire in the mid-1970s, Gotterher formed a production company called Instant Records. Here he worked with a series of punk and new wave acts, including The Go-Go's, Blondie, Richard Hell and Marshall Crenshaw. Also embracing rockabilly, Gotterher oversaw projects by Robert Gordon and Link Wray.

Strangeloves member Jerry Goldstein worked for Uni Records and was instrumental in the pairing of Eric Burdon with the soul-funk group, War. Later, Goldstein operated a management company, Far Out Productions, and a record company, LAX.

The third member of The Strangeloves, Bob Feldman, continued to work as a songwriter and producer, collaborating with acts such as Johnny Mathis, Jay And The Americans and Freddy Cannon. Two of Feldman's five children, Corey and Mindy, had careers in acting.

In addition to The Strangeloves and The McCoys, Bang Records had a strong roster which included Neil Diamond and Van Morrison. The Bang subsidiary labels, Shout and Bullet, generated hits by Erma Franklin and Freddie Scott. Eventually, Bang Records chief Bert Berns sued Atlantic for breach of contract and cut his ties to the label.

But at the age of 38 on December 30, 1967, Bert Berns died of heart failure. Just like singer Bobby Darin who suffered from the same malady, Berns perished during his prime. Berns' son, Brett, told *The Chicago Sun-Times*: "He was living on borrowed time. We heard stories that sometimes he would get excited in the studio when he felt he had a hit record. He would snap his fingers, shout ole! and check his pulse to make sure he wasn't overdoing it." One of the last recording sessions Berns oversaw was a salsa version of "Hang On Sloopy" by Cuban bandleader Arsenio Rodriguez. Berns had discovered Rodriguez while visiting pre-Castro Cuba.

Berns' widow, Ilene, took over the reigns of Bang Records. The label's successes in the 1970s were limited to singer-songwriter Paul Davis, Elton John sideman Nigel Olsson, and a few other acts. Bang was acquired by CBS in 1982. Berns' children, Brett and Cassandra, later managed their father's publishing company, Sloopy II.

Berns' songwriting partner formed a production firm in 1966 called the Wes Farrell Organization. Farrell churned out numerous pop hits such as, "Come On Down To My Boat" (Every Mothers' Son), "Come A Little Bit Closer" (Jay & The Americans), as well as several Partridge Family hits such as "I'll Meet You Halfway," "C'mon Get Happy" and "Doesn't Somebody Want To Be Wanted." Also a successful music publisher, Farrell scored hits by Tony Orlando, Wayne Newton, The Cowsills, Paper Lace and The Rascals. After a stint as the head of Bell Records, Farrell started Chelsea Records, where he worked with Rick Springfield, Lulu and Johnny Whitaker. Also involved in the advertising field, Farrell launched Coral Rock Commercials, a Cleo Award-winning operation. Providing the musical scores for several feature films, Farrell contributed to the Academy Award-winning picture, *Midnight Cowboy*. Farrell was married twice, first to Frank Sinatra's daughter, Tina, and then to actress Pamela Hensley. Farrell succumbed to cancer in 1996.

Meanwhile, music arranger John Tatgenhorst would later write the Buckeyes anthem, "Go Bucks." Subsequently working in commercial advertising, he also composed and arranged music for television programs such as *Live With Regis & Kelly* and *The Adventures Of Batman & Robin*.

As for OSU marching band director Charles Spohn, he was succeeded in 1970 by Paul E. Droste. In 1973, the band admitted its first female musicians. Currently, the band consists of 225 members – 192 on the field and 33 alternates. Meanwhile, "Hang On Sloopy" is now synonymous with the OSU marching band, and is performed during time-outs, at the close of the third quarter and during critical situations on the field.

In addition to its status as an Ohio State University football anthem, "Hang On Sloopy" emerged as a 1960s garage-rock classic, alongside party gems such as "Wooly Bully," "96 Tears" and "Louie Louie." "Sloopy" is regularly heard at sporting events around the state, particularly at professional football games in Cleveland and Cincinnati. By the late-1970s, OSU fans began incorporating an "O-H-I-O" chant and arm gestures at the end of each chorus of "Sloopy." In 2006, Columbus pop group Saving Jane recorded an updated version of the song, which incorporated the sing-along chant.

Sloopy also hit the literary world in Richard Price's 1974 novel, *The Wanderers*. The coming-of-age narrative is set in the Bronx and features a character named Hang On Sloopy. The book was later adapted into a feature film by director Philip Kaufman.

And lastly, Dorothy "Sloopy" Heflick passed away at the age of 84 on July 28, 1998, in Pass Christian, Mississippi. Aside from her musical career, Heflick would earn a Master's degree in English and later teach exceptional children in St. Petersburg, Florida. Several of Heflick's relatives would attend Ohio State, including her nephew, Frederick Ruland, who worked at the university as a statistician. Heflick's longtime musical partner, Yvonne "Dixie" Fasnacht, sold Dixie's Bar of Music in 1964.

CHAPTER 2
ALAN FREED
AND THE RISE OF ROCK AND ROLL IN CLEVELAND

The city of Cleveland earned the right to the Rock and Roll Hall of Fame because of the foresight of pioneering deejay Alan Freed. "At 11:15 at night, after the news and sports, after Mom and Dad turned off the lights, he hit the airwaves at WJW like a renegade evangelist, selling sin instead of salvation, barking his message over choruses of strip-show horns and crap-game crooners, pounding his palm raw on a telephone book to bring home the beat," *Life* magazine proclaimed.

"Hello everybody, how y'all tonight? This is Alan Freed, the old 'King of the Moondoggers,'" the golden-throated deejay would begin his evening radio show in the early-1950s. Crosstown deejay Joe Finan recalled: "The first time I heard him, I didn't know who he was. This guy's voice made me feel like he was in the room, that this is somebody I want to know. He came across three-dimensionally. Most disc jockeys were vanilla; he wasn't." First calling the music he played "rhythm and blues," Freed was crucial in the genesis of the revolutionary musical form called "rock and roll," and gave the youthful music its name.

Born Albert James Freed on December 15, 1921, near Johnstown, Pennsylvania, he moved several times as a young child before settling in Salem, Ohio, a small industrial city located between Youngstown and Akron. The son of a clothier, Freed played the trombone in his high school orchestra and led a New Orleans-style jazz band called The Sultans of Swing. At home, Freed's musically proficient family would gather around a piano to play swing-style jazz.

Attending Ohio State University in 1940, Freed majored in mechanical engineering. Though never stepping foot in the studios of the campus radio station, he often spoke of getting his start there. Young and impatient, Freed left school in 1941 to join the army. But after training for the ski patrol, he received a medical discharge a year later.

After returning to Salem and attending broadcasting school, Freed landed his first radio job at nearby WKST in New Castle, Pennsylvania, a station he would later describe as a broom closet. But by 1943, Freed had worked his way to the area's radio powerhouse, WKBN in Youngstown, landing the job by exaggerating his experience. Playing classical music – including his favorite composer, Wagner – Freed also provided the play-by-play announcing for local football games.

Hired as a newsman in 1945 by ABC-affiliate WAKR in Akron, Freed soon landed an evening deejay position, given the job when the scheduled announcer was fired for calling off. Playing contemporary pop music for the first time, Freed was an immediate hit, with his program sponsored by the now defunct O'Neil's department store. Dominating the airwaves at his peak of popularity, Freed attracted an amazing 60-percent share of the local radio market.

Every Saturday night, Freed hosted WAKR's *Request Review* program, which was broadcast from the station's basement studio inside the city's tallest building, First Central Tower (now called First Merit Tower). In front of a live in-studio audience of about 70 dancing teenagers, Freed spinned hot jazz and big band swing, as well as pioneering rhythm and blues discs by artists such as Louis Jordan. Hiring Erich Schrader, a local 17-year-old pianist with a penchant for upbeat boogie-woogie music, Freed would sometimes play along with his trombone.

First using the term "rock and roll" in early 1946, Alan Freed would signal his young musical partner, "'Are you ready to *rock and roll*' or 'let's get *rockin'*,'" recalled Schrader.

Adopting his first radio nickname, Knucklehead Freed, the charismatic deejay became a local celebrity who was often mobbed by autograph seekers. Emceeing teen sock-hops at a rented Catholic church hall in the Firestone Park section of Akron, Freed first donned his trademark, plaid sport coat and bowtie, and played records for the sons and daughters of the region's tire-factory workers.

With his star on the ascent and the tripling of his weekly salary from $60.50 to a then-hefty $200, Freed signed a contract containing radio's first-ever non-compete clause in 1948, prohibiting him from working within a 75-mile radius for a year, should he quit or be fired.

After hiring Lew Platt as his personal manager, Freed was fired in 1949 for demanding another raise. Walking out of WAKR's cellar studio, Freed marched across the street to the since demolished two-story structure that housed WADC and transplanted his popular request program. Taken to court by WAKR's attorney-owners, Freed was taken off the air the very next day and legally barred from radiowork in both Akron and nearby Cleveland. Taking the case all the way to the Ohio Supreme Court, an incredulous Freed tried to take over the questioning from his own lawyer. (Meanwhile, Freed had been replaced at WAKR by Scott Muni, who later worked his way to WMCA in New York City, but is better known for his longtime stint at the city's FM rock powerhouse, WNEW.)

Losing his court case, Freed was then hired by a new Cleveland television station, WXEL channel 9. Billed as a "teejay," he played mostly Bing Crosby and other pop schmaltz. While the station was within the forbidden 75-mile radius, Freed's previous contract failed to mention television. (When Freed signed his radio contract, Ohio had only two operating television stations). Attempting to adapt his radio show to the small screen, Freed would direct the cameraman to zoom in on the spinning records while they played. With the program a failure, Freed was then cast as the co-host of an afternoon film matinee.

Returning to radio in June 1951, at 50,000-watt WJW in Cleveland, Freed was hidden away in the late-night graveyard shift. Initially playing a fare of classical music, Freed had secured the job with the assistance of his friend, record store owner Leo Mintz.

Mintz had operated the landmark Record Rendezvous store since 1939, initially selling used jukebox records which he purchased for a couple-cents each. Relocated several times before finally settling in downtown Cleveland, Record Rendezvous was one of the few places that sold records by Muddy Waters, Big Joe Turner, Wynonie Harris, and other similar blues, R&B and rock artists, who were popular in the city's large black community.

Record Rendezvous was the first record store in Ohio to introduce telephone-booth-like listening rooms, where customers could preview potential purchases. Beginning in 1951, Mintz noticed that white teenagers were entering the booths with R&B records in hand. A former Cleveland disc jockey and program director (and later a Kent State University professor), Robert West, recalled that "a lot of white kids went in there and bought R&B – I know I did; there were blacks too." Informing the skeptical Freed of the new trend, Mintz convinced the deejay to program the music on WJW. Building upon his teenage love of jazz and swing, Freed enjoyed playing upbeat, sax-heavy R&B discs by acts like Fats Domino and Earl Bostic.

Possessing charm and wit, Freed had a velvety-cool style that his fans wanted to identify with. "He would march around the room, and yell and shout, and would really get enthusiastic. He was brilliant on the air. He could grab an audience. He obviously enjoyed very much what he was doing – and he loved the music," recalls Robert West. "On occasion, if Alan had to go down the hall or go out to buy a beer, his brother David Freed would cover and nobody would ever know the difference; their voices were identical." Rival deejay Joe Finan remembers: "Alan always had a beer in the studio, and Erin Brew was the number one sponsor, so the station would look the other way."

From that brief overnight slot, Freed was quickly promoted to a several-hour-long evening shift. He soon owned the black radio market in Cleveland and Akron, and was slowly attracting a white audience. Cleveland alone claimed a population of 130,000 African-Americans in 1950, drawn to northern industrial centers during the wartime labor shortages. Only 8,500 blacks had called Cleveland their home 40 years earlier in 1910.

But with the strict segregation of postwar America, African-American musical styles had been mostly restricted to inner-city neighborhoods. But in Cleveland, Alan Freed provided blacks with an unlikely voice. "He was accepted with open arms" by the black community, "because he was the gatekeeper to a full three or four hours a night of the music which barely got on the air," recalled Joe Finan. Robert West remembered: "That's what blacks liked: A white guy playing their music. It made their music legitimate, it made it valid, that a white disc jockey would play nothing but black music, which in Cleveland was all that he played; he wouldn't play any white artists. He played 'blues and rhythm' as he called it." The promise of integration was seen as a victory for black America, which began to believe that equality was attainable.

But Freed was not the first deejay to play R&B records, just the most famous. At WLAC in Nashville, white deejay Gene Nobles was playing jazz and some proto-R&B in the early-1940s, with his program later evolving into the popular *Randy's Record Shop Show*. And while former jazz deejay Hunter Hancock was playing R&B on KFVD in Los Angeles, the bookwormish Zenas "Daddy" Sears spun blues and R&B discs on the state-owned station, WGST in Atlanta. The targets of racist groups, Freed and other white R&B deejays frequently received threats. Fellow WGST disc jockey Bill Lowery told author Wes Smith that Zenas Sears received many phoned-in "challenges for him to step outside because somebody wanted to blow him away."

During this period, few blacks hosted radio programs on prominent stations. On WDIA in Memphis, Nat D. Williams was billed as "the Mid-South's first Negro disc jockey." Because of its strong nighttime signal, WDIA had a near-monopoly of millions of black listeners across dozens of states, and became the most influential radio station in the country in terms of disseminating and popularizing African-American music, including gospel, blues and R&B.

Back in Cleveland, Mintz had given Freed an obscure record by an eccentric Manhattan street musician named Moondog, which featured a howling dog, homemade instruments and a jungle-boogie beat. Adopting the song as his theme, Freed would then segue into Todd Rhodes' 1948 hit "Blues For The Red Boy." Freed started to call himself the Moondog, and his show evolved into *The Moondog Rhythm And Blues House Party*. The term "rock and roll" was soon incorporated into the program's name to make the music more palatable to white America.

While both Leo Mintz and Alan Freed have been individually credited with coining the term "rock and roll" to describe the new music, Freed had been using the phrase on the air since 1946, during his first year at WAKR in Akron. With its origin remaining elusive, and its definition a far more complicated matter, the word "rock" was first used in the title of a hit record in 1922, when a blues singer named Trixie Smith, entered a primitive recording studio to record "My Man Rocks Me (With A Steady Roll)." The disc was released by Black Swan, the first-ever, black-owned record company, which included blues pioneer W.C. Handy on its board of directors.

For the first half of the century, the term "rock and roll" was also a euphemism for sex. The phrase appeared in the title of a song for the first time in 1934, by a popular, all-white vocal trio, The Boswell Sisters. But this typical showtune was anything but rock and roll.

By the late 1940s, pockets of southern blacks began calling rhythm and blues concerts, "rock and roll parties." And when vocalist Wynonie Harris recorded the Roy Brown-composed "Good Rockin' Tonight" in 1948, Harris became the first R&B artist to feature the term, "rock," in the title of a hit song.

But up to the late-1940s, the term "race music" was still being used to describe all nonclassical forms of black music; the terms "sepia" and "Harlem" – as in "Harlem Hit Parade" – were employed less frequently. Then in 1949, the editors of *Billboard* magazine decided that the phrase, "race music," was demeaning to blacks. As a staff project, the magazine spent much of the year deliberating a replacement. When a young staff writer, Jerry Wexler (later a co-owner of Atlantic Records), suggested "rhythm and blues," the term was immediately adopted and become the industry standard. An obscure, postwar phrase, its origin remains elusive. "R&B" was a combination of blues, hot jazz, and gospel, while rock and roll brought a touch of country music, which itself had a mutually-incestuous relationship with the blues.

R&B music's first star, Louis Jordan, began as a novelty act in the jazz and vaudeville traditions. Featuring a 2/4, shuffle-boogie beat, Jordan's swinging, up-tempo, danceable, saxophone-heavy sound was difficult to categorize. It was not jazz, big band or traditional, 12-bar blues.

Rock music was also the by-product of technological advances, as teenagers began carrying portable, Japanese-made, solid-state, transistor radios, which freed youth from the parental supervision of programming choices: teens could now secretly listen to an R&B or rock and roll station abhorred by their parents.

And with the money-spending teenager in mind, RCA introduced the microgroove, seven-inch, vinylite, 45-rpm record. (RCA was also reacting to the introduction of the 12-inch vinyl LP by rival label, Columbia Records.) Wanting to popularize the inexpensive "45," RCA sold compatible record players at below cost.

Meanwhile, within two years, the size of Freed's white radio audience at WJW surpassed that of his black listernership. But throughout the histories of ragtime, jazz, blues, and R&B, there has always been a tradition of hip whites venturing uptown to absorb black culture.

In Cleveland, adventurous whites frequented East Side and downtown, black nightclubs such as Gleason's Musical Bar and Leo's Casino. Nicknamed "black and tans," these clubs tolerated white visitors, giving them their first glimpses of blues and R&B.

During this same period, an unlikely, white, R&B-inflected singer named Johnnie Ray was honing his talent in a variety of Cleveland and Akron area nightclubs, before he would break out nationally with the hit, "Cry."

Expanding into concert promotion by 1951, Alan Freed and Leo Mintz were bankrolled by a pair of Akronites, Lew Platt and Milton Kulkin. Experiencing a rocky start, Freed was banned from the prestigious Meyers Lake Ballroom in nearby Canton after concertgoers – which the local paper described as a crowd of "2,500 negroes" – caused massive damage to the venue.

Considered the first rock concert, Freed's most notorious show took place on March 21, 1952, at the 15-year-old Cleveland Arena, a hockey venue that no one believed he could fill. Although Freed had sponsored a number of smaller concerts around northeast Ohio, the mere size of the Cleveland show, plus the fact that the audience consisted of both blacks and whites, earned it the designation as the first rock and roll concert.

Billed as "the Moondog Coronation Ball," Freed advertized the event only on his radio program. Remarkably, all 7,500 tickets were sold the same day they went on sale. Celebrating the success, Freed's partner, Leo Mintz, took his family to Florida for a brief vacation. But due to overeagerness and miscommunication, no one was prepared for what came next. Mintz's son, Stuart, told *Scene* in 1986: "On that same Tuesday, my uncle... had another 7,500 tickets printed up; he thought, 'If we sold that fast, we can sell another 7,500.' But he forgot to say 'second show' on the tickets. My dad got a call... in Florida with a voice begging, 'Leo, come home.'"

Arriving in a taxi directly from the airport, Leo Mintz was overwhelmed by the sight of thousands of well-dressed youth who had immobilized the boulevard for a block in each direction. When Mintz saw what was happening, he turned around and flew back to Florida.

As *Life* magazine recalled: "So they came. By foot. By bicycle. By streetcar and by bus. They came from beyond Cleveland, too, from Akron, from Canton, from all over the industrial north of Ohio, many of them the children of the great black northern migration, just a generation removed from the farm, from Mississippi and Arkansas and Louisiana and the holy hell of the rural South, gathered now for the biggest party in the history of Cleveland." Though the event was grossly oversold, Freed announced the previous night that an additional 2,000 tickets were to be made available the day of the show, thereby drawing thousands more to the scene.

The concert was co-headlined by The Dominoes and Paul Williams, whose 1949 hit "The Hucklebuck" had spawned a huge dance craze of the same name. The concert was scheduled to conclude with a grand ceremony in which Freed was crowned the "King of the Moondoggers."

Unequipped for music concerts, the arena lacked adequate security and crowd control. At the first sign of trouble, the suited, ticket-window workers left their posts. One attendee later recalled in *Q* magazine, "Me and three girlfriends rode the streetcar to the arena. It was supposed to start at 10 PM but when we got there at 9 PM they'd already closed the doors." Paul Williams, who was on stage at the time, later told deejay Norm N. Nite: "We played the first number and... I saw the doors and they looked like they were breathing." With the music starting, and thousands still outside – many without tickets – the steel doors buckled under the weight of those trying to get in, and bang, every door crashed to the ground, one after the other. A witness later told *Life* magazine: "Oh, Lord, how they poured into the hall, and soon the crowd began to move in enormous rhythmic waves, back and forth, then in a mad swirl. And then a fight started, and another, and another."

Opening act Paul Williams continued to play until the raging fans overtook the stage. Telling *Life* magazine, Williams recalled that as a performer, he was used to seeing people "killed every way you can imagine; Knives, guns, hammers, baseball bats – every way a person can die, I've just about seen it. And there's only one thing you can do, and that's keep on playing." With the large crowd spilling onto the streets, 40 police officers and 30 firemen were radioed to converge on the hall.

While *The Cleveland Plain Dealer* estimated the crowd size at 16,000, a suburban newspaper put the number at 25,000, and the local black newspaper, *The Call & Post,* referred to the audience as "some 20,000 rabid blues fans." *The Akron Beacon Journal* reported: "Hepcats jammed every inch of the Arena floor, took every seat, filled the aisles and packed the lobby and sidewalk, overflowing onto Euclid Ave. It was impossible to dance and the orchestra could not be heard over the din." *The Call & Post* provided the most sensational account, describing the event as a place where males "were wearing their hats inside a public place, guzzling liquor without restraint from pocket flasks, and, here and there, actually shooting themselves with narcotics in the midst of a crowd!" With politicians and civic groups in an uproar, Freed was threatened with prosecution.

Fearing imprisonment and the loss of his job, Alan Freed was unusually somber behind his microphone the next night. In a heavily-bootlegged recording of the broadcast, Freed apologized to his many listeners, "If you wish to lay the blame on me for what happened last night, you're certainly welcome." Begging for forgiveness, he asked his fans to telephone, and send letters and telegrams to station management to keep him on the air.

A prime reason for the concert's huge draw was Cleveland's popularity as a destination for jazz and R&B acts. The same week as the Moondog Coronation Ball, scores of touring acts were scheduled to perform in Cleveland. Lionel Hampton was playing the Towne Casino; John Lee Hooker headlined an "all star Harlem Revue" at the Circle Theater; The Orioles and Jimmy Forrest were at the Ebony Lounge; and the Coronation Ball's co-headliners, The Dominoes, were already in town, booked for a week of nightclub gigs. Cleveland radio legend Norm N. Nite told interviewer Jesse Wilder, "So many performers came here from the South or wherever because of Freed and because of the hotbed of entertainment – both East and West side: Acts like a Little Richard or a Fats Domino playing at some small club on Prospect or 55th Street or Moe's Main Street on 77th and Euclid. It was amazing, utterly amazing. It was all here." Independent record promoter Chuck Young told *Scene* magazine, "That was hip stuff.... On Friday and Saturday nights there would be more white people in these clubs than black people. You couldn't get in. There were lines outside."

Although Freed's concert promotion business was thriving, he further expanded his music empire. Launching his own record company, Champagne, he signed The Crazy Sounds, which he renamed The Moonglows, after his radio nickname. The group's lead singer, Harvey Fuqua, recalled in *Goldmine* magazine, "I thought [Freed] was wonderful, he was the only guy playing black music at the time... the kind of music I liked." The Moonglows went on to record a series of doo-wop standards including "Sincerely" and "Ten Commandments Of Love." Another local doo-wop group aided by Freed, The Coronets, scored a top-10 R&B hit in 1953 with "Nadine."

Angering his business partner Leo Mintz, Freed also opened his own record store. But more significantly, Freed's WJW radio program was now syndicated around the country and could be heard across most of New York City via a tiny station in Newark, New Jersey, WNJR.

But in April 1953, an overworked Freed nearly died in an automobile crash, when he drove his car into a tree. Suffering massive internal and facial injuries, Freed underwent extensive plastic surgery. Always wearing makeup to hide his facial scars, Freed would be nagged by the injuries for the rest of his life. "My father used to say to me 'I am living on borrowed time. I shouldn't be here so I have nothing to lose.' I think he had a feeling that you should live your life as a meteorite burning fast and furiously," son, Lance Freed, told interviewer Les Smith.

Bandaged, but back behind the microphone at WJW within two months, Freed also returned to his concert promotions. Hiring a pair of headlining acts, The Dominoes and The Drifters, Freed launched a record-setting, 30-city, all-star R&B revue, which turned away crowds at every stop, and attracted its biggest audiences in Cleveland. While the national press was caught off guard by Freed's success, the music industry bible, *Billboard* magazine, began reporting his every move. Nicknamed the "Pied Piper of Rock and Roll," Freed had become its ultimate salesman. "Alan Freed could sell tickets to the end of the world – to the first *and* second shows," Cleveland-born R&B pioneer Screamin' Jay Hawkins proclaimed in *Nowhere To Run*.

Thanks to Freed, Cleveland became a breakout city for new music. Deejay Joe Finan recalled that in Cleveland, a radio station could hype up a record on Monday, play it four or five times in an afternoon, and have people clamoring for the disc by Thursday: "There wasn't another city that was as fast at the retail level than Cleveland, and that's why [record companies] came here, that's why they spent their money here." Cleveland deejay and music historian Chris Quinn recalled: "Many, many, many acts were broken out of Cleveland. Cleveland was responsible for a lot of hits, a lot of careers over the years." Chuck Young, the first music director of the 50,000-watt outlet KYW, told *Scene* that, "we were the first radio station in the country to play Bobby Darin's first hit, 'Splish Splash,' 'Chantilly Lace' by the Big Bopper, Jackie Wilson's 'Reet Petite,' Bobby Day's 'Rockin' Robin' and Freddy Cannon's 'Tallahassee Lassie.' We were playing the first four Buddy Holly records before anyone in the United States. This was almost a weekly thing, that we'd be breaking million selling records. There had to be over 200 million [sellers] that our station was responsible for. We played them all first."

Freed shared the Cleveland airwaves with several other powerful radio personalities, including Tommy Edwards, Joe Finan, Phil McLean, and Carl

Reese; WJW's morning drive-time jock was a young Soupy Heinz, who later emerged as comic Soupy Sales. But Freed's main local rival was another nationally-renowned deejay, Bill Randle. Music historian Peter Guralnick wrote in *Last Train To Memphis*: "Bill Randle was a legend in radio at that time. Tall, scholarly-looking with black horn-rimmed glasses, he had just been written up in *Time*," which boasted that he "had predicted all but one of the top-five best-sellers of 1954, discovered Johnnie Ray, changed the name of The Crew-Cuts (from The Canadianaires) as well as finding them their first hit, drove a Jaguar, and made a $100,000 a year, with his Saturday-afternoon CBS network show in New York the latest in his series of unprecedented accomplishments." But refusing to quit his Cleveland radio gig, he flew to New York City every weekend. Randle later recalled in a *Plain Dealer* interview: "But it wasn't long before I realized the music we were playing in Cleveland was on the cutting-edge of the musical trends – it was miles and miles ahead of New York. So after a while, I just started taking the hot, popular records I had been playing for weeks in Cleveland, play 'em in New York and say, 'Trust me, folks, this song's gonna be a big hit.' And they would end up being hits in New York. People there thought I was some musical genius – but really, I was just shooting fish in a barrel. It was already a hit in Cleveland."

Like Freed, Randle was also challenging radio's color barrier. Once fired for playing a black gospel version of "Silent Night" by Sister Rosetta Tharpe, Randle was rehired after listeners clamored for his return.

Cleveland deejay Joe Finan later recalled that "every artist Randle played," he called "the most exciting. He even does that today." But Randle's most important discovery came in 1955, when he predicted the stardom of a southern hillbilly singer, and introduced the unknown artist on his program. When Finan was asked by Jud Phillips (brother of Sam Phillips) of Sun Records to play the Memphis-based singer, who had just landed on the country charts with his debut single "Baby Let's Play House," Finan balked: "Hearing Elvis Presley for the first time, as far as I was concerned he was a hilljack and I wasn't going to play him." But Randle did play Elvis Presley's early releases, becoming the first pop deejay north of the Mason-Dixon line to embrace the hip-shaking singer. But while Randle was leery of playing Elvis on his weekend program in New York, he knew Cleveland listeners would be receptive to the artist.

"The impact of Randle's spinning of [Elvis Presley's] Sun disks in Cleveland was unforeseen and quite shattering. Teen-age listeners seemed instantly to go berserk and kept calling the station for repeat plays of 'Mystery Train,' 'I Forgot To Remember To Forget,' and 'Good Rockin' Tonight.' The word spread like a contagion from Cleveland record distributors to executive home offices in New York, Chicago, and Los Angeles that there was a 'hot' new artist on the record scene," recalled R&B historian Arnold Shaw in *Honkers And Shouters*.

At Presley's third Cleveland concert on October 20, 1955 – as an opening act for Pat Boone, Bill Haley and The Four Lads – he asked Bill Randle to be his manager. With Randle declining the offer, Presley instead signed with former carnival huckster Colonel Tom Parker. Also on hand at the Cleveland concert was a camera crew from Universal Studios, who were there to film a short biography of Randle. Wisely, Randle paid the cameramen to also shoot Presley, who sang five songs that day. Forgotten in the nooks of the Universal vaults for nearly four-decades, the 16mm footage was later acquired by Randle for a pittance. He resold the film in 1992 for a reported $1.9 million.

Then three months after the Cleveland concert, Presley made his television debut on the CBS variety program, *Stage Show,* and was introduced by Randle, the guest emcee. By the following spring, Presley's debut RCA single, "Heartbreak Hotel," would be perched atop the pop charts for a two-month stay.

But Cleveland's most outlandish deejay was Pete "Mad Daddy" Myers. Dressing as a vampire while behind the microphone at WJW, he spoke in rapid-fire rhymes, played obscure rockabilly and R&B records, and coined catchphrases like "wavy gravy" and "mellow Jello." Myers also hosted a weekly horror flick on late-night television. A local celebrity, he drove around town in a pink Pontiac, while wearing a cape and winged sneakers. But when Myers made an off-color comment on his television program, he lost both his TV and radio gigs. But due to a contractual restriction, Myers was kept off the air for the next 90-days. Wanting to remain in the public eye, he hatched a publicity stunt. After attempting to fill a Cleveland harbor with Jello, he donned a Zorro outfit and jumped from an airplane into the choppy Lake Erie waters. It was a miracle he survived. Influencing a generation of youth, Myers also spawned a host of imitators.

Meanwhile, with rock and roll exploding around the country, Alan Freed drew further attention in the national press and was making a tremendous amount of money with his Moondog balls.

While blacks had constituted the majority of the audiences at Freed's early concerts, the racial makeup had reversed in just a few years. Co-emceeing a concert with Freed at the since-demolished Akron Armory, deejay Joe Finan recalled, "I can't remember seeing any blacks" in the crowd, which came to see Roy Hamilton, The Drifters, Frankie Lymon and Screamin' Jay Hawkins.

Taking notice of Freed's unprecedented successes, a New York radio station lured the deejay in September 1954. While he was still based in Cleveland, Freed had created a stir with his first East Coast Moondog ball in Newark, New Jersey. Promoting the concert on his syndicated program on WNJR, Freed drew 10,000 of his listeners to the event, a fifth of whom were white. Before leaving Cleveland, Freed hosted one final concert.

Working the late-evening shift at WINS, a then-low-rated 50,000-watt station, Freed was paid a base salary of $15,000 per year (the figure has been grossly exaggerated over the years), as well as a percentage of his program's advertising revenue. What Freed interchangeably called "rock and roll" and "rhythm and blues" was suddenly thrust upon millions of listeners, most of whom were white.

Packing several-hundred 45s into the trunk of his car, Freed sent shock waves throughout the music industry, which had settled into a pattern of banal, inoffensive, middle-of-the-road fare. (The top single of 1954 had been a light romantic ballad, "Little Things Mean A Lot" by Kitty Kallen.)

With the aid of a business partner, the heavy-handed Morris Levy, Freed was introduced to the movers and shakers in the New York music community. Levy was a notorious figure who was accused of associating with organized crime. Previously operating the legendary Birdland jazz nightclub, Levy expanded into all angles of the music industry, as he wheeled and dealed publishing houses, jukebox companies, and record labels like Rama, Gee, and Roulette.

With Freed taking WINS to the ratings forefront, he spawned scores of imitators. Emerging as a nationally-known celebrity, Freed hired two women to open his fan mail. Fellow deejay Wolfman Jack recalled in his autobiography: "As soon as he came to New York, *The Alan Freed Show* just tore up the town. Everybody went nuts, especially me." Singer Paul Simon told author Wes Smith: "New York was a pool of sounds, but only one station was playing rock 'n' roll, the station Alan Freed was on."

In New York, Freed was forced to drop his Moondog moniker after street musician Louis "Moondog" Hardin took him to court. Renaming his program *The Alan Freed Rock And Roll Show*, Freed was soon syndicated in two dozen cities. Losing another court fight, Freed and partner Morris Levy failed in their attempt to copyright the term "rock and roll." Soon buying a grand 16-room mansion in Stamford, Connecticut, Freed often broadcast his program from his home studio, which had been constructed inside a converted horse stable.

While continuing his national caravan-style concert revues, Freed also set up residency at the huge Paramount Theater in Brooklyn. Within two months, Freed was smashing attendance records that were set 25-years earlier by bobby-soxers who had jammed the Times Square auditorium to catch a glimpse of a young, rising, singing idol named Frank Sinatra.

"The excitement of being out in the audience was overwhelming.... Freed would come out in this really loud plaid jacket and blow kisses at the audience while the house band play[ed] some real down, aggressive blues vamp," Wolfman Jack wrote in his autobiography. One of the performers, singer Jo-ann Campbell, recalled in *When Rock Was Young*, "Alan had something like a twenty-five piece orchestra and two drummers for those shows, and when that band kicked off, let me tell you that the whole audience came to its feet and cheered. You just can't describe the sound and the feeling and the emotion that came alive in that room."

Paying his musical acts only nominal fees, Freed instead provided airplay on his radio program, ensuring consumer demand for records by LaVern Baker, Big Joe Turner, Chuck Berry and many others. Berry, who owed his initial stardom to Alan Freed, was summoned to New York in late 1955 for a one-week stint to promote his first hit, "Maybellene." Making his East Coast debut, Berry recalled in his autobiography: "We had five shows a day to perform, starting at one o'clock in the afternoon and continuing until one o'clock in the morning, with a one-hour movie between each show. Most shows held over seven thousand kids screaming through the live performances each of the seven days of that week." Berry also recalled his shock in seeing that "the audience seemed to be solid white." Within an environment of orchestrated mayhem, each act on the superstar bill was usually permitted to sing only three songs before yielding the stage to the next performer. When the pre-concert, filler movie was later dropped, each act was required to perform *seven* shows a day.

Meanwhile, when MGM film director Richard Brooks wanted a theme song for *The Blackboard Jungle*, he purchased the rights to Bill Haley And The Comets' "(We're Gonna) Rock Around The Clock" from Decca Records for one-dollar. (The song had been a moderate hit the previous year.) The first-ever rock song featured in a film, "Rock Around The Clock" became the first chart-topping single of the rock era in 1955, as the pudgy, spit-curled Haley became America's first rock star.

Premiering in New York City, *The Blackboard Jungle* was the first movie to expose modern, urban decay. Set in a rebellious public trade school, the big-screen feature captured what America feared about rock and roll music, as teacher Glenn Ford was assaulted by rock-crazed delinquents who challenged his authority. One of the delinquents was portrayed by a teenage Jamie Farr, best known for his role in *MASH*.

Music historian Marc Eliot observed: "The film's Bronx locale helped identify New York as the capital not only of rock and roll, but of the growing problem of juvenile delinquency." In a metaphoric sign of the times, the unruly and defiant students destroy old jazz 78s belonging to teacher Richard Kiley, behind a musical backdrop of the seemingly outdated music of Bix Beiderbecke. Other films like Marlon Brando's *The Wild One* and James Dean's *Rebel Without A Cause* romanticized youth rebellion, while at the same time, popularizing leather jackets, blue jeans, and motorcycles.

When violence broke out at theaters during the screenings of *The Blackboard Jungle*, the behavior was blamed on rock and roll. Some theaters responded by turning off the volume during the music scenes. Although the film made "Rock Around The Clock" a major hit and signaled the start of the rock era, it forever gave rock and roll a public relations problem.

Inspired by the success of *The Blackboard Jungle,* Alan Freed teamed with Bill Haley in the rock film, *Rock Around The Clock*. Using movies as a vehicle for defending both himself and rock music, Freed oversaw four cheapie rock flicks, including *Don't Knock The Rock*. These films usually employed flimsy plots and were built around performances by established rock acts. Another film, *Mister Rock And Roll*, gave Freed his new nickname.

Expanding his media empire, in 1956 Freed launched the first-ever, rock music program on network radio, *The Camel Rock And Roll Party*, which aired Saturday nights on CBS. Jumping on the rock and roll bandwagon, ABC television hired Freed to host a music program, which predated *American Bandstand*. Fellow deejay Hal Jackson recalled: "Alan just had a way of drawing people in, and he never played the race card. The kids were just kids to him. He didn't care if they were black kids or white kids. Of course, some people didn't like that. And when he got his television show going, they really hated it. But he was so powerful by then that no one could do anything to stop him." But Freed was indeed stopped in his tracks. When a television cameraman captured a black performer, 14-year-old Frankie Lymon, dancing with a white girl, the program was dropped by Southern stations. Two weeks later, advertiser jitters forced the show's cancellation. Soon after, ABC replaced the flashy and rebellious, integration-advocate, Alan Freed, with the affable, clean-cut and soft-spoken Dick Clark and *American Bandstand*, which enforced strict dress codes, with boys wearing suits and ties, and girls barred from wearing pants. Freed subsequently hosted a local music program on New York's WNEW.

With the country experiencing social upheaval, Freed and the entire rock and roll community were under constant attack from religious groups, law enforcement agencies, politicians, and, in the South, anti-integrationists. During an interview with a *New York Times* reporter, Freed mockingly drank not his usual bottle of beer but a tall glass of wholesome milk.

Also jumping on the anti-rock bandwagon was ASCAP – a powerful, monopolistic, Tin Pan Alley-era organization of music publishers that had previously excluded black songwriters. ASCAP's influence over radio airplay and record sales had suddenly been undermined by the fledgling, BMI service, which unlike ASCAP, welcomed R&B and country songwriters. By 1955, ASCAP composers accounted for only a quarter of the charted pop songs, down from 90-percent a decade earlier. With ASCAP members frantic to find a scapegoat, the brash Freed was the perfect target.

Rock also came under attack over the issue of bawdy lyrics. The fight was spearheaded by *Variety* magazine, ASCAP, and by the major record companies which were financially threatened by the growing market share of independent labels. Attacking what was sarcastically referred to as dirty "lee-rics" (the term coined by CBS Records executive Mitch Miller), a well-funded effort tried to stamp out rock and roll.

Dozens of early rock hits were targeted for their use of double-entendre lyrics, which euphemistically suggested sexual behavior. A frequent source of controversial material, Cincinnati-based King-Federal Records issued a number of bawdy singles such as "Work With Me Annie" by Hank Ballard And The Midnighters. Another contentious release, The Dominoes' "Sixty Minute Man" featured the bombastic boasting of a character named Lovin' Dan; banned by some stations and considered a novelty song by others, for most Americans it was their first exposure to rock and roll. Wanting to pacify their foes, radio stations and disc jockeys launched insincere and ineffective self-policing measures. Writing in a *Variety* editorial, King-Federal Records vice-president John S. Kelly promised to clean up his company's releases. Even black powerhouse WDIA promised to drop all "off-color" songs from its playlist.

But at the same time the music industry establishment was trying to suppress rock and roll, old-time record labels like Mercury and RCA were profiting from the music, by releasing their own watered-down renditions of R&B and rock hits. Called "cover versions," these songs usually surpassed the originals in both airplay and sales. While cover versions actually helped popularize rock music in the long run, they were financially crippling to both the original musical artists and their record companies.

Early R&B and rock artists such as LaVern Baker, Ruth Brown and Little Richard were supplanted on radio playlists by white cover acts such as The Crew-Cuts, Georgia Gibbs and The McGuire Sisters. Decades before his flirtation with heavy-metal, Pat Boone's foray into cover records gave middle-America sanitized versions of R&B songs that were so lame, they often bore little resemblance to the originals. Scoring numerous cover hits, beginning with Fats Domino's "Ain't That A Shame," Boone, an English and speech major in college, desperately wanted to change the title of the song to the grammatically correct, "Isn't That A Shame." Some deejays like Alan Freed exposed the fraud and refused to play cover versions.

But by the late 1950s, it became "increasingly difficult to separate white and black performers, largely because many black stylists [had] eliminated some of the coarser qualities from the blues and gospel styles, while a number of white performers [had] perfected their handling of black vocal accent, inflection patterns, and phrasing," recalled musicologist Johannes Riedel. In the end, major record companies reacted by luring leading rock acts with lucrative contracts and by buying out the pesky independent labels. With RCA Records purchasing Elvis Presley's contract for $35,000 from Sam Phillips, the label withdrew its financial and vocal support from anti-rock causes.

Meanwhile, the increasingly embattled Alan Freed saw his career mortally wounded in the aftermath of a May 1958, Boston stop of a multi-act concert tour. In a show headlined by Buddy Holly, Jerry Lee Lewis and Chuck Berry, dozens of heavy-handed police officers at the Boston Arena tried to corner Freed and challenge him to a confrontation. With the fiery Jerry Lee Lewis pumping out a headlining performance of "Great Balls Of Fire," the ecstatic "kids jammed the aisles and converged upon the stage. In the white heat of the frenzy, the house lights went up and the crowd ceased chanting and dancing, wondering at the cause for the intrusion. Boston police [were] streaming down the aisles in pairs with flashlights and nightsticks at the ready. Alan Freed cursed and raked his hands through his hair, then charged onstage. 'Hey, kids, take a look at this,' Freed cried. 'The cops don't want you to have a good time.' Catcalls and boos spread until the house groaned its resentment. Officers in riot gear froze with muscles tensed in anticipation of an attack.... A sergeant signaled retreat, and the bluebellies turned and filed out to the triumphant jeers of the teenagers," recalled Lewis' then-14-year-old wife, Myra, in the Jerry Lee Lewis biography, *Great Balls Of Fire*.

Wanting to make an example of Freed, the humiliated police force quickly regrouped. After confiscating the night's receipts from the box office, the police stopped the show. Attacking in force, police arrested Freed, charging him with anarchy and incitement to riot. With the young, racially-diverse crowd running through the streets, newspapers sensationalized the event, calling it a full-fledged riot.

With Freed's reported crimes becoming a national scandal, rock music had been further disgraced. Concert cancellations followed, and Freed lost hundreds of thousands of dollars in wasted advertising and already rented venues. In New Haven, Connecticut, Freed failed in his attempts to overturn a city ban of rock concerts. "My father was definitely a victim, in the sense that he was set up," Lance Freed told author Marc Eliot; ASCAP and the major record companies were "effective in convincing people there should be some investigation into how those 'nigger music' records could get to be hits." Former announcer Robert West was told by David Freed that his brother, Alan, "was totally innocent. They cracked down on him because he integrated the theater. He felt that was the real reason."

Fired by WINS, Freed moved to New York powerhouse WABC, where he toned down his antics. Bruised by the press, Freed had difficulty maintaining his public profile. With the tarnishing of "rock and roll," Freed began to call the music, "the Big Beat."

With his Boston trial postponed for a year, Freed cut back on his concert promotions. Evicted from the Paramount Theater, Freed moved to the Fox, where he set new box-office records. After grossing a hefty $207,000 in his first week at the Fox, Freed taunted his critics with a full-page ad in *Billboard* magazine. Although the horde of security guards and police stationed in the theater had expected trouble, the shows took place without incident.

Determined, Freed's enemies took another route – payola. In 1958, the Federal Trade Commission had launched a probe into payola, a practice whereby record companies would give deejays money, drugs or gifts in exchange for airplay. The practice was also prevalent among publishing companies, distributors and record stores. Inquiries into radio payola snowballed following the quiz show scandals of the late-1950s, when investigators discovered that popular contestants had been supplied with answers.

While payola was technically not illegal, an obscure 1934 FCC code loosely forbade the practice. The vicious rivalry between ASCAP and BMI was the catalyst behind the investigation, with ASCAP contending that without the payola payments, no radio station would ever play rock and roll. But in the 1950s, payola became a financial necessity for most deejays, who earned little in salaries. Euphemistically called "listening fees" by deejays, payola was considered a legitimate promotional cost by record companies.

Alan Freed would spend a full three-hours after his daily radio program, listening to new record releases. He likened payola to lobbying in Washington, D.C., with the money never guaranteeing airplay. Deejay Joe Finan, who was also implicated in the payola scandal, defended Freed, recalling that "the records he was playing, were the records he liked." Robert West recalled that Freed "had no sense of payola. He understood favors. He didn't take money to take money; he felt they were legitimate gifts."

But when Freed refused to sign a statement, declaring he had never accepted payola, he was dismissed by WABC. Also fired from his local television show on WNEW, Freed ended his last program by staring into the camera and rubbing a record between his fingers. Firing one final volley at the powerful music establishment, he said defiantly, "I know a bunch of ASCAP publishers who'll be glad I'm off the air."

As an omnipresent figure and rock's biggest cheerleader, Alan Freed became the chief target in a series of televised payola hearings in 1960. With the downfall of Freed seen as the key to stopping rock and roll, the proceedings resembled the McCarthy witch-hunts, which had riveted the country only a few years earlier. Powerful music industry players were hauled before stone-faced investigators, with Freed taking the brunt of the punishment for something that was commonplace in radio. Freed told the committee that he was paid $40,000 a year by WINS but returned $30,000 to the station to advertise his concerts.

The payola scandal dramatically changed the landscape of radio. While deejays had programmed their own music, all of that changed after 1960. Fearing FCC fines and license revocations, radio station owners took over the responsibility, which gave rise to "formula" or "top-40 radio," as playlists were determined by the record charts in *Billboard, Cashbox* and *Record World*. For the next decade, the deejay was little more than an announcer, a situation later rectified with the rise of underground FM radio.

Meanwhile, rock music was taking hits from all sides. An airplane crash outside of Clear Lake, Iowa, killed a trio of rock stars, Buddy Holly, the Big Bopper and the headlining 17-year-old singer named Ritchie Valens. Other rock stars saw their careers end in unusual circumstances. Both The Platters and Chuck Berry were scandalized in separate incidents involving women. Jerry Lee Lewis was heckled at his concerts after marrying his 13-year-old cousin, Myra Gale Brown. Little Richard experienced a religious conversion while on tour in Australia, convinced that rock and roll was the devil's music. More significantly, after Elvis Presley entered the service, his spirited persona was finally tamed. With the rise of clean-cut teen idols like Fabian and Ricky Nelson, even Freed's former employer, WINS, had abandoned rock and roll in 1961, changing its format to a middle-of-the-road fare of Frank Sinatra and Nat King Cole.

Left without an outlet to play records, Freed was abandoned by rock artists who saw no reason to perform at his concerts. Quietly leaving New York City in 1961, Freed was broke. An unskilled businessman who kept his money stacked in boxes inside a closet, Freed had grossed several-million dollars in just seven short years in New York, but was now bankrupt. "Alan was very free with his money. He would give it to anybody that was broke. If a musician he knew needed money, he would give it to him. He did not spend it on the wild life at all," defended former colleague Robert West.

Few other deejays or record industry heads were prosecuted, and even fewer lost their jobs. Dick Clark, who gave an impassioned defense, denied being involved in the practice of payola. But Clark had expanded into music publishing, acquired the copyrights of 162 songs, bought shares of record companies like the Philadelphia-based Jamie label, and had been accused of profiting from the songs he played on *American Bandstand*. Gene Vincent's former guitarist Jerry Merritt recalled in a *Blue Suede News* interview: "Dick Clark's people talked to Gene about promotion and tours with strings attached. Gene Vincent told Dick Clark to take it to the moon! To this day if Dick Clark has a 25th year special or whatever you don't see Gene on it." Though forced to sell off some of his holdings as part of a settlement, Clark emerged scot-free.

Exhausted and disheartened, Freed reluctantly pleaded guilty to bribery charges in 1962 and was given a suspended jail sentence. Left a broken man, Freed began to drink even more heavily. Drifting to the West Coast with his third wife and young son Lance, Freed arrived penniless. In California, Freed was financially aided by Bob Keane, who as the owner of Del-Fi Records was grateful to the deejay for helping ignite the career of Ritchie Valens.

Returning to the airwaves, Freed took the 22nd-ranked radio station in Los Angeles, KDAY, to 3rd place in the ratings. The station was owned by the same company which operated WINS in New York City. Pioneering Los Angeles deejay Art Leboe, who worked with Freed at KDAY, said in *Rockonomics*, "He loved being on the air again but was frustrated because he was unable to make the impact he had in New York. Kids liked him out here, but not the way they'd loved him in New York." Under the pressures of legal, tax and health problems, Freed resigned after several months. At the station, Freed was replaced by Tom Clay, a popular Detroit deejay. For a time, Freed drove around the country and promoted new releases for Mercury Records.

Then aided by his former business partner Morris Levy, Freed was again behind a microphone, this time at WQAM in Miami. But after clashing with the station owners over his independent concert promotions and his tendency to veer from the station's established playlists, Freed was fired.

Losing his properties and bank accounts to the IRS, Freed was left destitute. Returning to New York City for three months in 1963, Freed was met with cold shoulders by his former associates. When he was down and out, Freed "couldn't get his phone calls returned," recalled deejay Joe Finan.

Still hounded by the IRS, Freed was indicted by a federal grand jury in 1964 for income tax evasion, with the government claiming he owed $40,000 on unreported income of $57,000. Freed's son, Lance, recalled in *Rockonomics*: "Even today, all the performance money collected on the publishing of his music goes directly to the IRS. Originally, the debt wasn't quite a hundred thousand dollars, but with all the interest accrued over the years, it's headed toward the millions. There was nothing left at the end except the house in Palm Springs, which he was able to keep through the California Homesteading Act. Without that we would have been out in the street. Right up to the day he died he continued to make plans to someday return east." Suffering from uremia, Freed died of cirrhosis of the liver in 1965. Freed's funeral was paid for by Vee-Jay Records owner Randy Wood.

Wanting to forget the scar of payola, the music industry ignored Alan Freed's legacy well into the 1970s. But when historians began looking into rock and roll's origins, they rediscovered Freed's essential role. Paramount Pictures chronicled a week in the life of Freed's New York period in the 1978 biography, *American Hot Wax,* with Tim McIntyre in the lead role. In the film, Freed's character tells the district attorney: "Look, you can close the show. You can stop me. But you can never stop rock and roll. Don't you know that?" Unhappy with the movie's inaccuracies, R&B singer Screamin' Jay Hawkins, who portrayed himself in the film, said in *Nowhere To Run*: "History done Alan Freed wrong... and so did Hollywood."

With Alan Freed's meteoric rise synonymous with the birth of rock and roll, Cleveland was picked as the site of the Rock and Roll Hall of Fame and Museum in 1985. Freed was also inducted into the Hall of Fame in the Non-Performer category. In 1992, the 40th anniversary Moondog Coronation Ball in Cleveland included an appearance by Paul "Hucklebuck" Williams, the only act that took the stage at the original 1952 concert. In 2002, NBC aired the biopic, *Mr. Rock 'n' Roll: The Alan Freed Story*, with Judd Nelson in the title role.

Brenda Lee, who performed on some of Freed's revues, recalled in her autobiography, "Alan Freed was the epitome of what a rock 'n' roll disc jockey was at that time. I don't care what anybody says, he was a great man. He cared about us artists, and he cared about the music. His was a terribly sad story – he didn't deserve what became of him.... Dick Clark walked away unscathed. But Alan Freed became what many believe to be the music industry's fall guy to payola, a martyr to the rock 'n' roll cause.... How could anyone turn their back on the man who laid the foundation for the rock 'n' roll industry? It still makes me mad to think about it."

NORTHERN OHIO PIONEERS OF ROCK & ROLL

A number of rock and R&B acts emerged from the Northern Ohio cities of Cleveland, Youngstown and Toledo during the 1940s and '50s, including Bull Moose Jackson, Screamin' Jay Hawkins and The Poni-Tails. Many of these artists were aided in their careers by powerful deejays in Cleveland.

JUMP BLUES: TINY BRADSHAW & BULL MOOSE JACKSON

By the early-1940s, a new form of African-American music was emerging on the West Coast and in the Midwest called "jump blues." This new genre was danceable, performed by a combo or small jazz-styled orchestra, and was popular in urban areas. By the end of the decade, jump blues evolved into R&B.

Two pioneers of the genre, Ohio natives Tiny Bradshaw and Bull Moose Jackson both recorded for King Records. Born and raised in Youngstown, Bradshaw was drawn to jazz while attending Wilberforce University in 1932. Quitting school and moving to New York City, he joined a series of groups before forming his own orchestra in 1933. A popular entertainer who was frequently compared to one-time bandmate Cab Calloway, Bradshaw enjoyed long residencies in the house band at the Cotton Club in Cincinnati and at the Savoy in New York City.

During and shortly after World War II, Bradshaw rode out the Big Band era, often performing at military clubs. He eventually pared down to a small, R&B-style combo with a basic rhythm section. Signed by King Records of Cincinnati in 1949, Bradshaw finally reached the R&B charts, beginning with "Well Oh Well." His hit run at King continued in the early-Fifties with "I'm Going To Have Myself A Ball," "Walkin' The Chalk Line," "Heavy Juice," and his theme song, "Soft." Bradshaw would be best remembered for a song he composed and recorded, "Train Kept A-Rollin'." Reworked in 1956 by rockabilly act Johnny Burnette And The Rock 'n' Roll Trio, the song became a rock standard. It was later a hit for both The Yardbirds and Aerosmith.

After suffering a quick succession of strokes beginning in 1954, Bradshaw never fully recovered. Although his health had improved enough for him to return to the studio and stage, he passed away in 1958.

Another pioneering R&B star who began his career in the jump blues tradition, singer Bull Moose Jackson earned his nickname due to his oversized head. A native of Cleveland, he moved to New York City at age 18, and joined his first band, The Harlem Hotshots.

After returning to Cleveland, Jackson toured throughout the Northeast and developed a strong following in Buffalo, where he settled for a time. Eventually returning to his hometown, he was hired as a saxophonist by orchestra leader Lucky Millinder during a 1943 tour stop in Cleveland. Then following vocalist Wynonie Harris' departure from the orchestra due to illness, Jackson took over the lead vocal duties.

With King-Queen Records unable to sign Millinder who was already under contract, the label instead took a chance with Jackson. In 1946, Jackson would score his first solo with "I Know Who Threw The Whiskey (In The Well)," which was an answer record to Millinder's 1945 hit, "Who Threw The Whiskey In The Well." Luring away several members of Millinder's band, Jackson formed his own group in 1947, The Buffalo Bearcats.

Beginning with the chart-topping R&B smash "I Love You Yes I Do," Jackson enjoyed a solid run of hits over a brief two-year period with "All My Love Belongs To You" / "I Want A Bowlegged Woman," another chart-topper, "I Can't Go On Without You," "Cleveland Blues," "Little Girl Don't Cry," and a cover of a country song, "Why Don't You Haul Off And Love Me."

By the early-1950s, Jackson began recording bawdy songs like "Big Fat Mamas Are Back In Style," Leiber and Stoller's "Nosey Joe" and "Big Ten Inch Record" (which was revived in the 1970s by Aerosmith). But the arrival of doo-wop sounded the death knell for gritty, R&B shouters, and in 1955, Jackson was dropped by King Records. Then after recording for a series of labels, Jackson scored a surprise hit in 1961 with a re-recording of his earlier release, "I Love You Yes I Do."

Leaving music for more than two decades, Jackson worked in the commissary at Howard University in Washington, D.C. Making a minor comeback in the mid-1980s, Jackson was drawn back to the stage through the efforts of Pittsburgh oldies band, The Flashcats. Collaborating with the group, Jackson scored a minor hit with the comical single, "Get Off The Table Mable." An album's worth of material, *Moosemania*, was followed by a European tour. But falling ill, Jackson returned to Cleveland, where he spent his final days.

Another early R&B act, Youngstown-native Bobby Marchan found greater success after moving to New Orleans in 1953. As the lead singer of Huey Smith & Clowns, Marchan scored hits with "Rocking Pneumonia And The Boogie Woogie Flu" and "Don't You Just Know It." Pursuing a solo career, Marchan scored a pair of R&B hits with "Shake Your Tambourine" and the chart-topping "There's Something On Your Mind."

SCREAMIN' JAY HAWKINS

Screamin' Jay Hawkins was an accidental Clevelander. While riding on a Greyhound bus, his pregnant mother went into labor. Stepping off the vehicle in downtown Cleveland and delivering her child in the bathroom of the bus station, she gave up her son to the local orphanage and re-boarded another bus to complete her trip.

At the age of 14, Hawkins enlisted into the U.S. Army. During a subsequent stint in the Air Force, Hawkins became a successful boxer, winning a Golden Gloves middleweight championship in 1947. Abandoning sports for music, he had always yearned to become an opera singer. A self-taught piano player, Hawkins instead emerged as a blues shouter in the tradition of Louis Jordan and Roy Brown. After his military discharge, Hawkins joined Tiny Grimes' band, The Rockin' Highlanders. Eventually pursuing a solo career, Hawkins garnered a reputation as a shock-rocker, decades before Marilyn Manson.

Developing a flamboyant stage act which incorporated voodoo themes, Hawkins dressed in a Zulu costume and surrounded himself with ghoulish props including a cigarette-smoking, skull-on-a-stick nicknamed Henry. Hawkins usually began his performances by slowly emerging from a coffin, a gimmick conceived by deejay Alan Freed.

Hawkins recalled in a *San Francisco Chronicle* interview that Freed assured him, "You'll never have to worry about another hit record. People will stand in the rain to see you climb out of that coffin. They'll be gettin' three times the entertainment, and they'll always be back for more."

Hawkins scored his biggest hit with "I Put A Spell On You," an eerie, R&B romp which was punctuated by guttural moans and groans. Though the single sold well, it was banned by radio. Hawkins had written the song after he was dumped by a girlfriend.

Remaining a cult figure throughout his career, Hawkins opened up for The Rolling Stones in 1980 and enjoyed renewed popularity after his appearance in Jim Jarmusch's 1989 film, *Mystery Train*. Remarkably, Hawkins had sired several dozen children – many of whom had never met each other. Several months after his death in 2000, the Rock and Roll Hall of Fame attempted to organize a reunion of Hawkins' offspring.

LITTLE JIMMY SCOTT

A legendary Cleveland-based performer, Little Jimmy Scott led a difficult life, growing up in an orphanage after his mother's sudden death. Possessing a small, diminutive frame, Scott stood just under five-feet tall. His physical development was hampered by Kallmann's Syndrome, a chronic affliction which prevents the onset of puberty. The condition also gave Scott his distinctive, high-pitched voice.

After failing his first audition with Lionel Hampton's Orchestra in 1944, Scott was hired by the popular bandleader four years later. While with Hampton, Scott scored his only national hit in 1950, providing the local vocal on "Everybody's Somebody's Fool." Given his nickname by Hampton, Little Jimmy Scott possessed a gentle, emotional, vocal style that was legendary for making grown men cry.

Subsequently joining New Orleans-based R&B bandleader Paul Gayten, Scott continued to receive rave reviews. Leaving Gayten to pursue a solo career, Scott signed with Savoy Records in 1955. After battling label owner Herman Lubinsky over royalties, Scott recorded a series of unsuccessful singles for King Records. Then just as Scott appeared to get his big break – a 1962 album recorded for Ray Charles' label Tangerine Records – Lubinsky suddenly claimed that Scott was still under contract with Savoy. With Ray Charles unwilling to engage Savoy in a legal battle, the record was shelved. By the time Scott regrouped and issued his first solo album for Atlantic Records in 1969, musical tastes had changed. With his career floundering,

Scott spent decades in various low-paying jobs around Cleveland, including as an elevator operator at the Terminal Tower complex.

Then after giving a churning performance at the funeral of his longtime friend and ally, songwriter Doc Pomus, Scott drew the attention of a number of music-industry dignitaries in attendance. With the aid of rocker Lou Reed, Scott released his comeback album at Sire Records in 1992, *All The Way*.

Although Scott would achieve limited commercial success during his lifetime, he influenced a host of singers, including rock pioneers Sonny Til and Frankie Lymon. Soul legend Marvin Gaye once admitted to author David Ritz, "I heard Jimmy Scott back in the fifties when I sang doo-wop with Harvey Fuqua and The Moonglows. We looked to Jimmy as a master. My entire career I longed to sing ballads – like Frank Sinatra or Nat Cole or Perry Como – but with the depth of Jimmy Scott. He had that tear in his voice. That aching voice. When I finally got to record those ballads, I had a tape of Jimmy Scott at my side." Another R&B singer from Ohio, Nancy Wilson, would also acknowledge Scott as her chief influence.

ERNIE FREEMAN

A native of Cleveland, Ernie Freeman had a long and varied career as a solo artist, session pianist and arranger. Though his parents forced him to play the violin in a classical ensemble, Freeman was drawn to jazz and taught himself to play his father's saxophone. While in high school, Freeman joined his older sister's, popular, jazz combo, The Evelyn Freeman Swing Band.

Drafted into the U.S. Navy in 1942, Freeman and some of his former bandmates from Cleveland were assigned to a base in Indiana where they joined a military band, The Gobs Of Swing. After his discharge in 1945, Freeman returned to Cleveland and enrolled at the Cleveland Institute of Music. Leaving Cleveland for New York City, Freeman became an arranger for bandleader Woody Herman. Subsequently joining The Ernie Fields Orchestra as a pianist, Freeman toured across the U.S. for the next several years. By 1951, Freeman was moonlighting in another jazz outfit, The Billy Hadnott Sextette.

Forming his own combo in 1954, Freeman settled in Los Angeles. Emerging as a much in-demand session player, he was hired by the city's leading rock and R&B record labels, including Imperial, Modern, Specialty and Aladdin. During this period, Freeman worked on numerous hits – either as a pianist or arranger – including Ritchie Valens ("Come On, Let's Go"), Jan & Arnie ("Jennie Lee") and The Platters ("The Great Pretender").

As a solo artist, Freeman placed two instrumentals on the R&B charts in 1956, "Jivin' Around (Pts. 1 & 2)" and "Lost Dreams." The following year, Freeman topped the R&B charts with a cover of Bill Justis' instrumental, "Raunchy."

Heading a studio-only group, B. Bumble And The Stingers, Freeman scored hits in the early-1960s with the bouncy "Flight Of The Bumblebee," "Bumble Boogie" and "Boogie Woogie." Freeman did not appear on the group's 1962 hit "Nut Rocker" or participate in tours. Freeman's studio group also recorded as Billy Joe & The Checkmates and scored a top-10 hit with "Percolator (Twist)." Joining yet another studio-only group, The Marketts, Freeman scored a few hits with the Tommy Tedesco-led outfit. During this same period, Freeman recorded a number of upbeat, party albums such as *Limbo Dance Party* and *Comin' Home Baby*.

After a stint as the musical director at Liberty Records, Freeman was hired in the same position at Frank Sinatra's label, Reprise Records. At Reprise, Freeman collaborated with the Chairman of the Board on a number of recordings including, "Strangers In The Night." During this period, Freeman also worked with Dean Martin on hits such as "Everybody Loves Somebody." Freeman earned a Grammy for the arrangement of the Simon and Garfunkel, chart-topping ballad, "Bridge Over Troubled Water."

After leaving Reprise in 1971, Freeman worked infrequently. During his long career, Freeman performed on more than 100 chart hits, and worked with artists such as Sammy Davis Jr., Julie London, Paul Anka and Rosemary Clooney.

Another Cleveland-born talent, bandleader and composer Henry Mancini provided the hit scores for many films such as *The Pink Panther* and *Breakfast At Tiffany's*. Nominated for an amazing 72 Grammy Awards, he won 20. Meanwhile, Clevelander Eddie Platt was a one-hit wonder who reached the top-20 in 1958 with a rush-released cover version of The Champs' "Tequila." The session was the brainchild of deejay Bill Randle.

JOHNNY AND THE HURRICANES

Nicknamed "The Glass City," Toledo is located about 60-miles south of Detroit in the northwestern corner of Ohio. During the 1950s, Toledo spawned several hit acts: pop singer Theresa Brewer, R&B singer Annisteen Allen, jazz pianist Art Tatum, and a rock and roll combo, Johnny And The Hurricanes.

Formed in 1957 by several students at Rossford Catholic High School in Toledo, Johnny And The Hurricanes were headed by saxophonist Johnny Paris (born John Pocisk). Trained in jazz, Paris was drawn to rock and roll after hearing Bill Haley & The Comets.

Originally called The Orbits, the group emerged as an instrumental act because none of the members wanted to take on lead vocal duties. Renamed Johnny And The Hurricanes, the group signed with a small Detroit label, Twirl Records. After the group's debut 1959 release, "Crossfire," began garnering airplay throughout the Midwest, the single was leased to a larger label, Warwick Records. A national hit, the single was followed-up with the million-seller "Red River Rock," "Reveille Rock" and "Beatnik Fly." After switching to Big Top Records in 1960, the group would continue to chart but with none of the subsequent releases reaching the top-40.

By 1965, Paris was the last remaining, original member of the band. When gigs in the U.S. dried up, he began performing for European audiences.

Doo-Wop

A popular genre in the northeastern corner of the state, doo-wop had been popularized in the region by deejay Alan Freed. In addition to Freed's discoveries – The Moonglows and The Coronets – there were other successful, doo-wop groups in Northern Ohio.

One of these acts, The Edsels, emerged from the Youngstown suburb of Campbell. Recorded at a Cleveland studio, the group's single "Rama Lama Ding Dong" was issued in 1958. (Early pressings incorrectly read "Lama Rama Ding Dong.") Except for some activity in Baltimore, the song failed garner airplay. By 1960, the group was asked to perform on *American Bandstand* on the strength of another single, "What Brought Us Together." But when a New York deejay began playing their earlier release "Rama Lama Ding Dong," the song found renewed interest and raced up the pop charts.

Another Youngstown doo-wop act, The Students, relocated to Cincinnati. Formed in 1957, the group is best known for the upbeat single, "I'm So Young," which became popular a couple years after the group had disbanded in 1959.

The Steubenville-based group, The Stereos, traveled to New York City to find fame. Previously known as The Buckeyes, the group had issued a single on the DeLuxe label. Aided by songwriters Luther Dixon and Otis Blackwell, the group attracted only spotty airplay with a subsequent single, "Sweetpeas In Love." The group's only hit came with the self-composed ballad, "I Really Love You."

Formed in Cleveland, The Hornets were an obscure but highly-collectable, doo-wop quartet led by James "Sonny" Long. Members of the group also moonlighted as a gospel act, The Cleveland Quartet. While neither The Hornets nor The Cleveland Quartet had any success, the group's tenor Johnny Moore went on to front one of the leading acts of the early rock era, The Drifters. Moore was hired by The Drifters in late-1954, after a quick audition during a Cleveland tour stop.

Founded by legendary tenor vocalist Clyde McPhatter at Atlantic Records, The Drifters claimed nearly 40 members over their first two decades – including several different lead singers. But when McPhatter was drafted in 1954, the group had difficulty finding a suitable replacement.

In the late-1950s, Moore provided the lead vocals on The Drifters hits, "Adorable," "Ruby Baby," "Soldier Of Fortune" and "Fools Fall In Love." After leaving the group for a four-year military stint, Moore briefly attempted a solo career in the early-1960s under the name, Johnny Darrow. Eventually rejoining The Drifters, Moore initially alternated lead vocal duties with Rudy Lewis. But following Lewis' sudden death in May 1964, Moore fronted the band on a full-time basis and provided the lead vocals on hits such as "Under The Boardwalk," "I've Got Sand In My Shoes" and "Saturday Night At The Movies."

Hampered by constant infighting, The Drifters disbanded in 1970. With several splinter Drifters groups forming in the 1970s, Moore headed an official, European-based lineup. Adopting a more contemporary sound, Moore's version of The Drifters scored several British hits – none of which dented the U.S. charts. Leaving the group for a solo career in 1978, Moore later teamed with another former Drifters member, Ben E. King. Eventually securing the legal right to tour with his own Drifters group, Moore performed until shortly before his death in 1998. (Another Drifters member, Columbus-native Bobby Hendricks provided the lead vocal on the group's 1958 single, "Drip Drop." As a solo act, he scored a top-10, R&B hit with "Itchy Twitchy Feeling.")

GIRL GROUPS

During the big-band era, women in popular music were either dancers or featured vocalists. With women rarely hired as musicians, all-female orchestras or combos were treated as novelties. Among the all-girl vocal groups who emerged at the dawn of the rock era were the barbershop-styled Chordettes and Ohio's McGuire Sisters. Similarly, Toledo's Theresa Brewer was rooted in a pre-rock pop style. A former child prodigy who performed on radio since age five, Brewer first reached the charts in 1950 with "Music! Music! Music!" But like many of her contemporaries, Brewer survived into the rock era by recording sanitized cover-versions of rock hits such as "A Tear Fell," "You Send Me" and "Empty Arms."

Similarly, the doo-wop era of the 1950s was initially the domain of all-male groups. But that began to change. The first girl-groups to achieve any level of success were a pair of one-hit wonders, The Teen Queens and The Bobbettes. It took The Chantels to demonstrate any kind of staying power.

Most of the Buckeye girl-groups of this period emerged from the Cleveland area. The Poni-Tails – Toni Cistone, LaVerne Novak and Karen Topinka – were a trio of students at Brush High School in suburban Cleveland. The group was discovered by a local attorney at a school charity show.

Recording the single "Your Wild Heart," the group nearly had a hit on its hands until singer Joy Layne quickly recorded a cover version of the song. While Layne's rendition reached the top-20, The Poni-Tails' version failed to chart. Due to pressure from her parents, Topinka left the group and was replaced by Pattie McCabe.

Hiring a pair of managers and signing with ABC Records, The Poni-Tails scored a quick hit when influential Cleveland deejay Bill Randle began playing the B-side of an unissued acetate, "Born Too Late." Featuring Cistone's pleading and innocent lead vocal, the Don Costa-produced single was a top-10 smash in 1958. After touring across the country and appearing on *American Bandstand*, the group declined an extension of their three-year recording contract in 1960.

Another Cleveland girl-group, The Secrets were formed as a trio at Shaw High School. Expanded to a quartet, the group began performing around the city. But when classmate Tom King – the leader of The Starfires – asked the girls to join him at a number of local concerts, The Secrets drew the attention of talent agent Redda Robbins. Signing with Philips Records, The Secrets were whisked to the East Coast where their session for "The Boy Next Door" was cut in under half-an-hour. Although the single would reach the top-20 in 1963, the group became disenchanted with the music industry and disbanded in 1965.

Yet another Cleveland act, The Tracey Twins – Euni and Eudi – earned some national airplay with "Tonight You Belong To Me." The duo enjoyed stardom after winning a talent competition on *The Arthur Godfrey Show*. Over the next several years, the twins would appear on *American Bandstand*, *Merv Griffin* and *The Tonight Show*. And another sister act, Margy and Mary-Ellen Keegan formed The Short Cuts and scored a regional hit with "Don't Say He's Gone."

Another Cleveland native, solo singer Andrea Carroll was crowned "Little Miss Cleveland" and became a regular on a local, television variety program, *The Gene Carroll Show*. While in her teens, she scored several Midwestern hits including "Please Don't Talk To The Lifeguard," which was later recorded by Diane Ray. Backed by The Chiffons, Carroll nearly reached the top-40 with a composition written by a young Neil Sedaka, "It Hurts To Be Sixteen."

CODA

Meanwhile, many early R&B and blues artists had little to show for their chart successes. The July 1950 issue of *Ebony* magazine reported that singer Cow Cow Davenport "lives in obscurity in one of Cleveland's worst slum tenements. His apartment, a drafty three rooms, is in a sagging frame building just off a garbage-littered alley. Surrounded by faded photographs and mementos of his days of glory, he sits and broods about his past. Over a pot-bellied stove which in winter barely heats one room, he reminisces dolefully about the glories of yesterday" and recalling, "in those days none of us had any idea the things we wrote could make big money. We just sold them for what we could get. Sometimes it was as little as $25." He would earn no royalties for his hit "Cow Cow Boogie," which he sold to the Leed Music Co. for $500, lamenting: "They even took my name off the sheet music."

Meanwhile, Cleveland-born, gospel-reared singer Wynona Carr achieved only limited success. Originally the leader of The Carr Sisters, she later recorded as Sister Wynona Carr at Specialty Records. Changing musical directions, she scored an R&B hit in 1957 with "Should I Ever Love Again?" After recording an album for Frank Sinatra's Reprise label, she returned to Cleveland and died in obscurity.

Similarly, a pair of early rhythm-and-blues singing legends, Amos Milburn and former King Records artist Big Maybelle, spent their final years in Cleveland – both living in squalor. It would be decades before some of the major record companies would attempt to correct past financial wrongs.

CHAPTER 3
CINCINNATI: WLW AND KING-FEDERAL RECORDS

A cosmopolitan city in the southwestern corner of the state, Cincinnati was an amalgam of high European culture and Appalachian sensibilities. Earning many nicknames during the 19th century including The Queen City, Porkopolis and City Of Seven Hills, Cincinnati blossomed along the Ohio River, in a region originally purchased by land investor Judge John Cleves Symmes.

A large number of the city's first inhabitants arrived by flatboat, a rudimentary vessel constructed of logs. But by 1811, the modern steamboat made travel and trade possible up the Mississippi and Ohio Rivers. By the middle of the 19th century, Cincinnati was a booming trading town, as 3,000 steamboats visited the city annually, making it the busiest inland port in the nation.

One of the city's chief products was pork, which spawned the 1830s nickname, Porkopolis. As a byproduct of meat processing, soap was made by a number of firms, including Procter & Gamble, which continues to thrive today as a multinational firm with numerous product lines.

A city of immigrants, Germans and Irish descended on the region. One longtime resident, Harriet Beecher Stowe, chronicled Cincinnati's role in the development of the Underground Railroad, in her classic work, *Uncle Tom's Cabin*. When Abraham Lincoln finally met Stowe in 1862, he reportedly greeted her with the comment, "So you're the little woman who wrote the book that started this great war!"

The town also gave rise to the world's first professional baseball team. The Cincinnati Red Stockings were financed in 1869 by a group of investors, who began paying players and charging admission to games. A century later, the city came to idolize catcher Pete Rose, whose banishment from the Hall of Fame is still a sore point among baseball fans.

Cincinnati has also nurtured a rich musical legacy. The city was the capital of Christian music publishing in the 19th century. In an era before records, the printing of sheet music was a major industry, and in a period when faith played a more central role in the lives of Ohioans, singing religious songs at home and in church was a widespread practice.

Secular music also thrived in the city. Pittsburgh-born songwriter Stephen Foster moved to Cincinnati in 1846 and worked as a bookkeeper at his brother's steamship firm, Irwin & Foster. During his four-years in the city, Stephen Foster wrote the first of his many hit compositions, "Oh! Susanna," as well as a song later popularized by The Christy Minstrels, "Nelly Was A Lady."

At the turn of the century, the Cincinnati-based Baldwin Company emerged as one of the largest manufacturers of pianos in the world. In a time when owning a piano meant middle-class respectability, the proper American home prominently displayed the instrument in its parlor room. And while Cincinnati was America's buggy-manufacturing capital for several decades, its stature would be eclipsed by the arrival of the horseless carriage.

Beginning in the late-1910s, Cincinnatians were regularly exposed to a new musical form called jazz, as the result of the passing riverboats, which crept up from New Orleans. Meanwhile, Cincinnati's Mamie Smith would record a groundbreaking single in 1920, "Crazy Blues." Issued by Okeh Records, the single was considered the first-ever blues record. Purchased by both blacks and whites, the record spawned a host of imitators as competing labels cashed in on the emerging blues craze.

While Cincinnati had strict "blue laws," casino-style nightclubs featuring jazz and blues music flourished across the river in northern Kentucky, where former bootleggers went legit after the end of Prohibition. With relaxed laws and little in the way of police enforcement, these venues proliferated well into the 1960s.

But Cincinnati's greatest musical legacies were a radio powerhouse, WLW, and a record company, King-Federal. Established by a pair of visionaries, WLW was the brainchild of Powel Crosley II, while King-Federal was the creation of Sydney Nathan.

WLW: THE NATION'S STATION

Before the arrival of television, radio was king. Much like the state of television today, radio was dominated by a handful of networks. The programming on these networks ranged from dramas and comedies to soap operas and musical acts.

The Crosley family of Cincinnati was instrumental in the rise of radio broadcasting. Settling in Southern Ohio in 1810, the Crosley family toiled as farmers over the next several decades. One descendant, Powel Crosley, arrived in Cincinnati as a newly minted attorney in 1876. Fairly prosperous, Crosley dabbled in a variety of business ventures from the manufacture of stoves and automobile accessories to real estate development and the operation of a vaudeville theater. Eventually taking over the family business, Powel Crosley II would avoid his father's mistakes and live by the adage – pay cash and never borrow from a bank.

Then on a fateful afternoon on February 22, 1921 – George Washington's birthday – young Powel Crosley III was off from school and asked his namesake father to purchase a device he had just seen at a playmate's home – a "wireless." A wireless was an early name for a radio, and the boy's request stimulated the curiosity of his entrepreneurial father.

Later that day, Powel Crosley II took his son to a downtown Cincinnati manufacturer of radios. Crosley biographer Rusty McClure described the momentous event as the elder Crosley examined the device: "A salesman offered to demonstrate a Precision [brand radio] with a live program. He hooked up the batteries, attached the antenna, and handed over the headphones. Music filled Powel's ears. He listened a moment, then inquired about the price. The set, he was told, was a one-tube model, the cheapest in the store. Powel could have it for a hundred and thirty dollars – sans batteries, headphones, and antenna [which would be extra]. Powel was stunned. He looked at the set again. It was a wooden box with circuitry inside. Phonographs came in nicer boxes for far less money. A hundred and thirty dollars. About what the average workingman made in a month. Too much to spend on a child's toy.... Back home, Powel paced, hands behind his back, mumbling to himself. A hundred and thirty dollars. A third the cost of a Model T [automobile]. The least expensive set in the shop. Finally, he exploded. 'The idea of charging that much for that little thing,' he said. 'I could build that set for half the price!' And so, eventually, he did."

Initially, Crosley began selling only the wooden cabinets that housed these primitive radios. Next, he made radio parts for manufacturers. But Crosley yearned to construct radios. With a handful of firms such as General Electric and Westinghouse owning the majority of the crucial radio patents, Crosley had to overcome a series of challenges.

Despite the fact that he was booted from the engineering program at the University of Cincinnati, Crosley already had many patents to his name. Hiring a pair of engineering students, Crosley introduced his first radio, the Harko, in 1921. Quickly selling hundreds of thousands of radios, Crosley was unable to meet the endless demand. Some of the radios were manufactured by a firm in Iowa, which possessed a license to use a technology, which was unavailable to Crosley until he bought out a competitor in late-1922.

An innovator and astute businessman, Powel Crosley II saw another opportunity. With a scarcity of broadcasters in the Cincinnati area, Crosley launched his own radio station. On July 1, 1921, the Department of Commerce, which was headed by Herbert Hoover, granted Crosley the call letters 8XAA. Building a small, 20-watt transmitter, Crosley initially limited the fare to records, many of which he personally played. But since paid radio advertising was unheard of at the time, Crosley's sole reason for broadcasting was to sell more radios. But when the government ordered the end to all amateur broadcasts on January 1, 1922, 8XAA went off the air.

But after challenging the order, Crosley's radio station returned to the airwaves two months later as WLW. With the introduction of the limited-commercial license, WLW began broadcasting at 360 meters (the station would change frequencies a number of times). Challenging the dominance of the major players in the emerging broadcasting industry, WLW began producing quality, original programming.

But the leading players in radio soon regrouped. The first major radio network, The National Broadcasting Company (NBC), was formed in 1926 from a partnership between Westinghouse, General Electric and RCA, with a stated goal of establishing a radio monopoly. NBC operated two distinct networks, the Red and the Blue. The following year, NBC was challenged by an upstart venture. Originally called the United Independent Broadcasters, the network was purchased by David Sarnoff and renamed the Columbia Broadcasting System (CBS).

By 1927, WLW changed its frequency for the last time and settled at 700 kilohertz on the AM dial. Then after buying a competing station, WSAI, Crosley built a new transmitter for WLW north of the city. Instead of a mere 5,000 watts, WLW had received FCC approval to broadcast at 50,000 watts. Two matching 300-foot towers were constructed to handle the surge in power. When the switch was pulled, WLW adopted a new nickname, "The Nation's Station," and began targeting a national audience. While the NBC Blue network supplied about a third of WLW's programming, the remainder was produced in the station's studios or on location around the city. Meanwhile, Crosley's other Cincinnati station, WSAI, focused on the local market.

During this period, the Crosley empire was booming. Expanding far beyond radio, the company was manufacturing everything from refrigerators to airplanes. Surviving the stock market crash of 1929, the Crosley family had learned a valuable lesson decades earlier and owed nothing to the banks. While other firms shuttered, Crosley survived completely intact. Thriving during the Depression years, Crosley continued to introduce new products.

With many Americans no longer able to afford records or theater tickets, radio listenership boomed. Many of WLW's locally-produced programs were sold to network radio and independent stations around the nation. In 1933, WLW had a hit on its hands with a daytime drama called *Ma Perkins*. Sponsored by Procter & Gamble's Oxydol brand soap, the program gave rise to the phrase, "soap opera."

The Nation's Station would spawn a series of nationally-known personalities. In its first three decades of broadcasting, WLW was home to Red Skeleton, Doris Kappelhoff (better known as Doris Day), The Clooney Sisters (featuring Rosemary Clooney), Eddie Albert, Andy Williams, and The McGuire Sisters. Breaking the rigid color barrier of the period, WLW featured programs by African-Americans such as Fats Waller, The Mills Brothers and The Ink Spots.

Also embracing country and western music, the station produced numerous pioneers of the genre including Grandpa Jones, Minnie Pearl, Cowboy Copas, Merle Travis, Whitey Ford, Red Foley, and of course, Pa and Ma McCormick. Many of these performers appeared on the WLW program *The Boone County Jamboree,* which in 1945, was renamed *The Midwest Hayride.*

While AM radio stations in the United States were limited to 50,000 watts, WLW was briefly permitted to broadcast at ten times that level – 500,000 watts. Approved in June 1932, WLW's experimental license had to be renewed twice a year. After multiple trial and error efforts, engineers from WLW and General Electric designed and constructed the hulking, diamond-shaped, water-cooled transmitter, which was situated on former farmland between Cincinnati and Dayton. Powering up the transmitter on May 2, 1934, WLW could be heard across most of the country and into Europe. But with the increased wattage came problems. Neighboring farmers complained that light bulbs stayed lit and that the station's signal could be picked up by fences, poles and various other metal objects.

WLW was permitted to transmit at 500,000 watts until March 1, 1939. At that time, the FCC chose not to extend the station's experimental status. According to *The Cincinnati Post*: "The station's huge signal proved [politically] unpopular in Washington. Crosley's staunch anti-union attitude did not play well at the time, since he banned his news department from covering union issues.... Union organizing had indeed come to town and it was suddenly cheaper to produce radio shows in New York and Chicago. WLW performers, writers and musicians packed their bags [and headed] for those radio meccas. WLW produced far fewer of its own shows with NBC pressuring the station to carry more of its network programming." Losing his legal case, Crosley was denied an extension by the U.S. Court of Appeals for the District of Columbia. In a final blow, the FCC ruled that no AM station could increase its broadcasting power beyond 50,000 watts.

With no obvious heirs who could or would run the company, Powel Crosley II decided to sell the Crosley Radio Corporation in 1945. The Crosley family reaped $15.6 million in cash plus shares of the purchasing firm, AVCO. Though no longer a locally-operated, family-owned operation, WLW remained a media giant in Cincinnati.

By 1958, WLW expanded into television broadcasting with the licensing of WLWT, channel 5. The station became NBC's first affiliate. In the early days of the station, science fiction writer Rod Serling was a member of the staff.

Although banned from broadcasting at 500,000 watts, WLW maintained the colossal transmitter for the next three decades. Though repeatedly petitioning the FCC for approval to restart the massive beast, no such action would come. WLW later became the flagship of Jacor Communications. In 1998, Jacor merged with Clear Channel Communications.

SYDNEY NATHAN & KING-FEDERAL RECORDS

The most important independent labels of the 1950s were Atlantic and King-Federal. While Atlantic operated in one of the nation's music capitals, King-Federal thrived despite its isolated location in the lower Midwest. But while the label was conceived as a country-oriented endeavor, King-Federal quickly embraced urban musical styles such as blues and R&B. The King-Federal roster of the 1950s boasted some of the top acts in the nation, including The Dominoes, James Brown, Hank Ballard And The Midnighters, Little Willie John, Roy Brown and The "5" Royales.

In the years immediately following World War II, technological advances such as the invention of the tape recorder made it easier for entrepreneurs to start their own record companies. And with most non-mainstream, musical genres such as R&B and country ignored by major labels, a growing number of independent record companies were launched to meet the demand.

One of these entrepreneurs set up shop in Cincinnati. An unlikely cog in the rise of rock and R&B, Sydney Nathan established a musical empire at King-Federal Records. But unlike his rivals at Atlantic, Nathan was far more motivated by profit than in creating musical art. Surrounding himself with talented staff, Nathan was unstoppable for nearly two decades.

Born in Cincinnati on April 27, 1904, to a professional tailor, Nathan suffered from poor health throughout his life. Dropping out of school during the ninth grade in 1920, Nathan took a variety of jobs in his youth. Drawn to the entertainment industry, he worked at an amusement park, promoted wrestling matches and played drums in various jazz bands. At age 18, he briefly relocated to Arizona in an attempt to alleviate the symptoms of his chronic asthma.

Returning to Cincinnati, Nathan worked at a downtown Cincinnati radio wholesaler. During this period, he became enamored with the radio stars on WLW. Subsequently working at his brother's pawn shop, Nathan accidentally fell into the record business as the result of an unpaid debt. Lending an acquaintance $6, Nathan had trouble collecting the tab. Nathan told *The Cincinnati Enquirer*, "One night I saw the fellow at [the Beverly Hills Supper Club across the Ohio River in Kentucky] with a gorgeous babe. I figured he would be in the next day with my six bucks. He didn't show. For three weeks in a row I saw him at Beverly with the same babe. Finally on the dance floor, I grabbed his shoulder, told him that if he could afford Beverly, he certainly could repay me. He turned red, blue and green, and told me he didn't have it." Trying to make good on his debt, he gave Nathan 300 used records and insisted that at two-cents each, they would bring in six-dollars. Instead, Nathan made $18 in just one day. Buying more used records from local jukebox operators for two-cents a piece, Nathan had tapped a lucrative market.

Moving to Miami at the invitation of his physician brother, David Nathan, Sydney Nathan opened a photo-finishing business to cater to tourists. But following an abnormally chilly winter which had kept tourists away, Nathan was forced to shutter the business.

Returning to Cincinnati in 1939, Sydney Nathan opened his own record store (with a photo developing business in the rear). Though located in a rundown neighborhood, the store prospered. Realizing he could earn far more profit by issuing his own records, Nathan decided in 1943 to launch a record company.

Initially dabbling in country music, Nathan recorded a pair of radio performers from WLW, Merle Travis and Akron-native Grandpa Jones. Fearful of losing their radio jobs, Travis and Jones recorded under a pseudonym, The Sheppard Brothers.

Disappointed with the quality of the pressed records, Nathan raised $25,000 from family members to purchase record-pressing machinery. Despite the wartime shortages of shellac – a crucial material in the manufacture of records – Nathan somehow managed to hoard a large supply. Coming under scrutiny from the federal government, Nathan escaped prosecution.

By 1944, Nathan settled his record company inside a former ice warehouse on Brewster Avenue in the Evanston section of Cincinnati. Nathan used the building's metal rollers to ferry boxes of records instead of blocks of ice. Situated on a short, dead-end street, the inconspicuous, 9,000-square-foot brick building went generally unnoticed in the city. A prime location for distributing records, the building abutted a Baltimore & Ohio train line.

Knowing little about the record business, Nathan solicited the advice of WLW performer Alton Delmore, a member of the popular country act The Delmore Brothers. Also instrumental in the success of the label was local businessman Howard Kessel, who guided Nathan throughout the company's run.

Soon after, King had its first national success with the Cowboy Copas hit, "Filipino Baby." A popular performer, Copas was known for his stints on *The Grand Ole Opry* and WLW's *Midwest Hayride*. Over the next few years, King would have further successes in the country field with Wayne Raney, The Carlisle Brothers, Moon Mullican and Hank Penny. (While he did not record for King Records, Hank Williams Sr. came to Cincinnati in 1948 and '49 to record some of his early releases such as "Lovesick Blues.")

Sensing a demand, Nathan expanded into the African-American music market. With the black population of Cincinnati increasing from 7.5% in 1930 to 15% in 1945, the community was clamoring for R&B and blues records. Visiting the Cotton Club in the city's West End district, Nathan initially tried to sign jump-blues bandleader Lucky Millinder, who had scored a major hit in 1944 with "Who Threw The Whiskey In The Well." But since Millinder was contractually bound to another label, Nathan instead signed one of Millinder's vocalists, Bull Moose Jackson.

In August 1945, Syd Nathan launched a subsidiary label called Queen. The final Queen Records release – the last of 75 singles – was by orchestra leader and horn player, Earl Bostic. A jazz-rooted entertainer, Bostic remained with King until his death two decades later. Recording prolifically during this period, Bostic placed three singles on the charts, including a cover of Duke Ellington's "Flamingo." After folding the Queen subsidiary in 1947, Nathan introduced the King "race" series. Although "race" and "hillbilly" records were now both issued on the same King imprint, the race records featured blue and silver labels while the hillbilly records used red and gold labels.

A color-blind employer who hired a large number of African-Americans, Nathan would not allow skin color to get in the way of earning a profit. Former trumpet player and arranger Henry Glover was hired as an "A&R man," and had the authority to sign new acts. One of the first African-American executives at a large record label, Glover worked with both country and R&B acts at King-Federal. Also a songwriter, Glover often used the pseudonym, Henry Bernard.

Meanwhile, during the 1940s and '50s, black gospel acts began rivaling their secular R&B counterparts in terms of record sales, and Nathan was not going to ignore the economic opportunity. Some of the label's earliest gospel stars included, The Swan Silvertones, The Harmoneers and Wings Over Jordan.

In 1947, Nathan acquired a large financial interest in a competing, independent label, DeLuxe Records. The company had been formed three-years earlier by David and Jules Braun in Linden, New Jersey. By 1952, the label's headquarters were moved to Cincinnati. But with the Braun brothers devoting more time to their new label, Regal, Nathan assumed full ownership of DeLuxe as well as its back catalog. In the process, King also acquired the recording contract of New Orleans R&B singer Roy Brown. Initially reissuing a number of DeLuxe tracks on King Records, Nathan later revived the label.

Syd Nathan generated most of his profits from song royalties. Each time a song was played on radio, in nightclubs or on jukeboxes, royalties were paid to the songwriter and music publisher. Sending out talent scouts – often to the South – Nathan was constantly in search of original compositions. But instead of paying songwriting royalties, Nathan instructed his employees to pay flat fees of $50 or $100, and as such, King-Federal owned the compositions. On these releases, Nathan used various songwriter pseudonyms including Lois Mann and Sally Nix.

And when Nathan forced his R&B artists to record renditions of country hits, it wasn't because of some noble motivation. When Bull Moose Jackson was instructed to record the country song "Why Don't You Haul Off And Love Me," it was because Nathan owned the composition and wanted to maximize his profits. Nathan would often demand the same of his country artists, forcing them to record countrified renditions of the label's R&B releases.

Meanwhile, yet another former Lucky Millinder Orchestra vocalist, Wynonie Harris, released a series of groundbreaking records for King.

Recording the Roy Brown-composed "Good Rockin' Tonight" in 1948, Harris made rock and roll history by scoring the first R&B hit to feature the term "rock" in the title (the song would be reprised in 1954 by Elvis Presley). Nicknamed "Mr. Blues," Harris became a workhorse at King as he churned out hits such as "Lollipop Mama," "All She Wants To Do Is Rock" and "Good Morning Judge." Also in 1948, West Coast singer-pianist Ivory Joe Hunter recorded his first of several top-10 R&B hits for King Records with "Don't Fall In Love With Me."

The King-Federal roster also featured a number of female R&B singers. A growling, shouting and gyrating performer, Big Maybelle recorded for the label in 1948. Though she would have little chart success at King, she fared far better at Okeh and Savoy Records. Also briefly recording for King-Federal, teenage vocalist Little Esther Phillips would manage just one hit during this period, a top-10 R&B entry, "Ring-A-Ding-Doo."

In 1950, Nathan shrewdly purchased the Miracle Records catalog from the IRS for less than $5,000. Nathan also signed a vocalist from the label, Sonny Thompson. While Thompson would score only a few hits at King-Federal, he remained at the label as an A&R executive.

A notoriously thrifty businessman, Nathan manufactured everything involved in the production of records, with the exception of the inner LP sleeves. By establishing a national distribution network to avoid dealing with the major labels, Nathan overcame a crucial problem that plagued most independent record companies. Another advantage of being a full-service operation was the ability to issue a limited quantity of a record to test the market.

Hank Ballard, leader of The Midnighters, recalled in *When Rock Was Young*, "Syd Nathan was the stingiest man in the world. Nobody could get as much out of one dollar as Syd Nathan could. Just to prove a point once, he said, I'm going to show you how I can conserve $20,000 in one month. So he started cutting back on everything, even electricity. You'd go to the toilet and there [wasn't any] light on!"

Nathan understood the need to surround himself with talented producers. Leaving Savoy Records in 1950, producer Ralph Bass was hired by King Records. Generously rewarded, Bass was given his own subsidiary, Federal, and a half-stake in a lucrative publishing company. Initially launched to record West Coast R&B acts, the Federal subsidiary was supervised by Bass and the legendary, Los Angeles-based songwriter and bandleader, Johnny Otis.

The first major act to emerge from Federal was an R&B vocal outfit assembled by songwriter-manager Billy Ward – The Dominoes. Featuring the talents of tenor Clyde McPhatter and booming bass of Bill Brown, the group recorded a long string of hits including "Do Something For Me," "Have Mercy Baby" and "I'd Be Satisfied."

But it was The Dominoes' bawdy song, "Sixty Minute Man," which created a commotion. Though banned by radio for its risque lyrics, the song still managed to cross-over onto the pop charts and became the biggest R&B hit of the decade. But fearful of government regulation and a backlash from radio, Nathan was uneasy about releasing controversial singles, even if they sold in the millions.

At King-Federal's West Coast division, Bass also signed a group headed by Tony Williams called The Platters. The group's Federal recordings were rougher and more bluesy than their later pop-oriented releases, and as a result, fared poorly on the charts. But when the group's manager, Buck Ram, was negotiating a contract with Mercury Records for another of his acts, The Penguins (of "Earth Angel" fame), he demanded that Mercury also sign The Platters. While The Penguins would have limited success, The Platters developed into the most successful vocal group of the decade, scoring hit after hit, such as "Smoke Gets In Your Eyes" and "The Great Pretender." Meanwhile, Nathan continued to expand his empire by purchasing a Miami-based label, Glory Records.

Returning to Cincinnati in 1954, Ralph Bass assumed the production duties from Henry Glover of an up-and-coming R&B group headed by Hank Ballard called The Royals. But in order to avoid any confusion with another successful King Records act, The "5" Royales, Ballard's group was later renamed The Midnighters.

Discovered by King-Federal producer Johnny Otis at a Detroit talent show in 1951, The Royals/Midnighters broke onto the charts in 1953 with "Get It." Their subsequent hit, "Work With Me Annie," was one of the most influential hits of the era. Co-written by Bass and Ballard, the risque song employed a number of suggestive double-entendres. Milking the smash hit, The Midnighters released multiple followups such as "Annie Had A Baby" and "Auntie's Aunt Fannie." Other record labels joined the fray and issued answer songs such as "The Wallflower (Roll With Me Henry)" by teenage vocalist Etta James.

At the same Detroit talent show where Johnny Otis had discovered Hank Ballard, Otis was far more impressed with a 13-year-old singer named Little Willie John. Although Sydney Nathan would originally pass on the teenager, John would eventually sign with the label after touring with a popular bandleader, Paul Williams.

Barely five-feet tall and possessing a mean temper, Little Willie John commanded an emotionally-charged voice far beyond his years. With his jazz-inflected delivery, he scored a string of R&B hits beginning in 1955 with "All Around The World" and continuing with "Need You So Bad," "Talk To Me, Talk To Me," and a standard which would be re-worked on the pop charts by Peggy Lee, "Fever." But after killing a man during a bar scuffle, John would tragically perish behind bars.

With R&B morphing into rock and roll by the mid-1950s, Nathan began targeting the crossover-pop market. The Cincinnati-based doo-wop group, Otis Williams And The Charms, scored a series of cover hits beginning with a remake of The Fontaine Sisters' "Hearts Of Stone" and continuing with

"Ling, Ting, Tong" and "Two Hearts." But when Williams' backing group left the label over monetary issues, he hired a new group and continued his hit run with "That's Your Mistake," "Ivory Tower" and "United." The label's other pop hits included "Seventeen" by Boyd Bennett And The Rockets and the instrumental, "Honky Tonk," by Bill Doggett.

Meanwhile, Syd Nathan would berate Ralph Bass for signing an unknown, gritty vocalist from Georgia named James Brown. At the singer's first King session in February 1956, Nathan sat inside the glassed-in control booth with musical director Gene Redd, producer Ralph Bass and a recording engineer. But as Brown later recalled in his autobiography, the session was suddenly halted by Nathan who sprang from his seat during the first verse of "Please, Please, Please." Furious, Nathan shouted, "What's that? What in the hell are you doing? Stop the tape. That doesn't sound right to my ears. What's going on here?" Turning to Ralph Bass, Nathan continued his tirade, "I sent you out to bring back some talent, and this is what I hear. The demo was awful, and this is worse. I don't know why I have you working here. Nobody wants to hear that noise." Sensing no potential in the singer or the song, Nathan released the record only after producer Ralph Bass threatened to quit. Reaching the R&B top-10, the single would be a harbinger of things to come.

Similarly, Nathan refused to release another of Brown's self-composed songs, "Try Me." But with Brown funding his own session and sending out demos of the track to notable deejays, Nathan could not ignore incoming orders for the record. King would issue a newly recorded version of the song, which topped the R&B charts.

Meanwhile, after their contract expired in 1958, The Midnighters' were lured back to King-Federal. Now billed as Hank Ballard And The Midnighters, the group issued the single, "Teardrops On Your Letter." The B-side was a dance record called "The Twist." While both sides of the record did well on the R&B chart, neither song reached the pop top-40. Returning to the pop top-10 the following year with another dance record, "Finger Poppin' Time," Ballard also saw his earlier single, "The Twist" return to the charts, this time crossing over onto the pop top-40 thanks to a note-for-note, cover version by former chicken-plucker, Chubby Checker.

At the end of the 1950s, King-Federal was the sixth-largest record company in America with 400 employees. But with the music industry soon targeted by government investigators, the payola scandal would severely harm independent labels. Spending about $1,800 per month on payments to influential deejays around the country, Nathan was openly frank about the practice. But after deejay Alan Freed was prosecuted for accepting cash and gifts, Nathan deflected much of the blame onto his executives, Ralph Bass and Henry Glover. (By this time, Glover had left King and was working for Roulette Records in New York City.) In the wake of the scandal, King-Federal had difficulty in securing radio airplay and would begin a slow downward spiral.

Trying to adapt, Nathan changed the label's focus from singles to albums.

Reissuing much of the company's catalog on the LP format, he also began targeting overseas markets. A boost to the label's album format came through the acquisition of Bethlehem Records. A jazz-oriented label, Bethlehem had a strong roster with acts such as Nina Simone, Herbie Mann, Errol Garner, Carmen McCrae, Roland Kirk, Bobby Scott, Bobby Toup and Benny Carter. Meanwhile, with Nathan suffering from heart ailments, Hal Neely was promoted to vice-president.

Though frequently at odds with Nathan, James Brown kept King-Federal afloat throughout much of the 1960s. But despite his track record at the label, Brown continued to be misjudged by his boss. After Nathan repeatedly refused Brown's request to record a live album, the soul singer financed the project himself. Spending $5,700, Brown recorded *Live At The Apollo*. Just slightly over 30 minutes in length, the album was released in 1963 with an original print run of just 5,000 copies. But instead of playing a cut or two, deejays were airing an entire side of the LP at a time. With the album spending over a year on the charts, the label scored a massive hit.

In 1964, Nathan recorded a 35-minute motivational speech for his sales and publishing staff. In the oration, the gruffy-voiced, slow-speaking Nathan declared: "Somebody has to be the chief, and I am elected as the chief. I'm spending my money, not yours, so unless I change my ideas, it has to be as you hear on this record." He also reminded his staff about the way things are done in Cincinnati: "Don't forget, we're in the Midwest, and we are not contaminated by New York or Los Angeles or Chicago."

But Nathan soon faced a predicament when James Brown tried to leave the label. According to Brown, his contract with King-Federal covered only his vocal performances. Brown told *Rolling Stone*, "Mr. Nathan was the first one willing to take a chance on me, [but] we had differences. Mr. Nathan never did believe that I could play keyboards. Had it in my contract I couldn't play and sing on the same record. And he was dead wrong on that."

Wanting to record instrumental tracks and work as a producer, Brown signed with the Mercury Records subsidiary, Smash. An angry Nathan quickly filed suit. Subsequently, over the next two years, Brown had hits on both labels – while Brown recorded instrumentals for Smash, King issued a series of unreleased tracks from its vaults.

Brown recalled in his autobiography, "Meantime, it was a standoff between King Records and Mercury. I started to think there was something funny about it; Mercury seemed more interested in putting Mr. Nathan out of business than in recording me on vocals. The doors at King were all but closed; they had beat him, he had nothing to fight with. I felt bad about it, so I went to Arthur Smith's studio in Charlotte, North Carolina, cut 'Papa's Got A Brand New Bag,' and sent the tape to Mr. Nathan. It was done underground – I had to sneak the tape to him." By 1965, Brown had re-signed with King Records. But while Brown remained at the label, vice-president Hal Neely would leave to join Starday Records.

Struggling to keep the label afloat, Nathan merged King with Starday

Records in 1967. The new firm was called King-Starday. But a year later on March 5, 1968, Nathan would be dead after succumbing to heart disease and pneumonia at his condominium in Miami.

In October 1968, King was sold to Starday Records with an agreement that Starday would later be sold to Lin Broadcasting. Starday at the time was headed by Nathan's friend Don Pierce and former King Records executive Hal Neely (who had first option to buy King Records). The following month, Lin paid $5 million for Starday and King.

Then in 1971, a faction consisting of Neely, music publisher Freddy Beinstock and the songwriting duo of Jerry Leiber and Mike Stoller, formed Tennessee Recording and Publishing and purchased King-Starday. Not included in the deal were James Brown's contract and his past catalog, which were sold to Polydor Records. By 1973, Neely sold his interest in the firm.

Then in 1975, Tennessee Recording and Publishing sold the King-Starday catalog – minus the music publishing rights – to GML Inc. Over the next decade, much of the King-Federal catalog was reissued on the GML subsidiary, Gusto Records, often with added instrumentation in an effort to update the music. But the results enraged music purists. When Rhino Records began releasing the King-Federal catalog in its original, unadulterated form, the label often struggled to locate the original master recordings.

Then in 1995, a lawsuit over underpaid royalties was filed by a number of recording artists – Gene Pitney, Hank Ballard, The Shirelles and B.J. Thomas – against King/Gusto Records, GML Inc. and other related parties. In the end, the suit was settled for a reported $3.5 million.

Meanwhile, the city of Cincinnati would do little to honor the legacy of Sydney Nathan or King-Federal Records. James Brown lamented in a *Mojo* magazine interview – "I tried to put the studio back. The building is still there but they've gutted it. It would be like going to Memphis, where Elvis cut his records, and seeing the place boarded up. I'd rather have them tear it down then boarded up. Boarded up looks like it was a failure, you know? So you go there and it just hurts you to your heart." After Brown's death in 2006, his former sideman Bootsy Collins continued the crusade to honor the label's legacy. Collins told *The Chicago Sun-Times* in 2007, "We've been talking about saving King over the last seven years. At least the building is still standing. Someone has to step up and be the Henry Kissinger and pull it together. That's what my effort is. I'd not only like to restore the studio, but you have to tie in what's happening today. I'd like to have school programs involved. That way, it is still a work in progress."

Aside from its musical legacy, King-Federal also nurtured a number of talented record executives, including Seymour Stein of Sire Records, Jim Wilson of Sun Entertainment and Alan Leeds of Paisley Park Records.

Both Sydney Nathan and producer Ralph Bass have been inducted into The Rock and Roll Hall of Fame. As part of Ohio's 200th birthday celebration in 2003, the state honored King-Federal Records with a historic site marker.

FRATERNITY RECORDS

King-Federal's chief competitor in Cincinnati was a small label operated by classically-trained songwriter, Harry Carlson. After quitting the photography business, Carlson launched Fraternity Records in 1954. Assisted by his wife, he set up a studio in a room at the Sheraton-Gibson Hotel. The label's roster would include Jimmy Dorsey, Cathy Carr, Lonnie Mack, Charlie Daniels, 2 Of Clubs, The Casinos, Dale Wright and Bobby Bare.

A native of Ironton, Bobby Bare was drawn to the honky-tonk country of Hank Williams. But just as Bare's career was taking off, he was drafted into the U.S. Army in 1958. Before he left, Bare submitted a demo tape of the track "All American Boy" to Fraternity Records. But without his knowledge, the song was erroneously issued by Fraternity as by Bill Parsons, a singer that Bare had aided on a number of demo sessions. With the single becoming a top-5 smash hit, Parsons lip-synced the song on television programs. Meanwhile, Bare could not convince his army buddies that the song was really his.

Upon his discharge from the military in 1960, Bare returned to Fraternity Records and recorded a sequel to "All American Boy" called "I'm Hangin' Up My Rifle," a song inspired by the discharge of fellow soldier Elvis Presley. (Later moving to RCA Records, Bare recorded yet another sequel, "Brooklyn Bridge.") Enjoying a long career on the pop and country charts, Bare earned a Grammy in 1963 for "Detroit City."

A native of Cincinnati, rockabilly singer Carl Dobkins Jr. began his recording career at Fraternity Records. Initially nicknamed "The Teenage Rage," he was managed by local deejay Gil Sheppard. Switching to Decca, he landed a top-10 pop hit in 1959 with "My Heart Is An Open Book." Placing a few more singles on the charts, Dobkins scored his final top-40 hit with "Lucky Devil." (Another rockabilly artist from the Cincinnati area, Rusty York is best remembered for his King Records hit "Sugaree." He later operated his own label, Jewel Records.)

In 1975, Harry Carlson sold Fraternity Records – only the rights to the company's name – to longtime associate Shad O'Shea for $25,000. The rights to the label's master recordings were deeded back to the individual artists. O'Shea kept the label active, often releasing singles tied to local sports teams.

CHAPTER 4
POP-ROCK IN THE 1960s & 1970s

With the arrival of The Beatles, the era of girl groups and teen idols quickly faded. Almost overnight, The Beatles changed the landscape of American popular music. Suddenly, every rock band in America wanted to look and sound like the Fab Four, and Ohio bands like The Outsiders and The McCoys were no different.

THE BEATLES IN OHIO

The original "boy band," The Beatles performed in Ohio fours times in the mid-1960s, twice each in Cleveland and Cincinnati. Unfortunately, three of their four Ohio appearances were marred by problems.

During their first U.S. tour in 1964, The Beatles stopped in Cincinnati on August 27. Opening up for the visiting Liverpool natives were The Exciters, Bill Black's Combo, Jackie DeShannon and The Righteous Brothers. Staged at the Cincinnati Gardens, the group's debut Ohio appearance was before 13,326 fans, who paid between $2.75 and $5.50. Brought to town by WSAI deejay Dusty Rhodes, the concert was emceed by several of the station's deejays. With the venue lacking air conditioning, the summer weather made the room unbearably hot and muggy.

But it was a dispute with a local union, not the heat, which nearly torpedoed the concert. The Musicians Union demanded that local groups be added to the bill, or otherwise, the concert would be canceled. After hundreds of angry phone calls, the union relented and retracted its demands.

After giving a press conference, The Beatles took the stage at 9:35 PM. Concertgoer Dale Stevens recalled in *The Cincinnati Post*: "Once the crowd realized The Beatles were on the verge of coming through the curtain, it was bedlam to a remarkable, unbelievable degree.... You couldn't really hear The Beatles, of course. But that didn't stop John, Paul, George and Ringo. It might have looked as though they were pantomiming pandemonium but the grins were there, the massive heads of Beatle hair jiggled and bounced, and the more the girls yelled, the harder Ringo whapped his drums." After the concert was over, a stream of fans lined up to touch the stage where just minutes earlier, The Beatles had spun their rock and roll magic.

Although the Cincinnati concert went smoothly, the group's stop in Cleveland was a far different matter. A crowd of mostly teenage girls jammed the Public Auditorium on September 15, 1964. Brought to Cleveland by WHK-AM, the radio station guaranteed an upfront fee of $50,000 to the group's manager Brian Epstein, with tickets priced at $4.00 and $6.50. (Later, the appreciative Beatles included the station's logo, "WHK Good Guys," on the cover of their landmark album, *Sgt. Pepper's Lonely Hearts Club Band*.)

On the day of the concert, 500 police officers provided security, which cost the city more than $14,000. Arriving in Cleveland, The Fab Four were escorted by a 21-car police motorcade enroute to the downtown Sheraton, where a frenzied crowd of 5,000 fans had amassed. Opening up for the group was the same lineup as in Cincinnati, with the exception of Clarence "Frogman" Henry who had replaced The Righteous Brothers. When The Beatles hit the stage, hundreds of hysterical female fans swarmed toward the stage, with numerous concertgoers fainting or receiving minor injuries. At one point, the concert was stopped for more than 20 minutes by Cleveland police officer Carl Bare, who admonished the audience to calm down and return to their seats. During the unscheduled break, the WHK deejays were nowhere to be found, and instead, deejays from a competing radio station, KYW, saw an opportunity to commandeer the stage microphone and promote their own station! Eventually, The Beatles returned to the stage and finished their performance.

Following the completion of their concert at around 10 PM, The Beatles rushed to their limo and headed for the airport, enroute to their next show in New Orleans. The following day, *Cleveland Plain Dealer* music critic Robert Finn remarked that The Beatles "sang and played with all the subtlety of an artillery bombardment" and sounded much like "a battery of air raid sirens, cherry bombs and starving orangutans."

In the wake of the mayhem surrounding The Beatles concert and a similar frenzy at a subsequent show by The Dave Clark Five, Cleveland mayor Ralph Locher imposed a so-called "Beatle Ban," prohibiting all rock concerts in the city for the next 18 months. As a result, The Beatles skipped the city during their 1965 North American tour. But in 1966, the ban was rescinded and The Beatles returned. (Ironically, Locher would later campaign for Cleveland's selection as the host city of the Rock and Roll Hall of Fame.)

The Beatles' second performance in Cleveland took place on August 14, 1966. The group was originally scheduled to play Louisville, Kentucky, on that day, but the promoter was unable to book a suitable concert venue. The group was brought to Cleveland by a new radio station on the dial, WIXY-1260. But on the heels of John Lennon's off-the-cuff comment that the group was "more popular than Jesus," ticket sales suffered for the entire tour. Just three days before the Cleveland performance, Lennon offered up an apology. Nonetheless, the damage had been done, and instead of selling out the 80,000-seat Cleveland Municipal Stadium, just 24,600 tickets were sold.

With the show booked during the middle of baseball season, a small stage was constructed behind second base, a few hundred feet from the closest concertgoers. Behind the stage was a specially built trailer, which was accommodated with bathrooms and four beds. (After the show, The Beatles tried to purchase the trailer.)

At first, the concert proceeded without incident. Then as the group launched into the opening riff of the concert's fourth song, "Day Tripper," chaos erupted as nearly 5,000 fans raced onto the field and toward the band.

Those who reached the stage first were nearly crushed by the advancing mob. In an effort to protect the Fab Four, members of the overwhelmed police force began clubbing and throwing the surging teenagers from the small stage. Sensing the potential danger, Lennon signaled for his bandmates to retreat to their trailer. While Lennon and McCartney were amused by the commotion, Starr was shaken up after he had to be rescued by the WIXY deejays. After a 33-minute delay, the field was cleared. The Beatles had averted a disaster and would return to finish the concert.

Then with McCartney announcing that "Long Tall Sally" would be the "second to last song" of the night, out-of-control fans returned to the field. After ending the song prematurely, The Beatles ran to a waiting limo, slowly rode through a sea of fans, escaping unscathed from the stadium.

The Cincinnati stop of the tour was scheduled to take place a week later at Crosley Field. But the August 20th show was postponed by one day due to heavy downpours, which began shortly before the concert was to start. Despite pleas by the local promoter, Brian Epstein refused to allow the group to risk electrical shock by playing in the rain. The stage was not protected by a canopy and the equipment was soaking wet. While the Saturday night concert was scheduled to start at 8 PM, the postponement was not announced until 10:15. While some attendees were unable to return the following day, others claimed they had lost their tickets and were permitted inside the stadium for the noontime show.

Clandestinely driven to Crosley Field in a brown UPS van, The Beatles played the early-afternoon gig before just 23,000 fans. The Fab Four plowed through their poorest performance of the tour, with the sound marred by the rain-damaged equipment. In the following day's local paper, the reviewer complained that for their $60,000 fee, The Beatles should have played for more than 45-minutes.

Packing up and rushing to the newly built Busch Stadium in St. Louis for a scheduled concert later that same day, The Beatles were again met with strong rains and were forced to play in soggy weather under a canopy. The group would play its final paid concert at San Francisco's Candlestick Park, two weeks later on August 29, 1966.

With the British Invasion reshaping the musical landscape on both sides of the Atlantic, many American pop and rock artists were brushed aside. But that was not always the case.

With his recording career thriving well into the rock era, Buckeye-native Dean Martin was nicknamed "The Beatle Buster" when in 1964, he knocked the Fab Four out of *Billboard* magazine's number-one spot with "Everybody Loves Somebody." Not especially fond of rock and roll music, Martin rolled his eyes when he shared the bill with The Rolling Stones on the television show, *The Hollywood Palace*. Scoring nearly a dozen pop-hits in the 1960s, Martin would also enjoy great success with his variety program, *The Dean Martin Show*. Even during the Summer of Love in 1967, Martin's television program ranked in the top-10.

THE CLEVELAND SCENE

Much like the rest of the nation, rock bands around Cleveland were captivated by the British Invasion. One of these groups, The Outsiders, would record on the same label as The Beatles.

The origins of The Outsiders can be traced to an instrumental group patterned after The Ventures called Tom King And The Starfires. Formed in 1965, the group scored a local hit with the single, "Stronger Than Dirt," which was issued on Tom King's uncle's label, Puma Records. Wanting to add a vocalist to the group, saxophonist Mike Geraci recommended his younger brother, Sonny.

With Sonny Geraci on lead vocals, the group was co-managed by Capitol Records promotional representative, Roger Karshner. Renamed The Outsiders, the group recorded the Tom King co-composition, "Time Won't Let Me." But despite the fact that the single had been released as by The Outsiders, the group continued to perform around Cleveland as The Starfires. In order to get airplay on the local top-40 stations, Karshner promoted The Outsiders as a West Coast act. Breaking in two new members during this period, The Outsiders were unable to launch a national tour in support of the soaring single.

Geraci proudly recalled in a *Scene* interview, "One of the biggest thrills in my entire life was the day the first box of records came. I opened the box, and it was on the same label as The Beatles and The Beach Boys. My record looked just like theirs." The Outsiders followed up with another rocker, a cover of The Isley Brothers' track, "She's So Respectable." (Another of Roger Karshner's local acts, Cleveland-based Dick Whittington's Cats, scored a regional hit with the R&B chestnut "In The Midnight Hour," which was produced by future jazz star, Chuck Mangione.)

By November 1968, Sonny Geraci relocated to Los Angeles, and by early 1970, had formed a new version of The Outsiders. Initially joined by former Outsiders bassist Rick "Mugsy" D'Amata, Geraci later added another former bandmate, guitarist Walter Nims. Assisted by producer Ron Kramer, the group recorded four songs for Metromedia Records, including "Precious And Few." But when Kramer was fired from the label, the tracks went unissued. Landing at a division of Bell Records, Carousel, the group recorded a new version of the song. Geraci told *Scene* magazine: "We had been playing 'Precious And Few' for a year-and-a-half. We still did it in clubs, and it always got incredible reaction. But I was at the point where I was sick of it. Our hair was down to here [pointing to his shoulders], and I wanted a *rock* hit record. We were rocking. We were a rock 'n' roll band."

Meanwhile, in Cleveland, Tom King was still performing with his own Outsiders group and successfully sued Sonny Geraci over the ownership of the band's name. As a result, Geraci's group became Climax. A belated hit, "Precious And Few" took nearly a year to climb into the top-10 in 1972. But with no accompanying album, the group toured solely on the popularity of the single. Then with Arista buying out Bell Records, the group lost its momentum. A followup release, "Rock And Roll Heaven" was a flop, but soon reached the top-10 via a cover version by The Righteous Brothers. Returning to Cleveland in 1974, Geraci formed a series of bands and later recorded under the name Peter Emmett.

THE CHOIR AND THE RASPBERRIES

In 1964, four high-school friends from the suburban Cleveland community of Mentor formed a British Invasion group, The Mods. The group members were inspired to assemble a band after listening to a neighbor's Beatles record, which she had brought back from England in late-1963, a few months before Beatlemania would hit the U.S.

After a series of personnel changes, the group included Jim Bonfanti, Dave Smalley, Dave Burke, Don Klawon and Wally Bryson. (Making the local news, Bryson was suspended from his high school for refusing to cut his long hair.) By 1966, The Mods evolved into The Choir and opened up for one of their musical heroes, The Who. Fronted by Bonfanti on lead vocals and featuring Bryson and Smalley on guitar, The Choir scored a regional hit with "It's Cold Outside."

In 1967, Bryson left The Choir to join a young, classically-trained singer-pianist named Eric Carmen in a local group that was founded by a pair of Canadian natives, Cyrus Erie. Named after a bulldozer, Cyrus Erie recorded one single for Epic Records. Though a popular local draw, the group collapsed in 1969 after enduring frequent personnel changes.

After The Choir disbanded in 1970, Bonfanti teamed with Carmen and Bryson, along with bassist John Aleksic, to form The Raspberries. Within just a few months, the group was playing for one-thousand people every Sunday night at the Agora nightclub. After the replacement of Aleksic by Dave Smalley, who had just returned from fighting in Vietnam, the group was signed by Capitol Records.

Released in 1972, the group's self-titled debut album featured a scratch-and-sniff, raspberry-scented sticker. Wanting to distinguish themselves from other rock acts of the day, members of The Raspberries decided to adopt a cleancut image and wear matching suits – a throwback to the early Beatles era.

With most of the group's material written by the team of Carmen and Smalley, The Raspberries scored their debut top-40 hit with the million-selling "Go All The Way." Motivated by the censoring of The Rolling Stones' hit "Let's Spend The Night Together" on *The Ed Sullivan Show*, Eric Carmen sought to push the limits of pop airplay by employing vague, double-entre lyrics. Carmen recalled in *Blender* magazine: "I wanted it to have an intro that sounded like The Who, but when it hits the chorus, it should sound like The Beach Boys, so the line 'Go all the way' would be sung in these angelic voices, which I hoped might help disguise the openly erotic lyric."

But the song sounded incomplete and was nearly kept off their album until the producer added some special effects using a then state-of-the-art sound limiter. Released later in 1972, the group's second album, *Fresh*, spawned the hits "I Wanna Be With You" and "Let's Pretend."

In 1973, the group released the album, *Side 3*, which was highlighted by the hit, "Tonight." In the group's autobiography, Carmen recalled: "'Tonight' was my favorite Raspberries rock track. There was a little magic happening in the studio on that one. We were smokin' that day. There were flames coming out of the tape. It was the one track where we sounded on the record exactly like we sounded live." On a roll, the group performed at Carnegie Hall and appeared on several national television programs.

But with tensions intensifying within the group, Carmen fired Smalley. Unhappy with the move, Bonfanti quit in protest. (Smalley and Bonfanti would then form a group called Dynamite.) Later in 1974, Carmen and Bryson hired two replacements and recorded a fourth Raspberries album, *Starting Over*, which yielded the hit single, "Overnight Sensation." But due to flaring tempers – and a fistfight between Carmen and Bryson – the group disbanded in 1975.

Personally signed to a solo contract by Arista Records chief Clive Davis, Carmen initially took a pop turn. Backed in the studio by a local band called Magic, Carmen wrote all the songs on his debut solo album, *Eric Carmen*. The project spawned a trio of top-40 singles, "Never Gonna Fall In Love Again," "Sunrise," and an enduring ballad about unrequited love, "All By Myself." The song incorporated a portion of Russian composer Sergei Rachmaninoff's "Piano Concerto No. 2," and as a result, his estate earns a portion of the song's royalties. Regarding the success of "All By Myself," Carmen recalled in *Blender* magazine: "Eighteen-year-old boys despised us, but their 16-year-old sisters, and some rock critics, got it." The song has been recorded by dozens of artists including Frank Sinatra, Tom Jones, Sheryl Crow, Babes In Toyland, and Hank Williams Jr., and would return to the top-10 in 1997 thanks to Celine Dion.

Carmen continued his solo hit run with the Gus Dudgeon-produced tracks "She Did It" and "Change Of Heart." But unable to maintain his momentum, Carmen was dropped by Arista in 1980.

After taking a respite from the music industry, Carmen returned to the top-10 in 1984 as a songwriter, co-penning the Mike Reno/Ann Wilson ballad from the *Footloose* soundtrack, "Almost Paradise." Also returning to the studio, Carmen scraped the top-40 in 1985 with "I Wanna Hear It From Your Lips." Then in 1987, Carmen scored a top-10 hit with "Hungry Eyes," which was featured in the blockbuster film, *Dirty Dancing*. Enjoying newfound popularity, Carmen returned to the top-10 the following year with "Make Me Lose Control." That same year, he composed and performed NBC's Olympic theme. (Meanwhile, Raspberries guitarist Wally Bryson had teamed with former members of The Rascals to form Fotomaker.)

Reconciling with his former bandmates, Carmen reformed The Raspberries in 2004, to perform at the grand opening of the Cleveland House of Blues. Encouraged by the reaction of their longtime fans, The Raspberries would continue to perform on occasion.

SURF MUSIC: THE RIP CHORDS

With the sport of surfing uncommon on the usually tame waters of Lake Erie, surf music groups were equally rare in the Buckeye State during the 1960s. While future Beach Boys member Al Jardine had been raised in Lima, Ohio, he moved to Hawthorne, California, during his high school years.

One of the few surf acts with Ohio connections was The Rip Chords, a group which, at times, featured a Buckeye-native as the lead vocalist. While actress Doris Day was pursuing a career in Hollywood, her son Terry Melcher was raised by his grandmother in Cincinnati. After initially pursuing a solo career under the name of Terry Day, he then teamed with another future Beach Boys member, Bruce Johnston, to form the duo, Terry & Bruce.

Hired by Columbia Records as a producer, Melcher oversaw The Rip Chords. Co-writing a song called "Hey Little Cobra," Melcher decided to sing the lead vocal himself, and issue the single as by The Rip Chords; featuring the backing harmony of Bruce Johnston, the song reached the top-10 in 1963. Melcher and The Rip Chords followed up with a song co-written by Jan Berry (of Jan & Dean), "Three Window Coupe." Surprisingly, Melcher would turn down the Brian Wilson composition "Help Me, Rhonda." Neither Melcher nor Johnston would tour with The Rip Chords.

Also a successful singer-songwriter and producer, Melcher collaborated with The Byrds, helping to shape the group's innovative folk-rock sound on their first two albums. Melcher later worked with Paul Revere & The Raiders and Steppenwolf. After pursuing a solo career in the 1970s, Melcher was hired as the producer for his mother's popular television series, *The Doris Day Show* and *Doris Day's Best Friends*. A lifelong associate of The Beach Boys, Melcher would co-write their 1988 comeback hit, "Kokomo."

ONE-HIT WONDERS

In the field of popular music, numerous one-hit wonders have graced the charts. And a few, like the Ohio-based rock group, The Lemon Pipers, would manage to reach the number-one position but fail to return to the top-40.

THE HUMAN BEINZ

A popular Youngstown-area bar band, The Human Beinz were assembled in 1963 by members of various other local bands. A cover band that favored British Invasion music, the group nearly found success with an early version of the Van Morrison chestnut "Gloria," as by The Premiers. But a six-month delay between the recording session and the pressing of the 45-rpm record sabotaged the effort.

Featuring Richard "Dick" Belly on lead vocals and guitar, the group toured across the Midwest in the mid-1960s. Recording for a tiny label, Elysian Records, the group released several tracks as The Human Beingz (with a "g") and enjoyed regional airplay with a cover of The Yardbirds' "Evil Hearted You."

Soon, the group attracted the attention of a Capitol Records representative who was browsing the bins at a record store in the suburban Youngstown town of Boardman. Taken to a recording studio in Cleveland, the group unleashed an upbeat version of an obscure Isley Brothers track called "Nobody But Me." The single initially broke on black radio stations, which assumed the group was African-American. Reaching the top-10 in 1968, the song became a garage-rock classic.

While remaining a one-hit wonder in the U.S., The Human Beinz would score a followup hit in Japan with a cover of Bobby Bland's blues classic, "Turn On Your Love Light." Though deciding to dissolve after the release of a second album in 1968, the band regrouped the following year to tour Japan.

JOE JEFFREY GROUP

An ultimate one-hit wonder, Joe Jeffrey had one hit and then disappeared. Playing the clubs of his native Cleveland in the mid-1960s, the former Joe Stafford changed his name to Joe Jeffrey in order to avoid confusion with the 1950s pop singer, Jo Stafford.

Signing with Wand Records, Jeffrey scored a pop-soul hit in 1969 with "My Pledge Of Love." Followup releases floundered, including "My Baby Loves Lovin'," which was eclipsed on the charts by a competing version recorded by the British group, White Plains. By the mid-1970s, Jeffrey would leave music altogether.

THE CASINOS

Originally formed in 1958 as a doo-wop act called The Capris (not the famous group known for "There's A Moon Out Tonight"), The Casinos took nearly a decade before scoring their only top-40 hit. Popular around greater Cincinnati, the group also performed regularly on a local television program, *Five-A-Go-Go*.

Fronted by vocalist J.T. Sears, the group was befriended in 1961 by rockabilly singer Carl Dobkins Jr. Recording for Dobkins' label Name Records, the group scored several local hits beginning with "Do You Recall." Switching to another local label, Fraternity Records, the group churned out a series of singles, which were licensed to various record companies. But following the death of J.T. Sears in 1963, the group's manager/producer, Gene Hughes, took over the lead vocal duties.

After recording a cover version of King Curtis' "Soul Serenade" at the King Records studio, The Casinos took advantage of the remaining time to tackle another song, "Then You Can Tell Me Goodbye." The group had heard the John D. Loudermilk-composed ballad on a Memphis radio station, which had played an obscure rendition of the song by Johnny Nash.

A throwback to the doo-wop era, the song became a surprise, top-10 hit. Subsequently, The Casinos launched a series of high-profile tours and joined Dick Clark's Caravan of Stars. But except for a followup single that grazed the charts – a cover of Don Everly's "It's All Over Now" – The Casinos were unable to repeat their success. With an exhausted Hughes quitting in 1968, the group disbanded. Reforming two years later, The Casinos would continue to tour with various lineups into the 21st century. "Then You Can Tell Me Goodbye" returned to the charts thanks to country renditions by Eddie Arnold and Neal McCoy.

BUBBLEGUM ACTS

In general terms, "bubblegum music" is a pejorative label that refers to pop music aimed at pre-adolescents. More specifically, the phrase was coined in the late-1960s to describe the music of producers, Jerry Kasenetz and Jeff Katz, who in response to the growing seriousness of rock music, turned toward, simple, cheerful pop aimed at younger record buyers.

Hired by Buddah Records, the team of Kasenetz and Katz – also known as the Super K production company – worked with artists such as Ohio Express, 1910 Fruitgum Co., The Lemon Pipers and The Music Explosion. For some unexplained reason, a disproportionate number of these early bubblegum acts hailed from Ohio. Another Ohio-born act who relocated to Michigan, Tommy James began his hit streak with a slice of bubblegum pop, "Hanky Panky."

THE MUSIC EXPLOSION

Formed in 1964 as The Chosen Few in the city of Mansfield, the group was fronted by singer Bob Hallenbeck. But when Hallenbeck was recalled by the Navy in August 1966, he was replaced by Jamie Lyons. After auditioning for Katz and Kasenetz in New York City, the Ohio group was rushed to a recording studio just two days later.

Renamed The Music Explosion, the group bombed with its cover version of The Nightcrawlers' garage-rock standard, "Little Black Egg." As a followup, the group recorded "Little Bit O' Soul," a booming, percussion-heavy rendition of an obscure track by a British act, The Little Darlings. A million-selling smash, the single nearly topped the charts in 1967. A followup release, the pop-flavored "Sunshine Games" just missed hitting the top-40.

By early-1969, only one original member of The Music Explosion remained – drummer Bob Avery. Later that year, the group went on the road as the touring version of another Kasenetz and Katz studio-only act, Crazy Elephant, to promote the hit single, "Gimme Gimme Good Lovin'."

After The Music Explosion disbanded, Lyons issued some solo material and then joined the Columbus-based rock band, Mixed Water; the group would include guitarist-singer Eric Moore, who would later front the heavy-metal band, The Godz. In 1973, Mixed Water evolved into The Capital City Rockets and recorded an album for Elektra Records.

OHIO EXPRESS

After their success with Mansfield's Music Explosion, Kasenetz and Katz returned to that city to mine more talent. On the advice of The Music Explosion, the producers signed a young garage-rock band called Sir Timothy And The Royals. The group had won a number of regional battle-of-the-band competitions and had opened for several national acts in Columbus.

Shortly after signing with Kasenetz and Katz, the group was renamed Ohio Express and told that their first hit was already recorded. The group members were surprised to find that the single, "Beg, Borrow And Steal" (which was actually recorded by The Rare Breed), was re-issued in 1967 as by Ohio Express. The single did in fact become a hit and reached the top-30.

Then when songwriter Joey Levine sang a demo-record of a track he had co-written called "Yummy Yummy Yummy," Buddah Records chief Neil Bogart issued the demo as an Ohio Express single. A member of the group, Dean Katran, told *Citybeat,* "I remember we heard 'Yummy Yummy Yummy' over the phone and we said, 'Great, when are we going to record it?' They said, 'It's all done. It's going to come out next week.' They more or less promised us that we would get to do everything else after that." With the song hitting the top-10 in 1968, the members of Ohio Express took turns to see who could best mimic Levine's nasally vocal style. But while the Mansfield group would be permitted to record some of their album tracks, their songs were never issued as singles.

Over the next couple years, Kasenetz and Katz would replicate the same formula, with the touring group forced to learn Ohio Express songs by listening to the records. With Buddah continuing to employ Levine as the group's studio vocalist, Ohio Express' hit run continued with "Down At Lulu's" and "Mercy."

The touring version of the group would implode during the summer of 1968, when they heard *their* new hit single "Chewy Chewy" on the radio, enroute to a performance in Cincinnati. Angered that the label had failed to inform them about the release, and having to deal with disappointed concertgoers who kept requesting the song, two members of the band quit in protest.

Later, Kasenetz and Katz assembled a rock vaudeville act called Kasenetz-Katz Singing Orchestra Circus, which consisted of members from several bubblegum acts, including The Music Explosion and Ohio Express. The group scored a hit with "Quick Joey Small."

Joey Levine would also break his association with Kasenetz and Katz. Leaving for the West Coast, Levine worked as a commercial jingle singer; he would also join one-hit wonder Reunion and land on the charts in 1974 with "Life Is A Rock (But The Radio Rolled Me)."

THE LEMON PIPERS

Formed in Oxford, Ohio, The Lemon Pipers began as a college-town, garage-rock outfit. The group's lead vocalist, Ivan Browne, had previously led a popular regional band, Ivan & The Sabers, which he formed while attending the University of Cincinnati. By 1966, Browne replaced "Tony" in the Ohio University group, Tony And The Bandits. By year's end, the group shed itself of the "Tony" reference and emerged as The Lemon Pipers.

After releasing a local single, The Lemon Pipers were signed by Kasenetz and Katz to Buddah Records. Their debut Buddah release, "Turn Around And Take A Look," managed only spotty airplay.

Assigned to the songwriting/production team of Paul Leka and Shelly Pinz, the group reluctantly recorded "Green Tambourine." Initially rejecting the psychedelic, pop ditty, The Lemon Pipers relented when the label threatened to drop them. Taken to a studio in Cleveland, the group recorded the track along with several, similar, pop tunes. A surprise, number-one smash, "Green Tambourine" combined folk-rock and psychedelia within a light, bubblegum framework. A pair of similarly-styled, followup releases – "Rice Is Nice" and "Jelly Jungle" – just barely missed reaching the top-40. After recording two albums, the group was dropped by Buddah in 1969.

The group's lead guitarist, Bill Bartlett, returned to the pop charts in 1977 as a member of Ram Jam, and scored a hit with a hard-rock version of Leadbelly's folk standard, "Black Betty."

JOHNNY CYMBAL / DEREK

Though born in Scotland and raised in Canada, Johnny Cymbal was an adopted Ohioan who came to Cleveland at age 17. In 1963, he scored a novelty-styled doo-wop single with "Mr. Bass Man," which featured the backing, bass vocals of Ron Bright. A pair of followup singles – "Teenage Heaven" and "Dum Dum Dee Dum" – reached the lower portions of the charts.

Switching gears, Johnny Cymbal emerged as "Derek" (which was his younger brother's name) and scored a bubblegum hit in 1968 with "Cinnamon." Aside from the pseudonym Derek, Cymbal recorded under a host of names including Brother John, Dallas, The Non-Conformists and The Eye-Full Tower.

Also a prolific songwriter, Cymbal is best known for co-writing "Mary In The Morning," which was recorded by both Al Martino and Elvis Presley. By 1969, Cymbal would team with songwriter (and future wife) Peggy Clinger at Chelsea Records / The Wes Farrell Organization. One of their compositions, "Rock Me Baby," was a hit for David Cassidy.

Returning to Cleveland following the death of Clinger, Cymbal reunited with his former songwriting partner Mike Rashkow. Later settling in Nashville, Cymbal became a full-time songwriter. His compositions during this period were recorded by a variety of country artists including Aaron Tippen, David Frizzell and The Flying Burrito Brothers.

Bo Donaldson And The Heywoods

Formed in Cincinnati during the mid-1960s, pop group Bo Donaldson And The Heywoods originally found fame as guests on the Dick Clark television show, *Action '73*. The group's association with Clark began several years earlier after the mother of keyboardist Bo Donaldson, Bea Donaldson, began working at Clark's Cincinnati office. With his mother setting up an audition, Bo Donaldson and his group The Heywoods joined a series of Dick Clark's "Caravan of Stars" tours as an opening act.

The group's biggest hit came about by fortune and good timing. Though written by two British songwriters about the Civil War, "Billy, Don't Be A Hero" was taken as an anti-war song during the waning days of the Vietnam conflict. Forming a label in the U.K. to promote their own compositions, Mitch Murray and Peter Callander had signed the band, Paper Lace, to record the track. Issued in early 1974, the single topped the British charts.

But while Murray and Callander endeavored to find a label to issue the single in the U.S., ABC Records producer Steve Barri was determined to rush-release a cover version. Bo Donaldson And The Heywoods' rendition was issued just days after it was recorded and would quickly top the U.S. charts; the original version by Paper Lace was barely noticed by American record buyers. But while The Heywoods would return to the top-40 twice more in 1974 with "Who Do You Think You Are" and "The Heartbreak Kid," Paper Lace would score a major U.S. hit with "The Night Chicago Died."

Parting with ABC Records in 1975, Bo Donaldson And The Heywoods would record for a series of labels before disbanding by decade's end. Bo Donaldson launched a new version of The Heywoods in the mid-1990s.

CHAPTER 5
THE RISE OF ALBUM ROCK

With the arrival of the groundbreaking *Sgt. Pepper's Lonely Hearts Club Band*, The Beatles made history by not releasing any singles from the hit album. By the late-1960s, the music industry was experiencing a format shift, as the LP began to challenge the dominance of the 45-rpm single. And while the 12-inch LP was still king, the cassette and 8-track were both in their infancies.

Originally called "free-form" or "underground" radio, the genre was the antithesis of commercial AM radio. Songs were no longer limited to three or four minutes, album tracks were preferable to chart hits, and more significantly, deejays selected their own music. Additionally, the format condoned counter-cultural messages, political tirades and various public service announcements. Live broadcasts of concerts were also common.

While deejay Bob Fass at WBAI-FM in New York City is acknowledged as "The Father of Freeform Radio," other stations soon followed suit including WOR-FM in New York and WMMR-FM in Philadelphia. On the West Coast, a portly deejay named Tom "Big Daddy" Donahue brought the format to a commercial station, KMPX-FM, in April 1967. Later that same year, he took the format to KPPC-FM in Pasadena/Los Angeles. Though few American consumers owned FM radios in the late-1960s, the free-form format – later known as Album-Oriented Rock (AOR) – quickly spread across the country.

CLEVELAND ROCKS: WMMS IN CLEVELAND

Long before a character in the film *This Is Spinal Tap* blurted out "hello Cleveland," the city was a hotbed for all things rock and roll. Cleveland born-and-raised screenwriter Joe Eszterhas recalled in his autobiography that the place where he "had grown up in was a shot-and-a-beer town where the locals wore T-shirts that said, 'CLEVELAND – YOU GOTTA BE TOUGH!' It was, as Huey Lewis sang, 'The Heart of Rock and Roll' and boasted some of the best early rock and roll disc jockeys in the world: Alan Freed and Bill Randle and Pete (Mad Daddy) Myers. Cleveland was the home of such great smash-mouth rock and roll artists as Bocky Boo and the Visions, the James Gang, [Joe] Walsh, Sonny Geraci, Eric Carmen, Pere Ubu and Michael Stanley. It was the home of WMMS, which *Rolling Stone* magazine for many years called 'the best rock and roll station in America.'"

Cleveland-born singer-songwriter Marc Cohn recalled in *Scene*, "Basically, when I was 11 or 12, and my parents were asleep, I would listen to WMMS, especially early morning 'MMS on the weekend, which was usually pretty progressive radio. That was the first place I ever heard Van

Morrison, Jackson Browne, Bruce Springsteen. They wouldn't play the hits; they would play a whole side of an album. I, as a little kid, would call up a DJ and they'd tell me what records to buy."

Long before the arrival of WMMS, underground rock radio in Cleveland began in late-1966 when Martin Perlich hosted *The Perlich Project* on a classical music station, WCLV-FM. In 1969, David Spero – who worked behind the scenes on the locally produced, syndicated *Upbeat!* program – bought two hours of airtime on Friday nights at WXEN. There he would play records and interview the artists who were appearing on *Upbeat!*

Meanwhile, after the FCC mandated in 1968 that AM stations could no longer simulcast the same programming on their FM sister stations, WHK-FM adopted a free-form rock format and changed its call letters to WMMS. But due to low ratings, the station switched to a more mainstream format the following year.

Sensing an opportunity, WNCR-FM installed an AOR format in 1970. That same year, shock jock Don Imus arrived at WNCR's AM sister station, WGAR. At the time, WGAR became the first major-market outlet in the nation to play oldies music. As the morning-drive deejay, Imus was responsible for the station's dramatic jump in the ratings. Then with Imus' help, David Spero was hired as a deejay on WNCR. But after battling station management, a number of WNCR's employees – including Spero, Billy Bass and Martin Perlich – jumped to WMMS, which by 1970, had reverted to its original free-form rock format. With listeners also making the switch to WMMS, WNRC would shift to top-40 in 1973.

Purchased by Malrite Communications in 1972, WMMS came to dominate rock radio for the next two decades. Adopting a cartoon buzzard as its mascot, the station took the nickname, "Home of the Buzzard." Under the direction of program director John Gorman and station manager Billy Bass, WMMS settled into its classic on-air lineup of Jeff & Flash, Matt the Cat, Denny Sanders, Len "Boom Boom" Goldberg, Betty Korvan, the BLF Bash, and the potent afternoon jock, Kid Leo. A former engineering student, Kid Leo (born Lawrence Travagliante) broke acts such as Lou Reed, Mott The Hoople, Meat Loaf, Boston, Cheap Trick and Southside Johnny, and championed rockers such as David Bowie and Bruce Springsteen. At a February 1975 concert in Cleveland, Springsteen was shocked when the energized audience knew all the words to an unreleased track that Kid Leo had been promoting for months, "Born To Run." One of the station's most popular features was the live, midday "Coffee Break Concert" by artists such as Warren Zevon, John Mellencamp and Peter Frampton.

As the highest-rated station in Cleveland for more than a decade, WMMS spread its influence far beyond the borders of Ohio. But one aspect of the station's popularity was manufactured: WMMS won *Rolling Stone* magazine's "Best Radio Station" award, year after year, in part because the station management had organized an effort to manipulate the polling. A *Cleveland Plain Dealer* music critic exposed the sham in which the station would purchase several-hundred copies of the magazine and encourage its staff to send in the completed ballots. (Reliving some of its past glory in 2005, WMMS was voted Major Market Rock Station of the Year by the music industry magazine, *Radio & Records*.)

The emergence of album-rock stations like WMMS coincided with the rise of the Cleveland-based concert chain, The Agora. The original Agora opened near the campus of Case Western Reserve University in 1966 as a members-only club. The club's founder Henry LoConti Sr. was a former jukebox technician who noticed that the machines earned far more money at locations frequented by youth. In need of more space, the Agora relocated the following year to East 24th Street. Initially booking only local acts, the Agora scheduled its first national act in 1968, The Buckinghams.

By 1978, the Agora began syndicating the program, *Onstage At The Agora*. The club was also the site of the opening sequence of the 1980 Paul Simon film, *One-Trick Pony*. In 1981, the Agora was named as the nation's top rock club in Dave Marsh's *The Book Of Rock Lists*.

Perfecting his performance skills while leading the house band at the Cleveland Agora, Eric Carmen recalled in *The Cleveland Plain Dealer* how working at the venue was "probably the most fun I've ever had. Within two or three months, we were pulling 1,000 people a night into the place. It was very important in terms of honing what we did. We would be up there playing for hours. I relate it to what The Beatles did in Hamburg in the early '60s. You had to have a ton of material. It was a great testing ground."

But when the Cleveland Agora was destroyed by fire in 1984, the owners relocated to the former WHK Ballroom, which was built in 1913 as an opera house. Expanded into a national franchise, 13 Agora Concert Clubs were operating at the start of the 1980s, including Ohio locations in Columbus, Akron, Painesville, Toledo and Youngstown. But with the music industry struggling to survive during the rise of the video game era, the Agora empire imploded and LoConti lost $3 million. Although the Cleveland Agora continued to thrive, conglomerates such as the Clear Channel-spinoff Live Nation later dominated the concert industry.

Many visiting performers stayed at an infamous, downtown Cleveland hotel called Swingos. A traveling member of Kiss' large entourage recalled: "Swingos was one of the more intriguing curiosities of life on the rock 'n' roll circuit in the late '70s, a big city hotel that catered to rock bands. A squat, motel-style building in downtown Cleveland that was a stone's throw from the seediest part of the city, Swingos offered traveling bands all the amenities they craved – twenty-four-hour room service and a bar the size of a basketball court. Each of the rooms was done up in a special decor, from purple carpets, velvet chairs, oversized chandeliers, and upholstered walls in a palette of hues, which looked to me like Contemporary American Pimp, to Space Age Modernism, where all the rooms had white shag carpets, stark white walls, white modular couches, and chrome-framed beds." Elvis Presley was so intrigued by the facility that during one tour, he rented out 100 rooms on three floors, which became his Midwestern base of operation. A decade after the hotel closed, director Cameron Crowe paid homage to Swingos in the film, *Almost Famous*.

Like much of the industrial Midwest, Cleveland fell into severe decline during the late-1970s. Between gas shortages, court-ordered school bussing, union strikes and the decline of the auto and steel industries, the once proud city along Lake Erie became the butt of jokes.

Angered by a television comedian's attack on Cleveland, British-born rocker Ian Hunter penned "Cleveland Rocks" as a valentine to the city. A former member of Mott The Hoople, Hunter was fond of Cleveland because of the city's early support of his solo career. Hunter told *Relix* magazine, "In the '70s... on talk shows like *The Tonight Show* or *Mike Douglas*, people made Cleveland the joke town of the States, and we had the opposite experience. We'd been playing half-empty clubs and we would get to Cleveland and The Agora [nightclub] would be mobbed, thanks to deejays like Kid Leo at WMMS."

Aside from WMMS, a few other Ohio radio stations began experimenting with the album-rock format in the late-1960s. At the opposite corner of the state, Frank "Bo" Wood was also drawn to the emerging revolution in rock radio. Based in Cincinnati, Wood was a Harvard-educated, former concert promoter who had brought acts such as Janis Joplin, Arlo Guthrie and Sly And The Family Stone to the city's century-old Music Hall. At a time when few people owned FM receivers, Wood's father bought WEBN-FM in 1967 for a mere $5,000. Although the station was purchased by the elder Wood with the intention of airing jazz and classical music, his son had other ideas. Shortly after WEBN began broadcasting on August 30, 1967, the younger Wood began experimenting with an album-rock format during a Saturday night slot, which he dubbed "Jelly Pudding." Over the next two-years, the formats were reversed until WEBN became a full-time AOR station, and a classical program hosted by the elder Wood was relegated to a Sunday morning slot. In the process, WEBN went on to become the longest-running AOR station in the nation.

Four Dead In Ohio

At the core of the campus-based, counter-culture movement of the late-1960s was the opposition to the Vietnam War. With protest music challenging authority, America's youth felt emboldened. One such protest song – "Ohio" by Crosby, Stills, Nash & Young – was provoked by the shootings at Kent State University. Situated just several miles east of Akron in the city of Kent, the institution was founded in 1910, originally as a teacher's school.

With the U.S. military opening a new front in Cambodia, students launched massive protests on the campuses of nearly 440 U.S. universities in late-April and early-May of 1970. A number of the protests turned violent. At the University of Wisconsin, 83 students were arrested following a series of 20 fire bombings. But the protests at one Ohio institution had far deadlier consequences.

Wanting to make a political statement, busses carrying East Coast student radicals had decided to make their stand at Kent State. Hundreds of local protesters – most of them students – joined the fray.

The problems started on Friday night when reveling protesters decided to take over a main, downtown street. As *Time* magazine reported, "One irate motorist gunned his car's engine as if to drive through the dancers. Some students climbed atop the car, jumped on it, then led a chant: 'One-two-three-four, we don't want your war!' A drunk on a balcony hurled a bottle into the street – and suddenly the mood turned ugly. Students smashed the car's windows, set fires in trash cans, began to bash storefronts. Police were called, Kent Mayor LeRoy Satrom had ordered a curfew, but few students were aware of it. Police stormed into bars after midnight, turning up the lights, shouting 'Get out!' Some 2,000 more students, many of whom had been watching the Knicks-Lakers basketball game on TV, were forced into the street. Police and sheriff's deputies pushed the youths back toward the campus, then fired tear gas to disperse them."

"Saturday began quietly. Black student leaders, who had been demanding the admission next year of 5,000 more blacks to Kent State [up from 1970 total of 600], and leaders of the mounting antiwar sentiment on campus talked of joining forces. They got administrative approval to hold a rally that evening on the ten-acre Commons at the center of the campus. There, despite the presence of faculty members and student marshals, militant war protesters managed to take complete charge of a crowd of about 800, many still smarting from the conflict of the night before. They disrupted a dance in one university hall, then attacked the one-story Army ROTC building facing the Commons. They smashed windows and threw lighted railroad flares inside. The building caught fire. When firemen arrived, students threw rocks at them and cut their hoses with machetes until police interceded with tear gas. Without bothering to consult Kent State authorities, Mayor Satrom asked for help from the National Guard. Governor James Rhodes, still engaged in his tough – and ultimately unsuccessful – campaign for the Senate nomination, quickly ordered Guardsmen transferred from points of tension in a Teamster strike elsewhere in Ohio.

"Within an hour, about 500 Guardsmen, already weary from three nights of duty, arrived with fully loaded M-1 semiautomatic rifles, pistols and tear gas. They were in time to help police block the students from charging into the downtown area. Students reacted by dousing trees with gasoline, then setting them afire. Order was restored before midnight. On Sunday, Governor Rhodes arrived in Kent. He made no attempt to seek the advice of Kent State President Robert I. White and told newsmen that campus troublemakers were 'worse than Brown Shirts and Communists and vigilantes – they're the worst type of people that we harbor in America.' He refused to close the campus, as Portage County Prosecutor Ronald Kane pleaded; instead, he declared a state of emergency and banned all demonstrations on the campus. Late that night, about 500 students defied the order and staged a sitdown on one of Kent's busiest intersections. Guardsmen, their number now grown to 900, moved into the face of a rock barrage to arrest 150 students.

"By Monday, it seemed that the campus atmosphere had settled. Shortly after noon, nearly 1,000 protestors had gathered to challenge and harass the young guardsmen. In addition to the active protestors, another 2,000 spectators kept their distance as they watched the unfolding tragedy.

"Then the outnumbered and partially encircled contingent of Guardsmen ran out of tear gas. Suddenly they seemed frightened. They began retreating up the hill toward Taylor Hall, most of them walking backward to keep their eyes on the threatening students below.... When the compact formation reached the top of the hill, some Guardsmen knelt quickly and aimed at the students who were hurling rocks from below. A handful of demonstrators kept moving toward the troops. Other Guardsmen stood behind the kneeling troops, pointing their rifles down the hill. A few aimed over the students' heads.... Within seconds, a sickening staccato of rifle fire signaled the transformation of a once-placid campus into the site of a historic American tragedy."

Kent State student, and future Devo co-founder, Gerald Casale recalled in *Goldmine* magazine "We had no idea there was live ammunition in those guns. We didn't know what the hell they were doing. They were at a one-row kneel and one row standing, like in the Civil War. This guy in a gas mask, he gave a signal and bang!, they shot live rounds into the crowd, like a duck shoot. Some of the kids – they had nothing to do with the protest at all, they just happened to be coming out of the journalism building to see what was going on. It changed absolutely everything."

In the end, the President's Commission on Campus Unrest spread the blame all around: "The actions of some students were violent and criminal and those of some others were dangerous, reckless and irresponsible. The indiscriminate firing of rifles into a crowd of students and the deaths that followed were unnecessary, unwarranted and inexcusable."

But the war in Southeast Asia continued to rage and the Kent campus eventually re-opened. British singer Elton John recalled in *The Observer*, "When I first went to America it was going on and I remember playing Kent State University about six weeks after the students were killed there... and it was a really strange feeling – really odd."

Two lasting memories emerged from the shootings – the image of a hysterical 14-year-old runaway named Mary Ann Vecchio leaning over the body of a dead student, and the passionate, angry, protest song, "Ohio," by Crosby, Stills, Nash & Young. After viewing photographs of the tragedy in *Life* magazine, Neil Young wrote the lyrics to "Ohio," while staying at David Crosby's home near San Francisco. Rushing to a Los Angeles studio, the foursome quickly recorded the song in just a few takes. The track was delivered to Atlantic Records within 24-hours and released as a single a week later. Though the song was widely banned by top-40 radio, it still received a great deal of airplay.

A few weeks after the shootings, Crosby, Stills Nash & Young arrived in nearby Cleveland for a concert sponsored by the city's AM powerhouse, WIXY-1260. The following day, the band was joined by deejays from a local FM station, WNCR, for a morning trip to the scene of the bloodshed. Distressed upon his arrival at Kent State, Young stared in disbelief at the near-empty commons area.

It took three decades for the enrollment at Kent State University to recover to pre-May 4th levels. As for the song "Ohio," it continues to receive airplay on rock and oldie stations around the Buckeye State.

JOE WALSH & THE JAMES GANG

The James Gang originated in the Cleveland-Kent area in 1966, and built a following with their weekly gigs at JB's tavern in Kent. Formed by a pair of Kent State University students – drummer Jimmy Fox and guitarist Ron Silverman (formerly of Tom King And The Starfires) – the group experienced a rotating lineup, including a talented guitarist who had just completed a two-year army stint, Euclid-native Glenn Schwartz.

Spending less than a year with the group, Schwartz quit and sought fame on the West Coast. Turning down an offer by Duane Allman to join The Allman Brothers Band, Schwartz instead formed a hippie rock act, Pacific Gas And Electric. But just as the group's hit single, "Are You Ready," was climbing up the charts, Schwartz announced on stage in front of 80,000 people at the Miami Pop Festival that he was quitting drugs, leaving music and turning to Christianity. Returning to Cleveland, he initially teamed with his brother, Gene, as The Schwartz Brothers.

The very next day after Schwartz had quit The James Gang, a young guitarist named Joe Walsh approached the group to offer his services. At the time, Walsh was a member of a popular local act called The Measles. Hired after a short audition, Walsh soon emerged as the group's leader. A native of Kansas, Walsh was raised in Columbus and New Jersey, where he had formed a band called The G-Clefs; returning to Ohio, he attended Kent State University. While a student, he teamed with former members of a local band, The Choir, to form the shortlived act, The Power Trio.

A year after Walsh joined The James Gang, the group was pared down to a trio of Walsh, Jim Fox and former E.T. Hooley bassist Dale Peters. Soon after, The James Gang recorded their moderate-selling debut release, *Yer' Album*. In 1970, the group followed up with *Rides Again* (a half electric, half acoustic project), which spawned the group's first major hit, "Funk #49." Touring across Europe as the opening act for The Who, the surging James Gang honed a new fanbase. On the tour, Walsh was befriended by fellow guitarist, Pete Townshend. Released in 1973, Walsh's final album with the group, *Thirds*, was highlighted by the guitar-driven track, "Walk Away."

After a touring schedule of 300 gigs per year, Walsh amicably left The James Gang. Jim Fox recalled in *Rolling Stone*, "Pete Townshend told us to just find a kick-ass replacement, so we thought, 'Well, we'll just get another guitar player.' We were too stupid to understand the ramifications of Joe leaving.... But Joe Walsh isn't just a guitar player. He's a singer, a songwriter and more specifically a personality." Walsh was replaced in The James Gang by Italian-born guitarist Dominic Troiano, who had previously replaced Robbie Robertson in Ronnie Hawkins' backing band, The Hawks. While simultaneously working on his own solo projects, Troiano collaborated with The James Gang for two albums, *Straight Shooter* and *Passin' Thru*. Then in late-1973, The James Gang again lost their guitarist as Troiano joined Canadian rockers, The Guess Who. Troiano's replacement was yet another guitar virtuoso, Tommy Bolin, who would stay around long enough to record just one album, *Miami*. But with the group unable to maintain its classic sound following Walsh's departure, The James Gang disbanded after recording two more albums. Toward the twilight of the group, Fox was hired by Eric Clapton as a session player on his album, *461 Ocean Blvd*. But still wanting to salvage The James Gang, Fox rejected Clapton's invitation to join his band.

Meanwhile, Joe Walsh would settle in Boulder, Colorado, and team with Kenny Passarelli and former Measles bandmate, drummer Joe Vitale of Canton (who had been playing behind Ted Nugent), to form another power trio, Barnstorm. After releasing a moderate-selling debut disc, the group enjoyed greater success with its followup release. Issued as a solo Joe Walsh project, *The Smoker You Drink, The Player You Get* was highlighted the raucous track, "Rocky Mountain Way." With Barnstorm disbanding, Walsh moved to Los Angeles and turned to production work, overseeing albums by Joe Vitale (*Roller Coaster Weekend*) and Dan Fogelberg (*Souvenirs*). Vitale would later join Crosby, Stills and Nash's backing band. Subsequently, Walsh issued a series of well-received solo albums, including *So What* and the live project *You Can't Argue With A Sick Mind*.

By 1975, Joe Walsh would join The Eagles as the replacement for lead guitarist Bernie Leadon. Performing on the group's masterpiece, *Hotel California*, Walsh provided the skillful guitar-work on the smash hits, "Hotel California" and "New Kid In Town." Fondly recalling the album, Walsh told *Musician* magazine, "[The] thing I'm proudest about was to be in The Eagles and have a power base to make a valid artistic statement for the generation I represent. It was a special album for a lot of people, including me, to be able to affect that many people on the planet and to feel that album was good enough to justify being rich."

Under a great deal of pressure to match the success of *Hotel California*, The Eagles followed with *The Long Run*, which spawned the hits, "Heartache Tonight" and "The Long Run." But as Walsh recalled: "The thing that eventually became an incredible burden for The Eagles was trying to figure out what kind of intellectual statement you're gonna make about something. I was trying to get 180 degrees away from dwelling on anything, and just make music that would speak for itself." Maintaining a solo career during this period, Walsh reached the charts with a series of quirky hits including the autobiographical, "Life's Been Good." In 1979, Walsh launched a pseudo-presidential run with the platform, "free gas for everyone." But in the process, he managed to register 100,000 voters.

With The Eagles disbanding in 1980, Walsh continued to churn out solo albums such as *There Goes The Neighborhood*, *The Confessor* and *You Bought It, You Name It*. A track from the *Urban Cowboy* soundtrack, "All Night Long," gave Walsh a pop hit in 1980. By 1992, on the eve of the release of his comeback album *Ordinary Average Guy*, Walsh again toyed with political aspirations and announced his run for Vice President.

Walsh toured with the reformed Eagles in 1994. In 2006, he reformed the James Gang for their first tour in more than three decades.

THE MICHAEL STANLEY BAND

Although considered a superstar act in northern Ohio, The Michael Stanley Band (MSB) could manage only moderate success on the national scene. Often compared to Bob Seger who was a major star in his hometown of Detroit before gaining national recognition, heartland rockers MSB regularly filled large venues around Cleveland, Akron and Youngstown.

A native of suburban Cleveland, Michael Stanley (born Michael Stanley Gee) broke into music as a member of local British Invasion-style bands, The Sceptres and The Tree Stumps. The latter group would evolve into a folk-pop outfit called Silk. While earning a degree in comparative religion from Hiram College, Stanley recorded an album with the group, *Smooth As Raw Silk*.

Encouraged by New York City producer Bill Szymczyk, Stanley pursued a solo career. On his two solo albums, Stanley was aided in the studio by Joe Walsh, Todd Rundgren, Rick Derringer and other notable musicians. Stanley's self-titled 1973 debut garnered local airplay with the track, "Rosewood Bitters." Recalling his introduction to Michael Stanley, WMMS music director David Spero told *The Cleveland Plain Dealer*: "A salesman on the AM side [at] WMMS's sister station, WHK, named Stan Gee had been bothering me for ages to listen to this tape his kid had made.... You know, everybody gives you tapes to play when you're in radio. But he was telling me this guy Joe Walsh had played on it, and I'd known Walsh from when he was in the James Gang, an early '70s Cleveland group that produced a number of national hit singles and LPs. So I'm going, 'Yeah, yeah. Right.' And then I run into Walsh one day and he says, 'Well, you must know Michael Stanley.' And I say, 'No, I don't.' Joe says, 'I played on his record and all my guys are the backup band. Todd Rundgren is on it; it's really cool.' So I finally picked up the record and figured out that this was Stan Gee's kid.

I loved the record and I started playing it on the air. Then I met Michael and we became great friends."

Then after he was fired from his position as a regional manager of a record store chain in 1973, Stanley pursued a full-time music career and formed The Michael Stanley Band. Initially an acoustic trio, Stanley was joined by former Glass Harp bassist Dan Pecchio and guitarist Jonah Koslen. A veteran of two local bands, Koslen was previously a member of Jeep and Snake Eyes. (Snake Eyes included bassist Danny Sheridan, who later formed Eli Radish. A popular, local country-rock group, Eli Radish also included future MTV veejay Nina Blackwood on the harp.)

Expanded to a quartet with the addition of drummer Tommy Dobeck, The Michael Stanley Band released their debut album in 1975, the acoustic-rooted *You Break It, You Bought It*. Soon adopting a more rock-oriented sound, the group also hired David Spero as its manager. (Spero would later manage Harry Nilsson, Joe Walsh, Nelson, Nicky Hopkins, Sam Moore, Dickey Betts, Survivor, Don Felder and J.D. Souther.)

After the 1977 release of MSB's double-live album *Stage Pass*, Jonah Koslen left the band and was replaced by Gary Markasky; the project was highlighted by "Nothing's Gonna Change My Mind." Leaving Epic Records after three albums, the group would sign with Arista. For their 1978 album *Cabin Fever*, MSB was paired with hit producer Robert John "Mutt" Lange. Highlighted by the ballad "Why Should Love Be This Way," the album marked the departure of bassist Dan Pecchio and the addition of keyboardist Kevin Raleigh.

In 1980, MSB drew comparisons to Bruce Springsteen with the album, *Heartland*. Featuring Springsteen sideman Clarence Clemons on saxophone, the album spawned the local hit, "Lover." Another track, "He Can't Love You" became the group's first national top-40 hit and featured the lead vocals of Kevin Raleigh (who also composed the song). Reaching the height of its popularity in the early-1980s, MSB followed with the albums *Northcoast*, *MSB* and *You Can't Fight Fashion*; the latter album was produced by Bob Clearmountain and was highlighted by the group's ode to Cleveland, the top-40 rocker, "My Town."

In August 1982, over a four-night, sold-out run at the Blossom Music Center – an open-air venue located between Akron and Cleveland – The Michael Stanley Band drew a record-setting 66,000 concertgoers. Two years later, the group drew 76,000 to the parking lot of Municipal Stadium. But local fame didn't always translate into national success.

Then in 1983, Michael Stanley made an unfortunate career decision when he balked at EMI's offer to "extend" rather than negotiate a new contract. In the end, the group was dropped by the label. Subsequently issuing their own albums, MSB would lose their momentum. After releasing 13 albums, Stanley decided to call it quits. In 1986, the group performed a series of nine sold-out, farewell concerts at the Front Row Theater.

Meanwhile, after leaving The Michael Stanley Band in 1978, Jonah Koslen had formed Breathless. Issued by EMI Records, the group's debut album, *Breathless,* was well-received in Northeastern Ohio. Though touring as an opening act for Kiss, Breathless managed only spotty, national airplay of their single, "Takin' It Back." After Breathless disbanded in 1981, Koslen headed for Los Angeles but would return to Ohio for occasional MSB reunions.

In addition to Breathless, a number of Cleveland rock bands were on the cusp of breaking through onto the national level during the 1980s including Champion, Easy Street, Love Affair and Isuzu. Some like The B.E. Taylor Group and Beau Coup did manage to achieve some notoriety outside of Ohio. One manufactured rock act featuring three Clevelanders, The All Sports Band, was assembled by Cleveland sound engineer Tracy Coast; the group failed to live up to its hype with the release of a self-titled, major label album.

Following the breakup of MSB, Michael Stanley would emerge as a local media celebrity. After some local TV work, Stanley became a deejay, first at WMMS and later at WNCX (at this station, Stanley worked for a time with former Humble Pie drummer, Jerry Shirley). By 1993, Stanley returned to the stage with a new backing group, The Ghost Poets, which included former MSB bandmate Bob Pelander.

GLASS HARP

By the early-1970s, a number of rock musicians began taking a more serious, classical approach to the genre. Called "progressive rock," the movement spawned bands such as the Ohio-based trio, Glass Harp.

One of the most revered, Buckeye acts of the era, Glass Harp disintegrated just as they were poised for stardom. The group was formed in 1968 by a pair of Youngstown classmates, guitarist Phil Keaggy and drummer John Sferra, along with bassist Steve Markulin. The following year, the group would gel into its classic lineup, with Dan Pecchio replacing Markulin.

A guitar virtuoso who was missing part of a finger, Keaggy told *Guitar Player*, "I lost my middle finger before I began playing guitar in fourth grade, so I never missed it, because it wasn't there. I could still hold a plectrum. The only thing I had to get over was the embarrassment of playing in front of people, because, as a kid, you're self-conscious of things like that."

With the surging James Gang relinquishing its post as the house band at JB's tavern in Kent, Glass Harp was given the Wednesday night gig. Then at a performance just west of Akron at Chippewa Lake Park, Glass Harp drew the attention of a Decca Records representative.

Recorded at Jimi Hendrix's custom-built, Electric Ladyland studio in New York, the group's 1970 debut album, *Glass Harp*, was released the same week as Hendrix's sudden death. Glass Harp was soon opening for a series of leading rock acts, including Yes, Traffic, Mike Bloomfield, Ted Nugent and Alice Cooper. Opening for The Kinks at Carnegie Hall in 1971, Glass

Harp recorded the performance for a planned live album. But with their label balking, the tracks were belatedly issued 26-years later.

After the release of two more albums – *Synergy* and *Makes Me Glad* – Glass Harp ground to a halt. At age 21, Keaggy turned to God as a born-again Christian in the wake of his mother's death in an auto accident, and left the group. Though replacing Keaggy with Tim Burks and adding a fourth member, Glass Harp had lost its spark and was forced to disband in 1973. While Keaggy would later have a prolific career in the field of contemporary Christian music, Pecchio would join The Michael Stanley Band. Meanwhile, Sferra initially pursued a solo career, but later formed The Motion.

Glass Harp would later reunite for occasional performances. In 2003, the group issued a new studio album, *Hourglass*.

THE WHO TRAGEDY IN CINCINNATI

With the rise of arena rock during the 1970s, superstar acts began performing in large sport venues. Leading rockers such as Led Zeppelin and Kiss were filling massive arenas, playing for tens of thousands of fans at a time. Considered more than just ordinary concerts, these events would incorporate elaborate stage sets, pyrotechnics, light shows, extravagant stage costumes and deafening sound systems.

At the forefront of the 1960s British Invasion, The Who continued their momentum well into the 1970s. With innovative rock operas such as *Tommy* and album masterpieces like *Who's Next*, the group persevered despite the ever-changing tastes in popular music.

Able to fill large venues throughout much of their career, The Who launched a U.S. tour in September 1979. At the time, The Who were riding a wave of popularity, with two hit albums on the charts, *The Kids Are Alright* and the *Quadrophenia* soundtrack. The group graced radio playlists that year with the tracks, "Long Live Rock" and "5:15."

But just a year earlier, The Who suffered a pair of calamities when the group's outlandish drummer, 31-year-old Keith Moon, perished after an overdose, and longtime manager Pete Meadon committed suicide.

Then at a tour stop on December 3, 1979, at the Cincinnati Riverfront Coliseum, tragedy would strike the group again. The four-year-old venue had been constructed with sports, not music, in mind. Instead of utilizing assigned seating, the concert promoters employed a festival-seating format, where those arriving first, secured the best spots. The same seating format had been employed at the facility for other rock concerts. But at an earlier Led Zeppelin show, unruly fans broke through glass doors to get inside.

On that early December day, thousands of Who fans arrived hours early and waited outside the Coliseum, hoping to guarantee a good spot for the scheduled 8 PM show. But with the inclement winter weather, the uncomfortable wait was complicated by temperatures in the 30s. Despite the cold, there was a sense of anticipation in the air. By 7 PM, the crowd size was estimated at 12,000. But surprisingly, there were no crowd control procedures, barricades or designated lines. Although a squad of 25 police officers was in place around the building, they took a mostly hands-off approach with the massive crowd.

Then suddenly, a late sound-check by The Who triggered a charge toward the closed doors, with concertgoers thinking the show had started. Abruptly, some doors were opened and then quickly closed. This happened a few more times as confused ticket-holders surged forward. Another door had been broken by anxious fans, as frantic workers tried to repel the rush.

But with nowhere to go, those who were assembled near the line of doors were either trampled or crushed. "It was like everything went wrong at the same time. There was just too much mass chaos. The force just pushed you as hard as you've ever been squeezed and knocked the air out of you. We were stuck right in the middle of it where people were going down," a witness told *The Cincinnati Post*. But the pushing continued.

In the end, 11 people died, ages 15 to 27. All of them succumbed to suffocation. Two of the victims were mothers and three were high school students. Dozens of others were injured, many of them seriously.

One of The Who's associates, Richard Barnes, recalled what he witnessed upon arriving at the scene of human devastation: "I saw several firemen rush past the kids and assumed that there was a small fire somewhere. I thought that I could see and smell smoke. After a while I saw more police and paramedics rushing about and through the glass doors to the outside... I asked a woman usher whether there had been a fire. She noticed my official Who tour plastic pass. 'Don't you people know what's happened here tonight – fifteen people have been killed.' I was surprised, but for some reason didn't believe her. I thought perhaps there had been a couple heart attacks and a drug OD, and that the ushers had exaggerated the whole thing. We spotted a group of officials looking very clean-cut and worried, accompanied by top officers and firemen inspecting the place and I knew something was seriously wrong. I asked another uniformed usher why there were so many police and officials present. He told me that eleven people had been killed. Another elderly usher told me, almost with pride, 'Didn't you know? History has been made here tonight. The whole world will know about this in the morning.'"

When Richard Barnes arrived backstage, he first ran into The Who's manager Bill Curbishley, who thought it would be best if members of the group were not informed about the deaths until the close of the concert. Soon after, the city's Fire Marshall, Clifford Drury, arrived backstage and told Curbishley that the concert had to proceed as scheduled. Otherwise, the 18,000 fans in attendance might start trouble.

The Cincinnati Post reported: "By the end of that night, there was a pile of clothes several feet high that someone had swept up just inside the battered doors on the west side of Riverfront Coliseum. Hats, shoes, gloves, shirts, pants – a grim reminder of the force created when thousands of people crush together, clothes literally ripped from their bodies."

According to *Time* magazine, when members of The Who "came offstage, Curbishley told them the news. Kenney Jones slumped against a wall. John Entwistle tried to light a cigarette, which shredded in his shaking hands. Roger Daltrey began to cry. Pete Townshend went ashen quiet. Daltrey thought the whole tour should be canceled. Then Townshend spoke up. He said, 'If we don't play tomorrow, we'll never play again.'"

In his first interview after the tragedy, Who guitarist Pete Townshend told *Rolling Stone*, "The *problem* with Cincinnati was external security, external control: external people control. People in large numbers *need controlling*. They're – they're like cattle. But a lot of kids complained; everywhere they'd look there was a cop. It spoiled their evening for them. They felt, okay, it happened in Cincinnati, but *we don't need that*. There was an article in the paper in Seattle, complaining about the fact there was too much security."After the tragedy, Cincinnati banned festival seating. The ban stayed in place until 2004.

During a subsequent tour stop at Detroit's Pontiac Silverdome, The Who again encountered festival seating. At the start of the concert, tragedy nearly struck again. In front of the stage, bodies were crushed by those pushing in the back. Frantic ushers pulled distressed fans from the front of the entangled, human mass. Both Pete Townshend and Roger Daltrey pleaded with the throng of fans to step back and stop pushing. Among the nearly 50,000 fans in attendance, 20,000 were on the floor – all standing. Fortunately, there were no serious injuries.

Following the tragic tour, The Who slowly disintegrated. After staging a farewell tour in 1983, The Who would occasionally regroup for various projects. In 2006, the two surviving members of The Who – Roger Daltrey and Pete Townshend – released the album *Wire & Glass*. On the six-song set, Townshend provided the lead vocal on "They Made My Dreams Come True," which refers to the tragedy of 1979. The Who would never perform in Cincinnati again.

Other rock-related tragedies have occurred in the Buckeye State. A 2004 concert headlined by Pantera co-founder "Dimebag" Darrell Abbott ended in death when a 25-year-old gunman, Nathan Gale, jumped onto the stage at the Alrosa Villa nightclub in Columbus. While he was chased by bouncers, Gale shot and killed Abbott and three others. Two others were also shot but survived. In a matter of minutes, a police officer entered the club and fatally shot Gale, who at the time was holding a hostage.

In another calamity, guitarist Ty Longely perished along with over 100 others in an inferno at the Station nightclub in West Warwick, Rhode Island. A member of Great White since 2000, the Youngstown resident had been hired by the group's lead singer, Jack Russell. The out-of-control blaze began when the band's pyrotechnics display ignited the polyurethane insulation on nearby walls.

MEAT LOAF & BOSTON

The 1970s was the decade of the mega-selling rock album – Fleetwood Mac's *Rumours*, Pink Floyd's *Dark Side Of The Moon*, Peter Frampton's live effort *Frampton Comes Alive!*, Meat Loaf's *Bat Out Of Hell* and Boston's self-titled, debut release. Two of these albums had Ohio connections.

The group Boston was the brainchild of Toledo-born Tom Scholz, who was an electronics wizard during his youth. Also drawn to music, he was classically trained on piano. Discovering rock music in his mid-teens, he taught himself to play the guitar, bass and drums. Awarded a full scholarship in 1965 to the prestigious Massachusetts Institute of Technology, Scholz earned a Master's degree in mechanical engineering at age 21.

Remaining in Massachusetts, Scholz was hired by Polaroid as a product design engineer. Spending most of his income and spare time in his basement recording studio, he designed and built most of the equipment. Teaming with vocalist Brad Delp, Scholz devoted years to what would become the first Boston album. After a myriad of record label rejections, the pair signed with CBS/Epic in 1976. Scholz left his position at Polaroid only after he was certain the album *Boston* would be a hit.

Selling nearly 20-million copies, *Boston* came to define 1970s album-rock with tracks such as "More Than A Feeling" and "Long Time." Ironically, the album was a hit in Cleveland well before it was embraced in Boston. After following up with 1979's *Don't Look Back*, Scholz would belatedly release a third Boston album in 1986, *Third Stage*. Then after a decade of litigation over unpaid royalties, Scholz won millions of dollars from CBS Records.

Meanwhile, Cleveland nurtured two notable record labels during the 1970s, Cleveland International and Telarc. Cleveland International was started by a Pennsylvania-born musician, Steve Popovich. Previously a member of a local rock band called The Twilighters, Popovich had scored a regional hit in 1962 with "Be Faithful." After the group disbanded, Popovich was aided by Cleveland polka king Frankie Yankovic in landing a job at the local branch of CBS Records. Initially unloading trucks at the company's warehouse, Popovich worked his way up through the firm, and by 1970, was appointed vice-president of promotions. By 1974, Popovich was assigned to the A&R division of the CBS subsidiary, Epic Records, where he planned strategies to forge the careers of acts such as Boston, Cheap Trick, Ted Nugent, Michael Jackson and Cleveland rockers The Michael Stanley Band.

Unhappy living in New York City, Popovich resigned from CBS/Epic in 1976. Returning to Ohio, he launched his own label, Cleveland International Records (CIR). Leaving CBS/Epic on friendly terms, Popovich maintained his connections with the company, which agreed to manufacture and distribute his label's releases.

Popovich's major breakthrough came with the debut album by a former musical actor from Texas named Meat Loaf (born Marvin Lee Aday), who had previously starred in productions of *The Rocky Horror Picture Show*. But with Popovich initially unsure about signing the singer, guitarist Steven Van Zandt (a.k.a. Little Steven of Bruce Springsteen's E Street Band) began pestering Popovich on Meat Loaf's behalf. Writing in his autobiography, Meat Loaf recalled: "Popovich was a promotion guy who could get stuff on the radio. He walked around with a boom box everywhere he went, playing stuff. He didn't give you a tape to take home and listen to. He played it for you on the spot. Steve Popovich thought Little Steven was the genius in The E Street Band. I probably wouldn't argue with him on that. Little Steven told Popovich that the little fifteen-second interval at the opening of 'You Took The Words Right Out Of My Mouth' was the best intro in the history of pop music. Little Steven convinced him that *Bat Out Of Hell* was going to be a hit." But after receiving a rejection from Warner Brothers Records, Meat Loaf was about to abandon any hopes for a recording career.

But Little Steven remained persistent, with Meat Loaf recalling: "A couple days later he called Popovich again and said, 'Hey, you got one last chance!' Cleveland International had been the only other company we were courting. It was a new company – the only act they had on the label so far was Ronnie Spector! We played this game that we were getting ready to sign with Warner Bros., but we would really, really like to be with Cleveland International because we said we thought Warner Bros. was too *big*."

Released by CIR in 1977, *Bat Out Of Hell* featured dramatic readings of operatic-styled, hard-rock songs composed by Meat Loaf's collaborator Jim Steinman. Despite an absence of a promotional push from CBS Records, the album spawned rock classics such as "Two Out Of Three Ain't Bad," "You Took The Words Right Out Of My Mouth," and one of the most requested songs in the history of rock radio, the dynamic narrative of teenage lust, "Paradise By The Dashboard Lights."

With just one release, Popovich became a major player in the record business. But with the disappointing sales of the label's followup albums and the inability of CIR to secure royalties from CBS for Meat Loaf's smash album, Popovich shuttered the label in 1982 and went to work for Polygram's country division in Nashville.

Returning to Cleveland in 1993 to restart CIR, Popovich was unhappy with the royalty statements he was receiving from CBS's new owner, Sony Records. Meat Loaf, too, complained about the situation. Lawsuits were filed against Sony after an auditor hired by Popovich discovered that CIR and Meat Loaf had been shortchanged $20 million in royalties over two decades. In the end, the team of Meat Loaf and Jim Steinman received nearly $9 million, while Popovich settled for $5.4 million in past royalties and a $1.3 advance on future earnings. As part of the agreement, Sony agreed to place the CIR logo on all future printings of Meat Loaf recordings, which Popovich considered to be worth millions of dollars in exposure. But when Sony failed to add the CIR logo until a year later, Popovich again sued in 2002, winning another $5 million. With the album surpassing the 40-million mark in worldwide sales, *Bat Out Of Hell* helped put a small Cleveland label on the map. CIR would issue two more Meat Loaf albums, *Dead Ringer* and *Midnight At The Lost And Found*.

In addition to Meat Loaf, CIR signed a series of mainstream, usually Midwestern rockers, including Meat Loaf's backing singer Ellen Foley. The label's roster also included Ian Hunter, Chas & Dave, the Grammy-winning Brave Combo, and a country music outlaw from Akron, David Allan Coe. Another of the label's acts, a duo called The Euclid Beach Band, scored a local hit with "There's No Surf In Cleveland."

At the start of the 21st century, the biggest label in Ohio was situated in the suburban Cleveland city of Beachwood, Telarc Records. Formed in 1977 by Robert Woods and Jack Renner, the company began as a classical venture but eventually expanded to include jazz and blues music. In 2000, Telarc merged with another label, Heads Up, and added various world music genres to its offerings. After amassing 46 Grammy Awards, Telarc was sold in 2005 to Concord Music Group of Beverly Hills, California.

ODDS AND ENDS

One of the more creative, hard-rock bands from Ohio, The Damnation Of Adam Blessing were named after a pulp-fiction paperback. Founded in the Cleveland area by rhythm guitarist Jim Quinn and lead guitarist/vocalist Bill "Adam" Constable (formerly of The Society), the group was managed by a former radio executive from WIXY, Eric Stevens.

Signed by United Artists Records, The Damnation Of Adam Blessing released a psychedelically-tinged, debut album in 1968, with most of the material written by Constable. The often-rowdy group scored underground rock hits with melodic tracks such as "Back To The River" and a cover of the often-recorded rock standard, "Morning Dew." The group never recorded its concert showstopper, a cover version of Jimi Hendrix's "You Got Me Floatin'." Accentuated by long, drawn-out solos, the song typically took nearly an hour to perform. Fading by the time of the release of its third album, *Which Is Justice, Which Is The Thief*, the group disbanded in 1972. After briefly re-emerging under the name, Glory, the group broke up for good in 1974.

Also hailing from Cleveland, J.D. Blackfoot (born Benjamin Franklin Van Dervort) frequently employed American-Indian themes in his music. Previously using the stage name of Benny Van, he had fronted the Columbus-based garage-rock group, The Ebb Tides. Subsequently emerging as J.D. Blackfoot (which was also the name of his band), he recorded the single, "Who's Nuts Alfred." Veering from hard rock to psychedelia, Blackfoot followed with the album, *The Ultimate Prophecy*, which featured future Pure Prairie League founder Craig Fuller on guitar. After the group disbanded, Blackfoot recorded a series of solo albums, and then later settled in Missouri.

Meanwhile, during Alice Cooper's hit-producing years, he was backed by a pair of Akron-natives who had never met each other before teaming with Cooper in Arizona. Both drummer Neal Smith and guitarist Glen Buxton had moved to the Phoenix area with their families while in their mid-teens. Eventually, both men began performing with Cooper (then known as Vincent Furnier). A gifted blues-rock, slide guitarist, Buxton provided a number of inventive licks on Alice Cooper hits such as "No More Mr. Nice Guy" and "School's Out."

Based out of Detroit, Terry Knight And The Pack performed around Cleveland on a regular basis, and beginning in 1968, enjoyed a year-long residency at the famed Cleveland Agora. By the following year, the group was renamed Grand Funk Railroad. With Knight moving to the role of manager and producer, he recorded the group's albums in Cleveland. Although Knight parted with the band under hostile circumstances after the release of the album *E Pluribus Funk*, the group continued to record in Cleveland for a time.

Toledo-born Ruby Starr (born Constance Mierzwiak) released her first album in 1971 under the name Ruby Jones. Subsequently joining the Southern-rock band Black Oak Arkansas for several years, she provided the vocals on their biggest hit, "Jim Dandy." After leaving the group, she formed Ruby Starr & Grey Ghost. Signing with Capitol Records, she released a self-titled album in 1975. As a solo artist, she would release two more albums at the label. Starr later formed the groups, Grey Star and Henrietta Kahn.

A horn-based, soul-rock band from Cleveland, Rastus frequently toured with like-minded national acts such as Chicago and Tower Of Power. Although a favorite throughout the Midwest, Rastus never achieved widespread notoriety. Recording two albums in the 1970s, the group disbanded after experiencing a series of personnel changes.

Former Parma-native Neil Giraldo played guitar around Cleveland before joining Rick Derringer's band. Then in 1977, Giraldo was hired by Chrysalis Records as an arranger and guitarist for a young, new act – a petite, opera-trained vocalist named Pat Benatar. Giraldo backed Benatar on her long run of hits beginning with "Heartbreaker" and continuing with "We Live For Love," "You Better Run" and "Hit Me With Your Best Shot." Giraldo and Benatar would wed in 1982.

CHAPTER 6
THE ARRIVAL OF PUNK ROCK IN CLEVELAND

Festering in the urban enclaves of New York City and Los Angeles, as well as in the Midwestern cities of Detroit and Cleveland, punk represented a backlash against the manufactured stars of arena-rock and disco. Punk was a do-it-yourself movement embraced by music afficionados and disaffected outsiders. In the late-1980s, a *Washington Post* music writer examining the origins of punk, concluded: "Punk rock was fashioned in Manhattan in the mid-'70s, but it was often assembled from parts made in Ohio. Such seminal New York outfits as The Contortions, The Dead Boys, The Feelies, and Teenage Jesus And The Jerks relied on recent immigrants from Ohio. In fact, many of those musicians had done time in a little-known Cleveland band, Rocket From The Tombs, or its successor, Pere Ubu."

In the western suburbs of Cleveland, several students from Lakewood High School formed a rock group to explore their fascination with New York art rockers, The Velvet Underground. Calling themselves The Mirrors, the group initially performed only Velvet Underground songs. Formed in 1971 by Jamie Klimek, Jim Crook, Craig Bell (who didn't play an instrument at the time but quickly mastered the bass guitar) and Michael J. Weldon (a guitarist who was hired as the drummer), The Mirrors attracted very little interest, and at one bar, conceded to the owner's suggestion of giving away free draft beer as a means of drawing an audience.

As one band member later recalled in *Magnet*, "People hated us, you know? The only reason that people came was because we were giving them free beer. We're talking 25, 28, 30 people, and you knew every one of them by their first name." But one of their fans was a songwriter named Peter Laughner who penned glowing reviews of the band in the local music weekly, *Scene*. After experiencing a series of personnel changes as a result of the military draft, the group expanded its repertoire to include songs by garage rockers such as The Troggs and Detroit proto-punks, MC5 and Iggy And The Stooges.

After The Mirrors disbanded in 1976, the remnants of the group would team with drummer Anton Fier to form The Poli-Styrene Band, which would evolve into the better-known Styrenes.

Meanwhile, other like-minded groups were forming around Cleveland. Sharing a similar musical philosophy as The Mirrors, The Electric Eels were also probing the fringes of rock music. The group was assembled by a trio of friends – John Morton, Dave McManus and Brian McMahon – after watching an appallingly-awful performance by a local band at a Captain Beefheart concert. One of the first rock acts to exhibit the punk aesthetic – years before the rise of British punk – The Electric Eels sported safety pins and ratty, ripped clothes. Spouting obscenities and social commentaries, exploring dark themes and engaging in outlandish, onstage behavior, the group shocked audiences. But unable to find steady gigs in either Cleveland or Columbus, the group disbanded in 1975. Morton later told *Magnet*, "We really thought we were going to be popular and a big hit. We thought, 'The kids are ready for this.' We were quite astounded when we got booed."

Several of the group's members would find greater success in other projects: Nick Knox joined The Cramps; Jim Jones joined Guyana; and Anton Fier would next work with Pere Ubu. Meanwhile, Brian McMahon's brother, Kevin, would later form the new wave act Lucky Pierre, which at one time would include future Nine Inch Nails founder, Trent Reznor.

ROCKET FROM THE TOMBS & PERE UBU
An important cog in the rise of punk rock was a passionate and hulking Clevelander named David Thomas. A music critic for *Scene* magazine, Thomas wrote reviews under the name of Crocus Behemoth and was a huge fan of avant-garde rockers Frank Zappa and Captain Beefheart.

Also a musician, Thomas joined an art-rock act called Rocket From The Tombs. Formed in 1974, the group had been assembled as the house band for *Scene* magazine. Thomas told *The Cleveland Plain Dealer*: "I really wasn't interested in rock until I had to write about it for the *Scene*. I was going to college to be a microbiologist. I had worked all those years at Heights High. I was an A student. But when I got to college nobody was working. All they wanted to do was drink beer. So I quit school and got a job at [*Scene*].... I started writing soon after that and after a few years of having really intense feelings about the way rock should be, I started feeling like a hypocrite. I was inflicting these opinions on poor, stupid rock stars coming through town. I finally decided, 'If I'm so smart, I should do this.'"

Aside from Thomas, the group's other creative force was guitarist/songwriter Peter Laughner. Formerly in a band called Cinderella Backstreet, and then briefly a solo guitarist who performed in local folk clubs, Laughner was attracted to the musical experimentation of Rocket From The Tombs.

The group featured a somewhat revolving lineup which included Cheetah Chrome (born Gene O'Connor), Craig Bell, Steve Melman, Johnny Blitz (born John Mandasky), Stiv Bator, Charlie Weiner and others. The group's chief songwriters were Chrome, Laughner and Thomas – who often composed lyrics while working as a bouncer at the Viking nightclub. Although the group never recorded, bootleg versions of live tracks such as "Final Solution," "Sonic Reducer" and "Ain't It Fun" were heavily circulated, with a proper CD compilation finally issued in 2002.

Rocket From The Tombs made their debut at the Viking nightclub on the same bill as The Electric Eels and The Mirrors. Laughner viewed Rocket

From The Tombs as a revolutionary concept, and had convinced WMMS deejay Kid Leo to launch a local music program, with his group spotlighted on the first show. But despite Laughner's dedication, the group disbanded in late-1975. As Thomas recalls in *Magnet*, "It wasn't disagreements or fights that broke us up. It was simply that we all wanted very different things, and the only place we were in agreement was in the pursuit of [an] overdriven, hard Midwestern groove rock. It was doomed from the beginning."

The group splintered into two camps with Blitz, Chrome and Bator evolving into Frankenstein, which in 1976, emerged as the legendary punk outfit The Dead Boys.

The other camp morphed into Pere Ubu, which was headed by the team of Thomas and Laughner, and was named after a character in Alfred Jarry's play, *Ubu Roi*. Often performing at a Cleveland nightspot called The Pirates Cove – which was located in a grimy industrial district along the mouth of the Cuyahoga River – Pere Ubu built a small but loyal following among the urban, art crowd. The club owner soon set aside Thursday nights for Pere Ubu and similar acts.

Pere Ubu was partially financed by old money: the group's synthesizer player, Allen Ravenstine, spent a large portion of his trust fund to purchase a thirty-six room, gothic-styled edifice in downtown Cleveland, the Plaza Building. He converted the former office building into an artist colony, cheaply renting the apartments to bohemians, artisans, and musicians – including all the members of Pere Ubu except for David Thomas.

The group initially garnered attention in 1975 with its self-issued debut single, "30 Seconds Over Tokyo," one of several leftover tracks from the Rocket From The Tombs period. Though the single was intended as a farewell release, the group trudged on. Pere Ubu's originality was in part driven by the tension between the group's two creative forces, David Thomas and Peter Laughner. Leaving the group in June 1976, Laughner would die of acute pancreatitis the following year. He later achieved cult status.

Subsequent Pere Ubu singles, "Final Solution" and "Street Waves," fared well among the punk crowd in the U.K. but went mostly ignored in America. Then in 1978, the group signed with the Mercury subsidiary, Blank Records, and released the album, *Modern Dance*.

After Pere Ubu disbanded in 1982, David Thomas recorded a number of solo albums and worked with folk-rocker Richard Thompson. (Thomas was joined on his solo projects by an early Pere Ubu member, drummer Anton Fier. Fier had moved to New York City around 1978, and formed The Feelies. In 1980, Fier teamed with Arto Lindsay to launch The Lounge Lizards; by 1982, Fier and Lindsay would form the seminal indie band, The Golden Palominos.)

After spending four years in London, Thomas and his wife returned to Cleveland for an extended stay. Thomas recalled in *Newsday*: "I've been a whole lot of places, and realized that everybody has [an idea of] the perfect place to be, where the land, atmosphere, people are just so. Many people never find that place, but I found it at an early age. In England, I would sit on the banks of the Thames and weep when I remembered [Lake] Erie."

After forming a pair of similar groups – The Pedestrians and The Wooden Birds – Thomas wisely decided to resurrect the Pere Ubu moniker in 1987. Beginning with the album *The Tenement Year*, Pere Ubu continued to sporadically tour and record. But after Mercury Records refused to finance a trip to New York City for an appearance on *Late Night With David Letterman*, the group parted with the label under acrimonious circumstances. By the 1990s, Pere Ubu finally managed to score a pair of radio hits with "Waiting For Mary" and "Sleep Walk."

THE DEAD BOYS

Fronted by vocalist Stiv Bator, The Dead Boys were punk-rock pioneers whose sound, ethos and attitude came to define the genre. In addition to the surly Bator, the quintet included drummer Johnny Blitz, bassist Jeff Magnum and guitarists Jimmy Zero and Cheetah Chrome. After a concert in Youngstown, The Dead Boys were convinced by fellow punkers The Ramones to move their act to New York City. Magnum refused to leave Ohio, but would later rejoin the band.

Arriving in New York in July 1976, The Dead Boys found appreciative crowds at CBGB's, a pioneering punk bar in the seedy Bowery district. Performing a number of originals, the group also reworked some Rocket From The Tombs tracks into their set, including "Sonic Reducer," "Down In Flames" and "Ain't It Fun." Bator became the focus of the group's performances with his brash and violent stage antics, which included slashing his stomach and hanging himself from overhead pipes.

With CBGB's owner Hilly Kristal becoming their manager, The Dead Boys were poised to record for Kristal's new label. In need of a bass player, the group employed Bob Clearmountain for the sessions. Instead issued by Sire Records, the group's critically acclaimed, debut album, *We Have Come For Your Children*, made waves in the rock press. In late-1977, The Dead Boys toured across the U.K. as the opening act for The Damned.

In the wake of The Dead Boys' departure for New York City, another Cleveland band, The Pagans, was pushed to the forefront of the city's growing punk scene. Formed in 1977 by music journalist Mike Hudson, the group originally included guitarist Denny Carleton (formerly of 1960s pop band The Choir) who was replaced by Mike Metoff. (Metoff would later form a local new wave act called The Clocks, before changing his name to Ike Knox upon joining The Cramps.) Hudson told *The Cleveland Plain Dealer*, "Punks hated hippies, the '60s thing, the whole change-the-world thing. By the mid-'70s, the '60s generation already had a dominant role in the culture, and they were worse than the parents they were rebelling against in setting the agenda." Performing around Northeastern Ohio and releasing a few angst-driven singles including "Six And Change," The Pagans once opened up for a then-unknown British trio called The Police. But following a series of gigs in New York City, The Pagans disbanded in 1979. (The group would reunite in 1982.)

While in New York City, members of The Dead Boys crossed paths with guitarist Robert Quine, an Akron-raised guitarist, who quit his job as a lawyer to pursue a career in music. For a time, Quine worked in a New York movie memorabilia store along with punk musicians, Richard Hell and Tom Verlaine. Later asked to join Hell's group The Voidoids, Quine appeared on the seminal punk album, *The Blank Generation*. Quine later worked with Lydia Lunch, Tom Waits, Matthew Sweet, Lloyd Cole, and regularly toured and recorded with Lou Reed.

Meanwhile, with Sire Records wanting a more commercially-oriented album, The Dead Boys were paired with heavy-metal producer Felix Pappalardi for their second release. Issued in 1978, the album *We Have Come For Your Children* was highlighted by the track, "Ain't It Fun." But with Pappalardi failing to grasp the punk spirit, the album was a near-fiasco and sold even fewer copies than its predecessor.

In April 1978, The Dead Boys were sidelined when drummer Johnny Blitz was stabbed multiple times during an altercation with five men. A fundraiser for Blitz was staged at CBGB's, and featured The Ramones, John Belushi and members of Blondie. Then with the departure of Chrome and Zero in March 1979, The Dead Boys soon disbanded. But due to contractual obligations, the group was forced to reunite to record one more album, a live project taped at CBGB's. But with an angry Bators purposely singing off-mic, the resulting mix was unusable. A number of years later, Bators re-recorded the album's vocals when the tracks were issued by Bomp Records. Subsequently pursuing a solo career and flirting with new wave, Bators released the album, *Disconnected*.

Moving to London, Bators teamed with members of Sham 69 to form The Wanderers. Bators later joined forces with Brian James of The Damned to form the goth-flavored, punk supergroup, The Lords Of The New Church. The group scored an unlikely, MTV hit in 1982 with the grim track, "Open Your Eyes." After issuing three albums, the group disbanded in 1988. Meanwhile, the original line-up of The Dead Boys reformed for a brief tour in 1987, giving their final performance in suburban Cleveland.

After moving to Paris, Bators appeared in two films, including *Tapeheads*, where he portrayed Dick Slammer, the leader of a fictional, heavy-metal group called Blender Children. But after failing to seek medical treatment when the motorcycle he was riding was struck by a car, Bators passed away in 1990.

In 1993, Guns N' Roses recorded a cover of The Dead Boys' "Ain't It Fun." Meanwhile, Rocket From The Tombs would reform in 2003. Original members David Thomas, Craig Bell and Cheetah Chrome were joined by Richard Lloyd of Television and Steve Mehlman of Roue.

THE CRAMPS

With their twisted humor, oddball music and command of the visual image, a pair of Cleveland television movie-hosts would shape the creative processes of numerous musicians in northeastern Ohio. Decades before Elvira graced the small screen, deejay Pete Myers hosted a horror movie on WJW Channel-8. With his ghoulish black cape, eerie persona and dark humor, Myers invented a much-copied character.

Another Cleveland deejay, Ernie Anderson, built upon Myer's character and emerged as Ghoulardi, the host of *Shock Theater*. In between cheapie, monster B-films, Anderson puffed away on a cigarette, spouted off-the-wall beatnik poetry, rode his motorcycle through the studio and blew up props – all while blasting rock and jazz instrumentals such as Hank Marr's "Greasy Spoon," Duane Eddy's "Desert Rat," The Baskerville Hounds' "Space Rock" and Tom King And The Starfires' "Stronger Than Dirt." Paying homage to the Cleveland broadcasting legend, Akron-raised film director Jim Jarmusch proclaimed: "Ghoulardi was my hero.... Ghoulardi was really an amazing cultural figure who opened up all our imaginations.... I remember when he used to insert himself into films in some primitive kinescope way and he would be standing in the tunnel and the giant crabs would be coming up behind him. 'Look out. The giant crabs!'"

One teenager who preferred staying home on Friday nights to watch Ghoulardi was Eric Purkhiser, the future leader of the "psychobilly" punk band, The Cramps. Much of the macabre humor originated by Ghoulardi would later show up in the performances of The Cramps, Devo and Pere Ubu. (Ghoulardi was forced off the airwaves in 1966 after a successful three-year run. Anderson relocated to Los Angeles and later became the on-air voice of the ABC television network.)

Meanwhile, according to legend, Eric Purkhiser picked up Kirsty Wallace, who in her short-shorts and vintage blouse, was hitchhiking in her hometown of Sacramento. The two soon realized they were enrolled in the same course at Sacramento City College, "Art and Shamanism." Soon sharing an apartment as well as a love of early rock and roll, the pair decided to form a band. Purkhiser took the stage name of Raven Beauty, then Vip Vop, and finally, Lux Interior, which was taken from a Cleveland television commercial. Meanwhile, Wallace claimed that her stage name – Poison Ivy Rorschach – came to her during a dream.

After a brief stint in the Navy, Interior convinced Ivy to relocate to his hometown of Akron in 1974. There, the pair honed their musical craft in a large turn-of-the-century home in the city's artsy, Highland Square district, home to clubs like Annabell's and The Bucket Shop. (Later, Interior's younger brother, guitarist Mike Purkhiser, was a member of a pair of notable regional acts – a power-pop group called The Action and a neo-rockabilly act, The Walking Clampetts.)

A fan of rockabilly 45s, shock rocker Alice Cooper, the gender-bending band The New York Dolls and campy monster movies, Lux Interior merged his influences into a stage act. Realizing that New York City offered better opportunities for their offbeat brand of music, The Cramps left Akron. Ivy later told *The Los Angeles Times*, "We were arrogant enough to think, 'Let's move to New York and play at CBGB.'"

While working in a New York City record store, Interior convinced fellow employee Greg Beckerleg to join the band on second guitar (as Bryan Gregory). Also joining the group was his sister Pam Beckerleg on drums (as Pam Balam). By 1976, Balam was replaced by Ohio-native Miriam Linna.

The Cramps' first-ever public performance came at CBGB's as the opening act for Cleveland punksters, The Dead Boys. Standing at nearly seven-feet in his elevated stage shoes (six-foot-six in bare feet), Lux Interior was a menacing sight. But not impressing the club's owner Hilly Kristal, the group instead landed a weekly gig at a nearby, like-minded club, Max's Kansas City.

Teaming with producer Alex Chilton, The Cramps recorded their earliest tracks at the Sun Records studio in Memphis, and then garnered exposure through an opening slot on a Ramones tour. Soon after, Linna quit and was replaced by Clevelander Nick Knox, formerly of The Electric Eels.

Signed to I.R.S. Records and opening up for The Police on a British tour, The Cramps were poised for stardom. But instead, misfortune struck: Bryan Gregory quit and stole the group's van and equipment. And while battling their label over royalties, the group was unable to issue any recordings for the next two years

The Cramps' lineup would later include former Gun Club guitarist Kid Congo Powers and former Pagans guitarist (and cousin of Nick Knox) Ike Knox. Cultivating a strong following, The Cramps pumped out offbeat songs such as "Bikini Girls With Machine Guns" and "Ultra Twist."

The Cramps' 1989 album *Stay Sick!* was titled after one of Ghoulardi's on-air catchphrases ("stay sick, turn blue"), and their 1980 track "The Mad Daddy" was a nod to Pete Myers. (In the wake of Ghoulardi, one of his stage hands, Ron Sweed, created a similar, long-running character named the Ghoul. Originating from Cleveland, the Ghoul was syndicated in several other markets including Boston and Detroit.)

Eventually achieving a level of mainstream success, The Cramps performed two songs on a Halloween episode of *Beverly Hills 90210*. Also, Lux Interior would provide the voice for a character on the animated series, *SpongeBob SquarePants*.

*   *   *   *   *   *

Cleveland was not the only location in Ohio with a thriving punk scene. Cincinnati's contributions included punk acts such as Sluggo and The Ed Davis Band. The places to play and be seen were The Jockey Club and

Bogart's. Meanwhile, Columbus spawned punk groups such as Human Sufferage, Screaming Urge and The Jet Boys. And the best known punk act to emerge from the Toledo area was Necros. Popular in Toledo and nearby Detroit, the group recorded for Touch And Go Records.

Although a number of Northeastern Ohio bands had left for Los Angeles or New York to make their mark, the Cleveland punk scene persisted. The second wave of Cleveland punk bands would spawn The Starvation Army, The Floyd Band, The Offbeats and The Terrible Parade. The movement would later be chronicled in Brad Warner's 2007 documentary, *Cleveland's Screaming*.

Although punk rock continued to flourish in the clubs of Cleveland well into the 21st century, fewer of the city's acts managed to make a dent on the national scene. Some like underground Cleveland punkers This Moment In Black History and Death Of Samantha were known outside of the state boundaries. More notably, Death Of Samantha can boast that both Nirvana and The Smashing Pumpkins were at one time *their* opening acts. Fronted by singer-guitarist John Petkovic, Death Of Samantha would later evolve into a similar art/punk outfit called Cobra Verde. Petkovic later moonlighted as a *Cleveland Plain Dealer* columnist.

By the start of the 1980s, punk rock had given way to a commercially-accessible offshoot called new wave. Soon, the epicenter of new music moved from Cleveland, south to Akron.

CHAPTER 7
NEW WAVE AND THE AKRON SOUND

Shortly after punk reared its mohawked head in Cleveland, new-wave was emerging in nearby Akron. With the distinctions between the two genres not obviously apparent, bands from both camps performed at the same clubs and were paired on the same bills. While punk rock tended to be an aggressive, angst-motivated, guitar-driven genre, new wave music was more melodic and danceable, and usually employed synthesizers. And while punk rockers donned torn, dark jeans and leather, new wave artists favored bright shirts, skinny ties and checkered sneakers. The term "new wave" was coined by Seymour Stein, the head of Sire Records.

An industrial center, Akron is a city whose existence and growth were tied to advances in transportation. Constructed between 1825 and 1832, the Ohio-Erie Canal ran 308-miles from Portsmouth to Cleveland, with Akron the highest point along the route. These man-made canals helped distribute Akron-manufactured products such as agricultural reapers and Quaker Oats cereals. Then with the rise of the automobile industry in Cleveland and nearby Detroit, Akron was transformed into the Rubber Capital of the World, as virtually every major American tire-maker was based in the city. For decades, most of the city's residents worked for companies such as Goodyear, Goodrich, General, Firestone, Seiberling and Mohawk. Drawing workers from Southeastern Europe and all over the nation, the tire factories even lured a young and virile Clark Gable from the Appalachian hills of Southern Ohio.

In celebration of the ebony-colored compound which was used to manufacture tires, Akron held a formal gala called the Rubber Ball. The affair attracted the city's movers and shakers, who dressed in elaborate outfits made completely from rubber. Launched in the late-1930s and staged every year until the wartime rubber shortage forced an end to the event, the Rubber Ball was held in the aptly named "Rubber Room" nightclub, located in the since-demolished Portage Hotel. The hotel was also the site of the founding of the United Rubber Workers union in 1935. That same decade, dance-marathons were outlawed in the city after one competition continued for several weeks.

For a time, Akron was also considered the trucking capital of the world, home to firms such as Roadway and Yankee Lines. The city was also the one-time residence of Civil War-era abolitionist John Brown and the birthplace of Alcoholics Anonymous. Akron was also the center of the sports world for three events: from 1962 to 1998, Firestone Country Club hosted the World Series of Golf; attorney and broadcaster Eddie Elias founded the Professional Bowlers Association (PBA) and launched the Firestone Tournament of Champions, which ran from 1965 to 1993 (with General Tire as the sponsor in 1994); and after just one-year in Dayton, the Soap Box Derby made Akron its permanent home in 1935.

Akron prospered into the 1970s, at which time, big labor was unable to adapt. Overnight, the Rubber City lost most of its economic cornerstones including Firestone, General Tire and Goodrich. Ironically, this bleak environment gave rise to an upbeat, musical movement called new wave.

DEVO AND THE RISE OF NEW WAVE

Raised in the Akron area, Mark Mothersbaugh received a Mr. Potato Head for his 7th birthday, a toy which would later evolve into Devo's mutant "Spud Boy" character. In his teen years, Mothersbaugh attempted to launch a rock band. Creatively inclined, Mothersbaugh would later study art at Kent State University.

Remarkably, Devo was born from a violent incident. When four students were shot dead by Ohio national guardsmen, future Devo-members Mark Mothersbaugh and Jerry Casale were there to witness the abrupt deaths of two of their friends. Casale later recalled, "I would not have started the idea of Devo unless this had happened. It was just the defining moment. Until then, I might've left my hair long and been a hippie. When you start to see the real way everything works, and the insidious nature of power, corruption, injustice, brute force, you realize it's just all primate behavior."

The brainchild of Bob Lewis, Devo was formed specifically to perform at a 1973 event in Kent, the inaugural Creative Arts Festival. Though considered too mainstream for the outfit, former Joe Walsh bandmate Fred Weber was originally hired as the lead vocalist. The group also added Jerry Casale's brother, Bob, on guitar. Needing a name, the group initially chose Sextet Devo. A month later, Weber left the band.

Shortening their name to Devo, the group would not perform in public again until the following year's festival in 1974. While Jerry Casale assumed most of the vocal duties, Mark Mothersbaugh's brother Jim, an electronic whiz, joined on drums (but would leave two years later). Also joining at the time was another Mothersbaugh brother, Bob, on guitar. (To differentiate between Bob Mothersbaugh and Bob Casale, they took the stage names, Bob 1 and Bob 2.)

Meanwhile, after earning a pair of degrees from Kent State, Jerry Casale was hired as a part-time art instructor at the University of Akron. But he would lose his position after only one semester for showing his class some of Mark Mothersbaugh's unconventional artwork, which had offended a student.

During this period, members of Devo began devising a philosophy. The ideology behind Devo – short for de-evolution – was formulated from a series of eclectic sources: a strange nonscientific treatise on the evolution of human beings by Oscar Kiss Maerth which was titled *The Beginning Was The End*; an oddball religious pamphlet called *Jocko-Homo Heavenbound*; and a 1948 *Wonder Woman* comic book depicting a "deevolution" device, which was capable of reversing the evolutionary process.

Devo made their nightclub debut as the opening act for The Numbers Band at a downtown Kent nightspot. After building a studio behind a car wash, Devo would record sporadically. Assembling a 16-song demo tape, the group tried to use its contacts in the music industry. But an acquaintance from their days at Kent State, Joe Walsh, was unimpressed with the material.

Though polishing their songwriting, musicianship and stage act, Devo was usually met with confusion – if not outright hostility – by the public. Mark Mothersbaugh told author Simon Reynolds about this period: "We'd say, 'Here's another one by Foghat' and then play one of our tunes like 'Mongoloid.' Angry hippie factory workers charged the stage trying to stop us. Often we'd get paid to quit. Sometimes the police would be called." Hired as the opening act for a Cleveland radio station-sponsored Halloween party in 1975, Devo managed to offend nearly everyone in attendance and cleared several-hundred people from the auditorium before the headlining band had played a single note.

In 1976, Devo released a short 10-minute film, *In The Beginning Was The End: The Truth About De-Evolution*, which included the performances of two songs – a cover of "Secret Agent Man" and a quirky, autobiographical anthem, "Jocko Homo." Filmed at a number of Akron-area locales – a conference room at Kent State, the Goodyear World of Rubber museum and JB's tavern in Kent – the project would receive little attention at the time.

Then with two members leaving the group, Devo nearly disbanded. But with Mark Mothersbaugh assuming the lead vocal duties and Alan Myers joining on drums, Devo were poised for a breakthrough. Adopting a new stage look, members of Devo bought matching, yellow, industrial suits for four-dollars apiece from a local janitorial-supply manufacturer. As a final touch, the suits were accessorized with the word "DEVO" spelled out in black electrical tape.

Over a very short period, similar rock bands were sprouting all over town. Alan Myers' former bandmate, saxophonist Ralph Carney, would join the group Tin Huey. Founded by Harvey Gold in 1972 as a progressive rock/jazz outfit, Tin Huey also included Mark Price, Michael Aylward and Stuart Austin. Recording for a local label operated by musician Nick Nicholis, Clone Records, the group began garnering airplay on college radio. After adding bassist Chris Butler in 1978, Tin Huey were noticed by respected, New York City-based music critic, Robert Christgau. By year's end, the group was signed by music impresario Jerry Wexler to Warner Brothers Records.

Meanwhile, Tin Huey-member Chris Butler would have greater success with a side-project called The Waitresses. The inspiration for the group's biggest hit came from a cramped but noisy watering-hole in Akron's Highland Square district called the Bucket Shop where "girls danced on the bar" and "the floor was always sticky with spilled beer." For decades, Highland Square was a semi-gentrified neighborhood where musicians and students lived side-by-side with both professors and the urban poor. (Just three decades earlier, the Highland Square area was frequented by Alan Freed, who met his future wife at a dance school above a bar.) Devo biographers Jade Dellinger and David Giffels recalled that "Chris Butler, who had played with The Numbers Band and would soon be playing with Tin Huey, eventually wrote a song about the Bucket Shop girls who liked to flirt with all the boys. The song became the hit that propelled his later band, The Waitresses... 'I Know What Boys Like.'" Featuring the dry, sarcastic lead vocals of Patty Donahue, the song became a new wave standard. (Aside from Butler, The Waitresses included saxophonist Mars Williams, Television's Billy Ficca on drums and future B-52's member Tracy Wormworth on bass).

Tin Huey, Devo and a host of new wave bands honed the Akron sound at a tiny club called the Crypt. Located near the Goodyear factory complex on the city's east side, the beer-and-shot dive was co-owned by a Goodyear blue-collar laborer, Bill Carpenter. Struggling to keep the business afloat after a lengthy labor strike in 1976, Carpenter poured cheap draft beers for his co-workers.

But when members of a local hard-rock group, King Cobra, approached Carpenter about performing there, he offered them a remarkable deal – if they took over the lease payments and kept the bar open from morning to night, they could book any band they wanted. Taking on new duties as bartenders, King Cobra-members Ward Welch and Buzz Clic spent their days working in the basement-level establishment. Within months, King Cobra abandoned heavy metal and stepped to the forefront of the new wave / punk movement as The Rubber City Rebels. Wanting a more appropriate moniker, Welch took the stage name Rod Bent, and later, Rod Firestone. Then after the factory workers were finished drinking for the day, the bar became an incubator for Akron and Cleveland bands such as Pere Ubu, The Dead Boys, Devo and The Bizzaros.

One new wave act was formed by a pair of regulars at the Crypt, Sue Schmidt and Debbie Smith. (Schmidt and Smith were previously members of a 1960s, all-girl band at Akron's Firestone High School called The Poor Girls. Established long before pioneering, all-female rock bands such as Fanny and Joan Jett's early group The Runaways, The Poor Girls played their own instruments. The group had toured throughout Ohio, opening a number of times for Joe Walsh and later working with Peter Laughner.) Then following a Devo performance at the Crypt, Schmidt and Smith were introduced to drummer Rich Roberts. Formed in 1978 as Chi-Pig, the trio was named after a local barbecue restaurant. A similar group, Unit 5, was formed by a pair of record store employees; more polished than their contemporaries, the Tracy Thomas-fronted band was inspired by Devo.

In addition to the Crypt, new wave and punk music also thrived at a downtown Akron nightclub called the Bank. Nestled inside a former bank branch, on the ground floor of the crumbling Anthony Wayne Hotel, the Bank nightclub booked both local and national acts. (The club owner used the bank's steel vault to store bottles of liquor.)

Meanwhile, Devo decided to press 2,000 copies of the single, "Jocko Homo"/"Mongoloid," on their own Booji Boy label. Then winning the prize for best short film at the Ann Arbor Film Festival for their earlier project, Devo began garnering national attention. After impressing audiences at a pair of New York City clubs – CBGB's and Max's Kansas City – Devo was inundated with offers from major labels, including a deal involving David Bowie. Desperately wanting to sign the band to his Island Records roster, label chief Chris Blackwell flew to Akron in the middle of the century's worst snowstorm. Devo was also courted by Richard Branson of Virgin Records, who tried to convince the group to hire former Sex Pistols frontman Johnny Rotten.

Following a lawsuit, Devo was signed by Warner Brothers for U.S. distribution and Virgin for non-U.S. territories. Released in 1977, the group's debut album *Q: Are We Not Men? A: We Are Devo* was produced by Brian Eno. The cover featured an altered cartoon drawing of golfer Chi Chi Rodriguez, taken from the side of a golf ball package. Aside from their early single "Jocko Homo," the album was highlighted by a barely recognizable rendition of The Rolling Stones' classic "(I Can't Get No) Satisfaction." But because the song was so unlike the original version, it was considered a derivative musical piece, and as such, Devo had to secure permission to record the song from one of its composers, Mick Jagger. The song's video featured a contorting punk rocker from Los Angeles named Spazz Attack.

Meanwhile, Nick Nicholis kept his label, Clone Records, active and released the 1977 album *From Akron*, which featured one side by Nicholis' own band, The Bizarros, and the other side by The Rubber City Rebels. The son of a tire factory worker, Nicholis took the group's name from a Superman comic book. Formed by students at the University of Akron, The Bizarros were not performing the kind of mainstream rock their classmates were hearing on local commercial radio. After music critic Robert Christgau compared The Bizarros to avant-garde rockers The Velvet Underground (one of Nicholis' chief influences), the group signed with the Mercury subsidiary, Blank Records.

Meanwhile in 1978, the premier U.K. punk label, Stiff Records, issued *The Akron Compilation* – a collection of tracks by a number of Akron new wave acts. Assembled with the aid of local musician Liam Sternberg, the album featured a scratch-and-sniff, tire-scented sleeve. (Sternberg would later write the chart-topping Bangles' hit "Walk Like An Egyptian" and the theme for the Fox television series, *21 Jump Street*.) Also in 1978, the British rock magazine *Sounds* teamed with Stiff Records to launch a contest offering a trip to Akron, where the lucky winner would "tour a Firestone tire plant." More attention to the Akron sound came with a pair of multi-artist sampler albums issued by Clone Records, *Bowling Balls From Hell, Vols. 1 & 2*.

By 1978, The Rubber City Rebels had relocated to Los Angeles. The group's drummer Mike Hammer recalled in *Scene* magazine, "At our first gig in California, we came out being real punkers, really offending the crowd and doing a masterful job of putting everyone off. The first words out of our singer Rod Firestone's mouth were, 'We're the Rubber City Rebels from Akron, Ohio and we hate LA!' They took it real personally, at first, but we eventually made friends and met this guy who worked at Sire Records." Creating a buzz, the group headlined shows in Sunset Strip nightclubs, and shared bills with acts such as The Plimsouls and Dickies.

Four months later, The Rubber City Rebels were signed by Sire Records. But due to a series of unfortunate events – including their manager's insistence on recording in a Los Angeles studio – the group was dropped by the label before recording any material.

By year's end, The Rubber City Rebels splintered into two camps. Disheartened by the Los Angeles music scene, members Mike Hammer and Donnie Damage returned to Akron and formed the self-described "power-pop" group, Hammer Damage. Aside from performing original material, Hammer Damage also relied on an assortment of Rubber City Rebels songs. But after the departure of the group's singer-guitarist George Cabaniss in late-1979 for The Dead Boys, Hammer Damage endured a series of personnel changes before disbanding in 1982. During this time, Akron's new wave scene continued to spawn groups such as The Hi-Fis and The F-Models.

Meanwhile in Los Angeles, The Rubber City Rebels were befriended by members of an emerging new wave band, The Knack. With the aid of The Knack's vocalist Doug Fieger, the Akron group was signed to Capitol Records. In 1980, The Rubber City Rebels issued a self-titled album, which was produced by Fieger. But while The Knack's explosive, debut disc would sell six-million copies, The Rebels' album was ignored.

Similarly, Tin Huey also failed to arouse widespread interest. Following the poor sales of 1979's *Contents Dislodged During Shipment*, Warner Brothers renegotiated Tin Huey's contract, paying the band $50,000 to *not* record a scheduled second album. The group disbanded later that year, and in 1982, reformed without Chris Butler. Tin Huey member Ralph Carney would later work with The B-52's, before joining Tom Waits' band.

Meanwhile, Devo had finally achieved some notoriety. As the *Saturday Night Live* musical guests on October 14, 1978, the group unleashed its herky-jerky, robotic version of "(I Can't Get No) Satisfaction." While most viewers were unnerved by the irreverent rendition of the rock standard, hipsters were mesmerized. And while American audiences were slow to embrace the group, European audiences – which were raised on the electronic dance music of Kraftwerk – welcomed the Spud Boys from Akron.

Around this time, Devo came to the attention of rock veteran Neil Young, who wanted the group to appear in his avant-garde art film, *Human Highway*. Flown to California, Devo performed several songs – most notably, a deconstructed version of Young's "Hey Hey My My" – and appeared in various roles throughout the film. Though production began in 1978, the film would not be completed until 1982. (Devo would also appear in Young's 1979 performance film, *Rust Never Sleeps*.)

With the release in 1980 of the album *Freedom Of Choice*, Devo finally broke into the pop market. The project was highlighted by a straightforward, new-wave ditty called "Whip It." The song was based on an expression the Mothersbaugh brothers frequently heard at home during their childhood. Adopting a new look, the members of Devo donned gray, vinyl suits and wore inverted, red "flower pot" hats that were dubbed "energy domes." For their followup album *The New Traditionalists*, Devo dropped the flower pots for black, plastic, pompadour wigs. Although the new wave genre was burgeoning in the early-1980s thanks to MTV, Devo's followup albums – *Oh, No! It's Devo* and *Shout* – were far less successful. As a result, the group was subsequently dropped by Warner Brothers. With Alan Myers leaving the band, Devo took a two-year respite. Though reforming in 1987, Devo was met with indifference by radio.

After disbanding again in 1991, Devo would reunite for occasional tours. Mark Mothersbaugh later emerged as a thriving jack-of-all-trades, launching a Los Angeles-based production company called Mutato Muzika. A much in-demand session artist, he also provided the musical scores for films such as *Herbie: Fully Loaded*, *Rushmore* and *Lords Of Dogtown*, and supplied the music for dozens of television programs, beginning with the Paul Reubens, Saturday-morning, children's program, *Pee-Wee's Play House*. Expanding into commercial advertising, Mothersbaugh worked with Nike, McDonald's and Coca-Cola.

In 2006, Disney introduced Devo 2.0 – a new version of the band. More than 1,000 children auditioned to join what Gerald Casale described as the "next generation spud." Dressed in modified Devo costumes, the five youths recorded a 12-track CD and accompanying DVD. While Devo has not performed in their hometown since 1979, the youthful offshoot would play one of their first shows in Akron. In 2008, a reunited Devo belatedly returned to Akron for a fundraising concert.

Meanwhile, The Waitresses' 1981 yuletide track "Christmas Wrapping" belatedly became a Christmas favorite, emerging as a radio staple, two-decades after its release. The group's original lead singer, Patty Donahue, passed away in 1996.

And as for Akron's two pioneering new wave clubs, the Crypt was forced to shutter after the bar's owner sold the liquor license to a national chain restaurant for $14,000. The site was later bulldozed and paved over by a car dealership. The Bank nightclub suffered a similar fate and was demolished to make way for a minor-league baseball stadium. (The Bank nightclub was the setting of the 2008 novel *Punk Rock And Trailer Parks* by one-name author Derf.)

CHRISSIE HYNDE & THE PRETENDERS

In the mid-1960s, future Devo-member Mark Mothersbaugh briefly dated a shy, cross-town, dark-haired beauty with musical aspirations. Her name was Chrissie Hynde, and once she overcame her shyness, she became a rock lioness. Pouting, menacing and alluring, Hynde emerged as one of the most vital female bandleaders in all of rock history. Although Hynde was born and raised in Akron, she failed to ignite her musical career until reaching England.

Attending Firestone High School on Akron's west side, Chrissie Hynde was a classmate of the budding all-female rock quartet, The Poor Girls. At age 17, Hynde formed her first band – the shortlived Sat.Sun.Mat. – which also included Mark Mothersbaugh.

Beginning her studies at nearby Kent State University in the fall of 1968, Hynde pursued a degree in art for three years and briefly worked as a graphic designer. During this period, Hynde also spent a great deal of time hanging out in her brother Terry's downtown Kent apartment, where he often practiced with his group, The Numbers Band.

Heading for London in 1972, Hynde dated notorious rock journalist Nick Kent of *New Musical Express*. Aided by Kent, Hynde published some record reviews in the magazine. During this period, Hynde also worked as a clothing store clerk and as a model at St. Martin's School of Art.

Eventually, Hynde's parents flew to London and pleaded with their daughter to return home and finish her degree, and even tried to bribe her with a car. After briefly teaming with session player Chris Spedding in a Paris rock band called The Frenchies, she became disenchanted with the music industry and returned to Akron in 1975.

But while working as a cocktail waitress in a trendy disco in Cleveland called the Last Moving Picture Show, Hynde was deluged with music she despised. Then briefly fronting a Cleveland, cover band called Jack Rabbit, Hynde wore rubber skirts and blouses adorned with political messages.

Regaining her confidence, Hynde soon returned to London. There she launched various bands beginning with The Loveboys, featuring Richard Hell and Sylvain Sylvain. Also going nowhere was a group with future Clash member Mick Jones called Big Girls' Underwear. Hynde subsequently teamed with the future members of The Damned to form Masters Of The Backside.

Hynde told *Uncut* magazine, "I'd been in England five years and thought I was too old to be in a band, but I finally met the right guys... They were these rural thugs from Hereford. Really, they were like the guys in *Straw Dogs*. That was the beauty of The Pretenders. We had this image of being a nice pop band, but we were really pretty hardcore."

By 1978, Hynde had formed The Pretenders with guitarist James Honeyman-Scott, bassist Pete Farndon and drummer Martin Chambers. Featuring Hynde on guitar and lead vocals, the group scored a pair of U.K.

hits in 1979 – "Kid" and a cover of The Kinks' "Stop Your Sobbing."

Releasing a self-titled debut-album in 1980, The Pretenders would reach the U.S. top-10 with the lead-off single, "Brass In Pocket." But tragedy would soon strike the group with the drug-related deaths of Honeyman-Scott in 1982 and Farndon in 1983.

Bouncing back, The Pretenders thrived during the 1980s. The group's third album, *Learning To Crawl*, spawned the hits, "Middle Of The Road," "Back On The Chain Gang," and the Christmas classic, "2000 Miles." Another track from the album – "My City Was Gone" – was intended as a statement against the politicians who were destroying Hynde's hometown. The opening riff of the song was appropriated by talk show host Rush Limbaugh as the theme of his syndicated radio program.

The group's 1986 release, *Get Close*, was highlighted by "Don't Get Me Wrong" and a touching tribute to Hynde's second child, "Hymn To Her." Hynde had two daughters, the first with Kinks frontman Ray Davies in the early-1980s. Married to Jim Kerr of Simple Minds, Hynde had her second daughter; the marriage ended after five years.

Subsequent albums – *Packed*, *Last Of The Independents* and *Viva El Amor!* – were all fine efforts but only moderate sellers. In 1985, Hynde teamed with reggae band UB40 for a hit cover of Sonny & Cher's "I Got You Babe." Three years later, another collaboration between the two acts, "Breakfast In Bed," reached the U.K. top-10.

Yearning for a connection to her hometown, Chrissie Hynde rented a small apartment and opened a vegetarian restaurant in 2007. Hynde told *Billboard* magazine: "I wasn't there to stop the bulldozers. I think Akronites were pissed off at me for criticizing what had happened to Akron. But I'm going back. I want to establish the Jim Jarmusch Theater in Akron. I want the city to have an art house theater. I'm telling friends, 'Don't buy a place in Woodstock. Buy a place in Akron where you can get a great big wooden house for not a lot of money.' Flights to Akron are cheap. I have no sense of patriotism, but I do have a sense of community. And there is something geographically amazing there. Also, as you get older, your relationship with your hometown changes."

Although Chrissie Hynde would reach great musical heights, her brother's group endured a different fate. The Numbers Band (15-60-75) were launched in 1970 by brothers Bob and Jack Kidney during the wake of the Kent State shootings. Initially a blues outfit, The Numbers Band began infusing elements of rock, jazz and R&B, into their music, after adding a number of new members such as saxophonist Terry Hynde (Chrissie's older brother), bassist Chris Butler and drummer Jerry Casale. During a 1978 performance at Kent's JB's tavern, The Numbers Band were unable to attract the interest of Atlantic Records executive Jerry Wexler, who had made the journey to Ohio to sign Tin Huey, which were playing in the club's main room.

When The Pretenders made their Northeastern Ohio debut in 1980, Terry

Hynde joined his sister's group for an encore of "Stop Your Sobbing." In the end, The Numbers Band had become a breeding ground for talent – Chris Butler would join Tin Huey and form The Waitresses, while Jerry Casale would co-found Devo.

OTHER NEW WAVE ACTS

Another Akron-area new wave singer, Rachel Sweet, was a child prodigy who began singing at age five. By age nine, she opened up for pop legend Frankie Valli. At 16, she was signed by Britain's premiere punk label, Stiff Records. With her pristine delivery, Sweet drew critical praise for her first two albums, *Fool Around* and *Protect The Innocent*. Though best known for a quirky track about her sweetheart, "Tonight Ricky," Sweet would reach the top-40 with "Everlasting Love," an unlikely duet hit with heart-throb Rex Smith.

Sweet later composed and recorded material for a pair of offbeat, John Waters films, *Hairspray* and *Cry-Baby*. She later turned to acting and voice-over work. Having dropped out of Firestone High School, she used her music industry experience to earn admission to Columbia University.

Meanwhile, Sweet's Akron-born cousin was the leader of the punk-flavored act, Jane Aire & The Belvederes. Aided by producer Liam Sternberg – who had worked with both Rachel Sweet and British singer Kirsty MacColl – Jane Aire (born Jane Ashley) supplied a pair of tracks for *The Akron Compilation*, before signing with Virgin Records. Though moderately successful across Europe, Jane Aire was relatively unknown in her native country. Married for a time to Boomtown Rats bassist Pete Briquette, Aire later returned to Akron.

One of the more creative new wave acts of the period, Human Switchboard was formed in Kent. Releasing several records beginning with a 1976 EP produced by Pere Ubu's David Thomas, the group was signed by I.R.S. Records in 1980. Issued on the label's Faulty Products subsidiary, the group's only full-length studio album, *Who's Landing In My Hangar?*, went generally unnoticed. More popular on the East Coast than in Ohio, Human Switchboard relocated to New York City in 1981. With the group disbanding in 1982, lead singer-guitarist Robert Pfeifer was hired as an A&R representative by Epic Records. After briefly pursuing a solo career, he later headed the Disney-owned label, Hollywood Records.

Meanwhile down in Columbus, Ronald Koal was a charismatic and consummate showman whose stage act featured numerous wardrobe changes. As the leader of Ronald Koal And The Trillionaires, the deep-voiced singer issued a handful of records with his constantly evolving, backing band. Though incredibly talented and deserving of fame, Koal barely made a name for himself outside of Ohio.

The roots of the Boston-based new wave band, The Cars, reach back to Ohio. Ben Orr (born Benjamin Orzechowski) was a member of The Grasshoppers, the house band of the syndicated Cleveland-based television program, *Upbeat!* Orr had joined the band in 1964 as the replacement for departing lead singer-guitarist, Dante Rossi.

During the 1960s, The Grasshoppers were stars around Cleveland, scoring a pair of local hits with "Mod Socks" and "Pink Champagne (And Red Roses)." But with the Vietnam War raging, the group was forced to disband when two of its members were drafted. After joining two more local groups, Orr formed a series of bands with another Clevelander, Ric Ocasek (born Richard Otcasek). A native of Baltimore, Ocasek had moved to suburban Cleveland at age 16, after his father was hired by NASA's Lewis Research Center. Before teaming with Orr, Ocasek performed in the folk clubs of the city's artist community in the Coventry district.

After stints in Cleveland, Columbus and New York, Orr and Ocasek settled near Boston. There, they would form a folk group with Greg Hawkes called Milkwood. Adding two more members, the group evolved into the pioneering new-wave act, The Cars. Beginning with the 1978 hit "Just What I Needed" (which borrowed the opening riff of "Yummy Yummy Yummy" by The Ohio Express), The Cars churned out a string of synthesizer-heavy, usually upbeat hits over the next decade. Orr provided a rare, lead vocal on the group's highest-charting single, "Drive." Later pursuing a solo career, Orr scored a hit with "Stay The Night."

CHAPTER 8
HARD ROCK AND HEAVY METAL

Dotted by steel, tire and automobile factories, Ohio is a blue-collar state with a sizable hard rock and heavy metal fanbase. Long before Lollapalooza and Ozzfest, Cleveland hosted the World Series of Rock, a series of multi-act, musical spectaculars in the 1970s. Staged at the since-demolished Cleveland Municipal Stadium, these daylong events featured rock stalwarts such as The Rolling Stones, Pink Floyd, Ted Nugent, ELO and Foreigner. But despite Ohio's appreciation of classic, guitar-oriented rock, relatively few Buckeye acts achieved national acclaim.

TIM "RIPPER" OWENS & JUDAS PRIEST
One of the most remarkable stories in the history of rock and roll took place in Akron. As one of the thousands of bands in the nation making a living as a tribute act, British Steel was belting out cover versions of Judas Priest hits such as "You've Got Another Thing Comin'" and "Living After Midnight."

A disciple of the group since age 16 when his older brother played Judas Priest's 1982 album *Screaming For Vengeance* on their home stereo, Tim Owens began dressing like the group's leader singer, Rob Halford, and donned leather vests and studded bracelets. When Owens began performing in a series of local metal bands, he even followed Halford's example of riding a Harley-Davidson onstage.

As a member of a local act called Winters Bane, Owens recorded an album which sold 8,000 copies overseas but was never released domestically. Then wanting to earn better money, the group concocted a plan to form its own opening act – a Judas Priest cover band called British Steel. Although fans quickly discovered the ruse, the concept was well-received.

Then in a spectacular chain of events, British Steel was filmed at Sherlock's Park Place nightclub in Erie, Pennsylvania, by a member of the audience – Christa Lentine, the girlfriend of Judas Priest drummer Scott Travis. In February 1996, Lentine gave the jumpy, amateur videotape to Travis, who was desperate to find a replacement singer. (After quitting the group in 1992 to pursue a solo career, Rob Halford formed the metal act Fight, which included former Toledo residents Jay Jay and Brian Tilse.)

Determined to continue Judas Priest, the remaining members held auditions. But upon viewing Lentine's tape, Owens was invited to a tryout in Wales. Then as *The New York Times* blustered: "In an extraordinarily improbable variant of the all-American success stories – a hybrid of Horatio Alger's rewarded hard work and Walter Mitty's fulfilled fantasy – Owens had risen from devotee to icon, from metal-head to medal-god.... It is as if a sandlot baseball player not only got a chance to play in the majors but got to be Cal Ripken Jr. A young man whose life for a decade had revolved around a particular persona had been given license to assume that identity."

The revived Judas Priest was signed to CMC International Records, a division of BMG. Generally accepted by the group's fans, Owens fronted Judas Priest on two albums, *Jugulator* and *Demolition*. But even though he was the visual epicenter of the group, Owens never felt he was on equal standing with his bandmates.

Sounding like a tale only Hollywood could invent, Tim "Ripper" Owens' story hit the big screen. Based on a 1997 *New York Times* article, the feature film *Rock Star* took a number of liberties with the truth. A semi-fictional account which starred Mark Walhberg, the film was not well received by Owens or the other members of Judas Priest. Owens told *The Cleveland Plain Dealer*, "They made it seem like *Spinal Tap*. That's not what me or Judas Priest were all about. It was hard work. When I joined, they had been broken up for about five years. The band had lost its momentum, and it was hard to make up for lost time."

Then just days after Owens had a discussion with his wife about leaving Judas Priest, he received an e-mail message in July 2003, informing him of his ouster. The move was necessitated by Rob Halford's decision to rejoin the group. Judas Priest guitarist Glenn Tipton told *Classic Rock* magazine, "We finished with 'Ripper' on a friendly note and we all think the world of him. Even Rob and Ripper got on well when they met; there were no fist-fights or anything."

After leaving Judas Priest, Owens declared he no longer wanted "to be called 'Ripper,' the nickname the band gave him." Returning to his home in the Kenmore section of Akron, Owens fronted the heavy metal acts, Iced Earth and Beyond Fear, and toured with headliners such as Anthrax.

WARRANT

Headed by Jani Lane (born John Kennedy Oswald), the glam-metal band Warrant scored several hits beginning in the late-1980s. Raised in the Akron area, Lane took up the drums in his youth. Under the stage name Mitch Dynamite, he joined a series of bar bands during his teenage years. After graduating from high school in 1982, he formed his own group, Cyren. Relocating to Florida, he joined a band called Dorian Gray. During this period, he adopted the stage name, Jani Lane.

Then in 1985, Lane and drummer Steven Sweet left Florida and headed for Los Angeles. Lane had previously played in an Akron-area band with Sweet's older brother, David. Initially joining a punk/metal band called Plain Jane, Lane and Sweet attracted the attention of guitarist Erik Turner, who had formed Warrant in 1984. Soon after, Lane and Sweet were invited to join Turner's band. Then after providing a track for the soundtrack of *Bill & Ted's Excellent Adventure*, Warrant was signed by Columbia Records.

Emerging as the group's lead vocalist and chief songwriter, Lane penned all of Warrants' hits. Embraced by MTV, the group achieved instant fame with the release of its debut album, *Dirty Rotten Filthy Stinking Rich*. The project spawned the hits, "Down Boys," "Sometimes She Cries," and the million-selling power ballad, "Heaven."

On a roll, the group followed with another hit album in 1990. Lane told his hometown newspaper, "I wanted the title of that record to be 'Uncle Tom's Cabin,' which was a song I was really proud of at the time. But the label told me they needed me to write a song like Aerosmith's 'Love In An Elevator,' which did not interest me at all. But I did what they asked. I went home and wrote the song 'Cherry Pie' in one night. And somehow that became the title of the album, the first single, and the entire image of the band. Now, granted – they were right. We sold a million records in a month. But when the backlash eventually came, it wasn't against the guys at Columbia who were making those decisions. It was against Warrant." The album also spawned the hits "I Saw Red," and featuring Jani Lane's brother, Eric, on acoustic guitar, "Uncle Tom's Cabin." In 1991, Lane would marry one of the models who appeared in the video for "Cherry Pie," Bobbie Brown. The marriage ended after two years.

After the release of the more adventurous effort, *Dog Eat Dog*, Lane quit the band in 1992. But upon his return to the group in 1994, hair metal had been supplanted by grunge, and as a result, Warrant had difficulty garnering radio airplay.

In 2004, Lane left Warrant to pursue a solo career. He was aided on his debut album by guitarist Billy Morris, a fellow Ohio-native who had joined Warrant four years earlier. Morris had also worked with Kidd Wicked, Spoyld and former Mr. Big guitarist Paul Gilbert. In 2004, Lane teamed with former Quiet Riot leader Kevin DuBrow in the Bad Boys of Metal Tour.

THE GODZ

The hypnotic rock anthem "Gotta Keep A-Runnin'" kept The Godz on the road for many years. Fronted by guitarist-singer Eric Moore, the group experienced a huge turnover of personnel through its various incarnations. Moore had formed The Godz after passing through a series of 1970s Buckeye bands – Tree, Mixed Water (featuring Jamie Lyons of The Music Explosion), The Capital City Rockets and Sky King.

Signed to Casablanca Records in 1977, The Godz found themselves booked as the opening act for labelmates, Kiss. Though savaged by critics, The Godz's self-titled, debut album was highlighted by a hard-rocking, seven-and-a-half-minute homage to hedonism, "Gotta Keep A Runnin'." After the group disbanded, Moore spent a brief period behind bars. Upon his release, he fronted a hard-rock outfit called Black Leather Touch, which evolved into The Eric Moore Band. Then after a couple years, Moore formed a new version of The Godz.

Moore later joined Freddie Salem And The Wildcats, a group led by a former member of the Southern-rock act, The Outlaws. After experiencing several personnel changes, the band morphed into a new version of The

Godz. But just as the group was enjoying some international success with their 1985 album, *I'll Keep You Rockin'*, Salem left to rejoin The Outlaws.

A star in his own right, Freddie Salem began his professional career in the pioneering, black-hippie outfit, The Chamber Brothers, whose biggest hit came with "Time Has Come Today." Then in 1977, he joined The Outlaws as the replacement for guitarist Henry Paul. Salem appeared on the group's final chart hit, a frenetic cover version of the pop standard, "(Ghost) Riders In The Sky." Later turning to production work, Salem also recorded a solo album. Operating a series of nightclubs, Salem later headed his own group, The Gunslingers.

MUSHROOMHEAD

Started as a side-project in 1993 by members of various Cleveland heavy-metal bands – including Hatrix, State Of Conviction, Terror and Unified Culture – Mushroomhead became a surprise success. Not wanting to draw attention away from their other bands, the group's eight members adopted new stage names and wore frightening costumes and masks. One of the group's two lead vocalists, J. Mann, sported a wedding dress, football vest and crimson-colored devil mask. Mann's blunt, deep-voiced chants were complimented by Jeffrey Nothing's melodic but menacing vocals. Influenced by Nine Inch Nails, the group layered crunching guitars over brooding, atmospheric keyboards.

After Mushroomhead had cultivated a strong local following, the various members quit their parent bands. Releasing a pair of self-produced CDs in the mid-1990s, the theatrical group enjoyed healthy sales around Northeastern Ohio.

After rejecting overtures from several record labels because it would mean a cut in merchandising revenues, Mushroomhead was shocked to discover that one of these prospective labels, Roadrunner Records, had released an album by an Iowa rock act, Slipknot, which adopted a suspiciously-similar stage act. In response, Mushroomhead dropped its jumpsuits and latex masks for more gruesome, horror-film-style masks with twisted "X" logos above the eyes. (When Slipknot made their first Cleveland appearance in 1999, the group was pelted by the audience with batteries and had to retreat from the stage.) Ironically, when Mushroomhead finally achieved national acclaim, the band was accused of copying Slipknot.

In 2000, Mushroomhead signed with Eclipse Records, which released the album *XX*, a compilation of tracks from the group's four self-issued albums. The group soon jumped to Universal Records, which issued an updated version of *XX*. By 2003, the group released *XIII*, a moderate seller which was highlighted by the track, "Sun Doesn't Rise." After the completion of a world tour, vocalist J. Mann (a.k.a. Jason Popson) left the band in August 2004, and was replaced by former 3quartersdead frontman, Waylon. In 2005, Mushroomhead signed with Megaforce Records.

Mushroomhead later spawned a pair of side projects, metal act 216, which was fronted by J. Mann, and a party-rock band called Tenafly Viper.

CHIMAIRA
Named after a lion-headed monster in Greek mythology, Cleveland-based Chimaira was at the forefront of American heavy-metal during the first decade of the 21st century. Headed by singer Mark Hunter, the melodic thrash band formed in 1998. Also the group's chief songwriter, Hunter based many of his lyrical themes on horror flicks such as *The Shining*.

Hunter told *The Akron Beacon Journal*, "I take things very personally. Some of the things other people might just blow off, I hold inside. I used to be a guy who never wanted to leave the house, and I was angry all the time. But by listening to bands like Alice in Chains, I found other people who felt the way I did. That's what I want to offer our audience. I'm a sensitive guy. I still cry when I watch the movie *E.T.* But I can turn that sensitivity into hatred really fast when I'm on stage."

Avoiding musical trends, Chimaira built a fanbase by churning out solid, thrash-based metal in the tradition of bands like Slayer and Pantera. Chimaira's debut EP, *This Present Darkness*, was issued in 2000 by East Coast Empire Records. After experiencing a number of personnel changes, the group was signed by Roadrunner Records.

Garnering national exposure on the Ozzfest tour in 2003, Chimaira reached the charts with their second album, *The Impossibility of Reason*. Their 2005 followup album, *Chimaira*, fared even better, and was highlighted by the tracks "Nothing Remains" and "Save Ourselves."

Parting with Roadrunner Records in 2006 over the label's inadequate promotion of the group, Chimaira instead entered into relationships with two labels to distribute the group's self-produced albums. The successful strategy resulted in Chimaira's fourth album, *Resurrection*, reaching the *Billboard* top-20 in 2007.

THEY SERVED TOO
More often than not, Ohio metal musicians have joined established, out-of-state acts. Formerly a member of a popular Cleveland band called Beau Coup, drummer Eric Singer (born Eric Messinger) of Euclid left for California in 1983 and joined the rock group, Kiss. An off-and-on member of the theatrical, fire-spitting, hard-rock outfit, Singer first worked with the band from 1991 to 1996. Singer also collaborated with Black Sabbath and shock rocker Alice Cooper.

Meanwhile, Guns N' Roses featured a pair of Buckeye natives, though not at the same time. Cleveland guitarist Gilby Clarke joined in 1991 as the replacement for Izzy Stradlin, and stayed for three years. Clarke told *Scene* magazine that he had only one week to learn the group's songs before going on tour, and was told by bandmate Slash: "Alright, well here's the deal. We're leaving next week. We play our first show in Boston at Boston Gardens, and you have to learn all 50 songs. And I ain't showing them to you.

If you wanna learn them, here's the records." Clarke appeared on only one studio album – a collection of cover songs *The Spaghetti Incident* – which was highlighted by an unlikely pop hit, a cover of the doo-wop standard "Since I Don't Have You," and an Ohio-rooted track originally recorded by The Dead Boys, "Ain't It Fun."

Fired by Axl Rose in 1994, supposedly because he was not contributing as a songwriter, Clarke would enjoy a successful solo career. He later joined the cast of the CBS music reality series, *Rock Star: Supernova*, which teamed an unknown lead singer with an all-star band featuring Clarke, Tommy Lee and Jason Newstead. Another Clevelander, Steven Adler was Guns N' Roses' drummer during their early years from 1985-1990. Moving to California as a teenager, Adler attended school with future bandmate, Slash. As the group's best known drummer, Adler appeared on the group's first two full-length albums, the smash debut *Appetite For Destruction* and a live project *G N' R Lies*.

Another Ohio native found fame only after leaving the state. Born and raised in Ravenna, where he lived with an older sister, Maynard James Keenan moved to Michigan after finishing 10th grade. Then after graduating from high school, he joined the army and attended the Military Academy at West Point. Quitting the Academy to study art, he enrolled at Kendall College of Art and Design in Michigan.

Drawn to the music of Kiss, Aerosmith and AC/DC, during his teen years in Ohio, Keenan formed the metal band Tool in 1989. An intense but melodic outfit, Tool released their debut, million-selling EP, *Opiate*, in 1992. By 1999, Keenan teamed with guitarist Billy Howerdel to launch a side project, the alternative-rock act, A Perfect Circle. As a means of differentiating between the two bands, the balding Keenan wore a wig when he performed with A Perfect Circle.

Neo-glam rockers Cherry Monroe formed in Youngstown in 2004. Fronted by singer-songwriter Matt Toka, the group signed with Universal Records and earned airplay with the track, "Satellites." Toka left the band in 2006 due to "creative differences."

A pair of Cleveland metal acts, Shok Paris and Neil Zaza, garnered national attention. Initially signed to the locally-based label Auburn Records, Shok Paris would later record a pair of albums for I.R.S. Records. With their videos airing on MTV, Shok Paris toured with the band, Lizzie Borden. And as the namesake of the band Zaza, guitarist Neil Zaza was renowned for his classically-rooted, melodic style. Later launching a solo career, he worked with legendary guitarist Joe Satriani and the 60-piece Cleveland Rock Orchestra.

Meanwhile, Cincinnati's Fireball Ministry was formed in the late-1990s by vocalist-guitarist James A. Rota II and guitarist Emily J. Burton. Settling in Los Angeles, the heavy metal act added Nick Raskulinecz and released the debut disc, *F.M.E.P.* The followup album, *The Second Great Awakening*, was highlighted by the tracks "Flatline" and "King." With their music included in various compilations and video games, Fireball Ministry toured with a series of notable metal acts including Disturbed, Dio and Uriah Heep.

CHAPTER 9
ALTERNATIVE ROCK: 1980s AND BEYOND

Evolving from punk and new wave, the terms "modern rock" and "alternative rock" were used as catch-all labels to describe a number of emerging musical styles in the late-1980s – grunge, techno, electronica, goth and Britpop. Initially ignored by mainstream radio, the genre was embraced by college hipsters and the counterculture crowd. Then when *Billboard* magazine quietly introduced a 30-position "Modern Rock Tracks" chart on September 10, 1988, the music industry was forced to acknowledge the emerging movement. In Ohio, there were three distinct, alternative-rock scenes: Dayton, Columbus, and the Akron-Canton-Cleveland region.

THE AKRON-CANTON-CLEVELAND SCENE
With its past history of spawning punk and new wave, the northeastern corner of the state was a fertile breading ground for alternative rock. Three dark-styled rock acts emerged from the region: Marilyn Manson, Nine Inch Nails and Filter. Although Mushroomhead could easily be described as an alternative rock act, the group's music was more rooted in heavy metal.

NINE INCH NAILS
The brainchild of the morose, dark-maned Trent Reznor, Cleveland-based, industrial-rock act Nine Inch Nails was a favorite among both fans and critics. Reznor recalled in *The Cleveland Plain Dealer*: "I spent a lot of time in Cleveland, thinking, formulating, banging my head against the wall. The music scene there was healthy when I was around."

Raised by his grandparents just across the state line in Mercer, Pennsylvania, Reznor studied classical piano but was reared on new wave music, and was a fan of Akron's Devo. After begging his family to buy him a Moog synthesizer, he was thrilled to be able to play one of his favorite songs, "Just What I Needed" by The Cars. Joining a series of rock bands, including new-wave outfits such as Option Thirty and The Urge, Reznor began toying with music composition. Dying his hair red and studying computer engineering for a year at nearby Allegheny College, Reznor would later utilize his computer skills in the recording studio.

With one of Reznor's bands frequently performing in nearby Cleveland, he moved to the city in 1984. Hired by a music instrument shop, Reznor was intrigued with the store's synthesizers and sequencers. Joining a series of local bands, Reznor flirted with hard rock in the band The Innocent, and was hired in time to appear on the cover (but not on the sessions) of their locally-issued album, *Living On The Streets*. Reznor subsequently joined Slam Bam Boo, Lucky Pierre, and a synth-rock act, The Exotic Birds, which also included his roommate from Mercer, Chris Vrenna. (The latter group was formed by percussionist Andy Kubiszewski, who later joined Stabbing Westward.)

But drawn to the more moody and complex, industrial-rock of Ministry and Skinny Puppy, Trent Reznor further immersed himself in electronic music. Quitting The Exotic Birds at age 23, a frustrated Reznor was determined to make it big. Driven to record his own material, Reznor entered into an agreement with the operators of a local studio, Right Track – he took on janitorial duties in exchange for studio time. Reznor told *Scene* magazine, "[Studio owner Bart Koster] said, 'If you want to come at night and mess around, go ahead.' So I pretty much taught myself engineering for what I needed to know, anything to do with computers.... I just gradually started doing some demos, and I gradually perfected them into something that was cohesive, that had a direction to it and that I felt strongly about." Unable to persuade fellow musicians to join him at the overnight sessions, Reznor was forced to play all of the instruments himself. But after completing some demos, he was angered when local club deejays refused to even listen to his music.

After signing with indie label TVT, Trent Reznor formed a band (which included Chris Vrenna) to recreate on stage what he had single-handedly created in the studio. Methodically recorded with four different producers, the debut Nine Inch Nails album *Pretty Hate Machine* was an instant smash with its breakout hit, "Head Like A Hole."

But experiencing problems with his record label, Reznor channeled his anger into his next project, the EP *Broken*. Recorded on the sly for fear that TVT would confiscate the tracks, the disc was issued by Interscope Records, with TVT receiving a portion of the profits. A track from the album, "Wish," earned a Grammy – oddly enough, for Best Metal Performance.

Leaving Cleveland, Reznor settled in Los Angeles, where he rented an infamous house in Bel Air, where Sharon Tate and four of her friends were slaughtered by the followers of Cincinnati-born cult leader, Charles Manson. Reznor later claimed he had no prior knowledge of the home's history. Constructing a home studio, he would begin work on *The Downward Spiral*.

Meanwhile, Reznor would start his own label, Nothing Records. The first act signed by Reznor was a macabre shock-rocker and fellow Ohioan, Marilyn Manson. Not surprisingly, some of the tracks on Manson's debut album, *Portrait Of An American Family*, were recorded at Reznor's home studio. (Other artists on Reznor's Nothing label included Coil, Meat Beat Manifesto, Pig, Pop Will Eat Itself and former Judas Priest frontman Rob Halford.)

With the owners of the Bel Air house demolishing the structure in 1994, Reznor relocated to New Orleans and constructed a state-of-the-art studio in a former funeral parlor. Wanting a memento from his Los Angeles home, Reznor took the blood-stained, front door.

Belatedly issued in 1994, *The Downward Spiral* was a smash hit, and was highlighted by the angry, churning track, "Closer." Also on the album was an introspective song about drug use, "Hurt," which was later reinterpreted by a dying Johnny Cash. A pair of followup Nine Inch Nails releases – *The Fragile* and *With Teeth* – were less enthusiastically received.

In 2004, Reznor successfully sued his former manager John Malm Jr. over breach of contract and fiduciary duty, and was awarded nearly $3 million. Around the same time, Reznor shuttered Nothing Records. The following year, Reznor sold his New Orleans home just months before the city was struck by Hurricane Katrina. But unfortunately, his recording studio took the brunt of the killer storm and was severely damaged.

When Trent Reznor returned to Northeast Ohio for a triumphal performance at Blossom Music Center in 2006, he told the audience: "Thank you Cleveland – this is where it all began."

MARILYN MANSON

When *The Canton Repository* asked its readers in 2006 to submit suggestions for future Football Hall of Fame festivities, the newspaper's entertainment writer had to admit, "I don't know if Canton is ready for a Marilyn Manson homecoming show." Former *Akron Beacon Journal* music critic Chuck Klosterman, who later joined the staff of *Spin* magazine, recalled how "people living in Canton did not particularly dig their native son... Whenever I'd write stories in the local newspaper about Mr. Manson walking around on 70-foot stilts and smoking human bones, readers from Canton would inevitably call me at the office and say, 'Why must you besmirch Canton's reputation by wasting ink on this transvestite hooligan? Our fine community has many other things to offer, such as the Pro Football Hall of Fame.'"

A misfit who rebelled against religion while attending a Christian school in Canton, Marilyn Manson (born Brian Warner) pulled a series of pranks with the objective of getting expelled. Later attending a public high school, Manson recalled in his autobiography, "I even joined the school band to meet girls. I started out playing macho instruments like bass and snare drums. But I ended up on the last instrument anybody who feels insecure about himself should be playing: the triangle." Manson would spend his teens years experimenting with the occult, shoplifting albums from a neighborhood record store and delivering pizzas for a popular, local restaurant.

With Manson's father finding work in Fort Lauderdale, Florida, the family was uprooted. In Florida, Manson enrolled in a community college and worked as a clerk in a record store. During this period, he also attempted to peddle poems and stories to literary publications. Turning to rock journalism, he concocted the character of Marilyn Manson – a contraction of Marilyn Monroe and Charles Manson. Forming his own band, Marilyn Manson And The Spooky Kids, he merged gothic imagery, hard rock and horrifying performance art.

Not too long after interviewing Trent Reznor for a magazine article,

Marilyn Manson had the fortune of opening up for Nine Inch Nails at a Florida concert. Then in 1993, Reznor invited Manson to join him at his Los Angeles home studio to shoot a video, which was never released.

Recording his debut album at The Bee Gees-owned Criteria Studios in Hollywood, Florida, Manson explored a number of morbid themes. The project was later tweaked by Reznor at his Los Angeles studio. But when Reznor delivered Manson's completed album, *Portrait Of An American Family*, to Interscope Records, the label refused to issue the project due to its subject matter. Eventually released in 1994, the album was unaltered except for the removal of one song, "Filth."

Spending a year on the road as the opening act for Nine Inch Nails, Marilyn Manson was met with outrage from many quarters, and in some instances, was paid *not* to perform. In an *Alternative Press* interview, the Canton singer insisted: "Marilyn Manson would have fit just fine right alongside Ziggy Stardust and Alice Cooper, The Stooges, T. Rex – any of that back then. And apparently I'm gonna be the one that has to break my back to make rock music exciting again, because not too many other people are making the effort." Ironically, Alice Cooper has often attacked Manson in the press.

With his career on the ascent, Manson yielded his biggest hit with a grizzly, maniacal version of The Eurythmics' "Sweet Dreams (Are Made Of This)." The track appeared on the uneven album, *Smells Like Children*.

Produced by Reznor, Manson's 1996 release *Antichrist Superstar* was more mainstream than his previous efforts, and spawned the hit, "Beautiful People." That same year, Manson was named Artist of the Year by *Alternative Press* magazine. In 1998, Manson followed up with the chart-topping album, *Mechanical Animals*, which strengthened his industrial-rock base.

A lightning rod for controversy, Marilyn Manson took pleasure in disturbing the establishment. But with the 1999 shootings at Columbine High School drawing unwanted attention to the goth-rock movement, Manson found himself at the center of a media storm due to the teenage shooters' affinity for goth music and clothing. Also that year, *Spin* magazine editor Craig Marks filed a criminal complaint after he was threatened and manhandled backstage at a Marilyn Manson concert.

In the end, Manson was unable to further push the envelope of outrageous behavior. It seemed that nothing he did or said was shocking anymore. And embracing a level of conformity, he married his longtime girlfriend, Dita Von Teese, in a ceremony at an Irish gothic castle. The couple would split in 2007.

FILTER

Marilyn Manson was not the only act to emerge from Trent Reznor's musical camp. Two former Nine Inch Nails associates launched their own band, Filter. Conceived during the sessions for the Nine Inch Nails album *Closer*, Richard

Patrick told *Scene* magazine: "The feeling to leave the Nails started creeping in around the summer of '93. I started to realize that I wasn't really going to have too much of a future outside of what I was doing in the band. I started to get motivated and decided that I should at least keep my options open. Once I started to get response... I mean, when I sent out that three-song demo to record companies and started to get responses, I realized what I should do." Forming Filter, Patrick provided the guitarwork and vocals, while Brian Liesegang programed the synthesizers and computers.

Holing up in a rented, suburban Cleveland house, the pair went jet-skiing on Lake Erie during the day and worked on their 1995 debut album, *Short Bus*, at night. From the project, the controversial track "Hey Man, Nice Shot" became a radio hit. Wanting to take their act on the road, the duo added guitarist Geno Lenardo, bassist Frank Cavanaugh and drummer Matt Walker.

Following Liesegang's departure from Filter in 1997, Patrick retained the group's name and recorded a cover version of the Three Dog Night hit, "One," for the film soundtrack, *The X-Files*. After further personnel changes, the group scored a hit in 2002 with "American Cliche."

Then after completing a rehab program in 2002, Richard Patrick teamed with brothers Dean and Robert DeLeo of Stone Temple Pilots to form the band, Army Of Anyone. Issuing a self-titled debut album in 2006, the group scored a hit with "Goodbye." (Richard's brother is actor Robert Patrick of *Terminator 2* fame.)

RELIENT K & SANCTUS REAL

Relient K was formed in 1997 by a trio of students – Matt Thiessen, Matt Hoopes and Brian Pittman – from three separate high schools in Canton. The musicians were longtime friends who met while attending Canton's First Friends Church. Naming their band after Hoopes' often-mocked car, the Christian alternative-rock group was discovered by Mark Townsend, a Cincinnati-born member of the Christian rock band DC Talk (and also the father of Matt Hoopes' girlfriend).

In 2000, Relient K issued a self-titled debut album produced by Townsend. The indie project was highlighted by the track, "(Marilyn Manson Ate) My Girlfriend." Later that same year, Relient K signed with Gotee Records, a label founded by former DC Talk member Toby McKeehan. Emerging as a superstar act in the contemporary Christian music field, Relient K released a pair of certified-gold albums – *The Anatomy Of The Tongue In Cheek* and *Two Lefts Don't Make A Right... But Three Do*.

Then when Gotee entered into a relationship with Capitol Records, Relient K was able to reach a wider audience. In 2004, the group landed in the top-20 of *Billboard* magazine's album chart with their fourth release, the Mark Townsend-produced *Mmhmm*. More solemn than its predecessors, the album spawned the radio hits, "Be My Escape" and "Who I Am Hates Who I've Been." The head of an Internet music-downloading measuring service told

Billboard magazine: "It was difficult in the beginning to convince programmers which format Relient K belonged in, whether it was alternative, adult top 40 or rock. But wherever it received airplay... it was downloaded like crazy." By the time of the group's fifth release – 2007's *Five Score And Seven Years Ago* – Relient K lost its bassist Brian Pittman and had expanded into a quintet with the additions of John Warne and Jonathan Schneck.

Another Ohio-based, early 21st century Christian-based rock act, Toledo's Sanctus Real, was also formed by high school students. A hard-rocking quartet fronted by guitarist-vocalist Matt Hammitt, the group gained notoriety after winning a citywide battle-of-the-bands competition in 2000. After releasing a series of albums, the group enjoyed its first secular hit in 2006 with "The Face Of Love."

Ohio hosts an annual Christian rock music event, the ALIVE Christian Music Festival, which draws thousands of music fans from around the nation. The weekend event is held annually at Clay's Park near the town of Canal Fulton. The biggest names in the field have performed at the 350-acre site including The News Boys, Michael W. Smith and Amy Grant.

THE DAYTON SCENE

A city of scientific discovery that at one time led the nation in patents, Dayton gave the world mechanized flight and modern business machines. In 1878, a Dayton saloon keeper named James Ritty designed a device called the "Incorruptible Cashier." After the patent was sold to John Henry Patterson, the machine was renamed the cash register. Forming the National Cash Register Company (NCR), Patterson established a thriving industry. One fired NCR employee, Thomas J. Watson, later emerged as the chairman of International Business Machines – also known as IBM. Another local manufacturing firm, Dayton Engineering Laboratories Co. – better known as Delco – was founded by former NCR employees Charles Kettering and Edward A. Deeds, and supplied auto parts to Detroit automakers.

Also the birthplace of aviation, Dayton spawned the inquisitive Wright Brothers who gave the world the gift of motorized flight. The proprietors of a bicycle shop, inventors Orville and Wilbur Wright spent their off hours studying aeronautical principals. Seeking optimal wind speeds, the brothers took their fixed-wing craft to Kitty Hawk, North Carolina, where they achieved their first manned, powered flight. Though lasting just 12-seconds, the December 1903 test flight would spark a scramble to develop the modern airplane.

Ohio has produced a number of aeronautical pioneers. Columbus-born pilot, Eddie Rickenbacker, was a celebrated, flying ace during World War I. Later, Newark, Ohio-native Jerrie Mock became the first woman to fly solo around the world. One of the first seven men to join the U.S. space program, Cambridge-native John Glenn became the first American to orbit the earth. Then in 1969, Wapakoneta-native Neil Armstrong was the first man to walk on the moon.

Situated in the Miami Valley, Dayton was nicknamed the Gem City. From this city of invention and creativity came a series of unique and creative musical acts. In addition to talents such as The Breeders and Guided By Voices, another Dayton band, Hawthorne Heights, was one of the first rock acts to take full advantage of the Internet as a marketing tool.

KELLEY AND KIM DEAL: THE PIXIES AND THE BREEDERS

Raised in a family of coal miners, Kim Deal recalled in *Spin* magazine, "My dad took guitar lessons when I was around 13. He would bring home tablature and I would pick up his acoustic guitar and play it before *he* would. He'd say, 'Oh, gosh, Kim, you're making me mad. You're picking it up so easy.' So I thought I was really cool playing stuff like 'King Of The Road' by Roger Miller – things dads would want to play. He never did learn how to play guitar."

By their mid-teens, twin sisters Kelley and Kim Deal formed the folk-rock duo, The Breeders. Playing old country and classic rock songs at truck stops and other low-rent venues around Dayton, the duo encountered many obstacles to success.

Then around 1985, Kim Deal and her husband, John Murphy, moved to Boston. After arriving, Deal spotted an advertisement in the local arts newspaper which read: "Looking for female bassist, high harmony, must like Hüsker Dü, Peter, Paul & Mary, no chops." The ad was placed by a pair of college friends, singer-songwriter Frank Black and guitarist Joey Santiago. With Deal the only one to audition, she was hired despite the fact she did not play the bass guitar at the time. The Pixies were soon completed with the addition of drummer David Lovering. While Frank Black took the stage name of Black Francis, Deal initially assumed the moniker, Mrs. John Murphy.

Writing their own material, The Pixies enjoyed challenging the status quo, even if it meant alienating audiences. Kim Deal told *The Guardian*, "It was '85 or '86 and in Boston there was something going round that was really weird – you would go to these stores where you could buy a $100 ripped T-shirt, because you were punk. And I just thought that was really funny. So at some of the shows, I would make sure not to change from my skirt and comfortable, sensible heels and the shirt with the bow on. Just to piss off the punks. And that's really thrilling. Because of course they hated it."

During their seven-year run, The Pixies recorded one EP and four highly-acclaimed albums, including *Surfer Rosa* – which was highlighted by "Where Is My Mind" and a track featuring Deal on lead vocals, "Gigantic." Moving to Elektra Records, The Pixies honed their sound on the 1989 release, *Doolittle*, which spawned the radio hits, "Monkey Gone To Heaven" and "Here Comes Your Man." But with tensions intensifying between Kim Deal and Frank Black, the group took a long break after the completion of a tour.

Yearning to grow as a vocalist, Kim Deal launched a side-project. Resurrecting the name of her teenage band, The Breeders, Deal teamed with friend Tanya Donelly (of Belly and Throwing Muses), and was joined by

David Lovering (of The Pixies), David Narcizo (of Throwing Muses), and later, Britt Walford (of Slint) and Josephine Wiggs (of Perfect Disaster). Working as a computer programmer in California at the time, Kelley Deal had hoped to join the outfit, but could not due to time constraints.

Recording their debut album *Pod* in 1990, The Breeders failed to garner attention. But with all of the group's members involved in active bands, The Breeders were considered a part-time venture.

Returning to The Pixies, Deal continued to quarrel with Black. In retaliation, Black blocked Deal from contributing ideas to the group's next two albums, *Bossanova* (featuring the tracks "Velouria" and "Dig For Fire") and *Trompe Le Monde* (highlighted by "Letter To Memphis" and "Head On").

Following the break-up of The Pixies in 1993, Kelley Deal replaced Tanya Donelly in time for the sessions of The Breeders' second album, *Last Splash*. A commercial breakthrough, the project spawned the hits "Saints," "Divine Hammer" and the quirky "Cannonball." After adding drummer Jim McPherson, the group joined the Lollapalooza tour.

But by 1995, The Breeders began to splinter. With Kelley Deal in rehab, the two remaining members – Kim Deal and Jim McPherson – formed a side-project called Tammy And The Amps. Adding two members and shortening their name to The Amps, the group recorded one album, *Pacer*, before disbanding in 1997. After completing rehab, Kelley formed her own group, The Kelley Deal 6000.

By 2000, the Deal sisters reformed The Breeders. Two years later, the group released its third album in 12 years, *Title TK*, which was characterized by Kim Deal's more gritty vocals. Then with Kim Deal and Frank Black reconciling, The Pixies reformed for a much-anticipated reunion tour in 2005.

GUIDED BY VOICES

A modern, lo-fi, indie-rock band, Guided By Voices (GBV) were known for their short songs and creative melodies. The brainchild of Robert Pollard, the group went through dozens of line-ups over two decades.

A former self-described jock who was obsessed with sports, Pollard also spent his youth drawing fake album covers for a series of fictitious bands he created. One of Pollard's high school classmates was Grammy-winning, country songwriter Frank Myers (of "I Swear" and "I'm Already There" fame).

While a freshman at Dayton's Wright State University, Pollard joined a heavy-metal outfit called Anacrusis. The band also included future GBV guitarist Mitch Mitchell. But inspired by the electronic, new wave of Devo, Pollard would soon change musical directions.

While employed as a fourth-grade teacher, Pollard spent his summers performing around Dayton as the leader of Guided By Voices. During this period, Pollard began issuing a series of self-financed GBV albums, never pressing more than a thousand copies.

After briefly disbanding, GBV were urged to reform by the owner of Scat Records, who had stumbled upon a copy of their 1992 album, *Propeller*. (Scat was launched by Robert Griffin, who ran the label from his apartment on the east side of Cleveland, before relocating the company to St. Louis.) Issued in 1993, the indie classic *Vampire On Titus* gave GBV new life. Embraced by college radio, the group began touring outside of Ohio for the first time. Poised for stardom, GBV continued to churn out critically-acclaimed albums.

In 1997, Pollard teamed with Cleveland alternative-rock act Cobra Verde for a new version of GBV. The configuration would last less than a year. Assembling yet another lineup of the group, Pollard retained Cobra Verde member Doug Gillard and added two former members of The Breeders. The group then teamed with producer Ric Ocasek on the album *Do The Collapse*, which was intended as the group's first major-label release. But with Capitol Records passing on the album, the new wave-flavored project was instead issued by TVT Records.

Though Pollard retired the GBV moniker at the close of 2004, he would continue to compose and record prolifically. By 2006, he had issued – under various monikers – nearly 50 albums.

HAWTHORNE HEIGHTS

One of the more successful, indie bands from Ohio, Hawthorne Heights straddled punk rock and the emerging emo movement. After earning a degree in communications from the University of Dayton, drummer Eron Bucciarelli worked for a cable company and moonlighted in a local punk band called A Day In The Life. Performing as often as possible, the group booked gigs far from home. Bucciarelli recalled in *Wire* magazine: "We went on tour every weekend. We'd pack up the van right after work on Friday, play a show that night in Pittsburgh, play the next night in Philly, wind up in Delaware somewhere on Sunday, and then drive all night to get back to Dayton by Monday morning." In addition to touring with the band, the group's lead singer, J.T. Woodruff, held down two day jobs and struggled to take college courses in the evenings. Though nearly disbanding, the group eventually evolved into Hawthorne Heights.

Posting two tracks on PureVolume.com, the group gained national exposure through a flurry of downloads. Following a series of label rejections, the group was signed in 2003 by Victory Records of Chicago. Subsequently utilizing the multimedia site MySpace.com, Hawthorne Heights nurtured a broad, loyal fanbase, with each group member answering hundreds of fan emails on a daily basis.

Without the benefit of radio airplay, Hawthorne Heights' 2004 album *The Silence In Black And White* sold nearly a million copies and was highlighted by the track, "Ohio Is For Lovers." Their followup release, *If Only You Were Lonely*, nearly topped the charts and featured the hit, "Saying Sorry."

In 2006, the band sued its Chicago-based record label, Victory Records, to void its contract and secure unpaid royalties. According to *Scene* magazine, "Hawthorne Heights says it hasn't received a penny from Victory, despite selling nearly 1.5 million sales of its first two records, which netted the label $10 million. Victory founder Tony Brummel countered in *Billboard* that Hawthorne Heights has yet to recover its advertising and promotional budget... and consequently still owes Victory $1 million as well as two more records." The lawsuit left Hawthorne Heights unable to release any material until the legal disputes were settled. Then after the group signed with Virgin-EMI, Victory filed a $20 million lawsuit. A court ruled that the band owed two more albums to Victory but was not exclusively bound to the label.

A number of other Dayton bands have also created waves on the national scene. Formed in 1992, Brainiac was headed by guitarist-keyboardist-vocalist, Tim Taylor. But on the cusp of stardom in 1997, Brainiac disbanded after Taylor was killed in a car accident.

Another notable Dayton band, Heartless Bastards, was formed in 2003. Fronted by vocalist Erika Wennerstrom, the group garnered glowing reviews in *Rolling Stone* and *Blender*, and was often compared to Akron-based, blues-rock act, The Black Keys. Other talented alternative rock acts from the city include Jayne Sachs and Shrug.

THE CINCINNATI SCENE

The Cincinnati modern-rock scene originated with groups such as Psychodots (formerly of Toledo) and The Wet Spots. By the 1990s, the city was churning out national acts such as The Afghan Whigs, The Ass Ponys and Over The Rhine. Another Cincinnati alternative rock act, Pay The Girl scored a moderate hit in 2003 with "Freeze."

THE AFGHAN WHIGS

A soul-infused, modern-rock quartet, The Afghan Whigs were known for their dark, sullen and self-loathing lyrics. Formed at the University of Cincinnati in 1987, the group featured singer-guitarist Greg Dulli, bassist John Curley, lead guitarist Rick McCollum and drummer Steve Earl (not the country singer of the same name). All of the members were college students except for Curley, who was working as a photography intern at *The Cincinnati Enquirer* (the position was arranged by his father, the publisher of *USA Today*).

Reared on soul music while growing up in Hamilton, Ohio, the group's chief songwriter Greg Dulli told *The Cleveland Plain Dealer*: "I would hear stuff like The Ohio Players and Earth, Wind And Fire. I used to ride my bike across the river to play hoops in the neighborhood that was basically Hamilton's ghetto. I went there to find a better basketball game.... That was where my R&B education began."

After issuing a self-produced album in 1988 on John Curley's Ultrasuede label, The Afghan Whigs drew the attention of the influential Seattle indie,

Sub Pop Records. Becoming the first non-West Coast act signed to Sub Pop, the group recorded a pair of albums and one EP at the label.

After emerging as a college-radio favorite, The Afghan Whigs were signed by Elektra Records. From their album *Gentlemen*, the group scored its first chart hit with "Debonair." A followup release, the EP *What Jail Is Like*, was issued the following year. With the group embarking on an extended hiatus in late-1994, Steve Earl left the band and was replaced by Paul Buchignani. But losing momentum, the group fared poorly with its 1996 followup, *Black Love*.

Moving to Columbia Records, The Afghan Whigs issued the album, *1965*. Around this time, the group would make a cameo appearance in the Ted Damme film, *Beautiful Girls*. In 2001, the group disbanded.

THE ASS PONYS

Formed in 1988, The Ass Ponys were fronted by former collectible-record dealer, Chuck Cleaver. After paying its dues in the clubs of Cincinnati, the group recorded its debut album *Mr. Superlove* at Ultrasuede Studio (which was operated by Afghan Whigs member John Curley). With their indie-rooted, country-rock stylings, The Ass Ponys churned out distinctive songs about backwoods Americana.

Signed by A&M Records in 1994, The Ass Ponys drew the attention of college radio with their third album, *Electric Rock Music*. But saddled with an off-color moniker, The Ass Ponys lost potential airplay for their hit, "Little Bastard," because many radio stations refused to utter the group's name. Then after replacing a key member, the group issued its second and final A&M album, *The Known Universe*. The group later signed with Checkered Past Records and issued the critically-acclaimed album, *Some Stupid With A Flare Gun*. Chuck Cleaver later formed the band, Wussy.

OVER THE RHINE

Formed by the husband-and-wife team of Karin Bergquist and Linford Detweiler (the son of a former Mennonite minister), the Cincinnati-based folk-rock act, Over The Rhine, was named after a historical but troubled neighborhood in the city. The couple had met while Bergquist was attending Malone College in Canton. Launched in 1990 as a four-piece rock band, the group issued two self-produced albums. In 1992, the group's second album, *Patience*, was reissued by I.R.S. Records.

Bergquist told *Paste* magazine: "We were blessed. We had no financial backing whatsoever. We built the band on my credit line. None of us had wealthy parents. When we first started playing, we went all-out and would rent this killer system and bring it into this little club, so we'd really sound good. And there were all these other jealous bands, saying, 'Oh, they're a bunch of rich suburban kids.' Nothing could have been further from the truth. We were going to go down swinging. And we did, or nearly went down a few times. But we were just so committed. It's like, if you're not gonna commit, go home."

After releasing two more albums on I.R.S., the group left the label, citing a desire for greater artistic control. Pared down to a duo of Bergquist and Detweiler, Over The Rhine frequently toured with the like-minded act, The Cowboy Junkies. After forming its own label in 2007, Great Speckled Dog, Over The Rhine released their 17th album, *The Trumpet Child*. Detweiler told *Cincinnati Magazine*, "There's something very Midwestern about what we do. We're not cool, we're not ironic, and we're not detached."

THE COLUMBUS SCENE

With a large college-age population and an independently-owned, alternative-rock radio station, WWCD, Columbus was a strong market for modern rock. The city produced acts such as O.A.R., The Royal Crescent Mob and The New Bomb Turks. Other notable, alternative rock acts from Columbus include V3, Gaunt, Scrawl, Watershed and Pica Huss.

And signed to Geffen Records in the late-1980s, The Toll were poised for stardom. Fronted by charismatic singer Brad Circone, the quartet was best known for the track, "Jonathan Toledo." After releasing two albums, the group was dropped by Geffen in 1992.

O.A.R.

A melodic, reggae-flavored "jam" band, Columbus-based O.A.R. (which stands for Of A Revolution) used a grass-roots ethos to achieve success. Formed in 1996 by several high school students in Rockville, Maryland, the group became popular in its hometown. Though the group's guitarist/vocalist Marc Roberge was drawn to reggae in his teens, he recalled in *The Washington Post*: "I couldn't relate to a lot of the lyrics. What you can relate to is the pulse of the music that comes out in such a positive light. That's what I took from reggae, not the way they speak or the history. I took my history and the way I am and evolved this pulse, tried to bring out this positive vibe." In 1997, the group spent just $1,700 to record an album, *The Wanderer*. The project was highlighted by a track which would later emerge as a sing-along at the group's concerts, "That Was A Crazy Game Of Poker."

In the fall of 1997, two of the group's members – Marc Roberge and drummer Chris Culos – left their Washington D.C. suburb to attend Ohio State University. The group had selected OSU in part because of its large enrollment, which translated into a huge potential audience. Joined in Columbus the following year by a pair of former bandmates – bassist Benj Gershman and electric guitarist Richard On – the group also added a sax player, fellow student and Ohio-native Jerry DePizzo.

Barred from performing at campus-area nightclubs because of their ages, O.A.R. decided to rent out a venue across from the Ohio State campus. But with O.A.R. selling out the hall on eight occasions, nearby club owners took notice and began booking the underage group.

In 1999, the group released another self-produced album, *Souls Aflame*. Encouraging fans to record their concerts and post the music on peer-to-peer file-sharing websites, O.A.R. cultivated a devoted following.

Wanting to take O.A.R. to the next level, the group's manager David Roberge (the brother of member Marc Roberge) launched a label, Everfine Records. Teaming with producer John Alagia (of Dave Matthews fame), the group issued its third album, *Risen*. Then with a followup album – the live project *Any Time Now* – selling in excess of 100,000 copies, major labels were aggressively courting the group. Despite objections from some longtime fans, the group signed with Lava Records.

The group's first Lava release, *In Between Now And Then*, featured the radio hit, "Hey Girl," and led to appearances in 2003 on both *Conan O'Brien* and *David Letterman*. The album also contained a track about the group's adopted hometown, "Road Outside Columbus." The followup studio album, *Stories Of A Stranger*, spawned the group's biggest hit to date, "Love And Memories." Then in 2006, O.A.R. sold out Madison Square Garden, with the performance captured on DVD.

A similar act from Cleveland, Oroboros, embraced 1960s-style psychedelia within a contemporary jam-band framework. Formed in 1980 as a Grateful Dead tribute band, Oroboros veered toward blues-rock and garnered a following on the HORDE festival circuit.

THE ROYAL CRESCENT MOB

A high-energy band that achieved some national success, The Royal Crescent Mob (TRCM) merged elements of funk with punk rock. Fronted by vocalist-harmonica player David Ellison and guitarist Harold "Happy" Chichester, the quartet was often compared to the California-based act, The Red Hot Chili Peppers. (In the mid-1980s, the visiting Red Hot Chili Peppers shared a bill with The Royal Crescent Mob at a small Columbus nightclub, Stache's.)

A native of Dayton, Ellison was influenced by a soul group from his hometown, The Ohio Players. Not surprisingly, TRCM's debut EP, *Land Of Sugar*, was named after Ohio Players member Leroy "Sugarfoot" Bonner. The EP was highlighted by a blistering version of The Ohio Players' funk standard "Love Rollercoaster," which became a TRCM concert staple.

Nicknamed "The R.C. Mob," the group signed with Sire Records in 1988. Recording a pair of albums at the label – *Spin The World* and the more rock-oriented *Midnight Rose's* – the group scored a hit on modern-rock radio with "Hungry." Already a very popular draw around Ohio, the group gained further exposure after touring with The Replacements and The B-52's. Despite being dropped by Sire in 1991, TRCM released two more albums. But after a nine-year run, the group disbanded in 1994. Chichester later formed a popular Buckeye band, Howlin' Maggie.

New Bomb Turks

Formed in Columbus by several Cleveland-born, Ohio State University graduates, New Bomb Turks were headed by vocalist Eric Davidson. Conceived by Davidson and guitarist Jim Weber in 1987, Davidson told *The Cleveland Plain Dealer*, "We were never just into punk. We came together because we were total music fans.... I didn't know how to play an instrument, or even sing. We just had a lot of ideas of what music should sound like." Surprisingly, none of the members knew each other while growing up in Cleveland, despite frequenting many of the same nightclubs.

Patterned after late-1970s, Cleveland bands such as Pere Ubu, New Bomb Turks were rooted in booming, garage-style punk. After a flurry of indie singles, New Bomb Turks signed with a German label, Crypt Records. Releasing four albums, the group regularly toured throughout the U.S. and Europe.

In 1996, New Bomb Turks signed with the famed, Los Angeles-based punk label, Epitaph (home of Rancid, Bad Religion and Offspring). After releasing three consistent albums – *Scared Straight*, *At Rope's End* and *Nightmare Scenario* – the group parted with the label in 2001. More rock-oriented than their punk/hardcore labelmates, New Bomb Turks fared poorly at Epitaph.

The group's final studio album, *The Night Before The Day The Earth Stood Still*, was issued on Gearhead Records in 2002. Though officially disbanding at the end of 2003, the group would reform for occasional performances, including a 2007 gig at the Rock and Roll Hall of Fame.

New Bomb Turks drummer Sam Brown later joined three other former Ohio State University students to form the Warner Brothers rock act, The Sun. The group's debut, *Love & Death*, was produced by Jay Bennett of Wilco.

Thomas Jefferson Slave Apartments

Formed in Columbus by vocalist Ron House and guitarist Bob Petric, Thomas Jefferson Slave Apartments (TJSA) were rooted in punk and lo-fi rock. A native of Wooster in Northeastern Ohio, House had previously led one of Columbus' top bands, the folk-punk outfit Great Plains. Launched in 1989, TJSA issued a series of self-produced singles. Releasing their debut album in 1995 on Onion/American Records, the group began garnering national attention with the garage-rock-accented *Bait And Switch*. The project contained the track "RnR Hall Of Fame," which advocated the bombing of the Cleveland museum.

Dropped by American Records, the group released the album, *Straight To Video*, on the indie label, Anyway Records. The group's final album, *No Old Guy Lo-Fi Cry*, was issued in 2000 by Rockathon Records, a label operated by Robert Pollard of the Dayton rock act, Guided By Voices. After TJSA disbanded, House formed The Ron House Band. Also a businessman, House is the co-owner of a record store near the Ohio State University campus, Used Kids.

THEY SERVED TOO

Though poised for stardom, Kent-based Dink never graduated to the big time. Formed in the early-1990s as a metal/industrial hybrid, Dink scored a moderate hit on alternative-rock radio with the frenetic track, "Green Mind." While working on their second album, the group experienced internal strife and was dropped by Capitol Records. Dink disbanded in 1999.

From the city of Alliance, Lovedrug signed with Columbia Records in 2004. But before issuing any material on Columbia, the quartet asked to be released from their contract and returned to their previous label, the Militia Group. Fronted by vocalist Michael Shepard, the alt-rock group made waves with the albums, *Pretend You're Alive* and *Everything Starts Where It Ends*.

Meanwhile, a number of musical artists left Ohio to find fortune. One of the more quirky acts to emerge from the 1980s, Deee-Lite was fronted by Youngstown native Kier Kirby. Better known as Miss Kier, the psychedelically-outfitted singer teamed with Ukranian-born deejay Dmitry Brill and Japanese-born deejay Towa Tei. Featuring the backing vocals of fellow Buckeye native Bootsy Collins, the trio's dance hit "Groove Is In The Heart" reached the top-10 in 1990, and became a club classic. Miss Kier and Brill later married.

Cleveland-native John Bell left for Georgia in 1980, where he would soon front the indie-darlings, Widespread Panic. Similarly, Toledo-born bassist Scott Shriner joined pop-punk act Weezer in 2001. Meanwhile, singer-harmonica player John Popper was born in Cleveland but raised on the East Coast. By the time he arrived in New York City, Popper had teamed with several high school friends to form the blues-rock act, Blues Traveler. Popper later founded the HORDE festival.

Meanwhile, Toledo native Gary Louris was a founding member of the Minneapolis-based folk-flavored alternative-rock group, The Jayhawks. As the group's lead singer and chief songwriter, he enjoyed a number of hits including "Waiting For The Sun" and "Take Me With You (When You Go)." Louris later joined a superstar side-project, Golden Smog.

Another longterm Toledo-area act, The Raisins emerged from a lively musical scene in the suburban city of Sylvania. Formed in the mid-1970s, the group quickly drew the attention of Adrian Belew, a guitarist who was raised just across the river from Cincinnati in Kentucky. Belew had previously worked with a series of leading rock acts such as David Bowie, King Crimson and Frank Zappa. By the late-1980s, Belew joined forces with The Raisins to form an avant-garde alternative act, The Bears. But while Belew later became a popular solo act, the rest of the group formed the Cincinnati-based, power-pop trio, The Pyschodots.

Situated just west of Cleveland, Oberlin College was the breeding ground of the rock act, The Yeah Yeah Yeahs. At the school, singer Karen O (born Karen Orzolek) dabbled in music and became friends with drummer Brian Chase. Transferring to New York University in 2000, she formed an acoustic, punk duo with guitarist Nick Zinner. After expanding to a trio called The

Yeah Yeah Yeahs, the group fired its original drummer and hired Karen O's Oberlin classmate, Brian Chase. Creating a national buzz, the unconventional group became a concert favorite. As the home of the nation's longest operating music conservatory, Oberlin also nurtured the musical acts, Liz Phair, Josh Ritter, Bitch Magnet and Marc Cohn. In 2007, the college launched its own record label, Oberlin Music.

But the act that changed alternative-rock from its post-new wave commercialism into a rougher, more coarse style called grunge, was Seattle's Nirvana. One of it members, drummer Dave Grohl, was born in Warren, Ohio, but raised in Virginia. Additionally, Stone Temple Pilots frontman Scott Weiland was raised in suburban Cleveland. Quitting high school during his freshman year, he moved to California. After the breakup of Stone Temple Pilots, Weiland co-founded Velvet Revolver, but was fired from the hard-rock band in 2008. Later that same year, Weiland reformed Stone Temple Pilots.

CHAPTER 10
SOUL AND R&B

By 1960, both doo-wop and blues music were falling out of favor in the African-American community. The new decade brought a rougher, more urban musical genre to the forefront – soul music. Soul prospered in two chief regions in Ohio: Dayton-Cincinnati and Akron-Canton-Cleveland. While Dayton and Cincinnati spawned pioneering artists like The Isley Brothers, Bootsy Collins and Tommy Tucker, the other corner of the state produced The O'Jays, James Ingram and Edwin Starr.

A large number of Dayton and Cincinnati soul acts recorded for Solar Records. Based in Los Angeles, the label was formed in 1977 by Dick Griffey. Previously the co-owner of Soul Train Records, Griffey had formed the label with *Soul Train* founder and host, Don Cornelius. Another notable Buckeye-born R&B artist, Anita Baker left Toledo at a young age and was raised in nearby Detroit.

THE CINCINNATI R&B SCENE

The Southwestern corner of the state produced a wealth of soul acts beginning with The Isley Brothers. Surprisingly, the group did not record for its hometown label, King-Federal.

The city also spawned a number of regional soul artists such as Kenny Smith. Despite never scoring a national hit, Smith was popular throughout the Midwest and emerged as a favorite in the British Northern Soul scene. Flirting with fame, Smith was also a member of a group called The Enchanters, which toured as the opening act for Tiny Bradshaw in 1956. Also a solo act, Smith recorded a series of singles for Fraternity Records. As a producer and songwriter, he worked with numerous artists such as Albert Washington and The Casinos. Smith was also the co-arranger of a minor chart hit by The Dolphins, "Hey-Da-Da-Dow." In the early-1970s, Smith hosted the shortlived television program, *Soul Street*.

THE ISLEY BROTHERS

One of the longest-surviving acts of the rock era, The Isley Brothers dominated the charts for several decades. Raised in the Cincinnati suburb of Lincoln Heights, four young brothers – O'Kelly, Ronald, Rudolph and Vernon – began harmonizing as a group at the Mt. Moriah Church in 1950. Ronald told *Discoveries* magazine: "My mother was a church director, and so was my grandmother, so they were the ones that put the group together in the beginning. We started doing gospel first, then they taught us everything right away – they taught us popular music at the same time. But our group started off doing gospel programs."

Chaperoned by their mother, the young brothers performed throughout Southwestern Ohio. But following the untimely death of Vernon Isley in a bicycle accident, the group disbanded. But at the urging of their family, the surviving brothers reformed the group a year later.

Leaving gospel for pop music, the group installed Ronald Isley as the lead singer. Making several bus trips to New York City, The Isley Brothers worked with record mogul George Goldner. Recording a series of singles – beginning with the 1957, doo-wop ballad "Angels Cried" – the group fared poorly.

Discovered at the Howard Theater in Washington D.C., The Isley Brothers landed at RCA Records in 1959. At the label, the group scored a career-making hit with the Ronald Isley-composed song, "Shout." At the Howard Theater, The Isleys were performing "Shout" as a medley with the Jackie Wilson hit, "Lonely Teardrops."

Taking its passion and call-and-response routine directly from the church, "Shout" also featured the group's former church organist, Professor Herman Stephens. Aided by the topnotch production team of Hugo Peretti and Luigi Creatore, the million-selling single became a rock standard, despite failing to reach the top-40. Another of the group's singles issued at the label, "Respectable," became a far bigger hit later in the decade for fellow Buckeye act, The Outsiders.

Switching to Atlantic Records, The Isley Brothers were teamed with superstar producers Leiber & Stoller. But surprisingly, none of their four Atlantic singles reached the charts. By 1962, the group found its way to the Scepter Records subsidiary, Wand, and was paired with songwriter-producer Bert Berns. That year, the group returned to the charts with an upbeat rocker, "Twist And Shout." The song was penned by Berns and had been previously recorded by another Atlantic artist, The Top Notes. Utilizing the same arrangement as The Isley Brothers, the song was later a hit for The Beatles.

In 1964, The Isleys formed T-Neck Records, taking the name from their adopted hometown of Teaneck, New Jersey. During this time, the group hired a bold, young guitarist named Jimmy (later Jimi) Hendrix. Ernie Isley told *The Cleveland Plain Dealer*, "Jimi Hendrix lived in our house when I was 12. He wasn't just a member of the band. He was a part of the household. I remember him practicing all the time. I didn't quite understand that because he was so good. But he was always trying to get more out of the instrument. He spent more time with his instrument than any of the other guys in the band. I don't remember him watching TV or reading a magazine or a book. Basically, he just played guitar. We bought him his first white Stratocaster."

Finding themselves on the Motown subsidiary, Tamla, The Isleys scored a crossover hit in 1966 with "This Old Heart Of Mine," a song written and produced by the team of Holland-Dozier-Holland. With the single reaching the U.K. top-10 in 1968, the group launched a British tour.

Leaving Motown, The Isleys reactivated T-Neck Records in 1969, and entered into a distribution deal with Buddah Records. Soon, the group was expanded with the addition of brother-in-law Chris Jasper and the two youngest Isley brothers, Ernie and Marvin. The new line-up would score the biggest chart-single of the group's career with the Grammy-winning "It's Your Thing" (the song would be resurrected in 1988 by rap act, Salt-N-Pepa).

Taking a turn toward funk and harder soul in the 1970s, The Isley Brothers enjoyed a string of hit singles and albums. The Isley Brothers were inducted into the Rock and Roll Hall of Fame in 1992.

BOOTSY COLLINS

One of the most prolific and creative musicians to emerge from Ohio, William "Bootsy" Collins was a founding father of funk. Inspired by James Brown, Collins begged his mother to buy him a guitar. After putting bass strings on his rhythm guitar, Bootsy teamed with his older brother Phelps "Catfish" Collins and singer Philippe Wynne to form The Pacemakers in 1967. Playing around Cincinnati, the group performed mostly James Brown songs. Recalling his teen years, Collins told *Goldmine* magazine, "We had started getting to the point of looking forward to each new James Brown record because it was going to be new and it was going to make us groove and it was going to set new ground as far as us becoming musicians."

Often hanging out at the King Records studios, members of The Pacemakers used the opportunity to learn from their musical mentors, especially James Brown. After a while, producer Bobby Byrd began hiring the band or individual members to work on an increasing number of James Brown spinoff projects. At the label, Collins also worked with Hank Ballard, Bill Doggett and others.

Then in 1969 when Brown's backing band refused to perform due to a monetary dispute, Brown telephoned Byrd, instructing him to fly The Pacemakers down to Columbus, Georgia. Gone was Brown's R&B orchestra, and born were The JBs, a pioneering, funk-defining rhythm section. Just 17-years-old at the time, Bootsy Collins recalled in *Waxpoetics* that the band already knew Brown's songs "inside and out. And he knew we knew them. So we hit the stage and sure enough, he calls out a song, drops his hand down, and we were on it! I mean we were onstage with the Godfather of Soul! Man we were going to wear that mutha out! We thought we were wearing it out. We hit every move. We knew all of his moves. If you noticed, it wasn't so much about his singing and screaming, it was all about his body. His moves." And beginning with the hit "Sex Machine," The JBs were also employed as Brown's studio band. Separately from Brown, The JBs recorded a series of instrumental singles.

Though Bootsy and Phelps Collins grew musically under Brown's strict, regimental system, the brothers quit in 1971 to form The House Guests, which included former bandmates from The Pacemakers. Then later in 1971, The House Guests headed for Detroit to consider an offer to join The Spinners and to meet R&B bandleader George Clinton. While singer Philippe

Wynne would join The Spinners, the rest of the band hooked up with Clinton, preferring a more free-spirited and informal musical environment.

By 1972, the Collins brothers were concentrating their efforts on George Clinton's pioneering funk collective, Parliament-Funkadelic. Over time, a number of other Pacemakers and House Guests alumni would join George Clinton's ensemble, including drummer Frankie "Kash" Waddy. But while the Collins brothers brought a greater level of creativity to the group – beginning with the album *America Eats Its Young* – the other members of Clinton's troupe were resentful of the new additions. Consequently, Bootsy Collins left the group for a two-year period.

Returning to the musical collective in 1974, Bootsy Collins performed on the hit Funkadelic album, *Up For The Downstroke*. By 1975, George Clinton added two more former James Brown sidemen, horn players Maceo Parker and Fred Wesley. The following year, Parliament would release its landmark album, *Mothership Connection*, which was highlighted by the funk standard, "Tear The Roof Off The Sucker (Give Up The Funk)." The followup album, *Funkentelechy vs. The Placebo Syndrome*, would feature the track, "Flashlight." A popular touring act during the 1970s, Parliament-Funkadelic employed a large, flying-saucer stage-prop, nicknamed "the Mothership."

Simultaneously pursuing a solo career, Bootsy Collins became a star in his own right. Nicknamed "Casper The Funky Ghost" and "Bootzilla," Collins cultivated a glitzy, outerspace persona. Playing his "space bass," Collins formed a successful offshoot band in 1976 called Bootsy's Rubber Band. Signing with Warner Brothers, he placed over a dozen hits on the R&B charts including "Stretchin' Out (In A Rubber Band)," "The Pinocchio Theory" and "Bootzilla." The backing musicians in Bootsy's Rubber Band launched their own successful act apart from the Collins brothers called The Brides Of Funkenstein.

Then with George Clinton battling his record label in court, Collins took an extended break from recording. After releasing a solo album in 1988, Collins formed The Bootzilla Orchestra for a Malcolm McLaren project.

In addition to his work with George Clinton, Bootsy Collins teamed with Roger Troutman to help the careers of several Ohio acts including the band, Dayton. A funk outfit named after its hometown, Dayton emerged in the late-1970s from the remnants of two groups, Sun and Over Night Low. Signed to Liberty Records, Dayton released a self-titled debut album in 1980. Fronted by vocalists Chris Jones and Jennifer Matthews, the group scored its biggest hit in 1982 with a cover of Sly & The Family Stone's "Hot Fun In The Summertime."

In the mid-1990s, Bootsy Collins began mentoring Cincinnati-based funk bassist, Chris Sherman. Nicknamed "Freekbass," Sherman founded the funk outfit, Shag. Simultaneously pursuing a solo career, Sherman issued his debut album in 1999, *Ultra-Violet Impact*. Collins would produce Sherman's next two albums, *Body Over Mind* and *The Air Is Fresher Underground*.

MEL CARTER

A former child singer, Cincinnati-born soul artist Mel Carter began performing at age four. By nine, he sang with bandleader Lionel Hampton. Also schooled in gospel, Carter joined The Raspberry Singers in the early-1950s. Then after a stint in his mother's gospel group The Carvettes, he joined The Gospel Pearls in the early-1960s.

As a solo artist, Carter scored his first hit in 1963 with "When A Boy Falls In Love," a song which was co-written by Sam Cooke and released on Cooke's Derby label. Switching to Imperial Records and teaming with producer Nick DeCaro, Carter recorded what would become his signature song, the timeless classic, "Hold Me, Thrill Me, Kiss Me." A remake, the song was originally a top-10 pop hit for Karen Chandler in 1953. Carter followed up with a few more moderate-selling hits, including "(All Of A Sudden) My Heart Sings" and "Band Of Gold."

Also an actor, Carter appeared on a number of television programs, including *The Rifleman*, *Sanford And Son* and *Magnum, P.I.*

MIDNIGHT STAR & CALLOWAY

One of the more successful R&B/dance bands of the 1980s, Midnight Star was formed at Kentucky State University in Frankfort. A native of Cincinnati, Reggie Calloway recalled in *The Lexington Herald-Leader* how the group came about in 1976: "I went around the school and picked out the best players I could find. We had played in marching band and jazz ensemble, so the players all knew what the others could do. We just found a room and started rehearsing." The group soon included Reggie Calloway's brother, Vincent, vocalist Brenda Lipscomb and four other students. The group created a stir on campus during its performance as the opening act for Natalie Cole's homecoming concert in 1977.

Unable to juggle both their studies and budding musical careers, members of the group dropped out of college in 1977. After a whirlwind tour of U.S. Air Force base clubs around the country and overseas, Midnight Star decided to test the waters of New York City. But finding little interest in the city's nightclubs, the group established a base in Cincinnati.

But while in New York, Midnight Star had caught the attention of Dick Griffey, the head of Solar Records. Signed to the label, the group managed only spotty airplay with its first three albums – *The Beginning*, *Standing Together* and *Victory*.

Adopting a more electronic sound, Midnight Star broke through in a big way with their fourth release, *No Parking On The Dance Floor*. The double-platinum album spawned a series of radio/club hits with "Freak-a-Zoid," "Wet My Whistle," "No Parking (On The Dance Floor)" and "Electricity." On a roll, the group followed up with *Planetary Invasion* in 1985, and scored the biggest chart hit of its career, "Operator." More hits would follow including "Headlines" and "Midas Touch."

Meanwhile, the Calloway brothers would quit Midnight Star to launch their own musical venture, Calloway. Not as successful as their previous group, Calloway reached the top-10 in 1989 with a leftover composition from the *No Parking On The Dance Floor* sessions, "I Wanna Be Rich." Followup singles such as "Sir Lancelot" and "All The Way" were less successful.

With the departure of the Calloway brothers from Midnight Star, Bobby Lovelace was added to the group. Releasing a self-titled album in 1988, Midnight Star landed on the R&B charts with "Don't Rock The Boat" (which featured a rap by a member of Whodini, Ecstasy) and "Snake In The Grass."

Aside from his membership in Midnight Star, Reggie Calloway worked as a producer with artists such as The Whispers, Gladys Knight, Natalie Cole and Teddy Pendergrass. As songwriters, the Calloway brothers composed Klymaxx's dance hit "Meeting In The Ladies Room," and Reggie Calloway earned a Grammy nomination for writing Levert's top-10 smash, "Casanova."

In 2004, Reggie Calloway issued his first solo album, *Walking Between The Raindrops*. The album was the first release from his namesake label, Calloway Records.

THE DEELE: L.A. REID AND BABYFACE

In the early-1980s, Reggie Calloway of Midnight Star came to the assistance of a talented Cincinnati-based R&B group, The Deele. Formed in 1981, The Deele featured a pair of then-unknowns named Antonio "L.A." Reid and Kenneth "Babyface" Edmonds. While Reid was born and raised in Cincinnati, Edmonds hailed from Indianapolis.

Produced by Reggie Calloway, The Deele's debut album, *Street Beat*, spawned the top-10 R&B hit "Body Talk." Reid later told his hometown paper, "Reggie Calloway, this guy probably doesn't even know how much impact he's had on my life. Reggie kind of taught me the importance of making sure that every song you record is the absolute best song that you can find and has the absolute best performance by the artist. It was that basic training. I like to think of it as boot camp that really sort of paved the way for what we do now at LaFace [Records], and so many of the other artists and labels that I associate with. But it all came from there."

But with Reggie Calloway preoccupied with his own group, The Deele produced their own followup album, *Material Thangz*. Though less successful than its predecessor, the album taught Reid and Edmonds the intricacies of the recording process. The Deele's third album, *Eyes Of A Stranger*, spawned a pair of top-10 R&B hits, an Edmonds co-composition "Two Occasions" and the retro-styled "Shoot 'Em Up Movies."

In 1987, Kenneth "Babyface" Edmonds released his first solo album, *Lovers*. Issued by Solar, the album spawned four chart singles, including the top-10 R&B hit, "I Love You Babe." Soon expanding their duties at Solar, Reid and Edmonds worked with labelmates The Whispers in 1987, helping to update the group's sound on the hit, "Rock Steady."

But it was Babyface's 1989 followup album, *Tender Lover*, which established the soul crooner as a major force in popular music. Rooted in traditional R&B, the album generated four top-5 R&B singles, beginning with "It's No Crime" and continuing with "Tender Lover," "Whip Appeal" and "My Kinda Girl." Now focusing their efforts on production and songwriting, Babyface and L.A. Reid parted with The Deele in 1988. (The remaining members of The Deele would issue a final album in 1993.)

As rising superstars, Edmonds and Reid became hot property in the music industry. Expanding their efforts, they were soon working with Paula Abdul, Whitney Houston, Bell Biv DeVoe, The Jacksons, Sheena Easton, Karyn White, and an act featuring Edmonds' two brothers and a cousin, After 7. Edmonds and Reid also aided the burgeoning career of former New Edition singer Bobby Brown, with Edmonds writing two of his early hits, "Don't Be Cruel" and "Every Little Step." Reid was briefly married to an artist he had produced, R&B singer Pebbles.

Though generating a string of hits, Reid and Edmonds earned little for their efforts. Reid told *The Cincinnati Enquirer*: "At that point I decided I wanted some ownership in this game. We were having a lot of success, making a lot of records, selling a lot of records, not making a lot of money. We wanted equity participation and you can't have an equity participation if you're work-for-hire. And as producers we were work-for-hire. So I figured it out. I want a label."

Forming LaFace Records in 1989, Edmonds and Reid entered into a distribution deal with Arista Records. Setting up operations in Atlanta, Edmonds preferred to focus on production and recording, while Reid became the company's president and CEO, and took on the responsibility of running the label.

From the soundtrack of the 1992 Eddie Murphy film *Boomerang*, the Edmonds composition "End Of The Road" topped the pop charts for nearly three-months and earned a Grammy for R&B group, Boyz II Men. The project also spawned the hit "Give U My Heart," a duet by Edmonds and Toni Braxton. The soundtrack would also net Edmonds a Grammy as a producer.

Issued in 1993, Babyface's next solo album, *For The Cool In You*, was co-produced with Reid. A solid R&B venture, the album spawned four hits including the gold-certified single, "When Can I See You." Throughout the 1990s, the duo continued to nurture a host of breakthrough acts including TLC, Usher, OutKast and Pink.

In the year 2000, Reid was named the president of Arista Records, replacing Clive Davis. Co-founded by Davis in 1975, Arista was later acquired by the BMG conglomerate. Although BMG would soon shutter LaFace Records, the label was reactivated in 2004. That same year, Reid left Arista and was named Chairman of the Island / Def Jam Group; he later headed Hitco Music Publishing.

Meanwhile, Edmonds continued his hectic recording and production schedule. In 1995, he composed most of the tracks on the *Waiting To Exhale* soundtrack; also that year, he co-wrote and co-produced Madonna's chart-topper, "Take A Bow." Then the following year, he issued his fifth solo album, *The Day*, and won a Grammy as producer of the Eric Clapton ballad, "Change The World."

Expanding into film production, Edmonds and his wife, Tracey, established the Edmonds Production Company. Their first effort was the 1997 comedy, *Soul Food*; they were later hired as the executive producers of the BET reality series, *College Hill*. And as Babyface, Edmonds continued to churn out hit albums – *Face2Face*, *Grown & Sexy*, and an innovative collection of mostly pop and rock cover songs, *Playlist*.

DAYTON FUNK & SOUL

For a city of its size, Dayton has produced a disproportionate number of nationally-known funk and soul acts such as The Ohio Players, Slave, Roger Troutman and Zapp. Though located just 60-miles north of Cincinnati, Dayton developed its own musical scene. Other Dayton R&B acts such as Sun, Faze-O and Platypus, recorded for major labels but did not fare as well.

Many emerging Dayton artists were aided by a pair of local radio stations. With Dayton radio station WDAO-AM going on the air in 1964, its FM counterpart, also known as WDAO, became the first R&B station on the FM dial. Throughout the 1970s, WDAO-FM remained a soul music powerhouse, with deejays such as John "Turk" Logan and Gene "By Golly" Berry.

OHIO PLAYERS

A hard-edged, funk-soul group best known for its ballads and engaging instrumentals, The Ohio Players struggled for over a decade before finally breaking through onto the national scene. Formed in 1959 as The Ohio Untouchables (named after the popular television program, *The Untouchables*), the group was headed by singer-guitarist Robert Ward. After floundering with a series of early singles, the group moved to Detroit. Working as session musicians, the group backed a young Wilson Pickett and The Falcons on their hit, "I Found A Love."

After The Ohio Untouchables dissolved in 1963, all of the members – minus Ward – returned to Dayton and reformed the band the following year. Eventually adding a pair of vocalists – Bobby Lee Fears and Dutch Robinson – the group emerged as The Ohio Players. Moving to New York, the group was hired as the house band for Compass Records.

After briefly disbanding again in 1970, The Ohio Players signed with Westbound Records in 1971. Adding vocalist-keyboardist Walter "Junie" Morrison, the group began its hit run with a pair of minor R&B entries, "Pain," and the obvious followup, "Pleasure." Then in 1973, the group scored a million-selling hit with the crossover single, "Funky Worm." With Morrison leaving for a solo career, he was replaced by tenor vocalist Leroy "Sugarfoot"

Bonner, formerly of Lonnie Mack's band.

Signing with Mercury Records in 1974, The Ohio Players took a turn toward funk beginning with the top-10 R&B hit, "Jive Turkey." Enjoying its greatest period of success, the group scored a pair of chart-topping, pop singles with the raucous "Fire" and the party-anthem "Love Rollercoaster." Other hits would include "I Want To Be Free," "Sweet Sticky Thing" and "Who'd She Coo?" And though only a minor chart hit, the song "O-H-I-O" became a concert favorite. Aside from their distinctive sound, The Ohio Players were renowned for their provocative album covers.

With the rise of disco, The Ohio Players disbanded in 1979. Three of the group's members would later form Shadow; though releasing a trio of albums on a major label, the group fared poorly. Following a brief reunion of The Ohio Players, Bonner released a solo album in 1985 under his nickname, Sugarfoot; the project was produced by Roger Troutman.

In 1988, The Ohio Players again regrouped. Meanwhile, rock act The Red Hot Chili Peppers would score a hit cover of "Love Rollercoaster" in 1997.

TOMMY TUCKER & DEAN AND JEAN

Shortly after graduating from high school in the mid-1950s, Tennessee-native Welton Young arrived in Dayton. There he joined a group of graduates from Dunbar High School to form a doo-wop act called The Corvettes. Heading to New York City in 1956, the group competed in Apollo Theater amateur shows and landed occasional club work. Soon renamed The King Toppers, the group was befriended by Orioles member (and fellow Ohio native) Aaron "Tex" Cornelius. But finding little success, the group disbanded shortly after the release of a single on Jubilee/Josie Records.

Back in Dayton, Welton Young teamed with Brenda Lee "Jean" Jones to form an R&B duo called Dean And Jean. The duo scored a trio of national chart singles in the early-1960s, two of which entered the lower reaches of the top-40 – "Tra La La Suzy" and "Hey Jean, Hey Dean."

Young and Jones also worked with a local band led by R&B singer, Tommy Tucker (born Robert Higginbotham). Raised near Dayton in the town of Springfield, the former high-school football star broke into music in the late-1940s as the pianist in a local band led by saxophonist Bobby Wood. By the early-1950s, Tucker formed a doo-wop act, The Cavaliers. Later assembling an R&B group, he began writing his own material.

In 1964, Welton Young would aid his former bandleader by providing the guitarwork on Tucker's self-composed, seminal R&B hit, "Hi-Heel Sneakers." Don Covay co-wrote Tucker's followup chart single, the often recorded ditty, "Long Tall Shorty." Attempting to reignite his career, Tucker traveled to Chicago in 1966 to work with legendary blues artist and producer Willie Dixon. Though frequently aided by Atlantic Records co-founder Herb Abramson, Tucker would fail to score another hit.

Meanwhile, Dean And Jean would join a Dick Clark "Caravan of Stars" tour. But soon after, the duo would leave the music industry altogether and return to Dayton. And in the 1990s, Tommy Tucker's daughter, Teeny Tucker, pursued a musical career.

ROGER TROUTMAN & ZAPP

A talented producer, multi-instrumentalist and singer-songwriter, Roger Troutman had a long and varied career. Raised in a musical family, Troutman teamed with his brothers in 1962 to form an R&B group. After experimenting with a series of names, the group surfaced as Roger And The Human Body. By 1975, the group released a self-financed debut album, *Introducing Roger*. A regional success, the album led to frequent opening slots for George Clinton's Parliament-Funkadelic.

Aided by their association with Clinton, the group signed with Warner Brothers Records. Renamed Zapp (after Terry Troutman's childhood nickname), the group recorded a self-titled album, which was produced by Roger Troutman and Bootsy Collins. A strong seller, the project spawned the top-10 R&B hit, "More Bounce To The Ounce." On most of the group's material, Roger Troutman used a Vocoder, which gave his voice an electronic tone. Though very successful on the R&B charts during the 1980s with hits such as "Dance Floor," "Doo Wa Ditty," "I Can Make You Dance" and "Computer Love," Zapp failed to garner crossover, pop airplay.

By the early-1980s, Roger Troutman was simultaneously pursuing a solo career. Using only his first name, "Roger" scored an R&B chart-topper with a cover of "I Heard It Through The Grapevine," and continued with "In The Mix" and the top-10 crossover ballad, "I Want To Be Your Man."

By the late-1980s, three of the Troutman brothers – Terry, Lester and Larry – had left Zapp to join another brother, Rufus Jr., in the family business, Troutman Enterprises. The multifaceted enterprise operated a limousine service, renovated houses, and also oversaw a thriving recording studio.

By the early-1990s, the group would add three new members – Roger Troutman Jr. and a pair of vocalists, Shirley Murdoch and Ray "Sting" Davis. Now called Zapp And Roger, the configuration had limited success. During this period, Roger Troutman guested on a number of hit records including "California Love" by rapper 2 Pac and "It's Your Body" by Johnny Gill.

Meanwhile, Shirley Murdoch would emerge as a successful solo singer. With Troutman's aid, she secured a recording contract with Elektra Records in 1985, and landed on the R&B charts with "No More," "Go On Without You," "Husband," "In Your Eyes," and her only crossover entry, "As We Lay." Murdoch later abandoned her career in secular music and returned to Toledo to work as an evangelist.

Tragedy struck the group when brothers Roger and Larry Troutman were found dead on April 25, 1999, near the family's Dayton recording studio. A murder-suicide, Roger fatally shot his brother, Larry, and then shot himself after fleeing the scene. The family grieved again when Roger Troutman Jr. died in 2003 from head trauma.

STEVE ARRINGTON & SLAVE

Created from the merging of two Ohio R&B groups, Slave had a complex history. After the Dayton-based act The Young Mystics disbanded in 1975, the group's drummer Steve Arrington relocated to San Francisco. Meanwhile, the remaining members of the group joined forces with a similar Ohio act, Black Satin Soul, to form Slave. Headed by trumpeter Steve Washington, Slave was soon at the forefront of the funk movement.

Slave first made waves with its 1977 hit, "Slide." Then in 1978, Arrington reunited with his former bandmates and joined Slave. Though originally hired as a backing vocalist, Arrington assumed the lead vocal duties from 1979 until 1982, and appeared on the R&B hits, "Just A Touch Of Love," "Snap Shot," "Watching You" and "Wait For Me."

Leaving Slave in 1982 for a solo career, Arrington placed over a dozen singles on the R&B charts including "Nobody Can Be You," "Feel So Real," and the title track of his 1985 album, *Dancin' In The Key Of Life*. But finding God, Arrington abandoned his music career in 1986 and became a minister.

Meanwhile, Steve Washington would form a spinoff group in 1979 called Aurra. The group featured a rotating lineup of personnel from Slave. With Starleana Young and Curt Jones sharing lead vocal duties, Aurra placed several singles on the R&B charts in the early-1980s, including "Are You Single" and "Make Up Your Mind." But after some disagreements over the ownership of the group's name, Young and Jones formed another outfit called Déja. Signed by Virgin Records, the duo nearly topped the R&B charts in 1987 with "You And Me Tonight." Quitting the duo in 1988, Starleana Young pursued a solo career. Meanwhile, Curt Jones teamed with replacement singer Mysti Day to release one more album as Déja. Two other Aurra members would later join the funk group, Mtume. During this period, Steve Washington also worked with P-Funk leader George Clinton on tracks such as "Hey Good Lookin'" and "Do Fries Go With That Shake."

LAKESIDE

One of the more underappreciated funk groups to emerge from Ohio, Lakeside employed multiple lead singers. The group originated in 1969, when guitarist Stephen Shockley formed The Young Underground in his hometown of Dayton. The group would soon add a second vocalist, Mark Wood.

Moving to Chicago and winning a talent contest, the group earned a recording contract with Curtom Records. But unfortunately, Curtom closed its doors shortly afterwards. Soon renamed Lakeside Express, the group borrowed the moniker from a Chicago newspaper.

Relocating to Los Angeles in 1974, the group experienced a series of personnel changes. Then after another dead-end recording deal, this time with

Motown, the group briefly recorded for ABC Records. But soon after, the label went under.

After drawing the attention of Solar Records, the nine-man group finally managed to reach the charts. Now called Lakeside, the group scored a top-10 R&B hit in 1978 with the disco/funk track, "It's All The Way Live (Part 1)." In 1980, the group released its signature hit, "Fantastic Voyage"; an R&B chart-topper, it was followed by a soul-ballad rendition of The Beatles chestnut, "I Want To Hold Your Hand." Also known for their fashion sense, members of Lakeside adopted a new look for every album cover.

After scoring two more top-10, R&B hits – "Raid" and "Outrageous" – Lakeside would disband in the late-1980s. Meanwhile, "Fantastic Voyage" would return to the charts in 1994, thanks to a hit cover version by rapper Coolio. The song also appeared in a P. Diddy television commercial for Pepsi.

NEO-SOUL: JOHN LEGEND & VAN HUNT

Situated just outside of Dayton is the town of Springfield, home of neo-soul singer John Legend (born John Stephens). A child prodigy, Legend began playing piano at age five. Initially home-schooled, he started attending a public high school at 12 and graduated four-years later. While still in his teens, he played the piano on Lauren Hill's 1999, million-selling hit, "Everything Is Everything."

While majoring in English at the University of Pennsylvania, Legend continued his musical pursuits. Directing a church choir and recording a pair of independently-issued albums, Legend drew the attention of R&B singer-songwriter Kanye West, who was the cousin of Legend's college roommate. After contributing vocals and musical accompaniment on West's hit album *The College Dropout*, Legend emerged as an in-demand session vocalist and was soon working with Jay-Z, Alicia Keys, Janet Jackson and The Black Eyed Peas.

In 2004, Legend released the Kanye West-produced album, *Get Lifted*. Highlighted by the self-composed, crossover soul hit "Ordinary People," the double-platinum album earned three Grammys, including the award for Best New Artist. With his sophisticated sound and old-school R&B charm, Legend leaped to the forefront of the neo-soul movement. Issued in 2006, Legend's follow-up album, the million-selling *Once Again,* spawned the R&B hits, "Save Room" and "Heaven."

Another neo-soul artist from the Dayton area, multi-instrumentalist Van Hunt emerged from a local band called Royalty. Inspired by the funk of The Ohio Players and the punk rock of Iggy Pop, Hunt infused elements of rock, R&B and jazz into his music. While attending Morehouse College in Atlanta, Hunt began producing demo recordings for local rappers.

Hunt's first success came as the writer and producer of the Dionne Farris track, "Hopeless." With the song appearing on the soundtrack of the film

Love Jones, Hunt soon joined Farris' band on piano and guitar.

By 2002, Hunt was managed by Randy Jackson (of *American Idol* fame) and was signed by Capitol Records the following year. Released in 2004, Hunt's self-titled, debut album spawned the hits, "Down Here In Hell (With You)," "Seconds Of Pleasure" and the Grammy-nominated "Dust." Producing, writing and playing nearly all of the instruments on his 2006 followup album, *On The Jungle Floor*, Hunt scored a pair of hits, "Character," and a duet with Nikka Costa, "Mean Sleep."

In 2006, Hunt joined Joss Stone and fellow Dayton soul singer John Legend on a hit cover of Sly & The Family Stone's "Family Affair." The track earned a Grammy nomination.

CANTON - AKRON - CLEVELAND

A more urban environment than the rest of the state, Northeast Ohio spawned a variety of R&B and soul entertainers. Many of these acts were reared on the classic R&B music of Cleveland radio station, WZAK. While Canton gave rise to the soul acts Macy Gray and The O'Jays, Akron spawned Howard Hewett, James Ingram and Ruby & The Romantics, and Cleveland produced Edwin Starr and The Dazz Band. Meanwhile, Youngstown native Robert "Kool" Bell would relocate to New Jersey and later form Kool & The Gang.

THE O'JAYS

Nicknamed the "Hall of Fame City," Canton is best associated with its role in the emergence of professional football. With its Pro Football Hall Fame, annual parade, induction ceremony and kickoff exhibition game, the city breathes all things football.

The first major musical act of the rock era to emerge from Canton was The O'Jays. After catching a performance by the doo-wop quartet Frankie Lymon & The Teenagers at the Canton Memorial Auditorium, several Canton teenagers decided to form their own similar group. Calling themselves The Triumphs, the group also sang gospel songs every Sunday morning on a local radio station. Consisting of Walter Williams, William Powell, Eddie Levert and two others, The Triumphs performed at local talent competitions, and often crossed paths with another budding local act from nearby Akron, Ruby And The Romantics. Heading to King Records in Cincinnati and changing names from The Triumphs to The Mascots, the group recorded a few tracks.

In 1961, The Mascots were aided in their career by popular Cleveland deejay, Eddie O'Jay. Frequently traveling to Cleveland, the group would lip-sync to the 45rpm record of their local hit, "Miracles," at high school sock-hops hosted by the deejay. In tribute to their mentor, the group changed its name to The O'Jays.

In 1963, The O'Jays teamed with producer/songwriter H.B. Barnum. Signing with Imperial Records, the group placed several singles on the R&B charts, including the top-20 entry, "Stand In For Love." On a roll, the group reached the R&B top-10 the following year at Bell Records with "I'll Be

Sweeter Tomorrow." But after the loss of member Bill Isles, the group disbanded for a short time.

Soon reforming, The O'Jays teamed with producers Kenny Gamble and Leon Huff at Neptune Records. But with the label closing its doors, Bob Massey left the group in 1971 to work as a producer. Pared down to a trio, The O'Jays signed with Gamble and Huff's new label, Philadelphia International Records. During this time, Eddie Levert was offered a solo contract by Motown, which he rejected.

Beginning with the 1972 hit single "Back Stabbers," The O'Jays reached their creative stride. Propelled to the forefront of soul music, the group continued its hit run with "Love Train," "For The Love Of Money," "I Love Music" and "Use Ta Be My Girl." Ironically, it took an Ohio group to help create what became known as "the Philadelphia Sound."

Following the death of longtime member William Powell in 1977, the group added Sammy Strain (formerly of Little Anthony And The Imperials). Then in the late-1970s, the group's career ground to a halt. "They were giving the best material to Teddy Pendergrass and Patti LaBelle. The songs they were giving us were mediocre at best. Consequently, we got no hits. We thought it was time to move on," Walter Williams later told *The Cleveland Plain Dealer*.

Though the group's chart run would ebb in the 1980s, The O'Jays continued to tour regularly. By the start of the 21st century, only Eddie Levert Sr. and Walter Williams would remain from the original lineup. In 2006, The O'Jays sued Philadelphia International over unpaid royalties. Meanwhile, two of the group's hits would gain new life, decades after their release – "Love Train" was used in a Coors commercial and "For The Love Of Money" became the theme song of Donald Trump's reality series, *The Apprentice*.

GERALD LEVERT

Ignoring their father's pleas not to pursue careers in music, two of Eddie Levert's children followed in his path. As a teenager, Gerald Levert had a goal of recording with his father. "I always wanted to do an album with him, but I wanted to wait until I had something to bring to the party. I couldn't do it when I first started because I would have been relying on his reputation, and I had promised myself that I'd never ride on his name. Before I could put the names Gerald Levert and Eddie Levert on the same album, I had to make the name Gerald Levert mean something," the younger Levert told *The Washington Post*.

In 1982, Gerald Levert teamed with his brother Sean and a childhood friend Marc Gordon to form the R&B trio, Levert. Signing with an independent label before landing at Atlantic Records in 1986, Levert scored a series of top-10 R&B hits such as "(Pop, Pop, Pop, Pop) Goes My Mind," "Addicted To You," "Just Coolin'" and "Baby I'm Ready." The group's only crossover, pop hit came in 1987 with the top-10 smash, "Casanova." In 1984, Gerald Levert teamed with R&B stars Keith Sweat and Johnny Gill to form the supergroup, LSG. Recording just one album, the trio scored an R&B hit with "My Body."

Simultaneously pursuing a solo career, Gerald Levert issued his fist solo album in 1991, *Private Line*. The project spawned a pair of number-one R&B hits, "Private Line," and a duet with his father Eddie Levert, "Baby Hold On To Me." In 1995, the pair would finally team up to record a duet album, *Father & Son*.

Also a producer, Gerald Levert worked with Barry White, Stephanie Mills, Troop, Mikki Howard, one-time Ohio resident Anita Baker, Akron singer James Ingram and The O'Jays. Discovered and managed by Gerald Levert, the Cleveland R&B group Rude Boys scored several hits including the 1991 R&B chart-topping ballad, "Written All Over Your Face." One of the group's members, Larry Marcus, is the cousin of blues legend B.B. King.

Also managed and produced by Levert, Cleveland-based Men At Large consisted of David Tolliver and Jason Champion. (David Tolliver's uncle, Lyn Tolliver, is a veteran Cleveland deejay). The duo scored several R&B hits in the mid-1990s, including "Use Me" and the crossover entry "So Alone."

Tragically, Gerald Levert died of a heart attack in 2005 at age 40. At the time of his death, he had just completed the posthumously-issued album, *In My Songs*, and co-authored an autobiography with his father, *I Got Your Back*. Tragedy struck again with the sudden death of Sean Levert in 2008.

RUBY AND THE ROMANTICS

Originally a member of a local girl-group, Ruby Nash began performing around the Akron-Canton area in the late-1950s. Then in 1961, Nash was asked to join an all-male, Akron-based group called The Supremes (not the Motown group of the same name), which consisted of Leroy Fann, George Lee, Ronald Mosley and Ed Roberts.

After performing around Ohio, the group headed to New York City in search of a manager and recording contract. After an audition for Kapp Records, the label asked Nash to move to the lead vocal role. Renamed Ruby & The Romantics, the group topped the charts in 1963 with its debut release, "Our Day Will Come." The group's hit run continued with "My Summer Love" and "Hey There Lonely Boy." Though placing several more singles on the charts, none would reach the top-40. Shortly after the group left Kapp for ABC Records in 1965, Nash's manager replaced the entire backing group.

In the end, the members of Ruby & The Romantics had earned little for their efforts. Returning to Akron, Ruby Nash later told her hometown newspaper: "We weren't very knowledgeable about some things.... I don't regret being a professional singer. My only regret is that I wasn't prepared to control my career or keep concert promoters and record producers from stealing thousands of dollars from us."

After retiring from music in 1971, Nash worked at AT&T for the next five years. A number of the group's songs enjoyed renewed lives through cover versions: "Hurting Each Other" by The Carpenters, "Our Day Will Come" by Frankie Valli, "Young And In Love" by The Marvelettes, and "Hey There Lonely Boy" was reworked as "Hey There Lonely Girl" by Eddie Holman.

HOWARD HEWETT

Hailing from Akron, R&B singer Howard Hewett was initially compared to legendary Motown crooner, Marvin Gaye. Breaking into music as a child, Hewett fronted a touring gospel group which also included his older sisters, The Hewett Singers. Drawn to the outrageous funk stylings of George Clinton, Hewett joined a pair of local R&B groups during his mid-teens, Soul Corporation and Lyfe, and played in area clubs such as the Tropicana and Silver Leaf. After graduating from Akron's Buchtel High School, Hewett moved to Los Angeles in the late-1970s.

While trying to jumpstart his musical career, Hewett began dating his soon-to-be first wife, *Soul Train* dancer Rainey Riley-Cunningham. During this period, *Soul Train* host Don Cornelius had assembled an R&B trio, Shalamar, which included Gerald Brown, Jeffrey Daniels and Jody Watley. Then upon Brown's departure in 1979, Hewett was added to the group as the lead vocalist.

Signing with Solar Records, Shalamar enjoyed a string of hits, including "Make That Move," "A Night To Remember" and the million-selling "The Second Time Around." The group's most enduring song, "Dancing In The Sheets," was featured in the Kevin Bacon film, *Footloose*. During this time, Hewett began duetting with a host of musical partners including Anita Baker, LaToya Jackson, Dionne Warwick and Stacy Lattisaw.

But with Shalamar imploding, Hewett left the group in 1985 to pursue a solo career. A hot commodity at the time, he received multiple offers from record companies. Signing with Elektra, Hewett released his debut album the following year, *I Commit To Love*. The project spawned the hits "I'm For Real," "Stay," and a surprise, gospel hit which became Hewett's theme song, "Say Amen." Though Hewett would find little crossover success, he enjoyed a strong hit run on urban radio with "I Commit To Love," "Strange Relationship" and "Show Me." Meanwhile in 1993, Hewett would end his high-profile, four-year marriage to his third wife, actress Nia Peeples.

In the mid-1990s, Hewett began working with jazz artists such as George Duke, Joe Sample and Brian Culbertson. Drawn to Christian music in the early-2000s, Hewett released a pair of gospel albums, *The Journey* and *The Journey Live: From The Heart*.

Blaming the lack of a Shalamar reunion on Jody Watley, Hewett told *The Akron Beacon Journal*, "I would love for it to happen, and so would Jeffrey [Daniels]. In fact, Jeffrey and I sometimes tour together in Japan, and we do Shalamar material. It's all Jody's decision. She says she doesn't want to revisit the past. To me, it's just business. I think it would do very well, and I think it would be an incredible show. I still feel that Shalamar is an unfinished book."

JAMES & PHILLIP INGRAM

Although Akron natives James and Phillip Ingram were both successful R&B artists, the brothers took different musical paths. While James developed into a pop-soul crooner, his brother Phillip was immersed in danceable funk.

A self-taught musician who was proficient on keyboards, guitar and electric bass, James Ingram teamed with Bernard Lawson to form a local R&B band called Revelation Funk. Dropping out of the University of Akron during his sophomore year in 1973, Ingram relocated to Los Angeles with his band. After the group dissolved, Ingram found plenty of session work. Hired as a backing vocalist by a variety of musical acts, Ingram joined Ray Charles on road dates and The Coasters on their Dick Clark oldies revues.

But when veteran producer/performer Quincy Jones heard Ingram's demo of the pleading ballad "Just Once," the Akronite was asked to record the song for Jones' 1981 album, *The Dude*. Issued as by Quincy Jones featuring James Ingram, the single was a crossover hit and earned three Grammy nominations.

After touring with Jones and a 50-piece orchestra, Ingram later teamed with Patti Austin and returned to the charts in 1982 with the chart-topping, million-selling, duet single, "Baby, Come To Me." Scoring a string of duet hits, James next paired with Michael McDonald on "Yah Mo B There." Then teamed with Kenny Rogers and Kim Carnes, Ingram charted with "What About Me?" Also a songwriter, Ingram collaborated with Michael Jackson to co-write the track "P.Y.T. (Pretty Young Thing)," which was included on the massively-successful, hit album, *Thriller*.

Ingram's most enduring hit came with a ballad from the animated film, *An American Tail* – a million-selling duet with Linda Ronstadt, "Somewhere Out There." Then in 1990, Ingram topped the charts with a rare solo hit, "I Don't Have The Heart."

Meanwhile, James Ingram's younger brother, Phillip, scored a series of R&B hits in the late-1970s and early-1980s as the lead vocalist of the Mansfield-based funk group, Switch. Four of the group's members, including Ingram, were previously in an Akron-based outfit called White Heat; the group recorded a Barry White-produced album for RCA Records, which failed to ignite interest. Formed in 1975, Switch also included a pair of former gospel singers from Michigan, brothers Bobby and Tommy DeBarge.

Discovered by Jermaine Jackson, the group signed with the Motown subsidiary, Gordy Records. In 1978, Switch scored its only crossover hit with the soulful ballad, "There'll Never Be." The group's R&B hit run continued with "I Wanna Be Closer," "Best Beat In Town," "I Call Your Name" and "Love Over And Over Again."

In 1980, the DeBarge brothers left Switch and joined their siblings in the pop-soul band, DeBarge. After leaving Switch in 1983, Phillip Ingram teamed with bandmate Attala Zane Giles to form a shortlived duo, Deco. Then in 1987, Ingram scored a minor, duet hit with Scherrie Payne, "Incredible."

BOBBY WOMACK

An often-overlooked singer-songwriter, Cleveland-born Bobby Womack had a diverse career. As a member of the family gospel act The Womack Brothers, Bobby Womack first performed professionally in 1953 after his father convinced Sam Cooke to let the five young brothers open up for Cooke's gospel group, The Soul Stirrers. Soon after, The Womack Brothers began touring with gospel acts such as The Staple Singers and The Five Blind Boys Of Mississippi. Bobby Womack served a duel role while touring with The Blind Boys, and was hired as the group's guitar player. Womack had learned to play the instrument at a young age by watching his musician father.

Meanwhile, Cooke had abandoned gospel in 1957 and began a successful solo career in pop music. Recommended to Cooke by The Blind Boys, The Womack Brothers were signed to SAR Records, a label launched by Cooke and his business partner J.W. Alexander. With their debut gospel release faring poorly, the brothers were convinced by Cooke to record some pop material. But upon hearing the news, the group's devout father wept and evicted his sons from their home in Cleveland. In response, Cooke wired the brothers enough money to purchase a car to take them to Los Angeles.

Forsaking sacred for secular music, the renamed Valentinos scored a top-10 R&B hit in 1962 with "Lookin' For A Love." That same year, Bobby Womack joined Cooke's backing group as a guitarist and performed on the hit, "Twistin' The Night Away." Continuing his membership in The Valentinos, Womack composed and provided the lead vocals on their 1964 release, "It's All Over Now," basing the lyrics on an uncle who was having marital difficulties. But upon hearing The Valentinos' unreleased track, The Rolling Stones would quickly record and issue the song, which eclipsed the original version on the charts.

Following the sudden death of Sam Cooke at the hands of a gun-toting motel clerk, Bobby Womack parted with The Valentinos and pursued a solo career. Then just three months after Cooke's funeral, the 21-year-old Womack wed Cooke's widow, Barbara, who was about a decade his senior. Though the marriage was her idea, Womack was attacked in the press, boycotted by radio and treated poorly by the public.

In 1965, Bobby Womack began a two-year stint behind soul singer Ray Charles. Then by the late-1960s, Womack emerged as a popular studio musician in Memphis and Muscle Shoals, Alabama, where he played behind Jackie Wilson, Aretha Franklin, Joe Tex, Dusty Springfield and countless others. Also backing Elvis Presley, Womack performed on the hits "In The Ghetto" and "Suspicious Minds."

A prolific songwriter, Womack penned the Wilson Pickett hits, "She's So Good To Me," "I'm Sorry About That" and "I'm A Midnight Mover." Briefly joining Pickett's band, Womack quit due to his boss' erratic and violent behavior.

After divorcing his wife in 1970, Womack began working with bandleader

Sly Stone. Issuing the self-produced album *Communication* – much of which was recorded at Muscle Shoals – Womack scored hits with "That's The Way I Feel About Cha" and "Woman's Gotta Have It." During this period, Womack contributed the composition "Trust Me" to Janis Joplin's album *Pearl*. Then after The J. Geils Band scored a hit with Womack's "Lookin' For A Love," Womack re-recorded the song and reached the pop top-10 in 1974.

But following his brother Harry's death in 1974, a devastated Bobby Womack faked blindness to get out of scheduled concerts. But with U.S. promoters threatening legal action, Womack spent the next few years touring across Europe. Taking a stylistic turn for the 1975 country-flavored album *BW Goes C&W*, Bobby Womack was joined on the recording sessions by his father and surviving brothers.

Issued in 1981, Womack's comeback album, *The Poet*, was marred by a lengthy lawsuit against his label over royalties. After winning the court case, Womack switched record companies and released *The Poet II* in 1984.

After befriending guitarist Ronnie Wood, Womack joined The Rolling Stones' entourage for several years and also provided the backing vocals on their 1986 hit, "Harlem Shuffle." In 1999, Womack released his first-ever gospel album, *Back To My Roots*. Then when Sam and Barbara Cooke's daughter, Linda, married Bobby Womack's brother, Cecil, Bobby Womack became the stepfather of his own brother.

EDWIN STARR

One the grittiest soul singers to emerge from the Buckeye State, Edwin Starr (born Charles Hatcher) is best remembered for the protest song, "War." A native of Nashville, Starr moved with his family to Cleveland at age three. While attending East Technical High School, Starr received vocal training from friend Sonny Turner, the leader of an established, local doo-wop group called The Metrotones. (Turner would find fame in the 1960s as the lead vocalist of The Platters on hits such as "With This Ring" and "I Love You 1000 Times.")

In 1956, Starr formed an 11-member doo-wop group, The Future Tones. After a 1959 performance on a local talent program, the group was selected as an opening act for visiting jazz legend, Billie Holiday.

But shortly after The Future Tones recorded a single, Starr was drafted into the army. After his discharge in 1960, Starr returned to Cleveland and rejoined his former group. But with the act losing its momentum, Starr accepted an offer to replace Howard Tate in Bill Doggett's touring band. Though hired as an organist in what had been an instrumental group, Starr was permitted to sing a song or two. But with Doggett refusing to allow Starr to record a song he had written, Starr quit to pursue a solo career.

Moving to Detroit and signing with Ric-Tic Records, Starr scored a top-10 R&B hit in 1965 with "Agent Double-O-Soul," which was inspired by the James Bond film series. Starr followed up with "Back Street" and "Stop Her

On Sight (S.O.S.)." Also having success as a songwriter, Starr composed the hit "Oh How Happy" for a Detroit group he had discovered, Shades Of Blue.

Angry that Motown session players were often moonlighting at Ric-Tic Records, Motown chief Berry Gordy purchased the tiny label in 1967. Although Starr had suddenly become a Motown artist, the label initially ignored the singer. Starr's first hit at Motown came two-years later with "25 Miles," which was produced by music veterans Johnny Bristol and Harvey Fuqua. The followup release, "I'm Still A Struggling Man" was a moderate R&B hit.

In 1970, Edwin Starr topped the charts with his signature piece, "War." Written by Norman Whitfield, the song was initially recorded as an album track by The Temptations. But when The Temptations' version began garnering radio airplay, Motown wanted to shield its superstar group from political controversy and chose Starr to record a new rendition. Recorded in just one take, the song was embraced by critics of the Vietnam War. (Ironically, Starr's brother was a U.S. Marine who was serving in Vietnam at the time.) Starr's followup release, "Stop The War Now," was similarly themed. Continuing his hit run, Starr scored a pair of R&B hits with "Funky Music Sho Nuff Turns Me On" and "There You Go."

In 1973, Starr hired an unknown act called Total Concept Unlimited as his backing band. By 1976, the group was renamed Rose Royce and would score hits with "Car Wash" and "I Wanna Get Next To You." Then a year after recording the soundtrack for the 1973 film *Hell Up In Harlem*, Starr left Motown over a royalty dispute.

Then after frequently touring across Western Europe, Starr settled in Warwickshire, England. He would subsequently record for a series of British labels as well as for Germany's WEA. Returning to the charts in 1979, Starr scored a pair of disco hits, "Contact" and "H.A.P.P.Y. Radio."

In 1986, Bruce Springsteen reached the top-10 with a live rendition of "War." In 1999, Starr joined Springsteen onstage in Birmingham, England, to perform a duet of the song. The following year, Starr teamed with Utah Saints to record an updated rendition of "Funky Music Sho Nuff Turns Me On."

THE DAZZ BAND

At the forefront of the electronic-funk movement of the early-1980s, The Dazz Band were a club favorite. Originally a jazz-fusion outfit called Telefunk, the group was formed on Cleveland's east side by saxophonist Bobby Harris in 1974.

Combining R&B with danceable funk, the group evolved into Kinsman Dazz, the longtime house band at the Kinsman Grill. Aided by local record distributor Joe Simone, the group signed with 20th Century Records in 1976. Paired at the label with producer Philip Bailey of Earth, Wind & Fire, the group scored a pair of minor R&B hits.

With Joe Simone now their manager, the renamed Dazz Band secured a recording contract with Motown. Then with trumpet player Sennie "Skip" Martin taking over lead vocal duties from Wayne Calhoun, the group topped the R&B charts in 1982 with the Grammy-winning, synthesizer-driven, funk-flavored hit, "Let It Whip." Though experiencing frequent personnel changes, the group continued its chart run with a series of dance-oriented releases, including "On The One For Fun," "Joystick," "Swoop (I'm Yours)," "Let It All Blow" and "Heartbeat."

After the departure of Martin in 1986, the group jumped to Geffen Records and scored its final hit in 1988 with "Single Girls." Over the next several-years, the group embarked on a number of well-received, overseas tours.

MACY GRAY

A neo-soul singer, Macy Gray possessed a unique, raspy voice reminiscent of Billie Holiday. With her retro-styled afro, funky clothes and charming persona, Gray quickly shot to fame. A native of Canton, the former Natalie McIntyre borrowed her stage name from a neighbor.

A gifted child who earned a scholarship to a prestigious boarding school near Akron, Gray was exposed to the rock music of her fellow classmates. Then while pursuing a film degree at the University of California, she found herself drawn to a clique of musicians.

Accidentally breaking into music, Gray was asked to write some song lyrics for a friend. But when her friend failed to appear for the scheduled recording session, Gray performed the songs herself. Despite the fact she disliked her own singing voice, Gray went from performing in the jazz clubs of Los Angeles to drawing the attention of major labels. But when Atlantic Records decided to pass on Gray's demo recordings, the dejected singer returned to Canton.

With her demo recordings still making the rounds, Gray found another suitor in 1998 – Epic Records. Taking nearly a year to record her debut album, *On How Life Is*, Gray was disappointed by the poor showing of the first single, "Do Something." But the second single, "I Try," would change Gray's life. A smash hit, it would propel the album to multi-platinum sales and earn a Grammy award for Best Female Pop Vocal Performance. Though Gray's 2001 followup album, *The Id*, was a commercial disappointment in her home country, it was a strong seller in the U.K.

Then with 20,000 fans packed into Canton's Fawcett Stadium on August 6, 2001, Macy Gray made national headlines with her pre-game annihilation of the national anthem. Forgetting the words and singing off-key, Gray was heckled and booed by those in attendance.

Released in 2003, Gray's third studio album, *The Trouble With Being Myself*, was highlighted by the track, "When I See You." Considered a comeback effort, Gray's fourth studio album, *Big*, was issued in 2007.

Also appearing on the big screen, Gray had roles in several films including *Training Day*, *Spider Man*, *Domino*, *Lackawanna Blues* and *Idlewild*. In 2005, Gray opened the M. Gray Music Academy in Los Angeles, to provide a musical education for latchkey children.

Another R&B female vocalist from Ohio, Vesta Williams, was born an hour south of Canton in the city of Coshocton, but raised in Los Angeles when her disc jockey father landed a radio job. After returning to Ohio in the late-1970s, Williams was hired by an R&B band in Dayton. Then after joining a group led by former Fifth Dimension member Ron Townsend, Williams emerged as a popular session vocalist.

Signed to a solo contract by A&M Records, Williams would place a dozen hits on the R&B charts beginning with "Once Bitten, Twice Shy" and continuing with "Sweet, Sweet Love" and "Special." In 1988, she dropped her last name and was simply known as "Vesta."

AVANT

A native of Cleveland, R&B vocalist, Avant (born Myron Avant), is best known for his romantic ballads. Inspired by a gifted uncle, Avant honed his musical abilities while attending the Cleveland School of the Arts. After winning a number of local talent shows, Avant signed with the MCA-distributed label, Magic Johnson Music.

An old-school R&B crooner, Avant possessed a pleasing, smooth tenor. Issued in 2000, Avant's debut album, *My Thoughts*, was a million-seller and spawned the hits, "Separated" and "My First Love." Also a million-seller, Avant's 2002 follow, *Ecstasy*, was highlighted by the track, "Makin' Good Love."

Continuing his hit run with the 2003 album, *Private Room*, Avant also reached the charts with the track "Don't Take Your Love Away" from the *Shark Tale* soundtrack. In 2005, Avant issued his fourth album, *Director*, which was highlighted by "You Know What." In 2006, Avant backed P. Diddy on the single, "Claim My Place."

BLUES IN OHIO

Although Ohio is far removed from the Delta region of Mississippi, blues music has flourished throughout the Buckeye State, particularly in areas with large populations of African-Americans such as Cincinnati and Cleveland.

Sometimes called the South's most Northern city, Cincinnati boasts a rich blues tradition. Cincinnati native Mamie Smith was the first artist to record a blues song. Issued in 1920, the 78rpm single, "Crazy Blues," was a sensation. A strong-selling record which was purchased by blacks and whites alike, the single spawned numerous imitators as record labels rushed to meet the unexpected demand.

During the 1920s, Cincinnati supported a thriving blues scene in the city's West End district. In these rough establishments, local bluesmen such as Sam

"Stovepipe" Jones and Bob "Kid Cole" Coleman entertained fellow African-Americans. A number of the city's blues artists ventured across the state border to Richmond, Indiana, to record for Gennett Records. Conversely, a few visiting bluesmen such as Walter Davis and Roosevelt Sykes recorded in Cincinnati, at a primitive studio inside a room at the Sinton Hotel.

By 1932, stride-style pianist Fats Waller came to Cincinnati and was hired by radio station WLW. Hosting his own radio program, *Fats Waller's Rhythm Club*, he also performed in area clubs. Legend has it that he was fired two-years later for pumping out boogie-woogie style jazz on an organ that had been dedicated to the station owner's mother. Leaving for New York City, Waller found greater fame with a program on the CBS radio network.

Meanwhile, when a young John Lee Hooker arrived in Cincinnati in 1933, he worked as a theater usher and joined a number of gospel groups including The Fairfield Four and The Big Six. Also honing his blues skills, Hooker performed at numerous house parties. After moving to Detroit in 1943, Hooker achieved national acclaim with hits such as "Boom Boom" and "Boogie Chillen'."

In the 1940s, blues music in Cincinnati was given a boost by a local record label. Shortly after Syd Nathan launched Cincinnati's King Records in 1943, he expanded from country into jazz, R&B and blues. Over the next two decades, numerous blues acts recorded at the label including Champion Jack Dupree, Memphis Slim, Albert King and former Cincinnati resident John Lee Hooker. One of the most successful blues acts at the label was Texas-born singer-guitarist Freddy King, who scored several hits including "Hide Away" and "I'm Tore Down."

Another notable Cincinnati bluesman, H-Bomb Ferguson, was notorious for both his musical prowess and his outrageous stage act. A native of Charleston, South Carolina, Ferguson was the 11th of 12 children of a Baptist preacher. Though honing his piano skills in the church, Ferguson was drawn toward the blues during his teen years. An explosive entertainer with a booming voice, he was initially nicknamed Cobra Kid, and then, H-Bomb. But after touring with B.B. King and scoring a few national hits in the 1950s, Ferguson had little to show for his hard work.

Leaving New York City for Cincinnati in 1957, Ferguson was lured by a recording contract with King-Federal Records. At the label, he would record the blues chestnuts, "Mary, Little Mary" and "Midnight Ramblin' Tonight." Ferguson also enjoyed a longterm residency at Cincinnati's Cotton Club. Located inside the Hotel Sterling, the Cotton Club was an early, racially-integrated nightclub. After the club's closure in the late-1950s, the city purchased the building, which was demolished in 1962.

Though retiring for a time in the 1970s, Ferguson returned to the stage after watching a television performance by R&B singer Rick James. Fascinated with James' elaborately adorned hair, Ferguson began wearing bright, outlandish wigs as a gimmick. Soon, he also wore grass skirts and wrapped himself with a live, boa constrictor named Boo Boo.

Another popular local bluesman, Albert Washington recorded for King's crosstown rival, Fraternity Records. A former gospel singer who had recorded with The Gospelaires, Washington became a fixture on the Cincinnati blues scene during his 16-year stint in the house band at the Vet's Inn. In 1969, Washington recorded a number of tracks with sideman Lonnie Mack. Though losing his sight to diabetes in the mid-1970s, Washington continued to record and perform.

Meanwhile, when Cincinnati music historian Steven C. Tracy began researching the city's blues history in the 1970s, he discovered that two long-forgotten bluesmen were still alive. With some prodding and gentle encouragement, Tracy managed to reignite the careers of both Big Joe Duskin and Pigment Jarrett.

At the other end of the state, Cleveland had its own thriving jazz and blues scene. With the auto and steel industries booming in the years following World War II, African-Americans migrated from the South to work in Cleveland's numerous, smoke-belching factories. A host of nightclubs opened to accommodate the influx, including the Cedar Gardens, Lindsay's Sky Bar, the Theatrical Grill, the Ebony Lounge and Gleason's. Visiting African-American musicians usually stayed at the Majestic Hotel, which also housed a jazz club. Targeting the urban market, Leo Mintz had opened the Record Rendezvous, which sold records by jazz and blues artists.

Cleveland nurtured a number of talented blues players. The legendary blues guitarist Robert Lockwood Jr. (occasionally spelled Robert Jr. Lockwood) was a fixture on the Cleveland musical landscape for decades. Called the last living link to guitarist Robert Johnson, Lockwood had received musical training from his stepfather. Following the poisoning death of Johnson in 1938, Lockwood found his way to Helena, Arkansas, where he played behind Sonny Boy Williamson on the radio program, *The King Biscuit Time*. Landing in Chicago by 1950, Lockwood worked as a session player behind some of the city's finest blues players including Sunnyland Slim, Eddie Boyd and Little Walter. Also a solo performer, Lockwood recorded for a series of labels.

But with the popularity of blues waning in the early-1960s, Lockwood settled in Cleveland and raised a family. At the time, the blues scene in Northeast Ohio was in a decline, except for a few acts such as Cleveland's Arbee Stidham and Akron's one-man band, Blind Joe Hill.

Regularly performing in Cleveland nightclubs such as Joe's Thing and Bar-Tees, Lockwood continued to record. Then in 1990, he won the very first W.C. Handy Award for Best Traditional Blues Album. After recording a trio of albums with bluesman Johnny Shines, Lockwood solidified his reputation. Then in 1998, Lockwood would earn his first of his three Grammy nominations. Performing until shortly before his death in 2006, Lockwood enjoyed a Wednesday-night residency at a downtown Cleveland nightclub,

Fat Fish Blue.

In the late-1980s, Robert Lockwood Jr. had befriended a transplanted, British slide-guitarist named Mr. Downchild, who made Cleveland his home. A classic Delta-styled player, Mr. Downchild would record with Lockwood, Pinetop Perkins and Sam Carr.

Another longtime Cleveland bluesman, Bill Miller, was celebrated in Chrissie Hynde's musical ode to the city of Cleveland, "Precious." Inspired by the pioneering, white bluesman Paul Butterfield, Miller began playing the blues harmonica as the leader of the local band Mr. Stress, and over the next few decades, emerged as a Midwestern institution. Eventually, Miller adopted the stage name, Mr. Stress.

One of the more creative Buckeye blues acts emerged from Akron. Rooted in the Delta-styled tradition, The Black Keys took the music world by storm. Often compared to the Detroit-based, blues-rock duo The White Stripes, The Black Keys were formed by singer-guitarist Dan Auerbach and drummer Patrick Carney.

Reared in a musical family, Patrick Carney is the nephew of Tin Huey saxophonist Ralph Carney. Hailing from Athens, Ohio, but settling in Akron, Auerback met Carney at Firestone High School. During this period, the pair occasionally performed together. By his mid-teens, Auerback was drawn to the music of pioneering blues players such as Robert Johnson and Son House.

After briefly enrolled at separate out-of-town universities, Carney and Auerbach reunited while attending the University of Akron. The two men then reconnected while working for the same landscaping firm. Quitting their day jobs at the same time, the pair subsequently formed a blues-rock quartet, which included a keyboardist and harmonica player. But after a few jam sessions, the outfit was pared down to a duo of Auerbach and Carney.

Signing with Fat Possum Records for a three-album deal, The Black Keys drew critical praise for their 2002 debut release, *Big Come Up*. Recording the album in Carney's basement, the duo spent next-to-nothing in production costs. Although Auerback and Carney later attempted to record at a San Francisco studio used by Green Day, the duo realized that their lo-fi, basement studio in Akron was more suited to the blues.

Building a following on both sides of the Atlantic, The Black Keys embarked on a series of tours. Their subsequent albums – *Thickfreakness*, *Rubber Factory* and *Magic Potion* – were throwbacks to the classic, Delta blues sound. One of the duo's songs, "Set You Free," was featured in the Jack Black film, *School Of Rock*.

In 2005, Carney teamed with local musician Jamie Stillman to launch a record label, Audio Eagle; the label showcased its entire roster of acts at a downtown Akron night spot, the Lime Spider. Also that year, *Classic Rock* magazine selected The Black Keys' rendition of the Junior Kimbrough standard "Everywhere I Go" as #87 on its list of the top-100 blues anthems. Released in 2008, the duo's album, *Attack & Release*, reached the top-20.

A somewhat similar act, The Soledad Brothers formed in 1998 from the ashes of a blues outfit called Henry And June. Based in the town of Maumee near Toledo, The Soledad Brothers began as a duo of vocalist Johnny Walker and drummer Ben Swank. Named after a trio of infamous prison convicts, The Soledad Brothers were a hit in the clubs of Detroit. The group was aided on some of its early recordings by Swank's former roommate, Jack White of The White Stripes. Expanded to a trio in time for their second album, The Soledad Brothers added former Greenhornes member Oliver Henry. Constantly on the road, the band told a British paper: "For two years it was just us three in the van. One year we drove 120,000 miles, by ourselves, without a tour manager – we'd sell our own merchandise, we'd unload our own equipment. We did our time." But shortly after the release of their fourth album in 2006, The Soledad Brothers disbanded.

Meanwhile, White Stripes frontman Jack White would also collaborate with members of The Greenhornes. Finding greater success in Detroit than in their native Cincinnati, The Greenhornes would make regular treks up Interstate-75 to perform for their growing fanbase. There, the group quickly drew the attention of the like-minded Jack White.

Then with White yearning to launch a side-project, he teamed with singer-songwriter Brendan Benson and two members of The Greenhornes, drummer Patrick Keeler and bassist Jack Lawrence. Calling themselves The Raconteurs, the hard-edged, blues-rock quartet was an immediate hit. The group's 2006 debut disc, *Broken Boy Soldiers*, was a strong seller and was followed by a sold-out tour. Keeler and Lawrence later teamed with Jack White in a studio band – informally dubbed The Do-Whaters – to back Loretta Lynn on her 2004 Grammy-winning album, *Van Lear Rose*.

DISCO IN OHIO

Emerging in the mid-1970s, disco dominated popular music for the remainder of the decade. Surprisingly, with the exceptions of Wild Cherry, Heatwave and La Flavour, not many Buckeye disco acts achieved national acclaim.

Formed in 1970 by guitarist-vocalist Robert Parissi and a number of fellow high school students in Steubenville, Wild Cherry began in the rock vein. Emerging as a popular bar band in Pittsburgh, the group disbanded in 1974. The following year, Parissi resurrected the group with a new line-up. Taking a turn toward disco but remaining in the rock and roll camp, Wild Cherry began performing throughout northeastern Ohio and would cultivate a following in Cleveland.

Signed by the Cleveland-based label, Sweet City Records – which was operated by producer Carl Maduri and concert promoter Mike Belkin – Wild Cherry recorded its debut album in 1975. During the sessions, Parissi hired local keyboard player Mark Avsec for just one track, "Play That Funky Music." Issued the following year, the single was constructed around a simple lyric written by the group's drummer, Ron Beitle. A surprise top-10 smash, the song was nominated for a Grammy. In the wake of the song's success, Avsec was hired as a full-time member. Veering toward rock on their followup album, Wild Cherry met resistance from radio.

In 1978, Wild Cherry added Pennsylvania-born, singer-guitarist Donnie Iris. (Iris was previously a member of the one-hit wonder, The Jaggerz). The following year, Avsec would team with Iris to form Donnie Iris And The Cruisers. The group would enjoy several hits including "Love Is Like A Rock," "My Girl" and "Ah! Leah!" In the late-1970s, Avsec also moonlighted in the Jonah Koslen-led rock band, Breathless.

As a songwriter and producer, Mark Avsec also worked with Massillon-based disco/show band La Flavour. Recording a self-titled debut album in 1980, the group scored a club hit with "Mandolay." The followup single, "Only The Lonely (Have A Reason To Be Sad)," dented the lower portion of the pop charts. Later signing with MCA Records, La Flavour were forced by their label to abandon disco, and under a new moniker, Fair Warning, recorded a second album. But when another producer heard the album's intended first single, "She Don't Know Me," the song appeared on the debut album by emerging New Jersey rockers, Bon Jovi. Consequently, MCA decided to shelf the Fair Warning project. Reverting to their original name and sound, La Flavour became a fixture on the East Coast showband circuit.

Another disco group with Ohio connections – the soul/funk-based outfit Heatwave – was formed in the mid-1970s on a U.S. military base in West Germany by two Dayton-reared brothers. Johnnie and Keith Wilder began their musical careers while still enlisted in the Army. Remaining in Europe following their discharges, the brothers hired several musicians to round out the group.

A favorite on the London nightclub circuit, Heatwave signed with GTO Records. With the aid of producer Barry Blue, the group's first recording sessions culminated in the 1977 disco smash, "Boogie Nights." Despite a number of personnel changes, the group continued its hit run with the ballad "Always And Forever" and "The Groove Line." Tragedy struck in 1979 when Johnnie Wilder was involved in a serious car crash. Though paralyzed, he continued to perform with the group. An updated version of the group's 1978 single, "Mind Blowing Decisions," reached the British charts in 1991.

Meanwhile, nearly three-decades after the release of the disco blockbuster, *Saturday Night Fever*, the legendary dance floor featured in the film was relocated to Akron.

RAP IN OHIO

Emerging from the urban neighborhoods of New York City during the early-1970s – but not catching fire until the end of the decade – rap music evolved from the rhyming tradition of immigrating, Jamaican, street deejays.

Another origin of rap music is the spoken-word tradition of the Harlem-based group, The Last Poets. Formed in 1968 during the rise of Black nationalism, The Last Poets initially shocked audiences with their blunt, political messages. By the time The Last Poets had settled into their classic line-up in 1969, the quartet included two Ohioans. Umar Bin Hassan had left his hometown of Akron for New York City, where he had hoped to prosper as a poet. The other Buckeye-born member, Abiodun Oyewole hailed from Cincinnati but was raised by his aunt in Queens, New York.

Releasing a self-titled debut album in 1970, The Last Poets scored a surprise hit, reaching the top-30 of *Billboard's* best-sellers chart. The project featured a combination of spoken and sung poetry over a background of jazz percussion. In a 2003 *Vanity Fair* piece, David Bowie would call the album "one of the fundamental building blocks of rap." Though the group's membership was in constant flux, The Last Poets would manage to place two more albums on the charts. The group's music was later sampled by a wide variety of rappers including A Tribe Called Quest, N.W.A. and Brand Nubian.

BONE THUGS-N-HARMONY

Although the state of Ohio is not known as a hotbed of hip-hop activity, several acts would reach national acclaim. Around 1990, a group of friends from Cleveland's Lincoln West High School would form a rap outfit called Faces Of Death. Originally consisting of Krazy Bone, Layzie Bone, Bizzy Bone and Wish Bone, the group issued a debut album in 1992.

Then while one of the group's members, Flesh-N-Bone (Layzie Bone's brother), was attending college in Los Angeles, he convinced his bandmates to join him. Traveling by bus to the West Coast, the aspiring rappers spent three months looking for a career break. Then after an over-the-phone audition, the group attracted the interest of Easy-E (formerly of the hit rap act, N.W.A.).

Mentored by Easy-E, the renamed Bone Thugs-N-Harmony were signed to his label, Ruthless Records. Issued in 1994, the group's EP, *Creepin' On Ah Come Up*, spawned the breakthrough hit, "Thuggish Ruggish Bone." The song's video was shot in Cleveland. The followup single, "Foe Tha Luv Of $," featured a guest rap by Easy-E.

But tragedy struck when Easy-E died shortly after the release of the group's album, *E. 1999 Eternal*. In tribute, the group recorded the track "Tha Crossroads" for inclusion on an expanded edition of the album. Becoming the group's defining moment, the song earned a Grammy in the Best Rap Performance by a Duo or Group category. The album also featured the rap classic, "1st Of Tha Month."

The group's followup albums – *The Art Of War* and *BTNHResurrection* – were solid, radio friendly outings, characterized by socially-conscious, street-savvy lyrics. During this period, member Bizzy Bone battled personal demons and began missing concert appearances and recording sessions.

In 1996, Bone Thugs-N-Harmony launched its own label, Mo Thugs Records. The label's first release, *Mo Thugs Family Scriptures*, showcased talent from around Cleveland. Then during a long hiatus, various members of the group recorded solo projects. But after reforming in 2004, the group would fire Bizzy Bone.

After parting with Ruthless Records, Bone Thugs-N-Harmony issued the 2006 album, *Thug Stories*. Pared down to a trio by 2007, the group released the comeback album, *Strength & Loyalty*, and returned to the top-10 with the track, "I Tried."

Bow Wow

Born and raised in suburban Columbus, Lil' Bow Wow (born Shad Moss) began his professional career at a very young age. Though yearning to become a basketball player, he was instead drawn to music. Landing his big break at age-six, he performed a set of freestyle rap during the intermission at the Columbus stop of Dr. Dre's Chronic Tour. Impressed by the performance, one of the headlining acts, Snoop Doggy Dog, gave the budding rapper the nickname, Lil' Bow Wow, and hired him as an opening act for the rest of the tour. Later, Lil' Bow Wow provided a cameo rap on Snoop Doggy Dog's 1993 hit album, *Doggystyle*.

At age-eight, the pint-sized rapper signed with the Atlanta-based label, So So Def/Columbia Records. With his mother, Teresa Caldwell, assuming managerial duties, the pre-adolescent entertainer was an immediate hit. Released in 2000, Lil' Bow Wow's multi-platinum selling, debut album *Beware Of Dog* was highlighted by the hits, "Bounce With Me" and "Bow Wow (That's My Name)." On the album cover, the young rapper wore a Cleveland Browns jersey.

Moving to Atlanta at age 14 in 2001, he began work on a more pop-flavored, followup album, *Doggy Bag*. Also hitting the big screen, he starred in the 2002 film about basketball stardom, *Like Mike,* and in the 2004 comedy, *Johnson Family Vacation*. During this time, he dropped "Lil'" from his name, switched labels and distanced himself from his parents.

After a few commercially-disappointing albums, Bow Wow reunited with his original producer, Jermaine Dupri, for the 2004 release, *Wanted*. But creating controversy with his song lyrics, Bow Wow was criticized for disparaging fellow performers, including Lil' Romeo, Will Smith and Ronald Isley. In 2007, Bow Wow made a guest appearance on the comeback album by fellow Buckeye rappers, Bone Thugs-N-Harmony.

KID CUDI

Dubbed a "flamboyant introvert" by *Spin* magazine, Cleveland-bred singer-songwriter Kid Cudi creatively merged hip-hop with various other musical genres. In 2004, he relocated to Brooklyn, New York, where he lived with an uncle, a part-time drummer.

Finally in 2009, Cudi scored a surprise, crossover-hit with "Day 'N' Nite." The track had been bouncing around the internet for a full year before mainstream radio took notice.

But even before his first album was released in late-2009, Cudi was co-writing songs with rappers Jay-Z and Kanye West. Also teaming with Cleveland rapper Chip Tha Ripper, Cudi formed a side project, Almighty GloryUS.

Also an actor, Cudi co-starred in the HBO comedy series, *How To Make It In America*.

OTHER OHIO RAPPERS

Cleveland rapper Ray Cash first came to prominence with his vocal contribution to the 1994, hit single by Bone Thugs-N-Harmony, "Thuggish Ruggish Bone." Cash was initially inspired to pursue a career in rap music after attending a Jay-Z concert. After belatedly reaching the charts in 2005 with the humorous track "Sex Appeal," Cash followed up with hits such as "Bumpin' My Music." Cash later tackled political issues on his 2006 album, *C.O.D. (Cash On Delivery)*.

Sentenced in 1992, Toledo rapper Lyfe Jennings served ten-years in prison for an arson conviction. But while behind bars, he was given an acoustic guitar by his brother. Then just days after his release, Lyfe Jennings was recording tracks and performing in Toledo clubs. A socially-conscience lyricist, the melodic rapper infused elements of traditional R&B on hits such as "Must Be Nice."

Meanwhile, Cincinnati-based producer Hi-Tek (born Tony Cottrell), worked with many of the nation's top hip-hop acts including The Game, D12, Common, 50 Cent, Xzibit, Busta Rhymes, Lloyd Banks, Young Buck and Snoop Doggy Dog. Hi-Tek first garnered attention after collaborating with Brooklyn rapper, Talib Kweli. In 2001, Hi-Tek released his first solo album, *Hi-Teknology*. Cincinnati is also home to the nation's largest, annual, hip-hop festival – Scribble Jam.

And although she's best known as a model and actress, Cincinnati's Carmen Electra broke into the entertainment field as a singer. Discovered by Prince, she was signed to his Paisley Park label and recorded a rap album in 1993. In 2003, she married Dave Navarro, the former guitarist of Jane's Addiction and The Red Hot Chili Peppers. The marriage ended after four years.

CHAPTER 11
SINGER-SONGWRITERS, ETC.

The singer-songwriter tradition in rock and roll can be traced back to folk music. Unlike most early rock artists, urban troubadours such as Bob Dylan and Joan Baez were composing their own songs and playing their own instruments. The tradition was continued by British Invasion acts such as The Beatles and Rolling Stones, as self-housed bands no longer needed to hire professional songwriters or backing musicians.

THE FOLK TRADITION

While Ohio has produced a number of nationally-known, folk-rooted artists such as Richie Furay and Phil Ochs, hundreds of other singer-songwriters toiled with little fanfare in the state's many folk coffeehouses and clubs. Notable folk artists from around the state include Jim Ballard, John Bassette, Charlie Weiner, Jon Mosey and Len Chandler. Singer-songwriter Alex Bevan scored a regional radio hit with an ode to his hometown, "Skinny (Little Boy From Cleveland, Ohio)." And though formed in upstate New York, experimental folk-rockers McKendree Spring frequently performed around Ohio and were sometimes considered a Columbus act.

Folk music is celebrated at Kent State University with a popular, annual folk festival. Launched in 1967, it is the second-oldest, college folk festival in the nation. After the university's student government ended funding in 2000, the event was promoted by the university's radio station, WKSU.

PHIL OCHS

One of Bob Dylan's contemporaries in the 1960s was Ohio singer-songwriter Phil Ochs. The two musicians were not the best of friends, and Dylan wrote "Positively Fourth Street," partly as an attack on Ochs.

Moving with his family to Columbus in 1954, Ochs studied music at Capital University Conservatory of Music. A skilled clarinet player at the age of 16, he was selected as a principal soloist of the college's orchestra. After a stint in military school, he returned to Columbus in 1958 to attend Ohio State University. Quitting after one semester, Ochs headed to Florida to try his luck as a singer. But arrested on vagrancy charges, he spent two weeks in jail and then returned to Ohio.

Resuming his studies at Ohio State University in the fall of 1959, Ochs would cross paths with another music enthusiast, Jim Glover. Over the next year, Glover would expose Ochs to the folk greats of the 20th century as well as to Leftist politics. Setting aside his rock and country records, Ochs became immersed in folk music. Formerly apolitical, Ochs became a campus activist as he led protests and penned newspaper editorials. But with his defense of

Fidel Castro considered too radical for university publications, Ochs started his own newspaper, *The Word*. (Around this time, the founder of The Youngbloods, Jesse Colin Young, briefly attended Ohio State University.)

Wanting to articulate politics through music, Ochs was taught to play the guitar by Glover. The pair soon formed two shortlived folk duos, The Singing Socialists and The Sundowners. But after a disagreement, the duo parted. Leaving Columbus for New York City, Glover performed in the coffee houses of Greenwich Village.

Pursuing a solo career, Ochs cultivated a repertoire of mostly folk standards and a few originals. Frequently performing at a new Cleveland folk club called Faragher's Back Room, Ochs opened up for a number of national acts including Judy Henske and The Greenbriar Boys. The summer before his college senior year, Ochs spent a week opening up for folk singer Bob Gibson. During this period, Ochs and Gibson collaborated on two songs, "That's The Way It's Gonna Be," and Ochs' first anti-war effort, "One More Parade," which would soon become popular on the folk club circuit.

Angry that he was not selected the editor of the OSU student newspaper, Ochs dropped out of college in protest during his final year. Heading for Greenwich Village, Ochs bunked with his former singing partner, Jim Glover. Welcomed by fellow folkies, Ochs drew attention in 1962 with the protest song, "The Cuban Invasion."

In the wake of Bob Dylan's newfound success, Ochs was signed by Elektra Records in 1964. With the Vietnam War intensifying, Ochs recorded the classic protest album, *All The News That's Fit To Sing*. His followup album, *I Ain't Marching No More*, was highlighted by the angry title track and "Draft Dodger Rag." Another Ochs composition from this period, "There But For Fortune," became a British hit for Joan Baez in 1965.

Now managed by his brother, Michael, and switching to A&M Records in 1967, Phil Ochs took a more mainstream course beginning with the album, *Pleasures Of The Harbor*. The following year, Ochs was involved in protest actions outside the 1968 Democratic National Convention.

In the 1970s, Ochs struggled with both his career and personal life. Suffering from depression, Ochs abused prescription drugs and alcohol. During this time, Ochs shocked his fans by appearing in an Elvis Presley-style, gold lamé suit. He would wear the same outfit on the cover of his album, *Greatest Hits*.

Disillusioned by the changes in the folk scene and music industry, Ochs withdrew from recording and would only occasionally perform. Traveling around the globe, Ochs suffered damage to his vocal chords as the result of a physical attack during a trip to Africa. In 1976, Ochs died by his own hand.

Phil Ochs' brother, Michael, later operated the world's largest, music photo archive. Meanwhile, Ochs' former singing partner, Jim Glover, formed a folk duo with wife, Jean Ray, and recorded three albums in the 1960s as Jim & Jean.

RICHIE FURAY

Future Buffalo Springfield guitarist Richie Furay was drawn to folk music in the early-1960s. A native of Dayton, he was raised in nearby Yellow Springs. While attending Otterbein College, he was captivated by the vocal harmonies and simple aesthetics of The Kingston Trio. After forming a campus folk trio called The Monks, Furay quit college to try his luck in the folk circuit of New York City's Greenwich Village.

Befriended by fellow folkie Stephen Stills in a Greenwich Village folk club, Furay joined the venue's house band, The Au Go-Go Singers. In 1964, the nine-member group recorded an album for Roulette Records. As Furay recalled in his autobiography, "By the time we got to Greenwich Village to do our folk music, the folk scene was already over. I had already seen The Beatles on *The Ed Sullivan Show* and the British Invasion thing had already taken hold." After the group disbanded, Stephen Stills traveled to Canada and met Neil Young at a coffeehouse in northern Ontario.

Inspired by The Byrds' revolutionary melding of the folk and rock genres, Furay sought out his former bandmate, Stephen Stills. Quitting his job at Pratt and Whitney Aircraft, Furay flew to Los Angeles in 1966 and began practicing songs which would later appear on the first Buffalo Springfield album. Formed by Furay, Stills, Neil Young, Dewey Martin and Bruce Palmer (later replaced by Jim Messina), the group was marred by constant infighting. Releasing three albums during their very short existence, Buffalo Springfield logged airplay with chestnuts such as "Mr. Soul," "Rock 'n' Roll Woman," and the Vietnam War-era protest song, "For What It's Worth."

With Buffalo Springfield disbanding in 1968, Furay and Messina formed the country-rock group Poco. Though enjoying critical success with tracks such as "Pickin' Up The Pieces" and "Good Feelin' To Know," the group failed to gain traction at the time. Leaving Poco in 1974, Furay formed the shortlived act, The Souther Hillman Furay Band.

Soon embracing Christianity, Furay released the spiritually-centered album, *I've Got A Reason*. By the late-1970s, Furay would leave popular music to focus on his ministry in Colorado. Furay would occasionally return to the stage as a solo artist and with various incarnations of Poco.

GENE COTTON

Another Buckeye folk artist who attended Ohio State University, singer-songwriter Gene Cotton was born into a large family in Columbus. Cotton became intrigued with music after receiving a guitar as a Christmas present. Inspired by the politically-charged music of Bob Dylan, Cotton began frequenting university-area folk clubs while still in high school.

After enrolling at Ohio State University in 1962, Cotton joined a folk group. Quitting school to perform in the clubs of Greenwich Village and throughout the East Coast, Cotton eventually returned to Columbus. Though resuming his college studies, he continued to occasionally record and perform.

After a stint at Myrrh Records, Cotton enjoyed some national success at ABC Records. Beginning in 1974, Cotton would place several singles on the *Billboard* pop charts, including "You've Got Me Runnin'," "Before My Heart Finds Out," "Like A Sunday In Salem (The Amos & Andy Song)," and a duet with newcomer Kim Carnes, "You're A Part Of Me."

Moving to Tennessee in the late-1970s, Cotton unsuccessfully ran for a seat in the state house of representatives. Cotton later embraced Christian music.

BREWER & SHIPLEY

As one half of the folk-rock duo Brewer & Shipley, Tom Shipley was born and raised in Mineral Ridge, Ohio. While pursuing a degree from Baldwin-Wallace College near Cleveland, Shipley performed in area folk coffeehouses like La Cave. Shipley told *The Cleveland Plain Dealer*: "I remember Buffy Sainte-Marie coming there with songs nobody had heard of. They were Bob Dylan songs. Nobody had heard of him."

After graduating in 1963, Shipley continued to perform in local clubs. Then in 1964, he met Oklahoma-born folkie Michael Brewer for the first time at the Blind Owl club in Kent. Soon leaving Ohio, Shipley and his new wife traversed North America, before settling on the West Coast. But along the way, the couple continued to run into Brewer.

In 1965, while employed as staff writers at A&M Records in Los Angeles, Brewer and Shipley formed a duo. Leaving A&M in protest after the label issued their incomplete demos, Brewer and Shipley signed with Buddah/Kama Sutra Records.

Then following a nightclub performance, Brewer and Shipley would compose their biggest hit. While relaxing backstage, the duo wrote "One Toke Over The Line." Despite being banned by many radio stations for its overt drug reference, the song reached the top-10 in 1971. The duo's subsequent singles – "Tarkio Road" and "Shake Off The Demons" – barely grazed the charts.

After disbanding the duo in 1979, both men settled in Missouri. Shipley became a television producer, documentary maker and recording engineer, and worked with artists such as Joni Mitchell. But after reuniting in 1986 for a well-attended concert sponsored by a Kansas City radio station, the duo decided to record and perform on a periodic basis. Brewer & Shipley's first album in two decades, *Shanghai*, was issued in 1995.

PURE PRAIRIE LEAGUE

A country-rock group, Pure Prairie League enjoyed a number of crossover hits. Experiencing frequent personnel changes, the group featured a series of lead vocalists including Gary Burr, Craig Fuller and Vince Gill.

Formed in 1969, Pure Prairie League moved its base from Cincinnati to Columbus. Signed to RCA Records, the group issued its debut album in 1971,

Pure Prairie League. Following the release of the group's second album *Bustin' Out*, Fuller left the band in 1972, and spent two-years in a Kentucky hospital, after claiming conscience-objector status during the Vietnam War. Soon after, the group was dropped by RCA Records.

Continuing to tour across the nation, particularly on college campuses, the group built a solid fanbase. Then when the three-year-old track "Amie" belatedly became a hit in 1975, RCA re-signed the band.

In 1979, 22-year-old Vince Gill joined in time for the album, *Can't Hold Back*. He would provide the lead vocal on the group's biggest pop hit, "Let Me Love You Tonight." Then from the group's tenth album *Something In The Night*, Pure Prairie League reached the top-40 with "Still Right Here In My Heart."

With Gill leaving for a solo career in country music, Pure Prairie League added vocalist Gary Burr. In 1985, Fuller rejoined the group and briefly shared lead-vocal duties. After the group disbanded in 1987, Fuller joined Little Feat. In 1998, Pure Prairie League was resurrected by Fuller and Mike Reilly.

MODERN TROUBADOURS

The singer-songwriter tradition continued in the 1980s. But unlike their predecessors, many of these artists did not tackle political issues. The leading, Ohio-rooted, singer-songwriters during this period included Jim Brickman, Marc Cohn and Joseph Arthur.

JIM BRICKMAN

Though initially considered a new age artist, Jim Brickman eventually veered toward mainstream pop. A native of Shaker Heights, Ohio, Brickman was trained in classical piano. During his high school years, he joined a local rock band which played cover songs.

While enrolled at Case Western Reserve University and the Cleveland Institute of Music, Brickman began writing advertising jingles. Settling in Chicago for ten years, he became a full-time jingle writer. During this period, his best-known commercial campaigns included, "Just for the taste of it – Diet Coke" and "G.E. – We bring good things to life." Landing in Los Angeles, Brickman worked with Muppets creator Jim Henson and wrote the 1979 novelty hit, "Rainbow Connection" by Kermit The Frog.

Signing a solo contract in 1994 with the jazz/new age label, Windham Hill Records, Brickman was an immediate sensation. While Brickman's early album releases were strictly instrumental projects, his later albums employed outside vocalists and were more pop-oriented.

Though initially reluctant to tour, Brickman emerged as a popular concert draw. A multifaceted entertainer, he was equally comfortable performing as a soloist on piano or with a full orchestra. During his career, Brickman would collaborate with artists such as Kenny Loggins, Michael Bolton, Carly Simon,

Olivia Newton-John, Donny Osmond and Collin Raye. Primarily a balladeer, Brickman is best known for tracks such "The Gift," "Love Of My Life," "Angel Eyes," "Rocket To The Moon" and "Peace." In 1997, Brickman scored a hit with country singer Martina McBride, "Valentine."

Also an author, Brickman published a pair of books, *Simple Things* and *Love Notes: 101 Lessons From The Heart*. Beginning in 1997, Brickman hosted a weekly, syndicated radio program, *Your Weekend With Jim Brickman*. He has also filmed three PBS specials, including *My Romance: An Evening With Jim Brickman*.

Signing with Disney in 2005, he issued the collection, *Jim Brickman: The Disney Songbook*. That same year, Brickman surprised his fanbase with a collection of updated hymns and spirituals, *Grace*; the album nearly topped *Billboard* magazine's Christian music chart and earned a Dove Award. Brickman's 2006 album, *Escape*, featured a number of musical guests, including his high school classmate, R&B singer Gerald Levert.

MARC COHN

Possessing a rich and soulful voice, Cleveland native Marc Cohn is best remembered for his atmospheric ode to a city in Tennessee, "Walking In Memphis." Growing up in suburban Cleveland – next-door to the musical director of the Cleveland Orchestra, the late George Szell – Cohn frequently eavesdropped on his neighbor. Cohn told his hometown newspaper: "I would listen for hours as he was playing the piano or as he was trying to work out a score that he was about to conduct. He was an incredible classical pianist. I've been surprised looking back at how much I really took in. I have no formal training whatsoever in music. And I certainly couldn't play a classical piece if my life depended on it. But sometimes when I hear my playing, it sounds a little classical. And I know that's where some of that comes from."

In the wake of losing his mother, at age two, and father, at age 12, Cohn turned to music as an outlet. Initially inspired by Irish rocker Van Morrison, Cohn began writing songs after his brother taught him to play Ray Charles' soul chestnut "What'd I Say" on the piano. While in high school, Cohn formed a rock band called Doanbrook Hotel. Enrolled at Oberlin College, just west of Cleveland, Cohn was prevented from majoring in music because he lacked a formal background in the subject and could not read music. But with access to the institution's music conservatory, he honed his piano skills. Heading off to U.C.L.A., Cohn completed a degree in psychology and began playing the coffeehouses and dinner clubs of Los Angeles.

Landing in New York City, Cohn formed a 14-piece R&B band in 1984 called The Supreme Court. Though in existence for only a few months, the group performed at Caroline Kennedy's wedding. Leaving the group for a solo career, Cohn moved to Memphis in 1986. There, he recorded demos for other artists. Also a session player, he performed on fellow Clevelander Tracy Chapman's album, *Crossroads*.

Signed to Atlantic Records in 1990, Cohn released his debut, self-titled album the following year. With his debut single, "Walking In Memphis," becoming a multi-format hit, Cohn emerged as an instant celebrity. From the same album, Cohn scored the radio hits, "True Companion" and "Silver Thunderbird." Nominated for three Grammys in 1992, Cohn took home the award for Best New Artist.

Though a similar-styled project, Cohn's followup album, *The Rainy Season*, would not fare as well. After taking a five-year hiatus to concentrate on family matters, he released *Burning The Daze*. The album featured several musical guests including Rosanne Cash and Patty Griffin.

Following a Denver concert in 2005, Cohn was shot in the head by a carjacker, but suffered only minor injuries. (The gunman later pleaded guilty to attempted murder charges.) Cohn is married to ABC News journalist Elizabeth Vargas.

JOSEPH ARTHUR

Just four days after graduating from Akron's Firestone High School (best known for alumni Chrissie Hynde, model Angie Everhart and astronaut Judith Resnick) in 1990, singer-songwriter Joseph Arthur left his hometown to advance his musical career. But while still in high school, Arthur had been making a good living as a bass player in a popular, local blues band led by Frankie Starr.

Settling in Atlanta with his group from Akron – a funk-rock outfit called Ten Zen Men – Arthur found a day job as a clerk in a music equipment store. Soon after, Arthur reverted to his teenage love of hard-rock and formed the band, Bellybutton. During this period, he began assuming occasional lead-vocal duties. With the group disbanding, Arthur began experimenting with the acoustic guitar. Then after six fruitless years in Atlanta, Arthur headed for New York City at the invitation of Peter Gabriel.

Discovered by Gabriel's A&R associate Harvey Schwartz, Arthur was often referred to in the press as Gabriel's protégé. Signing with Gabriel's label, Real World Records, Arthur also joined the lineup of Gabriel's annual WOMAD festival. (Gabriel would also record a cover version of Arthur's "In The Sun" for a Princess Diana tribute album.)

Issued in 1997, Arthur's debut solo album, *Big City Streets*, was ignored by radio. But with his introspective and clever lyrics, folk-rock delivery and unpretentious demeanor, Arthur slowly emerged as a college-radio staple. As a gimmick, Arthur often painted abstract works during his performances. (The artwork was later compiled in the book, *We Almost Made It*.)

Recording for a series of labels over the next several years, Arthur would release a host of EPs and full-length albums. Highlighted by the track "Chemical," Arthur's 2000 album, *Come To Where I'm From*, was critically-acclaimed but poor-selling project. That same year, Arthur toured as the opening act for labelmates, Ben Harper and Gomez.

Launching his own label in 2006 – Lonely Astronaut Records – Arthur released the album, *The Invisible Parade*. Wanting to tour in support of his fifth album *Nuclear Daydream*, Arthur assembled a backing band called The Lonely Astronauts (which included former Jayhawks guitarist, Kraig Jarret Johnson). The group would subsequently join Arthur in the studio for the followup album, *Let's Just Be*.

BLESSID UNION OF SOULS

A wholesome, pop-flavored act from Cincinnati, Blessid Union Of Souls was formed in 1990 by vocalist Eliot Sloan and guitarist Jeff Pence. With record executive Fred Davis describing the group's sound as "rural soul," Sloan insisted in *Scene* magazine, "[The description] didn't hit us right away, but it fits. He really inspired 'Virginia,' a song I think really epitomizes rural soul. It's not rock, it's not country, it's not R&B, but it's a combination of all those things."

Amazingly, the quintet had not performed in public before the release of their major-label debut album, *Home*. From the project, the group scored a pair of pop hits, "I Believe" and "Let Me Be The One." The group stumbled with the self-titled followup album, which included the radio hit, "I Wanna Be There." The group is best remembered for the uplifting track, "Hey Leonardo (She Likes Me For Me)."

Though recording only three albums in four years, the group was on five different labels during that period. After a long recording hiatus and the loss of two members, the group issued the 2005 album, *Perception*.

WOMEN TROUBADOURS

Ohio has produced a number of female troubadours, most notably rocker Chrissie Hynde of The Pretenders. Others include Marti Jones, Tracy Chapman, Maureen McGovern and Kate Voegele.

MARTI JONES

Aside from Macy Gray, the Canton area also spawned singer Marti Jones. A native of nearby Uniontown, Jones was rooted in the folk-rock tradition. Beginning her professional career in 1984, she was convinced by former Rubber City Rebels member Liam Sternberg to team with the Akron-based new wave band, Color Me Gone, as the vocalist on the group's debut release on A&M Records. Color Me Gone had been formed in 1982 by guitarist George Cabaniss (formerly of Hammer Damage and The Dead Boys). But with the album faring poorly, the group disbanded.

While the former members of Color Me Gone later launched The Village Idiots, Jones would emerge as a solo act. Retained by A&M Records, Jones recorded a trio of critically-acclaimed albums beginning with *Unsophisticated Times*. Though developing a loyal fanbase with her alternative/folk-rock stylings, Jones was unable to peddle many records.

In 1988, Jones married her longtime producer, singer-songwriter Don Dixon, who was best known for the quirky hit "Praying Mantis" and as the producer of the R.E.M. album, *Murmur*. After switching to RCA Records, Jones recorded the Dixon-produced project, *Any Kind Of Lie*, and then settled into a normal routine in Canton. Jones and Dixon were soon dubbed "Canton's cutest couple" by *Rolling Stone* magazine. After a four-year hiatus from music, Jones released a pair of albums in 1996, *Live From Spirit Square* and *My Long-Haired Life*.

TRACY CHAPMAN

A headstrong, folk-rock, singer-songwriter, Tracy Chapman bucked the traditional image of the rock star. Very guarded about her past, Chapman would rarely discuss her upbringing during media interviews. A classically-trained musician, she was born and raised in Cleveland. Making no career headway in her hometown, she attended Tufts University in Boston. During this period, Chapman joined an African drum ensemble and performed in local folk houses.

Following graduation, Chapman signed with Elektra Records. In 1988, she released a self-titled, debut album. From the project, Chapman scored an international hit with the atmospheric track, "Fast Car." That same year, she was nominated for six Grammy Awards and won three. Followup singles included, "Talkin' About A Revolution" and "Baby Can I Hold You." A politically-active entertainer, Chapman would perform at a number of high-profile events including Farm Aid and a Paris concert for Amnesty International.

Chapman returned to top form with the 1995 album, *New Beginning*. The project spawned the blues-inflected hit, "Give Me One Reason." Guesting on a duet project with B.B. King, Chapman scored the hit, "The Thrill Is Gone."

MAUREEN McGOVERN

A pop singer and Broadway actress, Youngstown-native Maureen McGovern is best remembered for her chart-topping single, "The Morning After." The song was prominently featured in the disaster film, *The Poseidon Adventure*. The Oscar-winning song was produced by Carl Maduri, who would later work with Wild Cherry on their hit, "Play That Funky Music."

Determined to break into music at a young age, McGovern performed around Youngstown in a folk act called Sweet Rain. In 1972, she was selected to sing "Morning After" after the head of 20th Century Records heard her demo recording. McGovern was later picked to record the themes for two more films, "Wherever Love Takes Me" from *Gold* and "We May Never Love Like This Again" from *The Towering Inferno*. McGovern appeared in the latter film, performing the song in a nightclub setting. The trio of recordings gave McGovern the unfortunate nickname, "The Disaster Theme Queen." Switching labels, she scored a final hit in 1979 with "Different Worlds," the theme from the television sitcom, *Angie*.

Turning to acting, McGovern appeared as a singing nun named Sister Angelina in the 1980 comedy film, *Airplane!* On Broadway, McGovern portrayed the role of Mabel in the Gilbert & Sullivan musical, *The Pirates Of Penzance*. She followed up with leading roles in two productions of the Pittsburgh Civic Light Opera, *The Sound Of Music* and *South Pacific*. Reviving her music career, McGovern emerged as a cabaret performer and recorded a series of albums for CBS Records.

BOY BANDS

The Boy Band movement of the late-1980s evolved from the doo-wop and teen idol traditions. The genre spawned a number of young, photogenic, well-dressed, all-male groups such as The Backstreet Boys and N-Sync, who awed young female fans with their good looks, tight harmonies and choreographed dance moves.

Another of these groups, 98 Degrees, had ties to Ohio. The quartet was formed by Massillon-native Jeff Timmons and a trio of singers from Cincinnati, Justin Jeffe and brothers Drew and Nick Lachey. Timmons told *Scene* magazine, "When I started the group with the guys, we modeled ourselves after Boys II Men, Take 6, doo-wop groups. As we progressed and got put into the boy-band category.... We started to follow into that: You gotta dance onstage, you gotta have explosions, pyro, all this hype. The shows weren't even satisfying for me, and it really did become about us being 98 Degrees and how we looked. It wasn't fulfilling." Beginning with "Invisible Man" in 1997, the group placed several hits on the charts including "Because Of You," "The Hardest Thing" and "Give Me Just One Night."

Meanwhile, Nick Lachey would become a media celebrity after his high profile marriage and subsequent divorce to actress-singer Jessica Simpson. Bandmate Jeff Timmons later pursued a solo career and toured with Ohio-born pianist Jim Brickman.

Not all Ohio-based boy bands were equally successful. During a revival of The Monkees in mid-1980s, a teenage version of the group called The New Monkees was assembled from a pool of 5,000 applicants. One of the members was Ohio-born, Michigan-raised Dino Kovas. Another member was 18-year-old, Columbus-born Larry Saltis, who was just about to begin his first semester at Kent State University. But with little in the way of promotion, the syndicated television series survived just 13 episodes in 1987. Saltis later worked as a restauranteur in Akron.

Another Ohio boy-band, Youngstown, also stumbled. Although the group's track "I'll Be Your Everything" was featured on the soundtrack of the children's film *Inspector Gadget*, the single barely dented the national charts. Similarly, Columbus-area native John Sutherland was a member of the boy band, B3. Though an overseas success, B3 remained unknown in their native country.

COUNTRY MUSIC

As one of the ingredients in the development of rock and roll, country music has thrived in Ohio. Most of the state's early, country and western artists were affiliated with the radio powerhouse, WLW in Cincinnati. With the station cultivating a demand for country music on programs such as *The Boone County* and its successor *The Midwest Hayride*, a host of performers received regional exposure, including Minnie Pearl, Cowboy Copas, Merle Travis, The Delmore Brothers and Grandpa Jones.

Born Louis Jones, Grandpa Jones won a talent show in 1929 while a high school student in Akron. After earning a spot on a local radio station as "The Young Singer Of Old Songs," he teamed with a harmonica player from Cleveland, Joe Troyan. During a longterm stint behind popular country singer Bradley Kincaid, Jones would earn his "Grandpa" nickname at the young age of 22. Wearing a grey wig and fake mustache, he quickly settled into his stage persona. By 1937, Grandpa Jones landed in Cincinnati, where he teamed with Merle Travis and The Delmore Brothers to form a Southern gospel quartet, The Brown's Ferry Four. While a staff performer at Cincinnati's WLW, Jones began his recording career at King Records in 1943. In 1969, he was hired as a charter cast member of the long-running television program, *Hee Haw*.

Meanwhile, Hollywood would cultivate a pair of silver-screen cowboys from Ohio – Roy Rogers and Hopalong Cassidy. Nicknamed "the King of the Cowboys," Cincinnati native Roy Rogers was teamed with his sidekick George "Gabby" Hayes and faithful horse Trigger, as he appeared in nearly 100 films. Backed by The Sons Of The Pioneers, Rogers recorded a string of Western classics including "Tumbling Tumbleweeds" and Cole Porter's "Don't Fence Me In." In 1947, Rogers married his singing and acting partner, Dale Evans. Hosting their own television series in the 1950s, the couple sang the show's closing theme song, "Happy Trails."

Meanwhile, fellow cowboy star Hopalong Cassidy emerged from the silent film era. Born in Cambridge, Ohio, the former William Boyd saw his career damaged in the late-1920s when a newspaper incorrectly ran his photo in an article about a similarly-named actor, William Stage Boyd, who was arrested for gambling and drinking liquor during Prohibition. Then in 1935, William Boyd was offered a career-defining role as Hopalong Cassidy. In all, Boyd would star in sixty-six Hopalong Cassidy films, most of which featured musical fare. Eventually purchasing the rights to the immensely popular screen character, Boyd licensed merchandise such as comic books, watches and cowboy outfits.

During the first part of his career, Akron's David Allan Coe was ostracized by his hometown country radio station. The son of an Amish mother and Mormon father, Coe was reared on R&B and blues. Heading for Nashville after his release from the Ohio Penitentiary at age 27 in 1967, Coe maneuvered to the forefront of the outlaw brand of country music. But Coe told *Scene* magazine that his reputation was unwarranted: "A lot of people think I'm a drug user and I've never done drugs. I've never been a drinker. When I was younger, I did a couple adults-only albums for *Easy Rider* magazine. A lot of people come to my concerts expecting to hear those songs. That was something I did in my 20s. It's not a part of my life now. All in all, I'm just a family person."

As a songwriter, Coe had his biggest success with "Take This Job And Shove It" by fellow Ohio native Johnny Paycheck. In 1975, Coe recorded a career-making hit with "You Never Even Called Me By My Name" – a song written by Steve Goodman of Chicago.

A fellow outlaw-style, country singer, Johnny Paycheck also spent time in prison. Born in Greenfield, Paycheck broke into music as a backing musician in the bands of Ray Price, George Jones, Porter Wagoner and Faron Young. Also a songwriter, Paycheck penned Tammy Wynette's breakthrough hit, "Apartment No. 9." Pursuing a solo career, Paycheck scored a series of country hits including "She's All I Got," "Mr. Lovemaker," and his signature piece which inspired a film of the same name, "Take This Job And Shove It." In 1989, Paycheck returned to prison for a two-year term after shooting a man.

Also hailing from Akron, Christy DiNapoli was the founder and creative force behind the country group, Little Texas. Beginning his career in the A&R department at Warner Brothers Records in Nashville, he later turned to management and production work.

Born in the Appalachian river town of Portsmouth, Earl Thomas Conley played in a series of country bands beginning in his teen years. Performing around Southern Ohio and adjacent West Virginia, Conley interrupted his budding musical career with a four-year army stint. Settling in Huntsville, Alabama, after his discharge, he made regular trips to Nashville. As a songwriter, he had his first success in 1973 with "Smoky Mountain Memories" by Mel Street; three years later, Conway Twitty topped the charts with Conley's "This Time I've Hurt Her (More Than She Loves Me)."

Aided by record producer Nelson Larkin, Conley was signed by GRT Records in 1974. Moving to Warner Brothers Records, Conley scored his first hit in 1979 with "Dreamin's All I Do." After a stint with Sunbird Records, Conley landed at RCA Records and unleashed a strong run of top-10 country hits in the 1980s, including "Heavenly Bodies" and "Don't Make It Easy For Me." After parting with Larkin in the late-1990s, Conley teamed with producer Randy Scruggs and took a stylistic turn toward classic-country.

In the vanguard of modern country music, Dwight Yoakam combined elements of rockabilly with classic, 1950s-style country. Born in Pikeville, Kentucky, but raised in Columbus, Yoakam spent his teenage years acting in school plays and performing in a series of garage-rock bands. Influenced by both country and rock, Yoakam traced his musical roots to Ohio State University's student radio station. "When FM finally broke in the 1960s, I was hooked into WOSU. It was progressive radio in all ways. You could just as easily hear an old Hank Williams Sr. cut played up against Jimi Hendrix. That's where I first heard Iron Butterfly and where I first heard Emmylou Harris and Linda Ronstadt and the Flying Burrito Brothers and Gram Parsons. I got an AM/FM stereo receiver and I rigged it up in my room. I was in junior high and it took me to another world. My style today is the result of that exposure to a variety of musical styles. I think it shaped a collage-like musical point of view for me," Yoakam told *The Cleveland Plain Dealer*.

After briefly attending Ohio State University, Yoakam moved to Nashville in the late-1970s to pursue a career in music. But finding resistence to his traditional, honky-tonk style, Yoakam relocated to Los Angeles.

Teaming with a fellow Midwestern transplant, guitarist-producer Pete Anderson of Detroit, Yoakam began honing a more polished, rockabilly-rooted sound. Releasing his major-label, debut album in 1986 – *Guitars, Cadillacs, Etc., Etc.* – Yoakam landed on the charts with "Guitars, Cadillacs" and a cover of Johnny Horton's "Honky Tonk Man." Enjoying a long hit-run well into the 21st century, Yoakam occasionally recorded cover versions of rock songs, including "Crazy Little Thing Called Love," "Suspicious Minds" and "I Want You To Want Me."

Meanwhile, another pair of Columbus residents – cousins Jay DeMarcus and Gary LeVox – teamed with Joe Don Rooney in 2000 to form the group, Rascal Flatts. An instant success, the Grammy-nominated trio scored a series of hits including "Bless The Broken Road" and "Fast Cars And Freedom." Eventually, Rascal Flatts crossed over into the pop market with the tracks, "What Hurts The Most" and "Life Is A Highway." Another Columbus-based act, country-rock outfit McGuffey Lane were a Midwestern institution for more than three decades.

A popular, modern-country group with Ohio roots, Sawyer Brown achieved fame in a non-traditional manner. While attending the University of Central Florida, singer-songwriter Mark Miller formed a duo in 1981 with keyboardist Gregg "Hobie" Hubbard. Raised on his grandfather's farm near Dayton, Miller had been reared on the old-time spirituals of the Pentecostal church. Moving to Nashville in 1982, Miller and Hubbard formed the group, Savannah. Wanting a more original moniker, the five-man outfit emerged as Sawyer Brown, taking the name from the street where they rehearsed.

Then after winning the top prize in the 1983 season of the syndicated television program *Star Search*, the group earned a recording contract with Curb Records. Embraced by country radio, Sawyer Brown placed numerous hits on the charts including "Step By Step," "The Walk," "Some Girls Do" and "Thank God For You."

NOVELTY ARTISTS

The novelty record has been around since the dawn of the music industry. From Spike Jones to Weird "Al" Yankovic, novelty artists have combined music with comedy. Beginning with his underground hit, "My Bologna" – a cheaply recorded spoof of The Knack's "My Sharona" – Yankovic came to dominate the genre in the 1980s. For nearly a decade, former McCoys' leader Rick Derringer collaborated with Yankovic as both a guitarist and producer.

Numerous other Ohioans have made contributions to the world of novelty music. In 1961, Cleveland disc jockey Phil McLean of WERE scored a national pop hit with "Small Sad Sam," a parody of the Jimmy Dean smash, "Big Bad John." But like many of Cleveland's more talented deejays, McLean left for New York City after the station changed formats in 1961. While in Cleveland, McLean had also hosted a local *Bandstand*-style music program, from 1955 to 1959. Meanwhile, Cleveland-born actor Jim Backus – known for his role as Thurston Howell III on *Gilligan's Island* as well as the voice of the cartoon character Mr. Magoo – scored a comedy hit in 1958 with "Delicious!"

Another Cleveland resident, one-hit wonder Daddy Dewdrop (born Richard Monda), reached the top-10 in 1971 with "Chick-A-Boom." He had written the track for the CBS cartoon series, *Sabrina & The Groovy Ghoulies*. Realizing its commercial potential, he quicky recorded the song with a group of studio musicians. (A former child actor, Monda had portrayed a young Eddie Cantor in the film biography, *The Eddie Cantor Story*.)

A pair of former Akronites, Jerry Buckner and Gary Garcia, relocated to Atlanta and scored a top-10 novelty hit with "Pac-Man Fever." Friends since their days at Simon Perkins Junior High School, the two men performed in separate rock bands around Akron before joining forces as producers and commercial jingle writers. Their followup single, "Do The Donkey Kong," failed to reach the charts. Additionally, Cleveland deejay Uncle Vic scored a regional hit with an ode to another video game, "Space Invaders."

Lorain-native Don Novello, better known as *Saturday Night Live's* chain-smoking priest Father Guido Sarducci, recorded a few comedy records beginning in the mid-1970s. Novello had created the character in 1973.

Although Joe Dolce was born in the northeastern Ohio town of Painesville, his 1981 single "Shaddap You Face" was a hit in his adopted homeland of Australia. While attending Ohio University in Athens during the mid-1960s, Dolce had formed a folk-rock band with Jonathan Edwards. Evolving into Sugar Creek, the band released one album in 1969. (After the group disbanded, Edwards went solo and topped the pop charts with his 1971 single, "Sunshine.")

A native of Cleveland and graduate of Kent State University, Arsenio Hall created a musical alter-ego – a morbidly-obese rapper named "Chunky A" – and scored a minor hit in 1989 with "Owwww!" The star of films such as *Coming To America*, Hall was once told by a college advisor to forget about a career in acting.

ETCETERA

Scott Savol came in fifth place in the 2005 season of *American Idol*. After touring with the show's cast, Savol returned to Cleveland and recorded for Cleveland International Records, the same label which spawned another heavyset crooner, Meat Loaf. Another Buckeye native, Charles Grigsby of Oberlin, reached the top-12 during season two.

A prolific singer-songwriter, Cincinnati-born Jimmy Griffin toiled as a solo artist and actor before joining David Gates in the soft-rock group, Bread. After scoring about a dozen hits, including "Diary" and "Everything I Own," Bread disbanded in 1977. Griffin later teamed with Randy Meisner and Billy Swan to form the country-rock group, Black Tie. Later, Griffin joined former Cymarron members Richard Mainegra and Rick Yancey in the country band, The Remingtons.

A pair of singer-songwriters – Boz Scaggs and Benny Mardones – were born in Ohio but raised elsewhere. Relocating to Oklahoma and then Texas, Scaggs had a prolific career during the 1970s with his pop-rock output. Conversely, Mardones was a Maryland-reared, one-hit wonder who scored an emotionally-wrenching ballad hit in 1980 with "Into The Night."

The Columbus pop-rock act, Saving Jane, scored a top-40 hit in 2006 with "Girl Next Door." Lead singer Marti Dodson was attending graduate school at Ohio State University when she formed the group with guitarist Pat Buzzard.

CHAPTER 12
ROCK ON TV:
WKRP IN CINCINNATI, DREW CAREY & UPBEAT!

Years before Cleveland-born comedian Drew Carey spotlighted the Buckeye State on his hit sitcom, Ohio was a breeding ground for television programs.

A native of Canton, Jack Paar hosted *The Tonight Show* from 1957 to 1962, before turning over the reins to a young Johnny Carson. Switching to prime-time television, Parr hosted a talk show for the next three years until he retired in 1965.

At KYW in Cleveland, Mike Douglas launched a talk show in 1961, and was initially paid a $400 weekly salary. Two years later, the show hit syndication. By 1965, the program was moved to Philadelphia. The following year, Douglas scored a surprise, pop hit with "The Men In My Little Girl's Life." Meanwhile, Cleveland-born Phil Donahue launched his daily talk show in 1967 at WLWD in Dayton, which was filmed in a studio that was converted from a roller rink.

One of the more colorful figures on television, Cincinnati councilman Jerry Springer became a successful, local newscaster before returning to elected office as the city's mayor. Later settling in Chicago, he emerged as the king of raunch with his daily slugfest, *The Jerry Springer Show*. Springer later toyed with the prospect of running for either governor or senator of Ohio on the Democratic ticket. Another Cincinnati television personality, Bob Braun scored a national hit in 1962 with "Till Death Do Us Part."

But the Buckeye television programs which made the most impact on the music world were the syndicated *Upbeat!* and the situation comedy *WKRP In Cincinnati*. Though not a musical program, *The Drew Carey Show* incorporated elements of Buckeye rock, and gave the nation an uproarious view of Ohio.

UPBEAT!

With the arrival of rock and roll in the 1950s, many television stations around the country began broadcasting their own locally-produced music programs, including *The Buddy Deane Show* in Baltimore and *The Milt Grant Show* in Washington. The ABC outlet in Cleveland, WEWS Channel 5, first aired a teen dance program from 1955 to 1959. Ohio's first, licensed television station, WEWS began broadcasting on December 17, 1947. The channel was launched by the Scripps Howard Company, also the owner of the newspaper, *The Cleveland Press*.

By 1963, WEWS featured a pop-music program produced by Herman Spero – a half-hour, Sunday-morning series called *The Johnny Holliday Show*. The show's host was a popular WHK deejay, who later provided the voice-over on the hit compilation album, *Cruisin' 64*.

Wanting to launch another musical project, WEWS introduced *The Big 5 Show*. Also produced by Herman Spero, the program would have an impact far beyond Cleveland. Originally hosted by a series of local top-40 deejays, the program debuted on August 25, 1964, with guest performances by Chubby Checker, Paul Anka and The Four Seasons.

But while visiting Toronto, Spero came across a similar show on Canadian television. Broadcast from nearby Hamilton, Ontario, the program was hosted by Don Webster, a Dick Clark look-alike. Webster recalled in a *Cleveland Plain Dealer* interview, "At that time... the only thing on television was *American Bandstand*. This was pre-*Hulabaloo*, pre-*Shindig*. In those days the artists weren't doing Coliseum dates and huge concerts; they were still trying to sell records, and doing smaller shows to promote record sales. So, Herman Spero, in conjunction with Don Perris, then the general manager [at WEWS], put this show together. It was Herman's idea to do a live show, bring all of the acts in live. Then Herman would put together a Cleveland gig for the acts."

Dropping black-and-white broadcasts for color, local radio emcees for Don Webster and changing its name from *The Big 5 Show* to *Upbeat!*, the new program was soon syndicated to 100 markets around the nation. More importantly for the city of Cleveland, numerous local acts – including The James Gang, The Outsiders and The Choir – were receiving national exposure. The program also featured a choreographer – originally Dick Blake – who devised new dance moves, which were copied by youth all around the country. The show's dancers came from local high schools and were required to wear white boots. Meanwhile, Herman Spero's teenage son, David, worked in various roles behind the scenes.

The program's original house band was a popular local act called Joey And The Continentals. But after *Upbeat!* hit syndication, Tom King And The Starfires took over the duties. The subsequent house band, The Grasshoppers, included Benjamin Orr (who later co-founded The Cars). Orr had joined The Grasshoppers in 1964 as the replacement for departing singer-guitarist Dante Rossi. (Rossi would later form The Tulu Babies, which morphed into The Baskerville Hounds.)

Although some of the program's musical guests lip-synched their songs on *Upbeat!*, most performers were recorded live. A frequent musical guest, Gary Puckett often co-hosted the program. Nearly all the big names in popular music appeared on the show, including Aretha Franklin, James Brown, Stevie Wonder, The Turtles and The Yardbirds. In 1965, folk-rock duo Simon And Garfunkel made their national television debut. In latter years, *Upbeat!* also featured hard-rock acts such as Deep Purple, Procol Harum, Iron Butterfly, Canned Head and even art-rockers The Velvet Underground. The program occasionally showcased jazz giants such as Lionel Hampton, Gene Krupa and Duke Ellington.

A tragic chapter of *Upbeat!* took place in December 1967. On an episode of the program, soul great Otis Redding sang a duet of "Knock On Wood" with Detroit rocker Mitch Ryder. Following the afternoon taping, Redding played three shows that evening at a local nightspot, Leo's Casino. Departing from Cleveland for a performance in Madison, Wisconsin, the airplane carrying Redding and members of his backing band, The Bar-Kays, crashed into icy Lake Monona. All aboard died, except for Ben Cauley.

After *Upbeat!* went off the air in 1971, Don Webster turned to meteorology and became the station's weatherman for three decades. As for Herman Spero, he was a visionary who pitched the concept of a music video program to HBO in 1979, two years before the advent of MTV.

WKRP IN CINCINNATI

Set in the offices and broadcasting studio of a fictional, money-losing, Midwestern, AM radio station, *WKRP In Cincinnati* was focused on the inner-workings of the music industry. The series was created by Hugh Wilson, who based the concept on the radio personalities he encountered at an Atlanta bar called Harrison's. Working as an advertising representative at the time, Wilson later switched careers and became a writer for *The Bob Newhart Show* and *The Tony Randall Show*. Given the green light by MTM chief Grant Tinker to develop a television pilot, Wilson returned to Atlanta to do research for the program. Aided by an associate Clark Brown, Wilson spent time interacting with the staff at radio station, WQXI.

When *WKRP In Cincinnati* debuted on September 18, 1978, the city's mayor was Jerry Springer. After a successful pilot, CBS ordered 12 episodes at a mere cost of $155,000 per show. The program was filmed in front of a live, studio audience. The first rock song to air on *WKRP* was "Queen Of The Forest" by Ted Nugent.

A number of prominent Cincinnati landmarks were featured in the show's opening sequence, including the German-made Tyler Davidson Memorial Fountain. *WKRP* had two theme songs. The opening theme was performed by Steve Carlisle. The song was composed by Tom Wells, with the lyrics provided by series creator Hugh Wilson. The song's lyrics refer to the career of the character, Andy Travis. When MCA Records wanted to extend the *WKRP* theme into a full-length song, the Akron-born team of Jerry Buckner and Gary Garcia (best known for their top-10 novelty hit "Pac-Man Fever") was hired to oversee the project.

For a closing theme, Atlanta musician Jim Ellis had provided Hugh Wilson a rough demo recording. Having written the music but not the lyrics, Ellis shouted out some gibberish, which he had planned on replacing with proper lyrics. Enamored with the song in its ragged form, Wilson used the original demo as the closing theme.

The program had a simple premise: A low-rated radio station was owned by the tyrannical Mrs. Carlson (originally Sylvia Sidney, and later Carol Bruce), but operated by her meek, insecure son, Arthur Carlson (Gordon

Jump). Program director Andy Travis (Gary Sandy) promised to improve the station's dismal ratings by adopting a rock format. But the elderly listeners of the station's previous elevator-music format initially protested the change.

The actor that portrayed laid-back deejay Johnny Fever, Howard Hesseman, had actually been a part-time jock at KMPX, the pioneering, free-form rock station in San Francisco. Two of the program's actors were Ohio natives, Gordon Jump and Gary Sandy – both from Dayton.

The other lead characters included the womanizing, sales executive, Herb Tarlek (Frank Bonner), the bumbling newsman who was obsessed with winning the fictional Buckeye News Hawk Award, Les Nessman (Richard Sanders), the vivacious secretary, Jennifer Marlowe (Loni Anderson), the bookwormish but lovely, Bailey Quarters (Jan Smithers), and the overnight deejay, Venus Flytrap (Tim Reid). Noted for its uncanny realism, *WKRP* was very popular in the radio industry.

In the program's best-remembered episode, "Turkeys Away," Mr. Carlson staged a promotion to drop live turkeys from a helicopter, where they unceremoniously fell like "sacks of wet cement." In response to the fiasco, Arthur Carlson pleaded: "As God is my witness, I thought turkeys could fly." A hysterical Les Nessman covered the spectacle, comparing it to the Hindenburg crash. According to Gordon Jump, the episode was based on a real-life turkey drop over a mall parking lot by a Dallas radio station.

The program even tackled serious subjects like The Who concert tragedy at the Riverside Coliseum where 11 fans were killed. The local CBS affiliate in Cincinnati initially threatened to pre-empt the episode, fearing it might somehow be disrespectful. But after station executives watched a preview of the episode, the program aired as scheduled.

In the final episode of the series, *WKRP* had moved up to sixth place in the ratings and was making money. An angry Mrs. Carlson considered changing the format because the station was expected to operate as a tax loss! After 90 episodes over four seasons, *WKRP* ended its run in 1982. After the cancellation was announced, the show's ratings soared during the summer reruns. In all, *WKRP* would earn 10 Emmy nominations.

The program was reprised in 1991 as a first-run, syndicated series. *The New WKRP In Cincinnati* featured the original characters, Mr. Carlson, Les Nessman and Herb Tarlek. The cast also included newcomer Tawny Kitaen as deejay Mona "Nightbird" Loveland. Most of the actors from the original series made guest appearance, with the exception of Jan Smithers and Gary Sandy. The program ran for two seasons.

When the original series aired in syndication, the licensing for the background music – which was an essential component of the program's realism – expired in the 1990s. Due to prohibitive licensing costs, most of the original music was also missing from the program's DVD releases and was replaced by nameless, generic pop songs.

THE DREW CAREY SHOW

As Cleveland's biggest booster on television, Drew Carey became the city's ambassador to the world. Frequently referencing his hometown and the Buckeye State, Carey decorated the walls of his favorite watering hole, the Warsaw, with various Cleveland memorabilia. Additionally, Carey donned t-shirts emblazoned with images of the Rock and Roll Hall of Fame, local television celebrity Ghoulardi and Cleveland sports teams.

Initially, the network was forced to pay a licensing fee to Major League Baseball every time Carey wore something with an Indians logo. But after acknowledging that the exposure meant free publicity, the fee was eliminated. Then when team owner Art Modell announced the move of the Cleveland Browns to Baltimore, Carey retaliated by tearing down all of the team's banners and colors from the set. Upon the team's return in 1995, Carey filmed a full episode at the Brown's new lakeside stadium.

Paralleling the storyline of his television show, Drew Carey purchased his childhood home from his mother. Carey's trademark crew-cut hairstyle and boxy, black-framed glasses were throwbacks from his stint in the U.S. Marines. Reared in the working-class Old Brooklyn area of Cleveland, Carey was blue-collar in every respect.

Carey broke into show business in 1986, when he was hired to write jokes for a friend who was a deejay. Carey told *Scene* magazine, "I didn't know how to write jokes, so I went to the Cleveland Public Library and got a book on how to write jokes and started giving jokes to him. I gave jokes to [legendary Cleveland deejay] John Lanigan, too, to see what he thought of them. He thought they were funny and gave me lots of encouragement. He took time to talk with me, which I thought was very nice of him."

Testing some of the material himself, Carey performed on amateur night at a downtown Cleveland comedy club. Initially a flop, he polished his act and was eventually hired as the club's emcee. In 1987, Carey drove around the country in an old station wagon, performing on the comedy circuit. Carey's first whiff of fame came when he competed on Ed McMahon's *Star Search*. Though victorious in his first appearance, Carey lost the following week.

After landing bit parts in the sitcom *The Torkelsons* and the film *The Coneheads*, Carey landed his own specials on HBO. Although Carey was poised for stardom, he experienced a few detours along the way. During this period, Carey had been considered as a replacement for David Letterman by NBC, but lost out to Conan O'Brien. Then after a disastrous Disney television pilot called *Akron Man*, Carey landed a role on the shortlived NBC series, *The Good Life*.

Then in 1995, Carey finally hit on a simple but brilliant concept. The brainchild of Carey and veteran, television producer Bruce Helford, *The Drew Carey Show* was intended as the celebration of the average, working man. The sitcom featured Carey as the assistant director of personnel at a fictitious downtown Cleveland department store called Winfred-Louder (which was patterned on the since-closed Halle's, which was also the namesake of Cleveland actress Halle Berry). By the time of the program's premiere, Cleveland's last downtown department store had already shuttered its doors.

The show's cast included Carey's sometimes paramour, Kate O'Brien (Christa Miller), and his dimwitted friends, Lewis Kiniski (Ryan Stiles) and Oswald Harvey (Diedrich Bader). Although Carey's arch-enemy Mimi Bobeck (Kathy Kinney) was scheduled to appear in just one episode, she remained through the show's entire run. Carey's boss at Winfred-Louder, Mr. Wick (Craig Ferguson), later hosted his own late-night talk show on CBS.

Debuting in the fall of 1995, *The Drew Carey Show* ranked a respectable 44th place for the season. By its second season, the show cracked the top-20. Though not a favorite of the ABC network brass, the program survived for ten seasons.

Much of the show took place in a neighborhood-style tavern, where Drew and his friends consumed bottles of Buzz beer. The exterior shot of the bar was taken from an establishment near Carey's Cleveland home called the Memphis Plaza Lounge. With the aid of computer graphics, the name on the sign was changed to the Warsaw Tavern. The show's original theme song, "Moon Over Parma," was discovered by Carey on a jukebox at a suburban Cleveland bar, the House Of Swing.

The program used multiple theme songs, including The Vogues' "Five O'Clock World" and "Cleveland Rocks" – not the original version by Ian Hunter, but a newly recorded rendition by a non-Ohio band, The Presidents Of The United States Of America. (During its entire run, the program used Hunter's version only a single time.) But as the song's composer, Hunter claimed he was able to purchase two homes with the songwriting royalties.

Carey also brought a number of Cleveland luminaries onto the program, including Mayor Michael White, Browns quarterback Bernie Kosar and rocker Joe Walsh. But when Indians slugger Albert Belle was unable to appear, the show's producers *settled* for Dave Winfield.

Beginning in 1998, Carey hosted the improvisational program, *Whose Line Is It, Anyway?* A similar, followup program on the Warner Brothers network, *Drew Carey's Green Screen Show*, did not fare as well. Carey returned to the small screen in 2007 to emcee the prime-time game show, *Power Of 10*. That same year, Carey was picked as Bob Barker's replacement on the long-running, television institution, *The Price Is Right*.

BUCKEYE FILMS

Though located far from the movie lots of Hollywood, Ohio boasts numerous ties to the film industry. In the first decades of the 20th century, the Warner family of Youngstown built an international, entertainment conglomerate. The term "silver screen" was coined in Akron, when the projectionist at the Majestic Theatre coated his movie screen with silver-colored paint in a successful effort to improve the picture quality. The technique spread across the country and the phrase "silver screen" became synonymous with Hollywood.

A large number of film directors emerged from the Buckeye State. Cleveland-native Wes Craven was best known for horror flicks such as *A Nightmare On Elm Street*. Akron-raised, independent director/actor Jim Jarmusch was responsible for a number of unconventional films such as *Mystery Train* and *Night On Earth*. Cincinnati's Steven Spielberg oversaw blockbusters such as *E.T.* and *Indiana Jones*. Emerging from the same city, Ted Turner built a film and television empire. And when former Cleveland residents Anthony and Joe Russo were shooting the Owen Wilson / Kate Hudson hit film, *You, Me And Dupree*, the brothers recalled a song from their youth. Popular around Cleveland in 1980, the humorous, reggae-infused track, "Funky Poodle" by Wild Horses, was included on the film's soundtrack.

Writing in his autobiography, Cleveland born-and-raised screenwriter Joe Eszterhas recalled going to a movie theater at age 13, to see the Russ Tamblyn feature, *High School Confidential!*: "The real star of the movie for me was Jerry Lee Lewis, who was already one of my true childhood heroes....[with] his long blond hair flying... on top of a piano that he'd literally set on fire." But Eszterhas insisted that "Russ Tamblyn, too, was close to my heart. Not just because he starred in *High School Confidential!*, the movie that influenced me more than De Sica and Rossellini. But because he starred in *The Kid From Cleveland*, which featured the entire Cleveland Indians world championship team of 1948!"

Many films associated with Ohio feature rock and roll themes. Following the surprise success of *Blackboard Jungle*, filmmakers rushed to churn out movies involving teenagers and rock music. Most of these films were low-budget efforts with lighthearted plots, and were intended as a vehicle to spotlight a series of rock and roll performances. Cleveland deejay Alan Freed oversaw four such films during the 1950s.

In 1987, Joan Jett and Michael J. Fox portrayed members of a struggling Cleveland bar band in the film, *Light Of Day*. Nine Inch Nails-founder Trent Reznor made a brief appearance in the film as a member of a fictional band called The Problems, and played a synth-rock version of Buddy Holly's "True Love Ways." The screenplay was written by director Paul Schrader, and was loosely based on a Cleveland band, The Generators. (Some of the film was shot at the since-shuttered Euclid Tavern.) The initial inspiration for the film occurred several years earlier when Schrader visited a new-wave/punk nightclub in Akron called the Bank. As musician Nick Nicholas recalled in *Scene* magazine, "He was having me take him around one night when we went to see Klaus Nomi, who was this really weird opera singer guy playing the Bank. Nomi was on stage and the place was packed. We were on the balcony just looking down on the stage at this guy performing in a tutu, all these strange lights were shining everywhere, a parachute was draped from the ceiling and 500 people were crammed in there dancing. It was really amazing – like being in a Fellini movie. We could've been in Japan, Germany, New York or anywhere that night." Another music-oriented film, *The Rocker* followed the exploits of an aging drummer from Cleveland who found fame as a last-minute replacement in his young nephew's surging rock band.

Meanwhile, the 2003 film *American Splendor* explored the mind of Cleveland writer Harvey Pekar. An employee of a U.S. Veterans hospital, Pekar had chronicled his mundane existence in comic book form since 1976. The award-winning film was shot in Cleveland and nearby Lakewood, and featured Paul Giamatti in the role of Pekar.

A seasonal classic, *A Christmas Story* was partially shot in Cleveland. Years after the film's release, a California movie fan purchased Ralphie Parker's home in Cleveland's Tremont neighborhood. The house was converted into a tourist attraction, with the interior replicated down to every last detail – including the leg lamp. (Conversely, while the Cleveland Indians were the subject of the comedy *Major League*, most of the film was shot in Milwaukee.)

Ohio's many Hollywood connections include screen legends Bob Hope, Doris Day, Dean Martin, Paul Newman, Clark Gable, Martin Sheen, Dorothy Dandridge, Jim Backus, Debra Winger, Burgess Meredith, Phyllis Diller, Tim Conway, Jonathan Winters, Halle Berry, and stars of the silent screen, sisters Lillian and Dorothy Gish.

CHAPTER 13
THE ROCK AND ROLL HALL OF FAME

"I thought I'd seen everything, but now we've got rock and roll at the Waldorf," producer Quincy Jones told the gathered audience of 1,000 rock dignitaries, who paid between $300 and $1,000, to salute the debut class of inductees at the first annual Rock and Roll Hall of Fame ceremony in 1986. Rock Hall board member and *Rolling Stone* publisher Jann Wenner added: "This is something that is long, long overdue. People are finally recognizing the fact that the music form known as rock and roll has become an integral part of 20th-century American history." Billy Joel later echoed the sentiment: "It's about time rock had a place of its own."

But at the time, the Rock and Roll Hall of Fame was still without a permanent home, as a site selection committee had been bombarded with generous offers from several deserving cities. But later that year, the Hall of Fame would land in Cleveland for the very same reasons that Springfield, Massachusetts, hosts the Basketball Hall of Fame, and Cooperstown, New York, the Baseball Hall of Fame. Behind an oversized microphone at 50,000-watt radio station, WJW 850-AM in Cleveland, deejay Alan Freed popularized the term "rock and roll" and launched a musical firestorm that survived long after his tragic and little-noticed death in 1965.

But in 1985, both Freed's legacy and the industrial North Coast city of Cleveland were experiencing a renaissance. As the nation's 12th largest metropolitan area, Cleveland was enjoying a building boom. Suddenly, the Rock and Roll Hall of Fame became the crown jewel amid new sports complexes, a science museum, two downtown malls, and a bustling waterfront entertainment district called the Flats, which was filled with concert venues, nightclubs and revelers on pleasure boats.

A turnaround city, Cleveland was shaking off several decades of decline. In the 1930s, Clevelander Bob Hope had left the city's vaudeville houses for New York, while a pair of local teenagers, Jerry Siegel and Joseph Shuster, created the Man of Steel, who was soon known to the world as Superman. The two friends based the fabled city of Metropolis on the downtown Cleveland skyline, which was visible from Siegel's home in the predominantly Jewish neighborhood of Glenville. (Siegel and Shuster sued DC comics in 1946 and 1978, in futile attempts to reclaim their ownership rights.) Ignoring the economic possibilities of promoting itself as the legitimate birthplace of Superman, Cleveland instead offered a collective shrug when the tiny town of Metropolis, Illinois, selected itself as the adopted home of the Man of Steel. Cleveland's only memorials to the pop culture icon are a tiny plaque at a neighborhood hall of fame and a small, streetside, historical marker.

A progressive city, Cleveland elected the country's first major-city black mayor, Carl Stokes, and later gave major league sports its first black manager when Frank Robinson was hired by the Indians. But the city was also saddled with national embarrassments, becoming the butt of jokes when an oil slick on the polluted Cuyahoga River caught on fire in 1969. Memorialized in the Randy Newman ode "Burn On Big River," the blaze set wooden railroad trestles afire, as the rust-belt city became a symbol of urban decay.

Later, Mayor Ralph Perk set his hair ablaze during a ribbon-cutting ceremony, and in 1978, the boy-wonder mayor, Dennis Kucinich, plunged the city into financial default. Another tragedy divided the region on May 4, 1970, when the Ohio National Guard fired shots at war protesters on the campus of nearby Kent State University.

The premise of a Rock and Roll Hall of Fame was offered as an alternative to the much maligned Grammy Awards. When the Grammys were hatched in the back room of a Los Angeles landmark, the Brown Derby restaurant, the established players in the music industry were reacting to their loss of power and influence, and were scheming to return popular music to the "sanity" of the pre-rock world of Patti Page and Perry Como.

Voting was limited to music insiders and previous Grammy winners, with music consumers completely shut out of the process. Consequently, at the premier Grammy ceremony in 1958, Elvis Presley did not win a single award. (During his lifetime, Elvis would win Grammys only for his religious recordings.)

Promoting highbrow snobbery, the Grammys chose to vilify rock and roll. After finally introducing a rock category in 1961, a jazz instrumental, "Alley Cat," won the award in 1962, the same year that Robert Goulet was voted the Best New Artist. During the height of Beatlemania in 1965 and 1966, Frank Sinatra twice won the Album of the Year award. Also in 1965, The Beatles lost in the Best Vocal Performance by a Vocal Group category to the since-forgotten Anita Kerr Quartet. Maintaining an anti-rock bias throughout the 1960s, the Grammys completely passed over Jimi Hendrix, Chuck Berry, Bob Dylan, The Who, and The Supremes. During a decade when Motown was dominating the pop charts, the label earned just one award.

Instead of celebrating artistic achievement, the Grammy Awards emerged as a popularity contest, and have consistently discriminated against innovative or new artists. Consequently, the Grammys have never achieved the impact nor the prestige of the film industry's Oscars or Broadway's Tony Awards.

As a result, many rival, music award shows have attempted to give rock and roll its deserved respect, including *The American Music Awards*, *The MTV Video Music Awards*, *The People's Choice Awards*, *The Soul Train Awards*, and *The Billboard Magazine Awards*. While Don Kirshner's *Rock Music Awards* faded in 1977 after three years, the *International Rock Awards* – complete with its Elvis statuette – also lasted just three years.

But when *Rolling Stone* publisher Jann Wenner was asked by *Billboard* why his magazine never established a televised award show of its own, he insisted: "I'm just not a TV person. We've done *Rolling Stone* TV specials, and I'm proud of all of that. But as much as I'd love the commercial gratification of doing our own awards show, now there are just too many award shows. I don't think there's much we could bring to the table. And there's not much money in it. You end up busting your ass, and the bulk of the money goes to the TV network. Forget it. I've got other things to do than work for a network."

In the early 1980s, an independent television-producer envisioned a new music award ceremony – a rock and roll hall of fame. As the head of Black Tie Productions, Bruce Branwin initially shared the idea with Suzan Evans, then a bankruptcy attorney in Manhattan. Becoming Branwin's business partner, Evans recalled in *Cleveland Magazine*, "I hated practicing law. I was always fascinated with the entertainment industry and when this came along I thought it was a dynamic opportunity. It was risky, foolish, impractical – all that. I didn't care."

According to *GQ* magazine, Branwin "approached Atlantic Records Co-chairman Ahmet Ertegun and suggested that Ertegun start a nonprofit organization using that name, [and] license the title to him for a small fee." Ertegun liked the idea of a rock award ceremony but hated the notion of a pay-per-view television show. After litigation, the producer was awarded a cash settlement (rumored to be $1 million), and Ertegun ran with the idea. Ertegun later told *Rolling Stone* in 1986, "We're not going to make this a rock and roll Disneyland. We have an obligation to the world of rock & roll, the artists and the fans, to make this a dignified place."

In early discussions, Ahmet Ertegun and Suzan Evans weighed the idea of a tiny hall of fame and museum honoring the founders of rock and roll. Needing music industry support, Ertegun corralled several of his colleagues, including Bob Krasnow of MCA, Jann Wenner of *Rolling Stone*, Seymour Stein of Sire Records, and entertainment lawyer, Allen Grubman. Quitting her law firm position, Suzan Evans became the Hall of Fame's first full-time employee.

Then with little fanfare in 1984, the Rock and Roll Hall of Fame Foundation was officially established in New York City, with the first year's inductees nominated by a 10-member committee, which included Krasnow, Ertegun, Stein, Wenner, Robert Hilburn, Kurt Loder, John Hammond, Nile Rodgers, Jerry Wexler, and, most importantly for Cleveland, their native son, deejay and author, Norm N. Nite. Then on August 5, 1985, an expanded 21-member board publicly announced the establishment of the Rock and Roll Hall of Fame, with the purpose of preserving the music and honoring its pioneers.

But 600 miles to the west, the like-minded K. Michael Benz – the executive vice-president of the Greater Cleveland Growth Association – simultaneously came up with the notion of constructing a rock and roll museum in Cleveland, and began soliciting radio stations and civic leaders for support. Little did he know that a similar project had been conceived in New York.

Likewise, rock impresario Bill Graham was also contemplating an identical structure in San Francisco. But predating all the others, the founder of the Agora concert clubs, Hank LoConti, was planning to build his own rock and roll hall of fame in Cleveland. Interviewed by Mike Olszewski in *Radio Daze,* LoConti recalled, "When we drew up plans for our new club that we were going to build across the street from the Agora, [the hall of fame] was supposed to be in there. I really got serious about it in 1978, '79. I went to New York and gave a presentation, figuring that if we got two major record companies to back us, that would be enough. I picked Columbia and Warner Bros. [Cleveland finance director] Joe Tegreene was working with me at the time, and I brought him too. After our presentation to Columbia, their answer to me was, 'There is going to be a Rock and Roll Hall of Fame someday, but when it's built, it will definitely be located in New York.'" Unfortunately, LoConti's proposal went nowhere.

Meanwhile, when Benz shared his proposal with Norm N. Nite (who maintained residences in both New York and Cleveland), Nite broke the news that a parallel effort was under way in the Big Apple. Benz told *Northern Ohio Live* that "they were going to have this small hall of fame, if you will, in a brownstone [on 42nd Street] that was being donated by [Mayor Ed] Koch."

But at a time when few people in the music industry had even heard of the project, then-Cleveland mayor George Voinovich and Ohio Governor Richard Celeste rushed to New York to learn more about the proposed Hall of Fame. As the first city to vie for the project, Cleveland had a head start over its competitors. While the notion of a rock museum remained hazy at best, it would mean bragging rights and tourist dollars for Cleveland, as well as the overdue recognition of Alan Freed as the music's originator.

While Michael J. Fox and Joan Jett were in Cleveland to shoot scenes for the film, *Light Of Day,* the city was spending $250,000 on a promotional campaign to lure the rock museum. Arriving in Cleveland, the Rock Hall selection committee was greeted by a large contingent of energized civic leaders. At one point, an excited Ahmet Ertegun ordered the guided bus tour to stop, so that he and other riders could buy records as souvenirs from the legendary Record Rendezvous store, where Alan Freed and store owner Leo Mintz had popularized the term "rock and roll" in the early-1950s.

With local support reaching rabid proportions, Clevelanders gathered 660,000 petition signatures in an attempt to win the Rock Hall (the city's population at the time stood at 536,000). Then on January 21, 1986, Cleveland tallied 110,315 votes in a *USA Today* telephone poll, asking readers to pick the city that most deserved the rock museum. Memphis came in a distant second with 7,268 votes. The newspaper had unprecedentedly extended the poll for a second day in a failed effort to give other cities a chance to narrow the gap. Meanwhile, a legendary tastemaker at WMMS, deejay Kid Leo called in favors to obtain endorsements from a number of music giants – including Bruce Springsteen, Michael Jackson and Pete Townshend – to build the museum in Cleveland.

Meanwhile, the music world would bestow instant credibility to the Rock and Roll Hall of Fame at the debut induction ceremony in January 1986. Honoring the pioneers of rock, the most powerful and influential members of the rock community had gathered at New York's Waldorf-Astoria Hotel. Billy Joel, Neil Young, John Fogerty, and Keith Richards were all on hand to witness the inductions of Chuck Berry, James Brown, Fats Domino, and Jerry Lee Lewis. More significantly for Cleveland, Alan Freed became the first non-performer inducted into the Hall of Fame. Mayor Voinovich had wisely sent a team of forty Cleveland boosters to the event, where they spent their time promoting the city.

Although the selection of the site was scheduled to be announced at the induction ceremony, the New York Foundation delayed picking a city as last-minute offers began pouring in from around the country. But backstage, Jann Wenner suggested that Cleveland was still the front-runner.

Memphis was offering to spend $8 million on a building, while San Francisco was conducting a $60,000 museum-feasibility study. In its proposal, Philadelphia pledged to open the museum in 18 months if selected, with Mayor Wilson Good unveiling a $45.7 million financial package. Chicago, meanwhile, launched an all-out effort to grab the hall from Cleveland. At an outdoor rally, Chicago mayor Harold Washington spoke with fervor when trying to invoke the name of the "Born To Run" rocker, mistakenly referring to him as Bruce Spring*time*.

But by the end of March 1986, the original field of eight cities was narrowed to Chicago, Cleveland, Philadelphia, and San Francisco. Dropped were Memphis, Nashville, New Orleans, and New York. The remaining cities were given a month to match Cleveland's $35 million package. Notable *Los Angeles Times* rock critic Robert Hilburn sided with Memphis, giving the second-place nod to both New York and Los Angeles. And in New York, two members of the selection committee were vehemently opposed to Cleveland. As Jim Henke later recalled in *Cleveland Magazine*, "Bob Krasnov hated the thought of it in Cleveland. Jon Landau was the same way... 'anywhere but Cleveland.'"

In an effort to bring the Hall of Fame museum to Cleveland, a massive, citywide celebration was launched to commemorate the 34th anniversary of the original Moondog Coronation Ball, with events organized all over town. Five television and nine radio stations simultaneously broadcast Bill Haley's "Rock Around The Clock." Cleveland native Eric Carmen released the single "The Rock Stops Here" as a Rock Hall anthem. But two weeks later, on April 6, *The Chicago Tribune* misreported that Los Angeles had been selected as the site of the Hall of Fame. Nonetheless, the following day, Ohio governor Richard Celeste signed the state's $584 million capital construction budget for fiscal 1987-88, which included $4 million for the rock museum.

Meanwhile, within the selection committee, Norm N. Nite was pushing his hometown as the only logical choice. Dick Clark told *Northern Ohio Live*, "I dare say, he was the guy standing yelling Cleveland at the top of his lungs at every free moment." A native of Cleveland, Nite was a respected deejay, promoter, and music historian who authored the pioneering, three-volume, *Rock On* encyclopedia series.

The son of a Cleveland civil-service employee, Norm N. Nite was 12 years old when, in 1952, he became absorbed with Alan Freed's radio program. Though fascinated with music, Nite instead pursued a degree in business administration at Ohio State University. Enamored with the campus radio station, he changed his major to broadcasting and built a loyal listenership with his oldies radio show.

After entering the military, Nite moonlighted as a nighttime deejay and released a pioneering oldies album, *Rock & Roll: Evolution Or Revolution*. The album was promoted by New York City deejay Pete "Big Daddy" Myers, who, like Freed, had first established his radio persona in Cleveland.

Discharged from the service, Nite returned to Cleveland, and at one time, held down deejay positions at three different stations. After making a name for himself as the host of *The Nite Train Show*, a popular, overnight, oldies show at WHK, Nite moved to WGAR, where his program propelled the station in the local ratings war.

A walking musical encyclopedia, "the other jocks on his station would kid [Nite] on the air, calling him Alan Freed's illegitimate son, or proclaiming him to be the lead singer of some long lost group, and ultimately out of this grew his title of 'Mr. Know-It All,' which evolved into 'Mr. Music,' as he is known today," recalled writer Ralph M. Newman. After syndicating his radio show, Nite landed in New York City behind a microphone at oldies powerhouse WCBS, which had just abandoned its progressive rock format.

Returning to Cleveland in 1978, Nite would alternate between his hometown and New York, at times holding down radio positions in both cities. While in Cleveland, Nite was instrumental in the relaunching of an annual Moondog Coronation Ball, with the rights granted by Alan Freed's younger brother, David, to Nite's Cleveland employer, WMJI. But more importantly for the city, Nite was convinced that the Rock and Roll Hall of Fame truly belonged in Cleveland.

With rumors hitting the local press about the imminent selection of the Rock Hall site, Clevelanders were uneasy about their chances of landing the museum. Then on May 5, 1986, Cleveland Mayor George Voinovich was met by a local rock band, Wild Horses, and hordes of media at Cleveland's downtown, Burke Lakefront Airport, and shouted, "We got it!" Joined by governor Richard Celeste, the usually conservatively-attired, elected officials donned t-shirts that read – "Cleveland: Home of the Rock 'n' Roll Hall of Fame." With radio stations blasting Ian Hunter's "Cleveland Rocks," as well as the state's official rock song, "Hang On Sloopy," local television stations broke away from scheduled programming for live coverage of the celebration.

At a news conference announcing Cleveland's selection, Ahmet Ertegun said, "We have been swayed by the incredible community enthusiasm that has come up in Cleveland." Essential to the decision was a generous financial package as well as a pledge by Cuyahoga Community College to develop a popular music program. The first *Rolling Stone* article on the selection of Cleveland as the Hall of Fame site warned that the cost could run as high as $20 million, with construction planned for early 1987. But even after Cleveland was picked as the site, there was grumbling abound. George Voinovich recalled in *The Akron Beacon Journal* that "the folks in New York were somewhat reluctant about it happening. They could never figure out why it was coming to Cleveland."

But many questions remained. As Thomas Kelly pondered in *Cleveland Magazine*: "There was nothing like a rock-music museum anywhere in the world. Without comparable data, there was no basis for predicting attendance, membership, sponsorship, museum sales or prices – no way to determine probable operating coasts, cash flow or budget. The same situation applied to the building itself. What was it? Where would it be? How big? How much to design and build? Furnish with what? From where? The city didn't need accountants to run the numbers, it needed David Copperfield."

Meanwhile, Cleveland civic leaders scrambled to find an appropriate site for the museum. Albert Ratner, the co-chairman of Forest City Enterprises' board of directors, was chosen by city officials to oversee construction. Donating a large, stately edifice in downtown Cleveland, Ratner was preparing to begin renovations. But the Rock Hall board in New York City had their own ideas, and without consulting Cleveland leaders, unveiled their own construction plans for the museum.

In January 1987, the New York City board members arrived in Cleveland to inspect prospective locations, including the site of the demolished Cleveland Arena, where the first rock and roll concert was staged by Alan Freed in 1952. The committee instead chose a compact, downtown lot, adjacent to the just-opened Tower City shopping center, on land donated by Albert Ratner. Plans called for the multi-use building to be built atop a parking garage and linked by underground tunnels to shield against Cleveland's sometimes fierce winters. Situated near a towering bluff and overlooking the industrial Cuyahoga River, the proposed museum was now estimated to cost $25 million. A separate Cleveland-based Hall of Fame board was formed to oversee the building's construction.

During the next several years, the Hall of Fame's price-tag kept increasing, forcing Cleveland officials to raise additional moneys. But on two occasions, the city nearly lost the museum over the slow pace of fund-raising. After mapping a financial strategy, members of the Cleveland Founders Club were dismayed by the absence of expected corporate donations. Also a disappointment, a proposed $5 million endowment from the television rights of the induction ceremonies never materialized due to network indifference. The concept of a live, televised ceremony was later ruled out. The New York board feared that many major stars would avoid the proceedings, with cameras destroying the induction's integrity, intimacy, and inclusiveness.

Selected to design the building was Chinese-born architect I.M. Pei. Rooted in modernism, Pei's previous designs included Boston's J.F.K. Library, Washington D.C.'s National Gallery of Arts East Building, and the expansion of the Louvre Museum in France. Educated at MIT and Harvard, Ieoh Ming Pei admitted to not liking rock and roll music when first asked to design the rock museum. Tutored in rock history by Jann Wenner, Pei was taken on guided tours of the entertainment districts in New Orleans and Nashville, and to Elvis Presley's Graceland mansion in Memphis.

Unveiling a model of the Rock and Roll Hall of Fame in January 1988, at an informal ceremony in New York City, the price tag for the sloping, 95,000-square-foot building had jumped to $45 million. With local business leaders rallying around Higbee Company chairman Robert Broadbent, the heads of BP America, U.S. Nestle and East Ohio Gas Company, corralled pledges and gifts of $15 million. The Rock Hall would remain in Cleveland only after officials secured the minimum $18 million interim goal demanded by the New York board. By year's end, the groundbreaking was again delayed, and the cost revised at $48 million.

Meanwhile, naysayers were multiplying both in Cleveland and in the national press. Richard Gehr charged in *The Village Voice*: "The museum's planning has also been a disappointment. An architect was hired and an extravagant building designed before anyone knew what it would contain or how it would be paid for. Major collectors of rock memorabilia are turning the project a cold shoulder. Rock and roll is here to stay, but its gonna take a miracle to build this funhouse." With Larry R. Thompson named the director of the Hall of Fame, the planned groundbreaking was again delayed, this time for two years, until 1991.

In early 1989, Cleveland mayor George Voinovich unveiled a plan to give $15 million in property taxes to the Rock Hall. But tempers flared during a colorful exchange among council members, who were concerned about public tax moneys being diverted away from the city's crumbling schools. The controversial president of the Cleveland City Council, George Forbes, threatened to torpedo funding for the museum if the ceremonies weren't brought to the city. During the vote, Forbes told the local Rock Hall board members in attendance: "I think you've been snookered by the crew in New York."

But with the money at hand, the New York-based Hall of Fame Foundation still refused to move the ceremony to Cleveland, citing "inconvenience." As one former Rock Hall board member admitted: "All these people in New York and Los Angeles didn't want to spend the money and time to fly to Cleveland. They would rather hop in a limo and go to the Waldorf, have their steaks and champagne, and then go home."

But noted Cleveland deejay Chris Quinn insisted: "The Hall of Fame is here, the ceremony should be here. It shouldn't be Cleveland this year, somewhere else next year, then Cleveland the year after that, and somewhere else after that. No, the Hall of Fame is here. This is the city that went to bat, that showed them that we deserve it. We won it, and it should be here." Meanwhile, *Cleveland Plain Dealer* rock critic Michael Norman observed that "getting the inductees to Cleveland wouldn't be the problem. Most of them would be happy to make the pilgrimage to receive such an honor. But it is unrealistic to suggest that regular Cleveland inductions would attract a crowd of other celebrities."

But nearly a decade after the Hall of Fame was conceived, the only physical evidence of the planned museum was a billboard. Situated in a weed-infested field, the message "CLEVELAND WELCOMES – FUTURE HOME OF ROCK AND ROLL HALL OF FAME," took on an eyesore status. Concerned but undaunted, Norm N. Nite told *Scene*: "Granted, there have been a lot of mistakes that have been made since Cleveland got this in May of 1986. We're talking about three-and-a-half years, all we've got up is a sign." With the revised cost now approaching $50 million, Cleveland managed to reach the $40 million interim goal and was then told to raise an additional $8 million. Jann Wenner told *GQ* magazine, "They tried to meet their financial commitments, but we kept escalating the price on them. I mean, we set very high standards. And they swallowed and said 'Okay.'"

Another roadblock occurred in March 1990, when the New York board demanded a site change, following the opening of a Record Town music store in the adjacent Tower City Mall. While hall officials publicly bemoaned the lack of potential expansion space, privately there was concern over the loss of revenue for the Hall of Fame's own proposed record store. But William Hulett later insisted that "the whole 'record store' thing was a red herring. It was just an excuse to move [the Rock Hall] to a higher-profile location."

But with Congresswoman Mary Rose Oaker lobbying for a site near the Municipal Stadium, museum officials relocated the Rock Hall to a lakefront location along the North Coast Harbor. The proposed area was a prime property at the end of a central thoroughfare, East Ninth Street. The site was previously home to a popular restaurant which served Lake Erie fish. In 1936, the area hosted the Great Lakes Exposition, which drew seven-million tourists to the city. In the 1970s, city leaders had planned to redevelop the East Ninth Street Pier – dubbed the Gateway Project – into a tourist destination with theaters, restaurants and museums. (Eventually, the revised Gateway Project was relocated to another part of downtown.)

But with the promise of a larger museum, critics complained that the building would block the view of Lake Erie. Meanwhile, a press release warned that with the expansion in the "size of the facility, we anticipate some increase in costs." With William Hulett hired as the Rock Hall's co-chairman, in January 1991, the hall's construction price was upped again, this time to $60 million.

By May, the San Francisco-based Burdick Group was hired to design the museum's interior, with the hall's cost again revised, now tagged at $60 to $70 million. (A rejected proposal by Malibu-based designer Barry Howard had called for moving sidewalks, with visitors wearing radio-controlled headphones at all times.)

Also in May 1991, University of Indiana at Bloomington professor Bruce Harrah-Conforth, was named director of curatorial and educational affairs at the Rock Hall. His main task was to fill the museum with artifacts, a difficult task in an environment where competition between collectors and commercial outlets like the Hard Rock Cafe had dramatically driven up the prices of memorabilia. Over the next several years, Harrah-Conforth convinced artists, their relatives, and others in the music industry to donate or lend historically vital pieces, including scribbled lyric sheets, school report cards, stage clothing, and the requisite guitars. Though his initial budget for acquisitions was nonexistent, funds were later allocated.

Meanwhile, using slides and drawings, architect I.M. Pei unveiled his revised plans for the Hall of Fame. The design featured a main tower surrounded by separate buildings, with the Hall of Fame chamber situated on the top level. But when local officials expressed their disappointment with the modifications, Pei offered another design in October. In the end, critics charged that the Hall of Fame's pyramid shape closely resembled Pei's designs of the Kennedy Library and Louvre addition. With Pei's contract finalized, his firm was paid $5.35 million. (Ironically, a pyramid-shaped Hard Rock Café opened its doors in Myrtle Beach, South Carolina, the same year as Cleveland's Rock Hall.)

At the seventh induction ceremony in 1992, hall officials again bemoaned the absence of major corporate sponsors, and feared that a planned autumn groundbreaking might be delayed yet another year. The hall's critics were leading a separate charge. Warwick Stone, the memorabilia buyer for the Hard Rock Cafe chain, told *GQ* magazine: "The Rock and Roll Hall of Fame doesn't exist. I mean, there is no Hall of Fame. Where's the property? Where's the collection? What is it earning?" Notable Cleveland deejay John Lanigan told *People* magazine, "It's very embarrassing." Concert promoter Bill Graham repeated the lament, "You have to wonder why there's such a problem." Meanwhile, in February 1992, K. Michael Benz succeeded Larry Thompson as the Rock Hall's executive director.

In May 1993, the New York-based Hall of Fame Foundation took several legal steps to consolidate its authority. With the Cleveland and New York boards entering into separate operations, the New York-based Foundation retained the rights to the Rock and Roll Hall of Fame, with the name licensed to the Rock Hall in Cleveland. The joint operating agreement gave the New York directors the right to move the museum to another city if funding goals were not realized. Privately, Cleveland officials were outraged by the actions but kept quiet for fear of losing the museum.

The New York Foundation also maintained its right to exclusively oversee the induction process. Meeting in a conference room at the posh Atlantic Records offices in New York City, a group of rock movers and shakers – mainly record company honchos – converged for annual, politically-charged shoutfests over who belonged in the Rock Hall.

With the New York board unable to line up the promised corporate funding for the construction of the museum, a member of the Cleveland Port Authority, Dennis Lafferty, exercised a never-before-used contingency – Port Authority bonds. With the remaining funding in place, all that was left to do was build the musical mecca.

Eventually, most of the Rock Hall's cost would be financed by the public sector, with Cleveland taxpayers especially burdened. Funding the bulk of the cost, The Cleveland/Cuyahoga County Port Authority issued bonds totaling $38.9 million, with the loan repaid by corporate sponsorships, a 10-percent, citywide museum admission tax, and an increase in the hotel bed tax. Additionally, Cuyahoga County pitched in $11.8 million, with the city of Cleveland coughing up another $11.2 million. The state of Ohio granted $8 million for the Rock Hall construction and $10 million for site improvements. Lastly, tens of millions of dollars were spent rerouting utility wires as well as constructing streets and a nearby rail line. (Former Cleveland Growth Association executive K. Michael Benz, later chairman of the Cleveland Rock and Roll Hall of Fame Museum Committee, had said in late-1985 that no public tax funds would be used to pay for the museum.)

The groundbreaking for the Rock and Roll Hall of Fame finally took place in June 1993, when Chuck Berry, Pete Townshend and Billy Joel turned over inaugural shovels of dirt, to the thumping background music of The Rolling Stones' "Satisfaction." Townshend, who had flown to Cleveland on the heels of his Tony Award win for the Broadway production of *Tommy*, told the jubilant summer crowd that he hoped the hall "doesn't become a monolith to a bunch of dinosaurs." But the turning over of dirt marked the hall's reality. Although delayed many times by funding, politics, and miscalculations, nothing could stop its completion now. In August 1993, the controversial Dennis Barrie was named the director of the Rock Hall, replacing Bruce Harrah-Conforth

In December 1993, James Henke was named the museum's new chief curator. Henke told *Billboard* that when he was hired, "there really wasn't much" of a collection, "it was more like some stuff from fans. There was very little of any substance.... Because Jann [Wenner] had a relationship with Yoko Ono and John Lennon, he had called Yoko and said, 'Jim is going to be the curator now.' I had met her a few times when I was at *Rolling Stone*. Through Jann's arrangements, we got Yoko to give us a nice collection of John Lennon memorabilia. It is on a long-term loan, but it is his *Sgt. Pepper* uniform and the leather jacket that he wore when The Beatles played in Hamburg and also some early song lyrics and school report cards. So that was the first big collection we got after I got onboard, and that sort of opened the door to trying to get more."

After making eight trips to Sam Phillips' home in Memphis, Henke managed to accomplish what both the Smithsonian and Hard Rock Café could not – convince Phillips to allow the museum to display his Sun Records artifacts, including the very piano used on Elvis' first hits. Other items in the museum's vast collection included: Alice Cooper's 10-foot-high guillotine prop; Jimi Hendrix's handwritten lyrics to "Purple Haze," retrieved from a waste basket; Janis Joplin's psychedelic Porsche; Jim Morrison's Cub Scout uniform; Buddy Holly's high school diploma; Ray Charles' sunglasses; Elvis Presley's leather suit from his 1968 comeback special; and Keith Moon's report card, which indicated "promise in music." The following year, fashion designer Stephen Sprouse was named the costume curator, in charge of the museum's 100 mannequins. Meanwhile, Dennis Barrie voiced his dissatisfaction with the museum's emphasis on lifeless rock memorabilia, and demanded more interactive, audio-visual exhibits. Barrie explained in *Scene* magazine, "We don't want to be the Hard Rock Cafe. I have a feeling that some people think that's what it's going to be." The resulting improvements added $8 million to the existing display budget of $14 million.

Meeting its target opening date of Labor Day weekend 1995, the Hall of Fame drew hundreds of thousands of visitors and two-thousand journalists to the opening festivities. Costing $92 million in the end, the museum had been tagged at $15 million nine years earlier. With board member Jann Wenner originally pegging the admission price at $2 or $3, the first-year entry price instead stood at $10.90.

The highlight of the weekend-long celebration was the Concert for the Rock and Roll Hall of Fame, which was staged at the 65-year-old, 80,000-seat Municipal Stadium, just 14 months before its hasty demolition and weeks before the announcement of the departure of the venue's sole tenant, the Cleveland Browns. Tickets ranged in price from $30 to $540, with live coverage provided by HBO on a pay-per-view basis. With the entire city ablaze in rock and roll fever, starstruck fans tailed the bumper-to-bumper limousines that packed the downtown streets.

Emceed by Cleveland deejays Len "Boom Boom" Goldberg and "Kid Leo" Travagliante, the monumental concert paired musicians in never-before combinations. Highlights of the seven-hour concert included John Fogerty performing his CCR classics and James Brown delivering his funk-soul chestnuts. But the night's crowd-pleaser was Buckeye-born singer Chrissie Hynde, who flew an Ohio flag from her amplifier as she shouted out a string of hellos to cities in Northeastern Ohio, starting with her hometown of Akron.

But not everyone was pleased with the all-star lineup. Sonny Geraci, the leader of the Cleveland rock band The Outsiders, told *Scene* magazine: "We all worked hard to get the Rock and Roll Hall of Fame built here, and they didn't even invite me or Eric Carmen or other people who had hit records out of Cleveland, Ohio. I know I'm not Bruce Springsteen, but you know what? It sure would have been nice for them to have us play on that bill." Closing the concert at 2:15 AM were Bruce Springsteen and Chuck Berry, joining forces on Berry's pioneering classic, "Rock And Roll Music."

A shimmering, futuristic, glass pyramid, the Rock and Roll Hall of Fame and Museum was constructed with 1,900 tons of steel, the frame built to withstand gale-force winds of up to 150 miles per hour. With the building's neon halo reflecting in the calm waters of the seven-acre, man-made harbor along the Lake Erie shore, the museum became an instant landmark. A reviewer for *Time* magazine declared: "The building is a rousing success. It bursts forth from the ground into several assertive geometric forms – a triangle, a cylinder, a rectangular box. A trapezoidal chunk of the museum brazenly juts out over Lake Erie."

The building was originally planned for 200-feet but was reduced in size to 167-feet because of its proximity to nearby Burke Lakefront Airport. The museum was originally neighbored on one side by the domed, state-of-the-art, Great Lakes Science Center, and on the other side by the hulking, 618-foot, William G. Mather freighter-turned-museum. In 2005, the Mather was relocated to the west side of the Rock Hall, near the Science Center.

In a recurring controversy, a brouhaha erupted at the 1996 induction ceremony as to whether or not Cleveland would stage the induction ceremonies the next year. Following promises by both Ahmet Ertegun and Rock Hall CEO William Hulett, Cleveland finally won the right to ceremonies in 1997, on a rotational basis, sharing the honor with Los Angeles, London and New York. But for the first 23 induction ceremonies, Los Angeles and Cleveland had each hosted the event just once. Then beginning in 2009, Cleveland began hosting the ceremony every three years.

Still, not everyone was happy with the Hall of Fame. David Bowie has called the museum "ludicrous," telling HBO: "Screw them. I'm not even remotely interested. I know my own worth. I don't need a medal. Would I turn it down? Absolutely." Although Bowie did not intend his induction in 1986, he accepted the award.

Similarly, when punk rock legends, The Sex Pistols, came to town in 1996, lead singer Johnny Rotten demanded that his group's memorabilia be removed from the museum. But when The Sex Pistols were actually inducted in 2006, the group had planned on attending the ceremony, but balked after the Rock Hall refused to supply free tickets for friends and relatives. Typically, an act's record label would pick up the cost of the additional tickets. Informed of the ticket policy, another inductee – Eddie Levert of The O'Jays – told *The Akron Beacon Journal*, "They want $2,000 for that ticket, man. I'll save that and pay rent."

Similarly, Ozzy Osbourne asked that the nominating committee remove his name from consideration, explaining in a statement: "It's a joke. It's about glad-handing and grandstanding and I don't want any part of it." But when he was inducted in 2006 as a member of the heavy-metal pioneers Black Sabbath, Osbourne was all smiles.

Other critics have suggested that the museum resembles a king-sized Hard

Rock Cafe. *Boston Globe* music critic Jim Sullivan typified the sentiment: "From an aesthetic viewpoint, there's always lurked the questionable desire to institutionalize what was never intended to be institutionalized or, especially, sanitized. When the Rolling Stones were inducted... some [people] wondered whether a Stones' exhibit would include Keith Richards' guitars and, maybe, a few old syringes from his days as a heroin addict?"

Even the Rock Hall's former curator, Robert Santelli, admitted that the very existence of such an institution is incongruent with the premise of rock and roll: "Depending on your point of view, the Cleveland-based Rock and Roll Hall of Fame and Museum is either the music's official house of history – the place where one can find proof of its artistic and cultural merit – or a triangular-shaped glass temple that has more to do with myth and mass consumption than the real story of rock 'n' roll. Ever since this museum dedicated to the music and abiding culture was conceived... the debate over whether it was a good idea or a bad one has kept many a critic and music historian engaged in vigorous discourse. The skeptics' fear that institutionalizing rock 'n' roll would kill the music's present and future and trivialize and compress its past into neat, carefully packaged modules was not to be taken lightly, even by the museum's proponents. After all, rock, by its very nature, has always been chaotic, incorrigible, and anti-institutional. Together the music and its culture represented the antithesis of establishment and order.... Attempting to explain the inexplicable and control the uncontrollable – in a museum, of all places – was nothing less than an assault on rock's most primal and sacred roots. Or so naysayers railed."

Another concern was voiced by Neil Young and others – the Hall of Fame has inducted far too many acts, somehow cheapening the honor. While the Baseball Hall of Fame has bestowed the honor on only a handful of players per year, former nominating committee member Jeff Tamarkin countered, "You have to weigh how many baseball players have been in the major leagues with how many people made rock and roll records." Noted *New York Daily News* music columnist David Hinkley lamented: "Among the hundreds of letters and e-mails I've received over the years about the Rock and Roll Hall of Fame, not one ever said, 'The Hall got it right!' All halls of fame feed on argument.... [But] somehow arguments over the Rock Hall often seem to take on an annoyed tone."

The Hall of Fame selection committee has also been criticized for its inconsistency in deciding which group members qualify for induction. While three-dozen singers can legitimately claim membership in The Drifters, only seven members were inducted. Meanwhile, Motown great Smokey Robinson was enshrined into the hall minus his backing group, The Miracles. Similarly, members of Bruce Springsteen's longtime backing outfit, The E Street Band, were also excluded by the Rock Hall.

When Buddy Holly was honored at a Rock Hall-sponsored symposium in December 2003, members of his backing band, The Crickets, boycotted the week-long event in Cleveland. The musicians were disgruntled over the Rock Hall's decision to exclude them from induction alongside Holly in 1986. Only guitarist Tommy Allsup – who played with Holly during his final tour – agreed to perform at the affair.

During his second and final year as a member of the selection committee, the former editor of *Goldmine* magazine, Jeff Tamarkin, recalled how the rules were changed: "The board asked us to choose a certain number of artists before we even came to the meeting. So by the time we got there in 1993, some of the nominees had already been chosen, and it was left to us to come up with the rest at the meeting. One interesting side effect of this change was that some committee members were willing to vote for certain artists in private that they would never advocate in public. For example, some of the people on the committee were appalled that The Doors and The Grateful Dead had received enough votes in advance to make the list, yet in a discussion that took place before the meeting among five or six committee members, none of them – except me – would admit to having voted for those artists. Had those names been bandied about at the open meeting, I'm convinced they would not have been nominated that year."

A number of acts – including The Moody Blues – were kept out of the Hall of Fame simply because one or two members of the committee opposed their induction. At the 2005 induction ceremonies, a reporter from *The Akron Beacon Journal* noted that, "one radio [industry] guy, who's a good friend of a voter, said once during a meeting, Canadian prog-pop trio Rush was mentioned and one of the rock hall foundation bigwigs stood up and declared 'Rush will not get anywhere near the Rock and Roll Hall of Fame as long as I walk this planet.'" A number of artists have tried to influence the induction committee. While Chubby Checker pleaded his case with a full-page ad in *Billboard*, hundreds of members of the "Kiss Army" descended on Cleveland in August 2006 to make their case for the theatrical rockers.

But the biggest controversy took place in 2007 when Fox News reported that The Dave Clark Five had allegedly received enough votes for induction, but were kept out of the hall because of a last-minute decision by Jann Wenner. Wenner and the Rock Hall vehemently denied the charge.

Later, the independent-minded Tamarkin lost his seat on the board, in part, for criticizing the induction process in a *Billboard* magazine editorial: "To the vast majority of rock fans, and even to most in the industry, the makeup of this committee and its selection process are shrouded in mystery – it often appears that one would have better luck uncovering who killed J.F.K.... Something is missing from that board room even as we bandy names about: the public. This is a vote by politburo, not a general election."

At times, even the identities of the nominating board was considered a guarded secret. When a Cleveland entertainment magazine tried to obtain the list of judges, they were told by the New York foundation that "they aren't allowed to give them out."

But still, the Rock Hall has thrived, and has added new exhibits on a regular basis. With a break-even point of 690,000 visitors, the Rock Hall had hoped to draw 900,000 annually. But just short of its one-year anniversary, the museum exceeded all projections, welcoming its one-millionth visitor. Of that number, 540,000 came from outside Ohio – including 50,000 from overseas. In contrast, the previously leading rock destination, Elvis Presley's Graceland mansion, draws 700,000 annually. But in the wake of the 9/11 attacks, the Rock Hall experienced a rough period in 2002, losing $900,000. Wanting to attract younger music fans, David Spero, the vice-president of Education and Public Programming, launched the MTV Summer Series, which brought emerging artists to the Rock Hall stage.

The original education director, Robert Santelli, was pivotal in organizing the Rock Hall's annual American Music Masters series, which brought artists, scholars and fans together to examine the legacies of pioneers such as Sam Cooke, Hank Williams Sr. and Jerry Lee Lewis. Additionally, Santelli and chief curator James Henke launched The Hall of Fame series, which brought scores of inductees as well as other notable music industry giants – including Little Richard, Ruth Brown, The O'Jays, Sun Records founder Sam Phillips and songwriters Leiber & Stoller – to the museum's intimate fourth-floor theater for interviews, performances and questions from the audience. These events were filmed for later use by music scholars.

But as much as he accomplished at the museum, Santelli told *The Cleveland Plain Dealer*, "We're still not where I think we should be. Sometimes people snicker or smirk at my position, What does the director of education at the Rock and Roll Hall of Fame mean? It doesn't carry the respect. I want to go out there and make a pitch that rock has had a profound impact on America and who we are as Americans. It is America's contemporary folk music."

The Hall of Fame experienced a series of personnel changes during its first decade of operation. In May 2002, the Rock Hall laid off one-fifth of its full-time staff, leaving just 92 paid positions. Slashing $2.4 million from its operating budget, the organization also cut the pay of its management level employees by 10-percent. But after twice refinancing the construction bonds to take advantage of lower interest rates, the museum shaved four years off the projected payoff date.

Robert Santelli left his position at the Rock Hall after a five-year run in 2000, and was belatedly replaced in 2003 by Warren Zanes. A former member of the 1980s alternative-rock band The Del Fuegos, Zanes later earned a Ph.D. in visual and cultural studies from the University of Rochester. (Zanes is married to Elinor Blake, a pop star in her own right who is well known in France.) In 2006, Warren Zanes resigned from his post at the Rock Hall, but remained affiliated with the institution as an educational advisor.

After a turbulent period in the Rock Hall's top position, Terry C. Stewart was hired as the executive director and CEO of the museum in January 1999.

A law school graduate and former chief executive of the comic book empire, Marvel Entertainment Group, Stewart became the Rock Hall's fifth head administrator in just four years. Stewart brought some of his personal rock memorabilia collection to the museum, including early concert posters.

And after three years as the co-chairman of the Rock Hall, Lee C. Howley stepped down from the position in 2000, and was replaced by former board member Jay Henderson. During his reign, Howley reduced the size of the Cleveland board from 50 to 34 members. The New York-based Rock and Roll Hall of Fame Foundation also saw a change in leadership. In 2006, Joel Peresman, a former concert promoter and booking agent, replaced executive director Suzan Evans.

Teaming with *College Music Journal* in 2005, The Rock Hall sought to organize an annual, world-class, multi-venue music festival in the spirit of the South By Southwest event in Austin, Texas. The inaugural CMJ/Rock Hall Music Fest was headlined by the reformed Pixies. But wracked by money woes, the event was staged just twice.

Marking its 10th anniversary in 2005, the Rock Hall formally announced plans for the construction of the long-awaited research library and archive. Construction of the $20 million, 70,000-square-foot facility began in 2007, on the campus of Cuyahoga Community College. Also that year, the museum launched an extensive renovation.

Then in August 2008, Clevelanders felt blind-sided by the surprise announcement of a Rock Hall annex in downtown Manhattan. The 25,000-square-foot, street-level facility was constructed in the city's fashionable SoHo district. While media reports in Cleveland called the New York project a temporary exhibition, *Rolling Stone* magazine referred to it as "a permanent outpost." Additional annexes were planned for Memphis and Las Vegas.

But despite dire predictions, the Rock and Roll Hall of Fame has thrived in Cleveland. Although attendance has dropped off somewhat from its first few years, music fans from around the world have continued to make the museum an essential destination.

CHAPTER 14
CONCLUSION

Chrissie Hynde of The Pretenders told *Scene* magazine, "Those people on the West Coast and those people on the East Coast were not nearly as cool as anyone in Ohio because we had the best radio, we were armed with our transistor radios, our little Westinghouse numbers, our little light blue and white numbers we got for Christmas, under our pillows at night. And we got more musical background and better stations than of those people on the West Coast put together. And where did Lou Reed come when he wanted to start his tour when he went solo? What's the first place he played? You got it. Cleveland. Where did David Bowie come on his first-ever appearance in America outside of the U.K.? Where did he go? You got it. Cleveland, Ohio. Because it always had the hippest, the coolest, the best music collectors, the people with the sharpest minds, and the most know-how about rock and roll were sittin' right there in Northeast Ohio."

Ohio's rich, musical heritage was celebrated by the Rock and Roll Hall of Fame with an exhibit in 2003. The display was showcased as part of Ohio's bicentennial celebration, and was partially funded by a state grant.

In addition to the Hall of Fame in Cleveland, a wealth of recorded music and related research material has been amassed by Bowling Green University in Northwestern Ohio. Housing the world's largest collection of rock and roll periodicals and books, the Music Library and Sound Recordings Archives are located on the third floor of Bowling Green's Jerome Library. The creation of Professor William L. Schurk, the facility has become an international mecca for music researchers.

*   *   *   *   *   *

In a rock and roll publishing world dominated by the likes of *Rolling Stone* and *Spin*, Ohio is home to *Alternative Press*. Launched by Kent State University student Mike Shea, the magazine came about after a series of quirky events. Shortly after the start of his freshman year, Shea came down with a serious case of mononucleosis. Dropping out of school to recuperate, he spent his time on what would become issue #1 of *Alternative Press*. But with Kent State closing its film department, Shea never returned to his classes. Initially a free "fanzine" with a press-run of one-thousand copies, the first issue of *Alternative Press* was distributed in June 1985 at a local punk-rock concert. Gradually building its circulation numbers and battling to stay afloat financially, the magazine was forced to suspend publication for a full year in 1987.

Over the next decade, Shea transformed *Alternative Press* into an influential and respected magazine. Then in 1997, Madonna's business partner Guy Oseary was unsuccessful in his attempt to purchase a stake in the periodical. By 2005, the monthly publication boasted nearly a quarter-million subscribers.

The Buckeye State also gave rise to *Billboard* magazine, an essential music-industry guide. Introduced by William H. Donaldson and James H. Hennegan in 1894, originally as *Billboard Advertising*, the Cincinnati-based weekly was initially priced at ten-cents. Renamed *The Billboard* in 1897, the magazine introduced its first music-related chart – a survey of sheet music sales – in 1913. By 1934, both *Billboard* and *Your Hit Parade* began tabulating the airplay of hit records on network radio. In coming years, *Billboard* would introduce a series of groundbreaking music charts including: "The Top Country & Western" (1949), "The Hot 100" (1958), and "The Harlem Hit Parade" (1942), which was later renamed "Top Rhythm & Blues" (1949). Although the magazine's dominance would later be challenged by *Record World*, *Cash Box* and *Radio & Records*, *Billboard* has remained the most influential publication in the music business.

Meanwhile, in the last decade of the 20th century, the music industry would undergo dramatic changes. Instead of radio stations and record stores keeping track of airplay and sales, computerized systems such as Broadcast Data Systems and SoundScan provided exact, empirical tallies. And while broadcasting conglomerates like Clear Channel would swallow up radio stations by the hundreds, Akron was one of only two cities in the top-100 U.S. markets not dominated by the firm.

The digital age also crippled the traditional record store, with North Canton, Ohio-based Camelot Music filing for Chapter 11 bankruptcy protection in 1996. The chain's original owner, Paul David, had sold the company three-years earlier. In 1998, Camelot was acquired by Trans World Entertainment, at which time, many of the chain's stores were renamed FYE.

* * * * * *

Though well outside the domain of rock and roll, classical and polka music are both celebrated with their own museums in Ohio. Following the hoopla surrounding the opening of Cleveland's Rock and Roll Hall of Fame, the politicians and city leaders of Cincinnati yearned for the prestige and economic impact of hosting a similar institution. Conceived in 1996 by businessman David A. Klingshirn, the American Classical Music Hall of Fame and Museum was constructed in the city's Over-The-Rhine district. Opening in 2000, the museum was adjacent to Cincinnati Memorial Hall, the home of the Cincinnati Symphony Orchestra, Cincinnati Pops and Cincinnati Opera.

And although Cleveland may be the Rock and Roll Capital, the city is also a celebrated polka center. An ethnic-rooted musical genre celebrated by the city's many Eastern European immigrants, polka in Cleveland had its own homegrown star, Frankie Yankovic. Born in nearby West Virginia but arriving in Cleveland at age five, Yankovic adapted his Slovenian brand of polka for American audiences. In 1948, Yankovic scored a million-selling hit with "Just Because." Playing more than 300 shows per year at his peak, Yankovic and his frequently changing cast of musicians became an institution, winning the first-ever Grammy for polka in 1986. In celebration of the music's legacy, the National Cleveland-Style Polka Hall of Fame opened in 1987. The competing Chicago-based, polka hall of fame had opened in 1969. Although the Chicago institution focused on the Polish form of the music, Frankie Yankovic was a first-year inductee. And despite persistent rumors, Weird Al Yankovic is not the offspring of Frankie Yankovic.

While Ohio can boast an internationally-known Rock and Roll Hall of Fame, the state has yet to establish any sort of institution honoring its own musical legacy. Despite a rich heritage, there are no present plans for an Ohio music hall of fame.

*   *   *   *   *   *

Lastly, why do some talented, musical acts from Ohio achieve widespread acclaim while others are ignored? While Chrissie Hynde became a rock legend, her brother Terry spent decades in The Numbers Band without ever attaining the fame or recognition his group deserved. With the right record company, personal contact or lucky break, numerous Buckeye artists – such as Max Wheel & The Shades, The Mary Martin Band, London Fog & The Continentals, Joey Leal or Rainbow Canyon – might have triumphed on the national level.

But the performers, deejays, producers and record label owners examined in this book have made an impact. And Sloopy is still hanging on.

BIBLIOGRAPHY

INTRODUCTION
Cornyn, Stan; & Scanlon, Paul. (2002). *Exploding: The highs, hits, hype, heroes, and hustlers of the Warner Music Group.* New York: Rolling Stone Press.
Ertegun, Ahmet. (2001). *What'd I Say: The Atlantic Story.* New York: Welcome Rain Publishing.
Martin, Deana; & Holden, Wendy. (2004). *Memories are made of this: Dean Martin through his daughter's eyes.* New York: Harmony.
Mazor, Barry. (2003, May-June). A soul forgotten. *No Depression.*
Soeder, John. (2004, June 17). That's Amore! *The Cleveland Plain Dealer.*
Warner, Jack L.; & Jennings, Dean. (1965). *My first hundred years in Hollywood.* New York: Random House.

CH. 1 – HANG ON SLOOPY: THE OHIO STATE UNIVERSITY TRADITION
Abrams, Malcolm X. (2007, January 6). OSU fans hanging on to "Sloopy." *The Akron Beacon Journal.*
Asakawa, Gil. (1992, March 6). The Strangeloves: Stranger-than-fiction story. *Goldmine.*
Dufresne Chris. (2003, December 29). Simple fist of fate. *The Los Angeles Times.*
Hoekstra, Dave. (2002, November 7). Something to twist & shout about. *The Chicago Sun-Times.*
Littlegreen, Curtis B., II; Mailer, David H.; & Yabroff, Marc S. (Eds.). (1989). *Script Ohio: The Ohio State University Marching Band.* Columbus: Ohio State University, Kappa Kappa Psi.
Lyttle, Eric. (2003, September). The real story of "Hang on Sloopy." *Columbus Monthly.*
Muise, Dan. (2002). *Gallagher Marriott Derringer & Trower: Their lives and music.* Milwaukee: Hal Leonard Corporation.
Pollard, James E. (1952). *History of the Ohio State University.* Columbus: The Ohio State University Press.
Shannon, Bob; & Javna, John. (1986). *Behind the hits.* New York: Warner Books.
Snypp, Wilbur; & Hunter, Bob. (1998). *The Buckeyes: Ohio State football.* Tomball, TX: Strode Publishers.
Wentz, Howard E. (1982). *Touchdown Buckeyes: My days with the Ohio State Buckeyes.* Defiance, OH: S/B Publications.
Wilson, Craig. (1988, October 24). Ohio State marchers strut their stuff with pride. *USA Today.*
Wexler, Jerry; & Ritz, David. (1993). *Rhythm and the blues: A life in American music.* New York: Alfred A. Knopf.

CH. 2 – ALAN FREED AND THE RISE OF ROCK AND ROLL IN CLEVELAND
Aiges, Scott. (2001, September). The crying game: A day of emotions with Jimmy Scott. *Down Beat.*
Belz, Carl. (1969). *The story of rock.* New York: Oxford University Press.
Berry, Chuck. (1987). *Chuck Berry: The autobiography.* New York: Harmony.
Bristol, Marc; & DeWitt, Dennis. (1992). Jerry Merritt interview. *Blue Suede News,* no. 20.
Dyer, Bob. (1990, October 14). Contract clause led to Freed's fame. *The Akron Beacon Journal.*
Eliot, Marc. (1993). *Rockonomics: The money behind the music.* New York: Citadel.
Finan, Joe. (1997, February 9). Interview with author.
George-Warren, Holly. (1994, March 24). Leader of the old school. *Rolling Stone.*
Guralnick, Peter. (1994). *Last train to Memphis.* Boston: Little, Brown.
Halasa, Joyce. (1990, September 13). Chuck Young, part I: Cleveland record promotions and payolas. *Scene.*
Harriott, Frank. (1950, July). Cow Cow Davenport. *Ebony.*
"Hepcats bay on trail of Moondog, Freed in jam." (1952, March 22). *The Akron Beacon Journal.*
Hirshey, Gerri. (1984). *Nowhere to run: The story of soul music.* New York: Times Books.

Horowitz, Carl. (1995, March 1). Showman Alan Freed. *Investor's Business Daily*.
Jackson, Hal; & Haskins, James. (2001). *The house that Jack built*. New York: Amistad Press.
Jackson, John A. (1991). *Big beat heat: Alan Freed and the early years of rock & roll*. New York: Schirmer.
Junod, Tom. (1992, December). Oh, what a night! *Life*.
Lee, Brenda; Oermann, Robert K; & Clay, Julie. (2002). *Little Miss Dynamite: The life and times of Brenda Lee*. New York: Hyperion.
Lewis, Myra; & Silver, Murray. (1982). *Great balls of fire: The uncensored story of Jerry Lee Lewis*. New York: St. Martin's.
Martin, Linda; & Segrave, Kerry. (1988). *Anti-rock: The opposition to rock'n'roll*. New York: Da Capo.
"Moondog madness." (1952, March 29). *The (Cleveland) Call & Post*.
Nite, Norm N. (1992, March 9). *Alan Freed special*. WMJI, Cleveland, OH.
O'Neil, Thomas. (1993). *The Grammys: For the record*. New York: Penguin.
Passman, Arnold. (1971). *The deejays*. New York: Macmillan.
Pollock, Bruce. (1981). *When rock was young*. New York: Holt, Rinehart and Winston.
Pratt, Ray. (1990). *Rhythm and resistance: Explorations in the political uses of popular music*. New York: Praeger.
Quinn, Chris. (1997, February 27). Interview with author.
Rathbun, Keith. (1986, March 20). The Moondog Coronation Ball: Happy birthday, rock 'n' roll. *Scene*.
Redd, Lawrence N. (1985, September). Rock! It's still rhythm and blues. *Black Perspectives in Music*.
Riedel, Johannnes. (1975). *Soul music black and white: The Influences of black music on the churches*. Minneapolis: Augsburg.
Ritz, David. (2002). *Faith in time: The life of Jimmy Scott*. Cambridge, MA: Da Capo Press.
Rutledge, Jeffrey L. (1985, February 1). Alan Freed: The fall from grace of a forgotten hero. *Goldmine*.
Sangiacomo, Michael. (1996, February 3). The men of steel. *The Cleveland Plain Dealer*.
Schrader, Erich. (1997, March 21). Interview with author.
Scott, Jane. (1982, March 14). 30 years ago, "Moon Dog" howled. *The Cleveland Plain Dealer*.
Scott, Jane. (1992, September 7). Lakewood deejay sells early film footage of Elvis. *The Cleveland Plain Dealer*.
Scott, Jane. (1993, May 28). Poni-Tails recall spotlight. *The Cleveland Plain Dealer*.
Scott, Jane. (1995, May 27). Light's out for Nite on radio in Cleveland. *The Cleveland Plain Dealer*.
Shaw, Arnold. (1974). *The Rockin' '50s*. New York: Hawthorne.
Shaw, Arnold. (1978). *Honkers and shouters*. New York: Collier.
Smith, Wes. (1989). *The pied pipers of rock 'n' roll*. Marietta, GA: Longstreet.
Snyder, Michael. (1985, April 14). Wild bluesman's revival. *The San Francisco Chronicle*.
Soeder, John. (2005, October 21). When Elvis rocked Brooklyn. *The Cleveland Plain Dealer*.
"The first rock 'n' roll concert." (1999, February). *Q*.
"Top jock." (1955, February 14). *Time*.
West, Robert. (1996, December 5). Interview with author.
Wexler, Jerry; & Ritz, David. (1993). *Rhythm and the blues: A life in American music*. New York: Alfred A. Knopf.
Williams, Valena Minor. (1952, March 29). Moon Doggers "break it up." *The (Cleveland) Call & Post*.
Wolfman Jack; & Laursen, Byron. (1995). *Have mercy*. New York: Warner.

CH. 3– CINCINNATI: WLW AND KING-FEDERAL RECORDS

Bird, Rick. (2002, November 22). Capturing WLW's heritage: A comprehensive history of WLW's golden years. *The Cincinnati Post*.
Blase, Darren. (1997, March 27). The man who was King. *(Cincinnati) City Beat*.
Brown, James; & Tucker, Bruce. (1986). *James Brown: The Godfather of Soul*. New York: Macmillan.

Dawson, Jim. (1995). *The Twist*. Boston: Faber & Faber.
Grendysa, Peter. (1990, September 7). King/Federal. *Goldmine*.
Hershey, Gerri. (2007, January 25). Funk's founding father. *Rolling Stone*.
Hoekstra, Dave. (2007, April 15). James Brown's death shines light on saving King Records. *The Chicago Sun-Times*.
Horstman, Barry M. (1999, February 24). Syd Nathan: He was rock music's unlikely legend. *The Cincinnati Post*.
Hurtt, Michael. (2004, August). The *Mojo* interview. *Mojo*.
McClure, Rusty; Stern, David; & Banks, Michael A. (2006). *Crosley: Two brothers and a business empire that transformed the nation*. Cincinnati: Clerisy Press.
Nager, Larry. (2003, March 9). Hank Ballard epitomized King Records sound. *The Cincinnati Enquirer*.
Perry, Dick. (1971). *Not just a sound: The story of WLW*. Englewood Cliffs, NJ: Prentice-Hall.
Pollock, Bruce. (1981). *When rock was young*. New York: Holt, Rinehart and Winston.
Radel, Cliff. (1994, November 6). King-sized dreams: Making former Cincinnati recording plant into museum would revive an era. *The Cincinnati Enquirer*.
Ramney, Jack. (1949, February 6). Juke box operator. *The Cincinnati Enquirer*.
Rumble, John W. (1992). Roots of rock & roll: Henry Glover at King Records. *The Journal of Country Music*.
Shaw, Arnold. (1978). *Honkers and shouters*. New York: Collier.
Sloat, Bill. (1997, May 4). Founder of King Records built mecca for Urban Music. *The Cleveland Plain Dealer*.
Talevski, Nick. (1999). *The unofficial encyclopedia of the Rock and Roll Hall of Fame*. Westport, CT: Greenwood.
Tracy, Steven C. (1993). *Going to Cincinnati: A history of the blues in the Queen City*. Urbana: University of Illinois Press.
Trotter Jr., Joe William. (1998). *River Jordan: African-American urban life in the Ohio Valley*. Lexington: University of Kentucky Press.
Winternitz, Felix; & DeVroomen Bellman, Sacha. (2000). *Cincinnati's insiders' guide* (4th ed.). Helena, MT: Falcon Publishing.

CH. 4 – POP-ROCK IN THE 1960s & 1970s
Black, Johnny. (2006, July). The greatest songs ever: Go All The Way. *Blender*.
Bronson, Fred. (1997). *The Billboard book of number one hits* (4th ed). New York: Billboard Books.
Gross, Larry. (2007, July 4). The pretenders. *(Cincinnati) CityPaper*.
Halasa, Joyce. (1991, August 22). Sonny Geraci: From Starfires to Outsiders. *Scene*.
Halasa, Joyce. (1991, September 5). Sonny Geraci, Pt. III: Hit records and a new start. *Scene*.
Hogya, Bernie; & Sharp, Ken. (2006). *Raspberries Tonight!* Cleveland: EricCarmen.com.
Lubinger, Bill. (2007, March 23). Still fired by love of rock. *The Cleveland Plain Dealer*.
O'Connor, Clint. (1995, August 27). Memorable moments. *The Cleveland Plain Dealer*.
Shears, Jake. (2006, November 12). When Elton met Jake. *The Observer*.
Soeder, John. (2006, February 12). One lonely song. *The Cleveland Plain Dealer*.
Soeder, John. (2006, February 26). Rock still beating a path to the door. *The Cleveland Plain Dealer*.
Stevens, Dale. (August 27, 2004). Beatles concert broke mold. *The Cincinnati Post*.
Tashian, Barry. (1997). *Ticket to ride*. Nashville: Dowling Press.

CH. 5 – THE RISE OF ALBUM ROCK
"At war with war." (1970, May 18). *Time*.
Barnes, Richard. (1996). *The Who: Maximum R&B* (Rev. ed.). London: Plexus.
Bird, Rick. (2004, December 3). 25 years ago tonight, 11 people died in a horrific crush outside the doors of the Coliseum. *The Cincinnati Post*.
Black, Judy. (1991, November 7). A conversation with Marc Cohn. *Scene*.
Budin, David. (1994, February 13). David Spero: Rock around the block. *The Cleveland Plain Dealer*.

Castro, Peter. (1994, February 28). Jammin' with... Roger Daltrey: Turning 50, the Dorian Gray of rock discovers he's still a Who at heart. *People*.
Cleveland, Barry. (October, 2006). Soulful 6-string excursions: Phil Keaggy. *Guitar Player*.
Conte, Andrew. (1999, November 27). The Who concert tragedy: After 20 years, scars remain. *The Cincinnati Post*.
Eckberg, John. (2004, April 11). Making Tracks: Bo Wood backs a magazine for grown-up music fans. *The Cincinnati Enquirer*.
Einarson, John; & Furay, Richie. (1997). *There's something happening here: The story of Buffalo Springfield*. New York: Cooper Square Press.
Flippo, Chet. (1980, January 24). Rock & roll tragedy. *Rolling Stone*.
Graham, Samuel. (1983, October). Joe Walsh goes back to barn-storming. *Musician*.
Harrington, Richard. (1993, July 4). Talkin' 'bout his regeneration: After the drugs, the tumult and the Who, Pete Townshend finds new life on Broadway. *The Washington Post*.
Hedegaard, Erik. (2006, August 24). Joe Walsh rides again. *Rolling Stone*.
Hunter, Ian. (2007, June). My page: Cleveland rocks. *Relix*.
Lendt, C.K. (1997). *Kiss and sell*. New York: Billboard Books.
Livingston, Sandra. (2005, March 6). Setting the record straight. *The Cleveland Plain Dealer*.
Loder, Kurt. (1982, November 25). The Who clean up at Shea. *Rolling Stone*.
Marcus, Greil. (1980, June 26). Interview with Pete Townshend, *Rolling Stone*.
Marsh, Dave; & Stein, Kevin. (1981). *The book of rock lists*. New York: Dell.
Meat Loaf; & Dalton, David. (1999). *To hell and back*. New York: HarperCollins.
Neer, Richard. (2001). *The rise and fall of rock radio*. New York: Villard.
Norman, Michael. (1992, June 14). Michael Stanley: Back to the music. *The Cleveland Plain Dealer*.
Olszewski, Mike. (2003). *Radio daze: Stories from the front in Cleveland's FM air wars*. Kent, OH: Kent State University Press.
Sharp, Ken. (1994, July 8). Look who's talking: A conversation with Roger Daltrey. *Goldmine*.
Sheff, David. (1994, February). Playboy interview: Pete Townshend. *Playboy*.
Soeder, John. (2006, February 26). Rock still beating a path to the door. *The Cleveland Plain Dealer*.
"10 questions for... Devo's Gerald Casale." (2006, December 8). *Goldmine*.
"The stampede to tragedy." (1979, December 17). *Time*.
Thompson, Dave. (1996, September). Quadrophenia – fourth time lucky. *Discoveries*.
Wolff, Carlo. (2006). *Cleveland rock & roll memories*. Cleveland: Gray & Company.

CH. 6 – THE ARRIVAL OF PUNK ROCK IN CLEVELAND
Boehm, Mike. (1995, June 30). No way to cramp their style. *The Los Angeles Times*.
Carney, Jim. (2006, September 25). Movie director is proud of Akron roots. *The Akron Beacon Journal*.
Norman, Michael. (1995, August 20). For Pere Ubu, time had come to elevate rock. *The Cleveland Plain Dealer*.
Petkovic, John. (2007, July 9). Punk rockers rebelled in 1977 with their own 'summer of hate.' *The Cleveland Plain Dealer*.
Reynolds, Simon. (2005). *Rip it up and start again: Postpunk 1978-1984*. New York: Penguin.
Robins, Wayne. (1988, September 16). Pere Ubu: Tying up the fringe. *Newsday*.
Soeder, John. (2003, June 1). Reigniting the Rocket. *The Cleveland Plain Dealer*.
Webb, Betty. (1992, March 6). Time goes easy on the Cramps beneath the band's black humor is a solid, rockabilly foundation. *The St. Louis Post-Dispatch*

CH. 7 – NEW WAVE & THE AKRON SCENE
Abram, Malcolm X. (2006, March 12). Devo's new devolution. *The Akron Beacon Journal*.
Angel, Johnny. (1995, August). Skinny ties & spiky hair: The guitarists of new wave remember. *Guitar Player*.
Christgau, Robert. (1978, April 17). A real new wave rolls out of Akron. *The Village Voice*.
Dellinger, Jade & Giffels, David. (2003). *Are we not men? We are Devo!* London: SAF.
Drexler, Michael. (1995, September 24). By the Numbers: Kent's longest-running band is still waiting

for its one big break. *The Cleveland Plain Dealer.*
Goddard, Simon. (2006, August). Chrissie Hynde lets *Uncut* in on the inspiration behind the motley gang's debut album. *Uncut.*
Hagelberg, Kymberli. (1991, April 4). Punk rock, the pink triangle and the birth of the Akron sound. *Scene.*
Holan, Mark. (1990, July 19). Chrissie Hynde's Cleveland. *Scene.*
Jenkins, Mark. (1989, June 28). Gems from the Rust Belt. *The Washington Post.*
Kadar, Dan. (2005, August 28). Tireless effort built this city on rock 'n' roll. *The Akron Beacon Journal.*
Paoletta, Michael. (2006, April 3). Q&A with Chrissie Hynde. *Billboard.*

CH. 8 – HARD ROCK AND HEAVY METAL
Batten, Steven. (1994, August 3). Gilby Clarke: Guitar pop his way. *Scene.*
Klosterman, Chuck. (2001, July 19). Glam slam metal jam: Bands from 1980s at Blossom tonight. *The Akron Beacon Journal.*
Klosterman, Chuck. (2001, November 15). Chimaira vocalist takes of things metal. *The Akron Beacon Journal.*
Ling, Dave. (2003, December). Rob is lucky to be back! *Classic Rock.*
Petkovic, John. (2003, July 20). Ousted singer for Judas Priest isn't bitter. *The Cleveland Plain Dealer.*
Revkin, Andrew C. (2003, July 27). Metal-head becomes metal-god. *The New York Times.*

CH. 9 – ALTERNATIVE ROCK: 1980s AND BEYOND
Barton, Laura. (2005, August 20). Misfits that fit. *The Guardian.*
Cherry, Robert. (2005, January 3). Canton band is rising in the charts while sitting around back home. *The Cleveland Plain Dealer.*
Clements, Paul. (2003, May). Urban legends. *Magnet.*
Hagelberg, Kymberli. (1995, November 16). Home is where their hearts are. *Scene.*
Harrington, Richard. (2004, December 24). The DIY attitude of O.A.R. *The Washington Post.*
Holan, Mark. (1989, December 21). Nine Inch Nails: Trent Reznor's big breakthrough. *Scene.*
Holan, Mark. (1995, May 4). Richard Patrick's sonic boom. *Scene.*
Howe, Jeff. (2005, November). The hit factory. *Wired.*
Kane, Dan. (2006, August 6). Who would you pick to perform at the ribs burnoff? *The Canton Repository.*
Klosterman, Chuck. (2006, February). February 1998. *Spin.*
Lockwood, Rod. (2007, April 29). The Bears: Sound collaboration. *The Toledo Blade.*
Manson, Marilyn; & Straus, Neil. (1999). *Marilyn Manson: The long hard road out of hell.* New York: ReganBooks.
Percorelli, John. (1997, February). Doing it for the kids. *Alternative Press.*
Petkovic, John. (2002, December 27). It's finale time for the New Bomb Turks. *The Cleveland Plain Dealer.*
Soeder, John. (1998, October 26). Rocking their soul: Afghan Whigs add raw edge to their music for new, mostly upbeat album. *The Cleveland Plain Dealer.*
Soeder, John. (2005, October 7). Secure nail. *The Cleveland Plain Dealer.*
Spitz, Marc. (2004, September). Life to the Pixies. *Spin.*
Taylor, Chuck. (2006, February 25). Download data. *Billboard.*

CH. 10 – SOUL AND R&B
Abram, Malcolm X. (2005, March 13). O'Jays flying on cloud nine and it's such a sweet trip. *The Akron Beacon Journal.*
Barton, Laura. (2006, March 3). "You wanna relish that bad feeling." *The Guardian.*
Chervokas, Jason. (1995, May 26). Make it funky: James Brown. *Goldmine.*
Conniff, Tamara; & Crosley, Hillary. (2006, August 26). Making of a Legend part. *Billboard.*
Ellis, Thomas. (2006, August-September). From the crib to the coliseum: Stretchin' out with bass

legend William "Bootsy" Collins. *Waxpoetics*.
Himes, Geoffrey. (1996, May 10). Levert: Like father, like son. *The Washington Post*.
Klosterman, Chuck. (2001, November 1). R&B man Hewett will showcase his inspirational album when he returns to Akron for two Tangier shows. *The Akron Beacon Journal*.
Nager, Larry. (1999, October 17). L.A. Reid: The man behind LaFace. *The Cincinnati Enquirer*.
Nickson, Chris. (2003, July). The Isley Brothers – 44 years of hits. *Discoveries*.
Paulk, Ralph. (1994, December 11). A song of success. *The Akron Beacon Journal, Beacon Magazine*.
Soeder, John. (1999, December 30). Isleys plan surprises to shout in New Year. *The Cleveland Plain Dealer*.
Soeder, John. (2005, March 13). O'Jays' soulful journey on R&B railroad. *The Cleveland Plain Dealer*.
Soeder, John. (2007, May 6). Finding harmony in life's struggles. *The Cleveland Plain Dealer*.
Talevski, Nick. (1999). *The unofficial encyclopedia of the Rock and Roll Hall of Fame*. Westport, CT: Greenwood.
Talevski, Nick. (2006). *Knocking on heaven's door*. London: Omnibus.
Tracy, Steven C. (1993). *Going to Cincinnati: A history of the blues in the Queen City*. Urbana: University of Illinois Press.
White, Glen. (1984, January 15). Midnight Star hits charts with hot-selling LP. *The Lexington Herald-Leader*.
Womack, Bobby; & Ashton, Robert. (2006). *Midnight mover*. London: John Blake Publishing.

CH. 11 – SINGERS-SONGWRITERS, ETC.
Bracelin, Jason. (2003, November 5). 98 Degrees and rising. *Scene*.
Norman, Michael. (1993, May 30). Rockin' the hard country: Yoakam's style was sparked while a youth in Columbus. *The Cleveland Plain Dealer*.
Norman, Michael. (1992, February 23). Local Grammy nominee hit it lucky in Memphis. *The Cleveland Plain Dealer*.
Obrecht, Jas; Barton, Geoff; Llewewllyn, Sian; Fielder, Hugh; Fortman, Ian; Yates, Henry; et. al. (2006, August). Top 100 blues anthems. *Classic Rock*.
Patterson, Brent. (2007, September). Brass tracks. *Cincinnati Magazine*.
Perry, Dick. (1971). *Not just a sound: The story of WLW*. Englewood Cliffs, NJ: Prentice-Hall.
Porter, Tim. (2003, October/November). Over The Rhine: Where Jesus is Lord and Elvis is king. *Paste*.
Scott, Jane. (1992, October 23). Brewer and Shipley hit the road. *The Cleveland Plain Dealer*.
Talevski, Nick. (2006). *Knocking on heaven's door*. London: Omnibus.

CH. 12 – ROCK ON TV: WKRP IN CINCINNATI, DREW CAREY & UPBEAT!
Black, Judy. (1992, January 23). Drew Carey: Cleveland's comedic hero. *Scene*.
Brown, Roger. (1996, January 7). Electrifying history: Early Cleveland television and radio led the way nationally with innovative and creative uses of 'new' media. *The Cleveland Plain Dealer*.
Budin, David. (1994, February 13). David Spero: Rock around the block. *The Cleveland Plain Dealer*.
Eszterhas, Joe. (2004). *Hollywood animal*. New York: Alfred E. Knopf.
Hagelberg, Kymberli. (1991, April 4). Punk rock, the pink triangle and the birth of the Akron sound. *Scene*.
Kassel, Michael B. (1993). *America's favorite radio station: WKRP in Cincinnati*. Bowling Green, OH: Bowling Green University Popular Press.
O'Connor, Clint. (1995, August 27). 'Upbeat' let newcomers rub elbows with stars. *The Cleveland Plain Dealer*.

CH. 13 – THE ROCK AND ROLL HALL OF FAME

Barry, Dave. (1986, August 24). Rolling out the rock artifacts. *The Washington Post*.
Belardo, Carolyn. (1986, May 1). Cleveland rocks, not Philadelphia. U.P.I.
DeCurtis, Anthony. (1986, June 19). Cleveland chosen as site for Hall of Fame. *Rolling Stone*.
Dunn, Jancee. (1995, October). Hail hail rock & roll. *Rolling Stone*.
Farley, Christopher John. (1995, September 4). Forever rockin': After years of planning, rock finally gets its own museum – in Cleveland! *Time*.
Farris, Mark. (1986, May 6). Rock hall of fame is Cleveland's. *The Akron Beacon Journal*.
Fricke, David. (1986, February 13). The Rock and Roll Hall of Fame: At last. *Rolling Stone*.
Gehr, Richard. (1988, April 5). The mart of rock and roll. *Village Voice*.
Greene, Andy. (2006, November 16). Clash hit Hall of Fame. *Rolling Stone*.
Harrington, Richard. (1988, January 27). Rock's induction production. *The Washington Post*.
Harrington, Richard. (1996, January 31). Hall of Fame director to move on. *The Washington Post*.
Hay, Carla. (2004, March 13). The last word: A Q&A with Jann S. Wenner. *Billboard*.
Hilburn, Robert. (1986, March 2). Misplacing rock's hall of fame? *The Los Angeles Times*.
Hinkley, David. (2007, March 14). Rock fans get no satisfaction. *New York Daily News*.
Holan, Mark. (1989, October 19). Norm N. Nite: The Rock Hall of Fame's unsung hero. *Scene*.
Holan, Mark. (1991, May 2). Five years and nothing to show for it. *Scene*.
Holan, Mark. (1993, September 15). Dennis Barrie: A conversation with the new Rock Hall director. *Scene*.
Holan, Mark. (1996, August 29). One year after. *Scene*.
Holan, Mark. (1997, June 12). Time is on his side. *Scene*.
Holan, Mark. (1998, January 8). How the Rock Hall voting process works. *Scene*.
Johnson, Kevin C. (1994, April 24). A cool head. *The Akron Beacon Journal*.
Kelly, Thomas. (1998, August). How the rock was won (Part One). *Cleveland Magazine*.
Kelly, Thomas. (1998, September). How the rock was won (Part Two). *Cleveland Magazine*.
Litt, Steven. (1995, August 27). Oh, for the right place. *The Cleveland Plain Dealer*.
Litt, Steven. (1995, September 10). Architecture critics mainly approve Pei's rock museum. *The Cleveland Plain Dealer*.
Litt, Steven. (1996, January 14). Artistic package on waterfront line an RTA letdown. *The Cleveland Plain Dealer*.
Lubinger, Bill. (1996, April 18). Rock hall so popular it needs to expand. *The Cleveland Plain Dealer*.
McGuire, Jack. (1990, March 12). Market profile Cleveland. *Advertising Age*.
Montanari, Richard. (1993, July). Exile on Ninth Street. *Northern Ohio Live*.
Newman, Ralph M. (1973). Norm N. Nite: New York welcomes "Mr. Music." *Bim Bam Boom*.
Norman, Michael. (1995, July 28). Out of the back room and into the fore. *The Cleveland Plain Dealer*.
Norman, Michael. (1996, January 20). Why rock induction isn't here. *The Cleveland Plain Dealer*.
Norman, Michael. (1996, January 24). Rock hall director resigns for new ventures. *The Cleveland Plain Dealer*.
Norman, Michael. (1996, September 1). Rock Hall a huge hit. *The Cleveland Plain Dealer*.
Norman, Michael. (1996, September 19). Cleveland to host Rock Hall inductions. *The Cleveland Plain Dealer*.
Norman, Michael. (1998, September 20). Man on a mission. *The Cleveland Plain Dealer*.
O'Malley, Michael. (1985, October 4). Rock 'n' roll officials come to Cleveland. U.P.I.
O'Neil, Thomas. (1993). *The Grammys: For the record*. New York: Penguin.
Olszewski, Mike. (2003). *Radio daze: Stories from the front in Cleveland's FM air wars*. Kent, OH: Kent State University Press.
Page, Clarence. (1986, March 19). A rock hall of fame for Chicago? *The Chicago Tribune*.
Palmer, Robert. (1985, August 5). Rock music will have its own hall of fame. *The New York Times*.
Pond, Steve. (1992, September). The Rock and Roll Hall of fame, prestigious figment of the Cleveland and music industry's imagination. *GQ*.
Powers, Ann. (1995, September 19). Cleveland rocks! *Village Voice*.

Propes, Steve. (1991, February 8). The Moonglows: The commandments of doo-wop. *Goldmine.*
Quinn, Chris. (1997, February 27). Interview with author.
Rathburn, Keith. (1986, May 8). We got it! *Scene.*
Roldo. (1996, January 31). Barrie forced out. *Cleveland Free Times.*
Sandstrom, Karen. (1995, August 27). What won this for Cleveland was Clevelanders. *The Cleveland Plain Dealer.*
Santelli, Robert. (1999). The Rock and Roll Hall of Fame and Museum: Myth, memory, and history. In Kelly, Karen & McDonnell, Evelyn (Eds.), *Stars don't stand still in the sky: Music and myth*. New York: New York University.
Sanz, Cythia; & Micheli, Robin. (1991, February 4). Stars partied and played for rock's Hall of Fame. *People.*
Schlager. Ken. (2006, March 18). Henke on curating: Serious, fun and filled with spirit. *Billboard.*
Soeder, John. (2002, May 25). Sponsors tune out, so Rock Hall lays off 21. *The Cleveland Plain Dealer.*
Soeder, John. (2005, November 26). Hall of Fame across the pond doesn't shun Black Sabbath. *The Cleveland Plain Dealer.*
"Souvenir Section." (1995, August 27). Rock and Roll Hall of Fame and Museum. *The Cleveland Plain Dealer.*
Sowd, David. (1981, October). Not fade away. *Northern Ohio Live.*
Stoffel, Jennifer. (1988, January 3). What's doing in Cleveland. *The New York Times.*
Strausbaugh, John. (2001). *Rock 'til you drop: The decline from rebellion to nostalgia*. London: Verso.
Sullivan, Jim. (1990, January 18). A hall of fame of differences. *Boston Globe.*
"Suzan Evans talks about the Rock and Roll Hall of Fame." (1996, November-December). *Liner Notes.*
Talevski, Nick. (2006). *Knocking on heaven's door*. London: Omnibus.
Tamarkin, Jeff. (1992, February 22). Rock hall of fame: An elitist club? *Billboard.*
Tamarkin, Jeff. (1997, March 6). Interview with author.
Van Matre, Lynn. (1986, March 23). Chicago still in the running to get Rock Hall of Fame. *The Chicago Tribune.*
Walsh, Ed. (1994, August 4). The Rock Hall is here to stay. *Scene.*
Weiskind, Ron. (1995, August 27). Why Cleveland: It's no mistake that the Roll Hall of Fame landed in the city by the lake. *The Pittsburgh Post-Gazette.*
Wilder, Jesse Bryant. (1993, July). Norm N. Nite: The Rock Hall's unsung hero. *Northern Ohio Live.*
Wise, Stuart. (1986, April 26). N.Y. is rocked and Frisco rolls. *The National Law Journal.*

CH. 14 – CONCLUSION
Rutlowski, Rex. (1997, March 13). The pen is mightier than the chord. *Scene.*
Soeder, John. (2005, May 22). Breaking with tradition: Alt-rock magazine turns 20 by taking chances on small bands. *The Cleveland Plain Dealer.*

INDEX

A

Abbott, "Dimebag" Darrell, 92
Abdul, Paula, 147
Abramson, Herb, 150
AC/DC, 122
Action, 102
Action '73, 78
Adler, Steven, 122
Aerosmith, 45, 46, 119, 122
Afghan Whigs, 134-135
After 7, 147
Agora, 81, 96
Jane Aire & The Belvederes, 114
Alagia, John, 137
Albert, Eddie, 56
Aleksic, John, 71
Alexander, J.W., 158
Alger, Horatio, 117
Alice In Chains, 121
ALIVE Christian Music Festival, 130
All Sports Band, 89
Allen, Annisteen, 49
Allman Brothers, 85
Allman, Duane, 85
Allsup, Tommy, 209
Almighty GloryUS, 170
Alrosa Villa nightclub, 92
American Classical Music Hall of Fame
 and Museum, 214
American Idol, 153, 185
Amps, 132
Anacrusis, 132
Anderson, Ernie, 102
Anderson, Loni, 190
Anderson, Pete, 183
Angels, 17-18
Anka, Paul, 43, 49, 188
Ann Arbor Film Festival, 109
Annabell's, 102
Anthony Wayne Hotel, 108
Anthrax, 118
April-Blackwood Music, 18
Armstrong, Neil, 130
Army Of Anyone, 129

Arnold, Eddie, 75
Arrington, Steve, 151
Arthur, Joseph, 177-178
Ashley, Jane, 114
Ass Ponys, 135
Attack, Spazz, 109
Au Go-Go Singers, 173
Auerbach, Dan, 165
Aurra, 151
Austin, Stuart, 107
Avant, 162
Avery, Bob, 75
Avsec, Mark, 166-167
Aylward, Michael, 107

B

B. Bumble And The Stingers, 48
B-52's, 110, 137
Babes In Toyland, 72
Backstreet Boys, 180
Backus, Jim, 184, 194
Bacon, Kevin, 156
Bad Religion, 138
Bader, Diedrich, 192
Baez, Joan, 171, 172
Bailey, Pearl, 8
Bailey, Philip, 159
Baker, Anita, 141, 155, 156
Baker, LaVern, 8, 37, 40
Balam, Pam. 103
Baldwin Company, 53
Ball, Ernest, 2
Hank Ballard And The Midnighters,
 39-40, 58, 61, 62, 63, 65, 143
Ballard, Jim, 171
Bank nightclub, 108-109, 111, 193
Bangles, 109
Banks, Lloyd, 170
Bar-Kays, 189
Bare, Bobby, 66
Bare, Carl, 68
Barker, Bob, 192
Barnes, Richard, 91
Barnstorm, 86

Barnum, H.B., 153
Barrie, Dennis, 205, 206
Baskerville Hounds, 188
Bass, Billy, 80
Bass, Ralph, 61-63, 65
Bassette, John, 171
Bator, Stiv, 98, 99-101
Bauman, Charlie, 13
Beach Boys, 70, 71, 73
Bears, 139
Beatles, 16, 19, 20, 23, 67-70, 79, 142, 152, 171, 173, 196, 205
Beau Coup, 89, 121
Beckerleg, Greg, 103
Beckerleg, Pam, 103
Bee Gees, 128
Behemoth, Crocus, 98
Beiderbecke, Bix, 38
Beinstock, Freddy, 65
Beitle, Ron, 167
Belew, Adrian, 139
Belkin, Mike, 166
Bell Biv DeVoe, 147
Bell, Craig, 97, 98, 101
Bell, John, 139
Bell, Robert "Kool," 153
Belle, Albert, 192
Belly, 131
Belly, Richard "Dick," 73
Bellybutton, 177
Belushi, John, 101
Benatar, Pat, 96
Benson, Brendan, 166
Boyd Bennett And The Rockets, 63
Bennett, Jay, 138
Benz, K. Michael, 197-198, 204, 205
Bergquist, Karin, 135
Berns, Bert, 15-17, 24, 142
Berns, Brett, 24
Berns, Cassandra, 24
Berry, Halle, 192, 194
Berns, Ilene, 24
Berry, Chuck, 37-38, 196, 199, 205, 207
Berry, Gene "By Golly," 148
Betts, Dickey, 88
Bevan, Alex, 171
Beyond Fear, 118
Big Bopper, 34, 42
Big 5 Show, 188
Big Girls' Underwear, 112

Big Maybelle, 52, 61
Billy Joe & The Checkmates, 49
Bishop, Joey, 6
Bitch Magnet, 140
Bizzaros, 108, 109
Bizzy Bone, 168-169
Black Eyed Peas, 152
Black Francis, 131
Black Keys, 134, 165
Black Leather Touch, 119
Black Oak Arkansas, 96
Black Sabbath, 121, 207
Black Satin Soul, 151
Black Tie, 185
Black Tie Productions, 197
Black, Frank, 131
Black, Jack, 165
Blackfoot, J.D., 95
Bill Black's Combo, 67,
Blackwell, Chris, 109
Blackwell, Otis, 50
Blackwood, Nina, 88
Blake, Dick, 188
Blake, Elinor, 210
Bland, Bobby, 74
Blender Children, 101
Blessid Union Of Souls, 178
BLF Bash, 80
Blitz, Johnny, 98, 99, 101
Blondie, 24, 101
Blood, Sweat And Tears, 23
Bloomfield, Mike, 89
Blue, Barry, 167
Blues Traveler, 139
Bobbettes, 51
Bocky (Boo) and The Visions, 79
Bogart, Neil, 76
Bogart's, 104
Bolin, Tommy, 86
Bolton, Michael, 175
Bon Jovi, 167
Bone Thugs-N-Harmony, 168-170
Bonfanti, Jim, 71-72
Bonner, Frank, 190
Bonner, Leroy "Sugarfoot," 137, 148
Boomtown Rats, 114
Boone County Jamboree, 56, 181
Boone, Pat, 17, 36, 40
Bootsy's Rubber Band, 144
Bootzilla Orchestra, 144

Bostic, Earl, 29, 59-60
Boston, 80
Boswell Sisters, 30
Bourhis, Ray, 22
Bow Wow Wow, 23
Bowie, David, 80, 109, 139, 168, 207, 213
Boyd, Eddie, 164
Boyd, William Stage, 181
Boyz II Men, 147, 180
Bradshaw, Tiny, 45
Brainiac, 134
Brando, Marlon, 38
Brandon, Ronnie, 19
Branson, Richard, 109
Branwin, Bruce, 197
Braun, Bob, 187
Braun, David, 60
Braun, Jules, 60
Brave Combo, 95
Braxton, Toni, 147
Bread, 185
Breathless, 89, 167
Breeders, 131-132
Brewer & Shipley, 174
Brewer, Michael, 174
Brewer, Teresa, 49, 51
Brickman, Jim, 175-176, 180
Brides Of Funkenstein, 144
Bright, Ron, 77
Brill, Dmitry, 139
Briquette, Pete, 114
Bristol, Johnny, 160
British Steel, 117
Broadbent, Robert, 202
Brooks, Richard, 38
Brother John, 77
Brown, Bill, 62
Brown, Bobbie, 119
Brown, Bobby, 147
Brown, Charlie, 11
Brown, Clark, 189
Brown, Gerald, 156
Brown, Jackson, 79-80
Brown, James, 58, 63-65, 143, 188, 199, 206
Brown, Les, 4
Brown, Paul E., 13
Brown, Roy, 30, 46, 61
Brown, Ruth, 8, 40, 210

Brown, Sam, 138
Brown's Ferry Four, 181
Browne, Ivan, 77
Bruce, Carol, 189
Bruder, Gustav, 14
Brummel, Tony, 134
Brungart, John, 14
Brutus Buckeye, 22
Bryant, Pure Prairie League, 11
Bryant, Rusty, 11
Bryson, Wally, 71-72
B3, 180
Bucciarelli, Eron, 133
Buchignani, Paul, 135
Bucket Shop, 102, 107
Buckinghams, 81
Buckner, Jerry, 184, 189
Buffalo Bearcats, 46
Buffalo Springfield, 173
Burdick Group, 203-204
Burdon, Eric, 24
Burke, Dave, 71
Burke, Solomon, 16
Johnny Burnette And The Rock 'n' Roll Trio, 45
Burr, Gary, 174-175
Burton, Emily J., 122
Busta Rhymes, 170
Butler, Chris, 107, 113
Butterfield, Paul, 165
Buxton, Glen, 96
Buzzard, Pat, 185
Byrd, Bobby, 143
Byrds, 173

C

Cabaniss, George, 110, 178
Cadets, 16-17
Caldwell, Teresa, 169
Calhoun, Wayne, 161
Callander, Peter, 78
Calloway, 145-146
Calloway, Cab, 45
Calloway, Reggie, 145-146
Calloway, Vincent, 145-146
Camel Rock And Roll Party, 39
Camelot Music, 214
Campbell, Jo-ann, 37
Canned Head, 188

Cannon, Freddy, 16, 17, 24, 34
Canton First Friends Church, 129
Joe Cantor Band, 4
Cantor, Eddie, 184
Capital City Rockets, 75, 119
Capris, 74
Captain Beefheart, 97, 98
Carey, Drew, 187, 191-192
Carleton, Denny, 100
Carlisle Brothers, 59
Carlisle, Steve, 189
Carlson, Harry, 66
Carmen, Eric, 71-73, 79, 81, 199, 206
Carnes, Kim, 157, 174
Carney, Patrick, 165
Carney, Ralph, 107, 110, 165
Carpenter, Bill, 108
Carpenters, 156
Carr Sisters, 52
Carr, Cathy, 66
Carr, Wynona, 52
Gene Carroll Show, 52
Cars, 114, 125, 188
Carson, Johnny, 187
Carter, Aaron, 23
Carter, Benny, 64
Carter, M.A., 12
Carter, Mel, 145
Carvettes, 145
Casale, Gerald, 84, 106
Casale, Robert, 106, 111, 114
Cash, Johnny, 127
Cash, Ray, 170
Cash, Rosanne, 177
Casinos, 66, 74-75, 141
Cassidy, David, 77
Cassidy, Hopalong, 181
Castro, Fidel, 172
Cauley, Ben, 189
Cavaliers, 149
Cavanaugh, Frank, 129
CBGB's, 100, 101, 103, 109
CCR, 206
Cedar Gardens, 164
Celeste, Richard, 198, 199, 200
Chamber Brothers, 120
Chambers, Martin, 112
Champion, 89
Champion, Jason, 155
Chandler, Karen, 145

Chandler, Len, 171
Chantels, 51
Chapman, Tracy, 176, 178, 179
Charioteers, 7, 8
Charles, Ray, 47, 157, 176, 206
Chas & Dave, 95
Chase, Brian, 139-140
Cheap Trick, 80, 93
Checker, Chubby, 16, 63, 188, 209
Cherry Monroe, 122
Chi-Pig, 108
Chicago, 96
Chichester, Harold "Happy," 137
Chiffons, 52
Chilton, Alex, 103
Chimaira, 121
Chip Tha Ripper, 170
Choir, 71, 85, 100, 188
Chordettes, 9, 51
Chosen Few, 75
Christgau, Robert, 107, 109
Christy Minstrels, 53
Chrome, Cheetah, 98, 99, 101
Chunky A, 184
Cincinnati Opera, 214
Cincinnati Pops, 214
Cincinnati Symphony Orchestra, 214
Cinderella Backstreet, 98
Circone, Brad, 136
Cistone, Toni, 51
Clapton, Eric, 86, 148
Dave Clark Five, 18, 20, 68, 209
Clark, Dick, 39, 43, 44, 75, 78, 150, 157, 188, 200
Clarke, Gilby, 121-122
Clash, 112
Clay, Tom, 43
Clear Channel Communications, 57, 81, 214
Clearmountain, Bob, 88, 100
Cleaver, Chuck, 135
Clemons, Clarence, 88
Cleveland International Records, 94-95, 185
Cleveland Municipal Stadium, 68-69, 88, 117, 203, 206
Cleveland Orchestra, 176
Cleveland Quartet, 50
Cleveland Rock Orchestra, 122
Clic, Buzz, 108

Climax, 71
Climax Blue Band, 24
Clinger, Peggy, 77
Clinton, George, 143, 150, 151, 156
Clocks, 100
Clooney Sisters, 56
Clooney, Betty, 4
Clooney, Rosemary, 4, 49, 56
CMJ/Rock Hall Music Fest, 211
Coasters, 16, 157
Cobra Kid, 163
Cobra Verde, 104, 133
Coe, David Allan, 95, 181
Cohn, Marc, 79, 140, 175, 176-177
Coil, 126
Cole, Lloyd, 101
Cole, Nat King, 42, 48
Cole, Natalie, 145, 146
Coleman, Bob "Kid Cole," 163
College Hill, 148
Collins, Bootsy, 65, 139, 141, 143-144, 150
Collins, Phelps "Catfish," 143
Color Me Gone, 178
Columbine High School, 128
Common, 170
Como, Perry, 48, 196
Conkling, Jim, 3
Conley, Earl Thomas, 182
Constable, Bill "Adam," 95
Contortions, 97
Conway, Tim, 194
Cooke, Barbara, 158, 159
Cooke, Sam, 145, 158, 210
Coolio, 152
Cooper, Alice, 89, 95-96, 103, 121, 128, 206
Copas, Cowboy, 56, 181
Copperfield, David, 201
Cornelius, Aaron "Tex," 149
Cornelius, Don, 141, 156
Coronets, 34
Corvettes, 149
Costa, Don, 51
Costa, Nikka, 153
Cotton Club (Cincinnati), 163
Cotton, Gene, 173
Covay, Don, 149
Cowboy Junkies, 136
Cowsills, 25

Cramps, 98, 100, 101-103
Craven, Wes, 193
Crazy Elephant, 75
Creative Arts Festival, 106
Creatore, Luigi, 142
Crenshaw, Marshall, 24
Crew-Cuts, 35, 40
Crook, Jim, 97
Crosby, Bing, 4, 5, 8, 28
Crosby, David, 84
Crosby, Stills & Nash, 86
Crosby, Stills, Nash & Young, 82-84
Crosley, Powel, 54
Crosley, Powel, II, 54-57
Crosley, Powel, III, 54-55
Crow, Sheryl, 72
Crowe, Cameron, 82
Crypt, 108, 111
Culbertson, Brian, 156
Culos, Chris, 136
Curbishley, Bill, 91
Curley, John, 134
Curtis, King, 74
Cymarron, 185
Cymbal, Johnny, 77
Cyren, 118
Cyrus Erie, 71

D

Daddy Dewdrop, 184
Dallas, 77
Daltrey, Roger, 91-92
Damage, Donnie, 110
D'Amata, Rick "Mugsy," 70
Damme, Ted, 135
Damnation Of Adam Blessing, 95
Damned, 100, 101, 112
Dandridge, Dorothy, 194
Daniel, Howard, 7
Daniels, Charlie, 66
Daniels, Jeffrey, 156
Daniels, Jerry, 7
Darin, Bobby, 24, 34
Darrow, Johnny, 50
Davenport, Cow Cow, 52
David, Paul, 214
Davidson, Eric, 138
Davies, Ray, 113
Ed Davis Band, 103

Davis, Clive, 72, 147
Davis, Fred, 178
Davis, Paul, 24
Davis, Ray "Sting," 150
Davis, Sammy, Jr., 6, 49
Davis, Walter, 163
Day, Bobby, 34
Day, Doris, 3-4, 5, 56, 194
Day, Mysti, 151
Day, Terry, 73
Dayton (band), 144
Dazz Band, 153, 160-161
DC Talk, 129
Dead Boys, 97, 99-101, 108, 110, 122, 178
Kelley Deal 6000, 132
Deal, Kelley, 131-132
Deal, Kim, 131-132
Dean And Jean, 149-150
Dean, Jimmy, 184
Buddy Deane Show, 187
Death Of Samantha, 104
DeBarge, 157
DeBarge, Bobby, 157
DeBarge, Tommy, 157
DeCaro, Nick, 145
Deco, 157
Deeds, Edward A., 130
Deee-Lite, 139
Deele, 146-147
Deep Purple, 188
Déja, 151
Del Fuegos, 210
DeLeo, Dean, 129
DeLeo, Robert, 129
Delmore Brothers, 59, 181
Delmore, Alton, 59, 181
Delmore, Rabon, 181
Delp, Brad, 93
DeMarcus, Jay, 183
DePizzo, Jerry, 136
Derek, 77
Derringer, Randy, 19
Derringer, Rick, 19-20, 22, 23, 88, 96, 184
DeShannon, Jackie, 67
Detweiler, Linford, 135
Devo, 84, 106-111, 114, 125, 132
Devo 2.0, 111
Diamond, Neil, 24

Dickies, 110
Diddy, P., 152, 162
Diller, Phyllis, 194
DiNapoli, Christy, 182
Dink, 139
Dio, 123
Dion, 16
Dion, Celine, 72
Dirck, Joe, 22
Disturbed, 123
Dixie and Sloopy, 15
Dixon, Don, 179
Dixon, Luther, 50
Dixon, Willie, 150
Do-Whaters, 166
Doanbrook Hotel, 176
Dobeck, Tommy, 88
Dobkin, Carl. Jr., 66, 74
Dr. Dre, 169
Dodson, Marti, 185
Doggett, Bill, 63, 143, 159
Dolce, Joe, 184
Dolphins, 141
Domino, Fats, 29, 33, 40, 199
Dominoes, 32, 33, 34, 39, 58, 61
Donahue, Patty, 108, 111
Donahue, Phil, 187
Donahue, Tom "Big Daddy," 79
Donaldson, Bea, 78
Donaldson, Bo, 78
Donaldson, William H., 214
Donelly, Tanya, 131
Doors, 209
Dorian Gray, 118
Dorsey, Jimmy, 66
Douglas, Mike, 82, 187
Drifters, 16, 34, 36, 50-51, 208
Droste, Paul E., 25
Drury, Clifford, 91
D12, 170
DuBrow, Kevin, 119
Dudgeon, Gus, 62
Duke, George, 156
Dulli, Greg, 134
Dupree, Champion Jack, 163
Dupri, Jermaine, 169
Duskin, Big Joe, 164
Dylan, Bob, 171, 172, 173, 174, 196
Dynamite, 72

E

E.T. Hooley, 85
Eagles, 86-87
Earle, Steve, 134
Earth, Wind And Fire, 134, 160
Easy Street, 89
Easton, Sheena, 147
Easy-E, 168
Ebb Tides, 95
Ebony Lounge, 164
Ecstasy, 146
Eddy, Duane, 102
Edison, Thomas, 2, 3
Edmonds, Kenneth "Babyface," 146-148
Edmonds, Tracey, 148
Edsels, 50
Edwards, Jonathan, 184
Edwards, Tommy, 34
Electra, Carmen, 170
Electric Eels, 97-98, 99, 103
Eli Radish, 88
Elias, Eddie, 105
Ellington, Duke, 7, 60, 188
Ellis, Jim, 189
Ellison, David, 137
ELO (Electric Light Orchestra), 117
Elvira, 102
Emmett, Dan, 2
Emmett, Peter, 71
Enchanters, 141
Eno, Brian, 109
Entwistle, John, 92
Epstein, Brian, 67, 69
Ertegun, Ahmet, 8, 17, 18, 197, 198, 201, 202, 207
Ertegun, Nesuhi, 17
Essington, C. Edwin "Tubby," 14
Eszterhas, Joe, 79, 193
Euclid Beach Band, 95
Eurythmics, 128
Evans, Dale, 181
Evans, Jack, 21
Evans, Suzan, 197, 211
Everhart, Angie, 177
Everly Brothers, 3
Everly, Don, 75
Every Mothers' Son, 24
Exciters, 16, 67

Exotic Birds, 125
Eye-Full Tower, 77

F

F-Models, 110
Fabian, 42
Faces Of Death, 168
Fair Warning, 167
Falcons, 148
Fann, Leroy, 155
Fanny, 108
Faragher's Back Room, 172
Farndon, Pete, 112-113
Farr, Jamie, 38
Farrell, Wes, 15-16, 24-25, 77
Farris, Dionne, 152-153
Fasnacht, Yvonne "Dixie," 15, 25
Fass, Bob, 79
Fat Fish Blue, 165
Faze-O, 148
Fears, Bobby Lee, 148
Feelies, 97, 99
Feinstein, Michael, 11
Felder, Don, 88
Feldman, Bob, 17-20, 24
Feldman, Corey, 24
Feldman, Mindy, 24
Fellini, 194
Ferguson, Craig, 192
Ferguson, H-Bomb, 163
Ficca, Billy, 108
Fieger, Doug, 110
Ernie Fields Orchestra, 48
Fier, Anton, 98, 99
Fifth Dimension, 162
50 Cent, 170
Fight, 117
Filter, 125, 128-129
Finan, Joe, 27, 29, 34, 35, 36, 42, 43
Finn, Robert, 68
Fireball Ministry, 122
Firestone Country Club, 105
Firestone High School, 108, 112, 165, 177
Firestone Tournament of Champions, 105-106
Firestone, Rod, 108, 110
Five Blind Boys Of Mississippi, 158
"5" Royales, 58

Flashcats, 46
Flatts, Rascal, 183
Fleetwood Mac, 93
Flesh-N-Bone, 168
Floyd Band, 104
Flying Burrito Brothers, 77, 183
Focus, 24
Fogelberg, Dan, 86
Fogerty, John, 199, 206
Foghat, 107
Foley, Ellen, 95
Foley, Red, 56
Fontaine Sisters, 62
Forbes, George, 202
Ford, Glenn, 38
Ford, Whitey, 56
Foreigner, 117
Forrest, Jimmy, 33
Foster, Stephen, 2, 53
Fotomaker, 72
Four Kings, 6
Four Lads, 36
Four Riff Brothers, 7
Four Seasons, 188
Fox, Jimmy, 85-86
Fox, Michael J., 193, 198
Frampton, Peter, 80, 93
Frankenstein, 99
Franklin, Aretha, 158, 188
Franklin, Erma, 24
Fraternity Records, 66
Freed, Alan, 9, 17, 27-44, 46-47, 79, 108, 193, 195, 199, 200, 211
Freed, David, 29, 41, 200
Freed, Lance, 34, 41, 43-44
Evelyn Freeman Swing Band, 48
Freeman, Ernie, 48-49
Frenchies, 112
Fuller, Craig, 95, 174-175
Furay, Richie, 171, 173
Furnier, Vincent, 96
Fuqua, Charlie, 7
Fuqua, Harvey, 33, 160
Future Tones, 159

G

G-Clefs, 85
Gable, Clark, 105, 194
Gabriel, Peter, 177
Gale, Nathan, 92
Gamble, Kenny, 154
Game, 170
Garcia, Gary, 184, 189
Garner, Erroll, 23, 64
Gates, David, 185
Gaunt, 136
Gaye, Marvin, 48, 156
Gayten, Paul, 47
Gee, Stan, 87
Gehr, Richard, 2002
Generators, 193
Geraci, Mike, 70
Geraci, Sonny, 70-71, 79, 206
Gershman, Benj, 136
Getz, Stan, 21
Ghost Poets, 89
Ghoul, 103
Ghoulardi, 102, 103, 191
Giamatti, Paul, 194
Gibson, Bob, 172
Gilbert, Paul, 119
Giles, Attala Zane, 157
Gill, Johnny, 150, 154
Gill, Vince, 174-175
Gillard, Doug, 133
Giraldo, Neil, 96
Gish, Dorothy, 194
Gish, Lillian, 194
Glass Harp, 88, 89-90
Gleason's, 164
Glenn, John, 15, 130
Glover, Henry, 60, 63
Glover, Jim, 171-172
Go-Go's, 24
Gobs Of Swing, 48
Godfrey, Arthur, 9, 52
Godz, 75, 119-120
Gold, Harvey, 107
Goldberg, Len "Boom Boom," 80, 206
Golden Palominos, 99
Golden Smog, 139
Goldner, George, 142
Goldstein, Jerry, 17-20, 24
Gomez, 177
Good, Wilson, 199
Goodman, Steve, 182
Gordon, Marc, 154
Gordon, Robert, 24
Gordy, Barry, 160

Gorman, John, 80
Gospel Pearls, 145
Gospelaires, 164
Gottehrer, Richard, 17-20, 24
Goulet, Robert, 196
Graceland, 202
Graham, Bill, 198, 204
Grand Funk Railroad, 96
Grand Ole Opry, 59
Milt Grant Show, 187
Grant, Amy, 130
Grasshoppers, 114, 188
Grateful Dead, 137, 209
Gray, Macy, 153, 161-162, 178
Great Plains, 138
Great White, 92
Green Day, 165
Greenbriar Boys, 172
Greenhornes, 166
Gregory, Bryan, 103
Griffey, Dick, 141, 145
Griffin, Archie, 12
Griffin, Jimmy, 185
Griffin, Merv, 52
Griffin, Patty, 177
Griffin, Robert, 133
Grimes, Tiny, 46
Grigsby, Charles, 183
Grohl, Dave, 140
Grubman, Allen, 197
Guess Who, 86
Guided By Voices, 131, 132-133, 138
Gun Club, 103
Guns N' Rose, 101, 121-122
Guthrie, Arlo, 82
Guyana, 98

H

Billy Hadnott Sextette, 48
Haley, Bill, 36, 39, 49, 199
Halford, Rob, 117-118, 126
Hall, Arsenio, 184
Hallenbeck, Bob, 75
Hammer Damage, 110, 178
Hammer, Mike, 110
Hammitt, Matt, 130
Hammond, John, 197
Hampton, Lionel, 47, 145, 188
Hancock, Hunter, 30

Handy, W.C., 30
Hard Rock Cafe, 204, 206, 207-208
Hardin, Louis "Moondog," 30, 37
Harmoneers, 60
Harper, Ben, 177
Harrah-Conforth, Bruce, 204, 205
Harris, Bobby, 160
Harris, Emmylou, 183
Harris, Wynonie, 29, 30, 60-61
Harrison, William, 1
Hassan, Umar Bin, 168
Hatrix, 120
Hawkes, Greg, 115
Hawkins, Ronnie, 86
Hawkins, Screamin' Jay, 34, 36, 44, 45, 46-47
Hawks, 86
Hawthorne Heights, 131, 133-134
Hayes, George "Gabby," 181
Hayes, Woody, 13
Heartless Bastards, 134
Heatwave, 166, 167
Heflick, Dorothy, 15, 25
Heflick, Fred, Jr., 15
Heflick, Jane, 15
Heisman Award, 12-13
Heisman, John W., 12
Helford, Bruce, 191
Hell, Richard, 24, 101, 112
Henderson, Jay, 211
Hendricks, Bobby, 51
Hendrix, Jimi, 89, 95, 142, 183, 196, 206
Henke, Jim, 199, 205, 206, 210
Hennegan, James H., 214
Herman, Pee-Wee, 111
Henry And June, 166
Henry, Clarence "Frogman," 68
Henry, Oliver, 166
Henske, Judy, 172
Hensley, Pamela, 25
Henson, Jim, 175
Herman, Woody, 48
Hesseman, Howard, 190
Hewett Singers, 156
Hewett, Howard, 153, 154-157
Hi-Fis, 110
Hi-Tek, 170
Hilburn, Robert, 197, 199
Hill, Blind Joe, 164
Hill, Lauren, 152

Hinkley, David, 208
Hobbs, Randy Joe, 19
Holiday, Billie, 4, 159, 161
Holland-Dozier-Holland, 142
Johnny Holliday Show, 187
Holly, Buddy, 34, 40, 42, 193, 206, 208
Holman, Eddie, 156
Honeyman-Scott, James, 112-113
Hooker, John Lee, 33, 163
Hoopes, Matt, 129
Hoover, Herbert, 55
Hope, Bob, 3, 5, 15, 193, 195
Hopkins, Nicky, 88
HORDE Festival, 139
Hornets, 50
Horton, Johnny, 183
House Guests, 143
House, Ron, 138
House, Son, 165
Houston, Whitney, 147
How To Make It In America, 170
Howard Theater, 142
Howard, Barry, 204
Howard, Mikki, 155
Howell, Thurston, III, 184
Howerdel, Billy, 122
Howley, Lee C., 211
Howlin' Maggie, 137
Hubbard, Gregg "Hobie," 183
Huber, Sally, 22
Hudson, Kate, 193
Hudson, Mike, 100
Huff, Leon, 154
Hulett, William, 203, 207
Human Beinz, 73-74
Human Sufferage, 104
Human Switchboard, 114
Humble Pie, 89
Hunt, Van, 152-153
Hunter, Ian, 82, 95, 192, 200
Hunter, Ivory Joe, 61
Hunter, Mark, 121
Hurricane Katrina, 127
Husker Du, 131
Hynde, Chrissie, 112-113, 165, 177, 178, 206, 213, 215
Hynde, Terry, 112, 113-114, 215

I

I Got Your Back, 155
Iced Earth, 118
Iggy And The Stooges, 97, 128, 152
Imus, Don, 80
Ingram, James, 153, 141, 155, 157
Ingram, Phillip, 157-158
Ink Spots, 6-7, 56
Innocent, 125
Interior, Lux, 102-103
Donnie Iris And The Cruisers, 167
Iris, Donnie, 167
Iron Butterfly, 188
Isles, Bill, 154
Isley Brothers, 16, 70, 74, 141
Isley, Ernie, 142-143
Isley, Marvin, 143
Isley, O'Kelly, 141
Isley, Ronald, 141, 169
Isley, Rudolph, 141
Isley, Vernon, 141
Isuzu, 89
Ivan & The Sabers, 77

J

J. Geils Band, 159
Jack Rabbit, 112
Jackson, Bull Moose, 45-46, 59
Jackson, Hal, 39
Jackson, Janet, 152
Jackson, Jermaine, 157
Jackson, LaToya, 156
Jackson, Michael, 93, 157, 199
Jackson, Randy, 153
Jacksons, 147
Jacor Communications, 57
Jagger, Mick, 109
Jaggerz, 167
James Gang, 79, 85-87, 188
James, Brian, 101
James, Etta, 62
James, Rick, 163
James, Tommy, 75
Jan & Arnie, 48
Jane's Addiction, 170
Jardine, Al, 73
Jarmels, 16
Jarmusch, Jim, 47, 102, 113, 193

Jarrett, Pigment, 16
Jarry, Alfred, 99
Jasper, Chris, 143
Jay And The Americans, 24
Jay, Jay, 117
Jay-Z, 152, 170
Jayhawks (doo-wop group), 16-17
Jayhawks (rock group), 139, 178
JBs, 143
JBs tavern, 143
Jeep, 88
Jeff & Flash, 80
Jeffe, Justin, 180
Joe Jeffrey Group, 74
Jennings, Lyfe, 170
Jet Boys, 104
Jett, Joan, 108, 193, 198
Jim & Jean, 172
Jive Five, 17
Jockey Club, 103
Joel, Billy, 195, 199, 205
Joey And The Continentals, 188
John, Elton, 24, 84
John, Little Willie, 22, 58, 62
Johnny And The Hurricanes, 49
Johnson, Jimmy, 16
Johnson, Kraig Jarret, 178
Johnson, Robert, 165
Johnston, Bruce, 73
Jones, Brenda Lee, 149
Jones, Chris, 144
Jones, Curt, 151
Jones, George, 182
Jones, Grandpa, 56, 59, 181
Jones, Jim, 98
Jones, Kenney, 92
Jones, Marti, 178-179
Jones, Mick, 112
Jones, Orville "Hoppy," 7
Jones, Quincy, 157, 195
Jones, Sam "Stovepipe," 163
Jones, Spike, 184
Jones, Tom, 72
Joplin, Janis, 82, 159, 206
Jordan, Louis, 31, 46, 210
Judas Priest, 117-118, 126
Jump, Gordon, 189
Justis, Bill, 48

K

Kahn, Gus, 5
Kallen, Kitty, 37
Kane, Ronald, 83
Karshner, Roger, 70
Kasenetz-Katz Singing Orchestra Circus, 76
Kasenetz, Jerry, 75-77
Katran, Dean, 76
Katz, Jeff, 75-77
Kaufman, Philip, 25
Kay, Ernie, 5
Kaye, Danny, 4
Kaye, Sammy, 4
Keaggy, Phil, 89-90
Keane, Bob, 43
KDAY (Los Angeles), 43
Keegan, Margy, 52
Keegan, Mary-Ellen, 52
Keele, Patrick, 166
Keenan, Maynard James, 122
Kelly, Dennis, 19
Kelly, John S., 40
Kennedy, Caroline, 176
Kenny, Bill, 7
Kent, Nick, 112
Kermit The Frog, 175
Anita Kerr Quartet, 196
Kerr, Jim, 113
Kessel, Howard, 59
Kettering, Charles, 130
Keys, Alicia, 152
KFVD (Los Angeles), 30
Kid Cudi, 170
Kid Leo, 80, 82, 99, 199, 206
Kidd Wicked, 119
Kidney, Bob, 113
Kidney, Jack, 113
Kimbrough, Junior, 165
Kincaid, Bradley, 181
King Cobra, 108
King Crimson, 139
King-Federal Records, 39-40, 45-46, 53, 58-66, 141, 143, 153, 163
King Toppers, 149
King, Albert, 163
King, B.B., 155, 163, 179
King, Ben E., 51
King, Freddy, 163

King, Tom, 52, 70-71, 85, 102, 188
Kingston Trio, 173
Kinks, 89, 112, 113
Kinney, Kathy, 192
Kinsman Dazz, 160
Kinsman Grill, 160
Kirby, Kier, 139
Kirk, Rahsaan Roland, 11
Kirshner, Don, 196
Kiss, 81, 119, 121, 122, 209
Kitaen, Tawny, 190
Klawon, Don, 71
Klimek, Jamie, 97
Klingshirn, David A., 214
Klosterman, Chuck, 127
Klymaxx, 146
KMPX (San Francisco), 79, 190
Knack, 110, 184
Knight, Gladys, 146
Knox, Ike, 100, 103
Knox, Nick, 98, 103
Koal, Ronald, 114
Koch, Ed, 198
Kool & The Gang, 153
Korvan, Betty, 80
Kosar, Bernie, 192
Koslen, Jonah, 88-89, 167
Koster, Bart, 126
Kovas, Dino, 180
KPPX (Los Angeles), 79
Kraftwerk, 110
Kramer, Ron, 70
Krasnow, Bob, 197
Krazy Bone, 168
Kristal, Hilly, 100, 103
Krupa, Gene, 188
Kubiszewski, Andy, 126
Kucinich, Dennis, 196
Kulkin, Milton, 31
Kweli, Talib, 170
KYW (Cleveland), 34, 68

L

La Flavour, 166, 167
LaBelle, Patti, 154
Lachey, Drew, 180
Lachey, Nick, 180
Lakeside, 151-152
Lakeside Express, 151
Lamour, Dorothy, 5
Landau, Jon, 199
Lane, Jani, 118
Lange, Robert John "Mutt," 88
Lanigan, John, 191, 204
Larkin, Nelson, 182
Last Moving Picture Show, 112
Last Poets, 168
Lattisaw, Stacy, 156
Laughner, Peter, 97-99, 108
Lawford, Peter, 6
Lawrence, Jack, 166
Lawson, Bernard, 157
Layne, Joy, 51
Layzie Bone, 168
Leadbelly, 77
Leadon, Bernie, 86
Leal, Joey, 215
Leboe, Art, 43
Led Zeppelin, 90, 91
Lee, Brenda, 44
Lee, George, 155
Lee, Peggy, 62
Lee, Tommy, 122
Leeds, Alan, 65
Legend, John, 152-153
Leiber & Stoller, 16, 46, 65, 142, 210
Leka, Paul, 77
Lemon Pipers, 73, 75, 77
Lenardo, Geno, 129
Lennon, John, 68, 205
Lentine, Christa, 117
Leo's Casino, 31, 189
Letterman, 23
Letterman, David, 100, 137, 191
Levert, 146, 154-155
Levert, Eddie, 153-155
Levert, Gerald, 154-155, 176
Levert, Sean, 154, 155
Levine, Joey, 76
LeVox, Gary, 183
Levy, Morris, 37, 43
Lewis, Barbara, 16
Lewis, Bob, 106
Gary Lewis & The Playboys, 6
Lewis, Jerry, 5-6
Lewis, Jerry Lee, 40-41, 42, 193, 199
Lewis, Myra, 40-41, 42
Lewis, Rudy, 50
Liesegang, Brian, 129

Light, Enoch, 4
Lil' Bow Wow, 11, 169
Lil' Romeo, 169
Limbaugh, Rush, 113
Lime Spider, 165
Lincoln, Abraham, 53
Lindsay, Arto, 99
Lindsay's Sky Bar, 164
Linna, Miriam, 103
Lipincott, Jesse H., 2
Lipscomb, Brenda, 145
Little Anthony And The Imperials, 154
Little Caesar & The Consuls, 20
Little Darlings, 75
Little Feat, 174
Little Miss Cornshucks, 8
Little Miss Share Cropper, 8
Little Richard, 33, 40, 42, 210
Little Texas, 182
Little Walter, 164
Live Nation, 81
Lizzie Borden, 122
Lloyd, Richard, 101
Locher, Ralph, 68
Lockwood, Robert, Jr., 164
LoConti, Henry, Sr., 81, 198
Loder, Kurt, 197
Logan, John "Turk," 148
Loggins, Kenny, 175
Lollapalooza, 117, 132
London Fog & The Continentals, 215
London, Julie, 49
Lonely Astronauts, 178
Long, James "Sonny," 50
Longely, Ty, 92
Lords Of The New Church, 101
Loudermilk, John D., 74
Lounge Lizards, 99
Louris, Gary, 139
Love Affair, 89
Loveboys, 112
Lovedrug, 139
Lovelace, Bobby, 146
Lovering, David, 132
Lowery, Bill, 30
LSG, 155
Lubinsky, Herman, 47
Lucky Pierre, 98, 125
Lulu, 25
Lunch, Lydia, 101

Lyfe, 156
Lymon, Frankie, 36, 48, 153
Lynn, Loretta, 166
Lyons, Jamie, 75, 119

M

M. Gray Music Academy, 162
Mack, Lonnie, 66, 149, 164
Madison Square Garden, 137
Madonna, 148, 214
Maduri, Carl, 166, 179
Maerth, Oscar Kiss, 106
Magnum, Jeff, 100
Mainegra, Richard, 185
Majestic Hotel, 164
Malm, John, Jr., 127
Malrite Communications, 80
Mancini, Henry, 3, 49
Mangione, Chuck, 70
Mann, Herbie, 64
Mann, J., 120-121
Manson, Charles, 126, 127
Manson, Marilyn, 47, 125, 126, 127-129
Marathons, 17
Marchan, Bobby, 46
Marcus, Larry, 155
Mardones, Benny, 185
Markasky, Gary, 88
Marks, Craig, 128
Markulin, Steve, 89
Marr, Hank, 102
Marsh, Dave, 81
Mary Martin Band, 215
Martin, Dean, 3, 5-6, 15, 49, 69, 194
Martin, Deana, 6
Martin, Sennie "Skip," 161
Martino, Al, 77
Marvelettes, 156
Mascots, 153
Massey, Bob, 154
Masters Of The Backside, 112
Mathis, Johnny, 24
Matt the Cat, 80
Matthews, Dave, 137
Matthews, Jennifer, 144
Max Wheel & The Shades, 215
Max's Kansas City, 103, 109
McBride, Martina, 176
McCabe, Pattie, 51

McCollum, Rick, 134
McCormick, Pa and Ma, 56
McCoy, Neal, 75
McCoys, 17-20, 22-23, 24, 67, 184
McCrae, Carmen, 64
McDonald, Michael, 157
MC5, 97
McGovern, Maureen, 179, 180
McGuffey Lane, 183
McGuffey, William Holmes, 2
McGuire Singers, 8-9, 40, 51, 56
McIntyre, Tim, 44
McKeehan, Toby, 129
McKendree Spring, 171
McLaren, Malcolm, 144
McLean, Phil, 34, 184
McLennan, Gene, 20
McMahon, Brian, 97, 98
McMahon, Ed, 191
McMahon, Kevin, 98
McManus, Dave, 97
McPhatter, Clyde, 50, 61
McPherson, Jim, 132
Meadon, Pete, 90
Measles, 85, 86
Meat Beat Manifesto, 126
Meat Loaf, 80, 93, 185
Mehlman, Steve, 101
Meisner, Randy, 185
Melcher, Terry, 73
Mellencamp, John, 80
Mellin, Bobby, 16
Melman, Steve, 98
Memphis Plaza Lounge, 192
Men At Large, 155
Merano, Silverno, 18
Meredith, Burgess, 194
Merseys, 22
Messina, Jim, 173
Metoff, Mike, 100
Metrotones, 159
Miami Pop Festival, 85
Midnight Star, 145-146
Midwest Hayride, 56, 59
Milburn, Amos, 52
Milkwood, 115
Miller, Bill, 165
Miller, Christa, 192
Miller, Mark, 183
Miller, Mitch, 39

Miller, Roger, 131
Millinder, Lucky, 45-46, 59, 60
Mills Brothers, 6-7, 56
Mills, Harry, 7
Mills, John, Jr., 7
Mills, John, Sr., 6-7
Mills, Stephanie, 155
Ministry, 126
Mintz, Leo, 29, 30, 31, 32, 164, 198
Mintz, Stuart, 32
Mirrors, 97, 99
Miss Kier, 139
Mitchell, Mitch, 132
Mitty, Walter, 117
Mixed Water, 75, 119
Mock, Jerrie, 130
Modell, Art, 191
Mods, 71
Monks, 173
Monroe, Marilyn, 127
Monroe, Vaughn, 4
Moody Blues, 208
Moon, Keith, 90, 206
Moonglows, 33, 48, 50
Moore, Eric, 76, 119
Moore, Johnny, 50-51
Moore, Sam, 88
Morgan, Russ, 8
Morris, Billy, 119
Morrison, Jim, 206
Morrison, Van, 17, 24, 73, 78-79, 176
Morrison, Walter "Junie," 148
Morton, John, 97
Mosey, Jon, 171
Mosley, Ronald, 155
Mothersbaugh, Bob, 106, 111
Mothersbaugh, Mark, 106-111, 112
Motion, 90
Mott The Hoople, 80
Mr. Big, 119
Mr. Downchild, 165
Mr. Magoo, 184
Mr. Stress, 165
Mt. Moriah Church, 141
Mullican, Moon, 59
Muni, Scott, 28
Muppets, 175
Murdoch, Shirley, 150
Murphy, Eddie, 147
Murphy, John, 131

Murphy, Mrs. John, 131
Murray, Mitch, 78
Mushroomhead, 120-121, 125
Music Explosion, 75-76, 119
Myers, Alan, 107, 111
Myers, Frank, 132
Myers, Pete "Mad Daddy," 36, 79, 102, 103, 200
MySpace.com, 133

N

N-Sync, 180
N.W.A., 168
Narcizo, David, 131
NASA's Lewis Research Center, 115
Nash, Johnny, 74
Nash, Ruby, 155
Nathan, David, 58
Nathan, Syndey, 54, 58-66, 163
National Cleveland-Style Polka Hall of Fame, 215
Navarro, Dave 170
Necros, 104
Neely, Hal, 64, 65
Nelson, 88
Nelson, Judd, 44
Nelson, Ricky, 42
New Bomb Turks, 136
New Edition, 147
New Monkees, 180
New York Dolls, 103
Newhart, Bob, 3
Newman, Paul, 194
Newman, Randy, 196
News Boys, 130
Newstead, Jason, 122
Newton, Wayne, 25
Newton-John, Olivia, 176
Nicholis, Nick, 107, 109, 193-194
Nicklaus, Jack, 15
Nightcrawlers, 75
Nilsson, Harry, 88
Nims, Walter, 70
Nine Inch Nails, 98, 120, 125-128
1910 Fruitgum Co., 75
98 Degrees, 180
Nirvana, 104, 140
Nite, Norm N., 32, 33, 197, 198, 200, 203

Nobles, Gene, 30
Nomi, Klaus, 193
Non-Conformists, 77
Norman, Michael, 203
North American Phono. Company, 2
Nothing, Jeffrey, 120
Novak, LaVerne, 51
Novello, Don, 184
Nubian, 168
Nugent, Ted, 86, 89, 93, 117
Numbers Band, 107, 112, 113-114, 215

O

O, Karen, 139-140
O.A.R. (Of A Revolution), 11, 136-137
Oaker, Mary Rose, 203
Oakley, Annie, 2
O'Brien, Conan, 137, 191
Ocasek, Ric, 115, 133
Ochs, Michael, 172
Ochs, Phil, 11, 171-172
Offbeats, 104
Offspring, 138
Ohio Express, 75, 76, 115
Ohio Players, 134, 137, 148-149, 152
Ohio State University, 11-25, 27
Ohio Untouchables, 148
O'Jay, Eddie, 153, 207
O'Jays, 141, 153-155, 207, 210
Olsson, Nigel, 24
Olympics, 17
On, Richard, 136
Ono, Yoko, 205
Option Thirty, 125
Orioles, 33, 149
Orlando, Tony, 25
Oroboros, 137
Orr, Benjamin, 114, 188
Osbourne, Ozzy, 207
Oseary, Guy, 214
O'Shea, Shad, 66
Osmond, Donny, 176
Oswald, Eric, 119
Otis, Johnny, 61, 62
OutKast, 147
Outlaws, 119-120
Outsiders, 67, 70-71, 188, 206
Over Night Low, 144
Over The Rhine, 135-136

Owens, Jesse, 13
Owens, Rick, 23
Owens, Tim "Ripper," 117-118
Oyewole, Abiodun, 168
Ozzfest, 117, 121

P

Paar, Jack, 187
Pacemakers, 143-144
Pacific Gas And Electric, 85
Pagans, 100-101, 103
Page, Patty, 196
Pantera, 92, 121
Paper Lace, 25, 78
Pappalardi, Felix, 101
Paris, Johnny, 49
Parissi, Robert, 166
Parker, Colonel Tom, 36
Parker, Maceo, 144
Parker, Ralphie, 194
Parliament-Funkadelic, 144, 150
Parsons, Bill, 66
Parsons, Gram, 183
Partridge Family, 24
Passarelli, Kenny, 86
Pastor, Tony, 4
Patrick, Richard, 128-129
Patrick, Robert, 129
Patterson, John Henry, 130
Paul, Henry, 120
Paul, Steve, 23
Pay The Girl, 134
Paycheck, Johnny, 182
Payne, Scherrie, 157
Pearl, Minnie, 56, 181
Pebbles, 147
Pecchio, Dan, 88, 89-90
Pedestrians, 100
Peeples, Nia, 156
Pei, I.M., 202, 204
Pekar, Harvey, 194
Pelander, Bob, 89
Pence, Jeff, 178
Pendergrass, Teddy, 146, 154
Penguins, 62
Penny, Hank, 59
Percolating Puppies, 7
Pere Ubu, 79, 97, 98, 108, 114, 138
Peresman, Joel, 211

Peretti, Hugo, 142
A Perfect Circle, 122
Perfect Disaster, 132
Perk, Ralph, 196
Perlich, Martin, 80
Perris, Don, 188
Peter, Paul & Mary, 3, 131
Peters, Dale, 85
Petkovic, John, 104
Petric, Bob, 138
Pfeifer, Robert, 114
Phair, Liz, 140
Phillips, Esther, 16, 61
Phillips, Jud, 35
Phillips, Sam, 35, 40, 206, 210
Pica Huss, 136
Pickett, Wilson, 148, 158
Pierce, Don, 65
Pig, 126
Pink, 147
Pink Floyd, 117
Pinz, Shelly, 77
Pirates Cove, 99
Pittman, Brian, 129-130
Pixies, 211
Plain Jane, 118
Platt, Eddie, 49
Platt, Lew, 28, 31
Platters, 42, 48, 61-62, 159
Platypus, 148
Plimsouls, 110
Poco, 173
Police, 100, 103
Pollard, Robert, 132-133, 138
Pomus, Doc, 48
Poni-Tails, 45, 51
Poor Girls, 108, 112
Pop Will Eat Itself, 126
Popovich, Steve, 93-94
Popper, John, 139
Portage Hotel, 105
Porter, Cole, 4, 181
Powell, William, 153
Power Trio, 85
Powers, Congo, 103
Premiers, 73
Presidents Of The United States Of America, 192
Presley, Elvis, 35-36, 40, 42, 61, 66, 77, 81-82, 158, 196, 202, 206

Pretenders, 112-113, 178, 213
Price, Mark, 107
Price, Ray, 182
Price, Richard, 25
Prince, 170
Procol Harum, 188
Procter & Gamble, 53
Professional Football Hall of Fame, 12
Professional Bowlers Association, 105
Psychodots, 134, 139
Puckett, Gary, 188
Pure Prairie League, 95, 174-175
PureVolume.com, 133
Purkhiser, Eric, 102
Purkhiser, Mike, 102

Q

Quiet Riot, 119
Quine, Robert, 101
Quinn, Chris, 34, 202-203

R

Rachmaninoff, Sergei, 72
Raconteurs, 166
Rainbow Canyon, 215
Raisins, 139
Raleigh, Kevin, 88
Ram Jam, 77
Ram, Buck, 62
Ramones, 101, 103
Ramsey Lewis Trio, 23
Rancid, 138
Randle, Bill, 35-36, 49, 51, 79
Raney, Wayne, 59
Rare Breed, 76
Rascals, 25, 72
Rashkow, Mike, 77
Raskulinecz, Nick, 122
Raspberries, 71-73
Raspberry Singers, 145
Rastus, 96
Rat Pack, 6
Ratner, Albert, 201
Ravenstine, Allen, 99
Ray, Diane, 52
Ray, Jean, 172
Ray, Johnnie, 35
Raye, Collin, 176

Record Rendezvous, 29, 164, 198
Red Hot Chili Peppers, 137, 149, 170
Redd, Gene, 63
Redding, Otis, 189
Reed, Lou, 48, 80, 101, 213
Reese, Carl, 34-35
Reid, Antonio "L.A.," 146-148
Reid, Tim, 190
Reilly, Mike, 175
Relient K, 129-130
R.E.M., 179
Remingtons, 185
Renaissance, 24
Renner, Jack, 95
Reno, Mike, 72
Replacements, 137
Resnick, Judith, 177
Reubens, Paul, 111
Reunion, 76
Revelation Funk, 157
Paul Revere & The Raiders, 73
Reznor, Trent, 98, 125-129, 193
Rhodes, Dusty, 67
Rhodes, James, 83
Rhodes, Todd, 30
Richards, Keith, 199, 208
Rick And The Raiders, 19
Rick Z Combo, 19
Rickenbacker, Eddie, 130
Righteous Brothers, 67, 68, 71
Riley-Cunningham, Rainey, 156
Rip Chords, 73
Ripken, Cal, Jr., 118
Ritter, Josh, 140
Ritty, James, 130
Riverfront Coliseum, 90-91
Robbins, Redda, 52
Roberge, David, 136
Roberge, Marc, 136
Roberts, Ed, 155
Roberts, Rich, 108
Robertson, Robbie, 20, 86
Robinson, Dutch, 148
Robinson, Frank, 196
Robinson, Smokey, 208
Rock and Roll Hall of Fame, 27, 65, 138, 143, 191, 195-211, 213, 214
Rockefeller, John D., 1
Rocket From The Tombs, 97, 98
Rockin' Highlanders, 46

Rodgers, Nile, 197
Rodriguez, Arsenio, 24
Rodriguez, Chi Chi, 109
Rogers, Kenny, 157
Rogers, Roy, 181
Rolling Stones, 22, 47, 69, 117, 158, 159, 171, 205, 208
Ronstadt, Linda, 157, 183
Rooney, Joe Don, 183
Roosevelt, Franklin D., 57
Rorschach, Poison Ivy, 102-103
Rose Royce, 160
Rose, Axl, 122
Rose, Pete, 53
Rossi, Dante, 115, 188
Rota, James A., 122
Rotten, Johnny, 109, 207
Roue, 101
Royal Crescent Mob, 11, 136, 137
Royal Guardsmen, 20
Royals, 62
Royalty, 152
Rubber City Rebels, 108, 109-110, 178
Ruby & The Romantics, 153, 155-156
Rude Boys, 155
Ruland, Frederick, 25
Runaways, 108
Rundgren, Todd, 87
Rush, 208
Russell, Jack, 92
Russo, Anthony, 193
Russo, Joe, 193
Ryder, Mitch, 188-189

S

Sachs, Jayne, 134
Sainte-Marie, Buffy, 174
Salem, Freddie, 119-120
Sales, Soupy, 35
Salt-N-Pepa, 143
Saltis, Larry, 180
Sample, Joe, 156
Sanctus Real, 130
Sanders, Denny, 80
Sanders, Richard, 190
Sandpipers, 23
Sandy, Gary, 189
Santelli, Robert, 208, 210
Santiago, Joey, 131

Sarducci, Father Guido, 184
Sarnoff, David, 56
Sat.Sun.Mat., 112
Satriani, Joe, 122
Savannah, 183
Saving Jane, 25, 185
Savol, Scott, 185
Sawyer Brown, 183
Scaggs, Boz, 185
Sceptres, 87
Schembechler, Bo, 13
Schmidt, Sue, 108
Schneck, Jonathan, 130
Scholz, Tom, 93
Schrader, Erich, 28
Schrader, Paul, 193
Schurk, William L., 213
Schwartz Brothers, 85
Schwartz, Gene, 85
Schwartz, Glenn, 85
Scott, Bobby, 64
Scott, Freddie, 24
Scott, Little Jimmy, 47-48
Scrawl, 136
Screaming Urge, 103
Scribble Jam, 170
Scruggs, Randy, 182
Sears, J.T., 74
Sears, Zenas "Daddy," 30
Secrets, 51-52
Sedaka, Neil, 52
Seger, Bob, 87
Serendipity Singers, 21
Sex Pistols, 109, 207
Sferra, John, 89-90
Shades Of Blue, 160
Shadow, 148
Shalamar, 156-157
Sham 69, 101
Shaw, Artie, 4
Shea, Mike, 213-214
Sheen, Martin, 194
Shepard, Chris, 144
Shepard, Michael, 139
Sheppard Brothers, 59
Sheppard, Gil, 66
Sheridan, Danny, 88
Sherlock's Park Place, 117
Shines, Johnny, 164
Shipley, Tom, 174

Shirelles, 65
Shirley, Jerry, 89
Shockley, Stephen, 151
Shok Paris, 122
Short Cuts, 52
Shriner, Scott, 139
Shrug, 134
Shuster, Joseph, 195
Sidney, Sylvia, 189
Siegel, Jerry, 195
Silver Leaf nightclub, 156
Silverman, Ron, 85
Simon and Garfunkel, 49, 188
Simon, Carly, 175
Simon, Paul, 37, 81
Simone, Joe, 160-161
Simone, Nina, 64
Simple Minds, 113
Simpson, Jessica, 180
Sinatra, Frank, 4, 6, 8, 25, 37, 42, 48, 49, 52, 72, 196
Sinatra, Tina, 25
Singer, Eric, 121
Singing Socialists, 172
Sir Timothy And The Royals, 76
Skeleton, Red, 56
Skinny Puppy, 126
Sky King, 119
Slam Bam Boo, 125
Slash, 121-122
Slave, 148, 151
Slayer, 121
Slim, Memphis, 163
Slint, 132
Slipknot, 120
Sloan, Eliot, 178
Sluggo, 103
Sly And The Family Stone, 82, 144, 153
Smalley, Dave, 71-72
Smashing Pumpkins, 104
Smith, Arthur, 64
Smith, Debbie, 108
Huey Smith & Clowns, 46
Smith, Kenny, 141
Smith, Mamie, 53, 162
Smith, Michael W., 130
Smith, Neal, 96
Smith, Rex, 114
Smith, Trixie, 30
Smith, Will, 169

Smithers, Jan, 190
Smithsonian, 206
Snake Eyes, 88
Snoop Doggy Dog, 169, 170
Snoopy, 11
Soap Box Derby, 105-106
Society, 95
Soledad Brothers, 166
Sonny & Cher, 113
Sons Of The Pioneers, 181
Soul Corporation, 156
Soul Stirrers, 158
Soul Street, 141
Soul Train, 141
South By Southwest festival, 211
Souther Hillman Furay Band, 173
Souther, J.D., 88
Southland Rhythm Girls, 15
Southside Johnny, 80
Spector, Ronnie, 94
Spedding, Chris, 112
Spero, David, 80, 88, 187-189, 210
Spero, Herman, 187
Spielberg, Steven, 193
Spinners, 144
Spohn, Charles, 21, 25
SpongeBob SquarePants, 103
Spoyld, 119
Springer, Jerry, 187, 189
Springfield, Dusty, 158
Springfield, Rick, 25
Springsteen, Bruce, 80, 88, 92, 94, 160, 199, 206, 207, 208
Sprouse, Stephen, 206
Stabbing Westward, 126
Stache's, 137
Stafford, Jo, 74
Stanley, Michael, 87-89, 93
Starfires, 70
Starr, Edwin, 141, 153, 159-160
Starr, Frankie, 177
Starr, Ruby, 96
Starvation Army, 104
State Of Conviction, 120
Steely Dan, 23
Stein, Seymour, 24, 65, 105, 197
Steinman, Jim, 94
Stephens, Professor Herman, 142
Steppenwolf, 73
Stereos, 50

Sternberg, Liam, 109, 114, 178
Stevens, Eric, 95
Stewart, Terry C., 210-211
Stidham, Arbee, 164
Stiles, Ryan, 192
Stillman, Jamie, 165
Stills, Stephen, 173
Stinziano, Mike, 22
Stokes, Carl, 196
Stone Temple Pilots, 129, 140
Stone, Joss, 153
Stone, Sly, 159
Stone, Warwick, 204
Stowe, Harriet Beecher, 53
Stradlin, Izzy, 121
Strain, Sammy, 154
Strangeloves, 17-20, 23-24
Street, Mel, 182
Students, 50
Sugar Creek, 184
Ed Sullivan Show, 71, 173
Sullivan, Jim, 208
Sultans of Swing, 27
Sun, 138, 144, 148
Sundowners, 172
Sunnyland Slim, 164
Superman, 109, 195
Supreme Court, 176
Supremes (Akron group), 155
Supremes (Detroit group), 196
Survivor, 88
Sutherland, John, 180
Swan Silvertones, 60
Swan, Billy, 185
Swank, Ben, 166
Sweat, Keith, 154
Sweed, Ron, 103
Sweet, David, 118
Sweet, Matthew, 101
Sweet, Rachel, 114
Sweet, Steve, 118
Swingos, 81-82
Switch, 157
Sykes, Roosevelt, 163
Sylvain, Sylvain, 112
Symmes, Judge John Cleves, 53
Szell, George, 176
Szymczyk, Bill, 87

T

T. Rex, 128
Take 6, 108
Tamarkin, Jeff, 208, 209
Tamblyn, Russ, 193
Tammy And The Amps, 132
Tate, Sharon, 126
Tatgenhorst, John, 21
Tatum, Art, 49
B.E. Taylor Group, 89
Taylor, Tim, 134
Tedesco, Tommy, 49
Teen Queens, 51
Teenage Jesus And The Jerks, 97
Teese, Dita Von, 128
Tegreene, Joe, 198
Tei, Towa, 139
Telarc Records, 95
Telefunk, 160
Television, 101
Temptations, 23, 160
Ten Zen Men, 177
Tenafly Viper, 121
Terrible Parade, 104
Terror, 120
Terry & Bruce, 73
Terry Knight And The Pack, 96
Tex, Joe, 158
Theatrical Grill, 164
Thiessen, Matt, 129
This Moment In Black History, 104
Thomas, B.J., 65
Thomas, Danny, 5
Thomas, David, 98-100, 101, 114
Thomas, Tracy, 108
Thompson, Larry R., 202, 204
Thompson, Richard, 99
Thompson, Sonny, 61
Tharpe, Sister Rosetta, 35
Thorpe, Jim, 12
Three Dog Night, 129
3quartersdead, 121
Throwing Muses, 131
Til, Sonny, 48
Tilse, Brian, 117
Timmons, Jeff, 180
Tin Huey, 107, 114, 165
Tinker, Grant, 189
Tippen, Aaron, 77

Tipton, Glenn, 118
TLC, 147
Toka, Matt, 122
Toll, 136
Tolliver, David, 155
Tony And The Bandits, 77
Tool, 122
Top Notes, 16, 142
Topinka, Karen, 51
Total Concept Unlimited, 160
Toup, Bobby, 64
Tower Of Power, 96
Townsend, Mark, 129
Townsend, Ron, 162
Townshend, Pete, 86, 91-92, 199, 205
Tracey Twins, 52
Tracy, Steven C., 164
Traffic, 89
Travis, Merle, 56, 59, 181
Travis, Scott, 117
Tree, 119
Tree Stumps, 87
A Tribe Called Quest, 168
Trigger, 181
Triumphs, 153
Troggs, 97
Troiano, Dominic, 86
Troop, 155
Tropicana nightclub, 156
Troutman, Larry, 150
Troutman, Lester, 150
Troutman, Roger, 144, 145, 149, 150
Troutman, Roger, Jr., 150-151
Troutman, Rufus, Jr., 150
Troutman, Terry, 150
Troyan, Joe, 181
Trump, Donald, 154
Tucker, Teeny, 150
Tucker, Tommy, 141, 149-150
Tulu Babies, 188
Turner, Big Joe, 29, 37
Turner, Erik, 118
Turner, Sonny, 159
Turtles, 188
Twilighters, 93
Twitty, Conway, 182
2 Of Clubs, 66
2 Pac, 150
216, 120
Tyler Davidson Memorial Fountain, 189

U

UB40, 113
Ultimate Prophecy, 95
Uncle Vic, 184
Unified Culture, 120
Unit 5, 108
Upbeat!, 80, 115, 187-189
Urge, 125
Uriah Heep, 123
Used Kids Record, 138
Usher, 147
Utah Saints, 160

V

Valens, Ritchie, 22, 42, 48
Valentinos, 158
Valli, Frankie, 114, 156
Van, Benny, 95
Vargas, Elizabeth, 177
Vecchio, Mary Ann, 84
Vee, Bobby, 17
Velvet Revolver, 140
Velvet Undergound, 97, 109, 188
Ventures, 19, 70
Verlaine, Tom, 101
Vet's Inn, 164
Vibrations, 16, 17, 18, 23
Village Idiots, 178
Vincent, Gene, 43
Vitale, Joe, 86
Voegele, Kate, 178
Vogues, 192
Voice Of America, 57
Voidoids, 101
Voinovich, George, 198, 199, 200, 201, 202
Vrenna, Chris, 126
V3, 136

W

WADC (Akron), 28
Waddy, Frankie "Kash," 144
Wagoner, Porter, 182
Waitresses, 107, 111, 114
Waits, Tom, 101, 110
WAKR (Akron), 27, 28, 30
Waldorf-Astoria Hotel, 195, 199

Walford, Britt, 131-132
Walhberg, Mark, 118
Walker, Johnny, 166
Walker, Matt, 129
Walking Clampetts, 102
Wallace, Kirsty, 102
Waller, Fats, 7, 56, 163
Walsh, Joe, 79, 85-87, 106, 107, 108, 192
Wanderers, 101
War, 24
Ward, Billy, 61
Ward, Robert, 148
Warne, John, 130
Warner Brothers, 2-3
Warner, Brad, 104
Warner, Jack, 3
Warrant, 118-119
Warwick, Dionne, 156
Washington, Albert, 164
Washington, Harold, 199
Washington, Steve, 151
Waters, John, 114
Waters, Muddy, 29
Watershed, 136
Sammy Watkins Orchestra, 5
Watley, Jody, 156
Watson, "Ivory" Deek, 7
Watson, Thomas J., 130
Watts, Gene, 22
Waylon, 120
WBAI (New York), 80
WCLV (Cleveland), 80
WDAO (Dayton), 148
WDIA (Memphis), 27
Weber, Fred, 106
WEBN (Cincinnati), 82
Webster, 188-189
Weezer, 139
Weigel, Eugene J., 14
Weiland, Scott, 139
Weiner, Charlie, 98, 171
Welch, Ward, 108
Weldon, Michael J., 97
Wells, Tom, 189
Wenner, Jann, 195, 196, 205, 206, 209
Wesley, Fred, 144
West, Kanye, 152, 170
West, Robert, 29, 41, 42, 43
Wet Spots, 134

WEWS-TV (Cleveland), 187-188
Wexler, Jerry, 16, 17, 31, 107, 197
WGAR (Cleveland), 80, 200
WGST (Atlanta), 27
Whispers, 146-147
Whitaker, Johnny, 25
Whitfield, Norman, 160
White Heat, 157
White Plains, 74
White Stripes, 165, 166
White, Barry, 155, 157
White, Karyn, 147
White, Michael, 192
White, Robert I., 83
Dick Whittington's Cats, 70
WJZ (Newark), 7
WHK (Cleveland), 67-68, 80, 81, 87, 187, 200
Who, 71, 90-92, 190, 196
Whodini, 146
Widespread Panic, 139
Wiggs, Josephine, 132
Wilco, 138
Wild Cherry, 166-167, 179
Wild Horses, 193, 200
Wilder, Johnnie, 167
Wilder, Keith, 167
William G. Mather Museum, 207
Williams, Billy, 7
Williams, H. Evan, 2
Williams, Hank, Jr., 72
Williams, Hank, Sr., 59, 183, 210
Williams, Mars, 108
Williams, Nat D., 30
Otis Williams And The Charms, 62
Williams, Paul "Hucklebuck," 32, 33, 44
Williams, Tony, 61-62
Williams, Vesta, 162
Williams, Walter, 153-154
Williamson, Sonny Boy, 164
Wilson, Ann, 72
Wilson, Brian, 73
Wilson, Hugh, 189
Wilson, Jackie, 34, 142, 158
Wilson, Jim, 65
Wilson, Nancy, 11, 48
Wilson, Owen, 193
Winfield, Dave, 192
Winger, Debra, 194
Wings Over Jordan, 60

WINS (New York), 41, 42, 43, 211
Winter, Edgar, 23
Winter, Johnny, 23
Winters Bane, 117
Winters, Jonathan, 194
Wish Bone, 168
WIXY (Cleveland), 68-69, 85, 95
WJW (Cleveland), 27, 28-29, 31, 34, 35
    36, 102, 195
WKBN (Youngstown), 27
WKRP In Cincinnati, 187, 189-190
WKST (New Castle), 27
WKSU (Kent), 171
WLAC (Nashville), 27
WLW (Cincinnati), 4, 7, 8, 54-57, 58, 59,
    163, 181, 187
WLWC-TV (Columbus), 13
WLWT-TV (Cincinnati), 53
WMCA (New York), 28
WMJI (Cleveland), 200
WMMR (Philadelphia), 80
WMMS (Cleveland), 79, 80-81, 82, 87,
    89, 198
WNCR (Cleveland), 80, 85
WNEW (New York), 28, 39, 42
WNJR (Newark), 34, 36
Wolfman Jack, 37
Womack, Bobby, 158-159
Womack, Cecil, 159
Womack, Harry, 159
WOMAD festival, 177
Wonder Woman, 107
Wonder, Stevie, 188
Wood, Bobby, 149
Wood, Frank "Bo," 82
Wood, Randy, 44
Wood, Ronnie, 159
Wooden Birds, 100
Woodruff, J.T., 133
Woods, Robert, 95
WOR (New York), 80
World Series of Golf, 105
World Series of Rock, 117
WOSU (Columbus), 182
WQXI (Atlanta), 189
Wray, Link, 24
Wright, Dale, 66
Wright, Orville, 130
Wright, Wilbur, 130
WSAI (Cincinnati), 56, 67

Wussy, 135
WXEN-TV (Cleveland), 80
WWCD (Columbus), 136
Wynette, Tammy, 182
Wynne, Philippe, 143-144
WZAK (Cleveland), 153

X

Xzibit, 170

Y

Yancey, Rick, 185
Yankovic, Frankie, 93, 214-215
Yankovic, Weird Al, 23, 184, 215
Yardbirds, 45, 74, 188
Yeah Yeah Yeahs, 139-140
Yes, 89
Yoakam, Dwight, 182
York, Rusty, 66
Young Buck, 170
Young Mystics, 151
Young Underground, 151
Young, Chuck, 33, 34
Young, Faron, 182
Young, Jesse Colin, 172
Young, Neil, 84-85, 110-11, 173, 199,
    208
Young, Starleana, 151
Young, Welton, 149
Youngbloods, 172
Youngstown (musical group), 180
Yuro, Timi, 16

Z

Zandt, Steven Van, 94
Zanes, Warren, 210
Zapp, 150-151
Zappa, Frank, 98, 139
Zaza, Neil, 122
Zero, Jimmy, 101-101
Zevon, Warren, 80
Zinner, Nick, 139

Also in the Ohio series:

The Ohio Book of Lists
by Dave Hudson

ISBN: 978-0980056129

www.ingramcontent.com/pod-product-compliance
Lightning Source LLC
Chambersburg PA
CBHW032039150426
43194CB00006B/344